CISO
Redefined

Revision Sub-title:
'Protecting Business'

Revision of Earlier Edition
Expect content duplication

Martin Gomberg

Published by Cyberite LLC
2023


ISBN 978-0-9987751-0-4



www.cisoredefined.com

martin.gomberg@cisoredefined.com

*Attack, breach, and data loss are increasingly significant issues, but not just technology issues, and technology alone regardless of spend will not fix this. Those tasked with the protection of business and community demand a broader requisite knowledge and skill set than ever before.*

## PUBLISHING

Published by Cyberite LLC, Boca Raton, Florida (most current published update © October 2023)

ISBN 978-0-9987751-0-4 (8.5" x 11") Portrait Format, Glossy Soft Cover Perfect Bound B/W Interior

This book is available in print, online for print-on-demand (www.cisoredefined.com) or in electronic copy. As update cycles differ, no assurance is made that each are the same as to the exactness of the material, layout, or design

## DISCLAIMER NOTICE

**Martin Gomberg is not an attorney, and nothing offered in this book constitutes legal guidance. For legal interpretation, opinion or advice of attorney consult appropriately specialized counsel.**

Matters of law, domestic or global, are presented and discussed from an operational 'non-lawyer' perspective. We need to understand what is required of the business to meet regulatory obligations. Often emerging laws are in flux and at best we can hope to get out in front of them with assumptions to be fixed later. Always affirm with legal counsel.

Corporate approaches to compliance vary. Size of company, industry and business goals differ. The opinions and approaches offered in this book may not be appropriate to all companies, or in all circumstances, or all times, and should not be taken as consultation, or acted upon without careful consideration of fit, and/or professional guidance.

Efforts have been made to cover a broad and complex area to accepted practice standards, but these vary as will company needs. No warranty in whole or in part is offered for this book, or to assuring the completeness, correctness, timeliness or currency of its contents, or its applicability to any specific or intended use, nor can be granted or extended by sales representatives or others, or in promotional or other printed sales, distribution, or marketing materials. No liability is accepted by the author, contributors, or publisher and none will be held liable for any loss of profits, incurred penalties, or other commercial damages attributable to the use or misuse of the information provided herein, consequential, incidental, or other.

Any similarity to the concepts presented by others in publication, presentation or practice is unintended except where identified as to source. Where the work of others is described or quoted, it is with best intentions for accuracy, but should be confirmed with original authors and sources.

No assertion of conformance, compliance, certification, or achievement to any standard, testing body, or regulation, domestic or global is made or assured. Remedy for verified mistakes, inaccuracies, misprints, or mis-edits is limited to provision of a corrected electronic copy upon notification of the error. Contact the author directly as noted below. Check the website for error notices and eligibility and provisions for replacement by electronic copy. No refunds are offered.

## SPEAKING ENGAGEMENTS, PRESS AND CONSULTING

Contact Martin Gomberg directly at mgomberg@cyberite.com or visit www.cisoredefined.com (Updates).

*To my family and friends*

*children and grandchildren*

*to babies*

*loving and lovable pets*

*to all those special*

*to the health and safety of nature and the environment*

*to timeless painted caves and that people are just people*

*to strength through diligence*

*animals domestic and wild*

*to peace in the world*

*to happiness*

*to peace and remembrance for those at rest*

*to democracy*

*the liberty to move freely again*

*to sybarites, digerati, and cognoscente everywhere*

*and to good wine*

# ACKNOWLEDGMENTS AND DEEPEST APPRECIATION

Richard A. Guida, CISSP, IANS Faculty and Author of The Entropy Police
for his expertise, friendship and offering comments in the Foreword
and for taking on the always difficult task of critical peer review


Mark Haimowitz, Former Director Business Continuity, Disney ABC Television
Mark Armour and David Lindstedt, Adaptive BC Manifesto


K-9 Trainer/Handler Keith Herron, Sr.,
for the contribution of photographs of Certified Dedicated Cadaver Detector Dog 'Vessa'


Tara M. Gomberg
assistance in the review of privacy materials and for providing the photograph of 'Pumpkin'


R.T. O'Brien, Principal, REINBO Consulting, UK
comments on the implications of Brexit and UK data transfer provisions


Janalyn Schreiber, Partner, Data Privacy & Security Advisors LLC
thoughts on the direction of US Privacy Policy


Chris Sumner, Co-Founder, Online Privacy Foundation
from the field comments on data inventory, mapping, and classification


Siarhei Varankevich
The Territorial Scope of the GDPR Flowchart
Published under Creative Commons License CC BY-SA 4.0


The Privacy Panel, a global cooperative 🌐
an unparalleled source of hands-on privacy and global data protection expertise


Trevor M. Gomberg, Esq., Levitt LLP
for his contribution of
"E-Discovery and the CISO: Why You Should Care"

# PREFACE

You have undoubtedly all heard of 'Picture-In-Picture' - a feature of almost all modern television.

This is 'Book-In-Book'.
One book embedded in another.

I have written a comprehensive compendium of information, experience, opinion, and knowledge. This comprises the bulk of the material in the book. This is for the mind. The table of contents is your guide.

But there is also a 'second book' embedded in these pages. A book of thought, quote, and career driving philosophies. CIO legacy. CISO wisdom. Executive leadership and guidance. My personal thought gems.

I have embedded and scattered these thoughts and phrases as 'callouts' throughout the book identified by the owl graphic that accompanies each.

This is for the heart. There isn't an index or guide. Thumb through the pages and find the owls. Even if you read nothing else in this book you will be a better CIO, CISO or transformational executive for having done so.

*Threats live where the business lives. There are no threats to technology, only to business, and the greatest threat to business is not recognizing this.*

# ABOUT THE AUTHOR:

## MARTIN GOMBERG, a.k.a. THE PRIVACY CIO

### CIO, CISO, CISSP, CIPP/E

**MARTIN GOMBERG,** a.k.a. THE PRIVACY CIO, is the Founder and Executive of CYBERITE LLC. He is an associate member of THE PRIVACY PANEL, a global collaborative of privacy expertise, a Senior Privacy Consultant, IANS Research faculty member, and a business advisor. He has spent over thirty years in technical operations as Chief Information Officer (CIO), and Senior Vice President and Global Director of Technical Security, Governance, Privacy, and Business Protection (CISO), for a major television and media brand, and prior, as Vice President of Global Technical Strategies for a major bank. He is a founding member of the CIO Executive Council, formerly Vice Chair of the U.S. State Department Overseas Security Advisory Council (OSAC) for the Media and Entertainment Industry Working Group and served as a member of several industry ISACS. An active speaker, author, and blogger on issues and practices in security, risk, business continuity and crisis management as well as global data protection, governance, and privacy, he has been recognized in citation and awards including the CIO Executive Council award for Outstanding Contribution to the Profession.

# FOREWORD

Martin Gomberg has produced, in this book, something that most writers can only dream of doing. He has taken experiences gleaned over a long and illustrious career in IT, information security and privacy, and turned them in to an eloquent description of what current Chief Information Security Officers, and those who aspire to become CISOs, should think about, worry about, and act upon.

This book is a comprehensive, engaging, and at times amusing picture of information security in the enterprise. Martin covers not only the current paradigms of information security, but also where the discipline is headed, especially with respect to its key practitioner, the CISO. He "redefines" the CISO as someone who does not just advise the business on information security but is truly *part* of the business in an intimate and profound way. This is a goal that all of us CISOs have long sought to achieve. We do not just want to "have a seat at the table," we want to be there with the full recognition by the other parties at the table that we belong there, that our contribution is critical to business success, and most importantly, that we are not just representing a "special interest" – i.e., information security – but instead have in mind the broadest interests of the enterprise as we offer our input into the deliberations.

Martin lays out a structure and a way of thinking that achieves these things. He provides both useful theoretical and practical advice on the topics that a CISO must deal with. While each chapter contains many gems, his material on incident management and response, drawn from his personal executive level experience, is especially important considering the serious data breaches that seem to afflict both the private and government sectors every year. And often every month, or even every week.

When I read a book, I always look for two things: (a) does it keep my interest – do I want to turn the page looking forward to what is on the next page; and (b) does it teach me something I did not previously know. Martin's book did both for me, and I hope and expect it will do likewise for anyone who reads it.

Thank you, Martin, for making such a noteworthy contribution to the field of information security, a profession that both you and I embrace. May your book have fair winds and following seas as it sails forth onto the oceans of many eager readers.

Rich Guida, CISSP

*Rich served in the U.S. Federal government for 28 years, most of that time in the Navy, and received a Presidential Meritorious Rank award in 1996. He then joined Johnson & Johnson as J&J's Chief Information Security Officer with the title of Vice President for Worldwide Information Security. He holds engineering degrees from MIT, and an MBA from George Washington University.*

# CISO
# REDEFINED

*Protecting Business*

Martin Gomberg, CISSP, CIPP/E

## ABOUT THIS BOOK

Some of you may remember a cartoon from 1969 still accessible online, Bambi meets Godzilla, by Marv Newland. To a background of soft flute music, Bambi, a peaceful little doe, is grazing in a field, nibbling flowers, sipping water from the brook, nibbling more flowers, when down comes this giant foot and the cartoon ends. With cyber threats, nation state actors, political unrest, breaches of privacy, fraud, supply chain and other third party risks, a barrage of discordant regulation, staffing issues, and concerns about the misuse and disruptive potential of generative AI, can't you almost feel that giant foot?

Given the attention and angst emerging to Generative AI as to whether a production enhancer, a job killer, a security threat, a violator of personal rights and privacy, a tool to be smartly used, a plagiarist, a hallucinating vomitus of self-perpetuating regurgitated thought, or the next step in our business evolution, I thought I would ask its opinion as to 'How to describe the global focus on cyber security, privacy and business protection, and if this were a war are we winning or losing?' Seems fair to ask the criminal how best to describe the crime. In full disclosure it sourced (1) Gartner, (2) Global security Report of the World Economic Forum and (3) McKinsey and Company in developing a very cogent response. I can imagine it speaking in a WARGAMES (1983) computer voice as it said "Generating answers for you…and produced"

*"Cybersecurity, privacy, and business protection are important topics that have gained global attention in recent years. The rapid development and adoption of new technologies, such as cloud computing, artificial intelligence, 5G and quantum computing, have created new opportunities and challenges for organizations and individuals. However, they have also increased the complexity and sophistication of cyberattacks, which can have devastating consequences for the economy, society, and national security.*

- *Geopolitics: The rise of cyber conflicts and espionage among nation-states, as well as the emergence of cyber militias and hacktivists, have increased the geopolitical tensions and risks in cyberspace. Organizations need to be aware of the potential impact of these activities on their operations, reputation, and supply chains, and adopt appropriate strategies to mitigate them.*

- *Emerging technology: The adoption of emerging technologies, such as privacy-enhancing computation, zero-trust architecture, extended detection and response, and secure access service edge, can help organizations improve their cybersecurity posture and resilience. However, they also introduce new vulnerabilities and challenges that require continuous monitoring and assessment.*

- *Emerging threats: Cyberthreats, such as ransomware, supply chain attacks, phishing, credential stuffing, and insider threats, have become more frequent, sophisticated, and targeted. Organizations need to invest in proactive threat intelligence, detection, and response capabilities, as well as in cyber awareness and education for their employees and customers.*

- *Laws and regulations: The proliferation of privacy laws and regulations across different jurisdictions, such as the General Data Protection Regulation (GDPR) in the European Union, the California Consumer Privacy Act (CCPA) in the United States, and the Personal Data Protection Bill (PDPB) in India, have increased the compliance requirements and obligations for organizations that collect, process, or store personal data. Organizations need to ensure that they adhere to these laws and regulations, as well as to the ethical principles and best practices of data protection.*

*The question of whether we are winning or losing the cyber war is not easy to answer. On one hand, we can see that there are many efforts and initiatives to improve cybersecurity at the global, regional, and national levels. For example, the World Economic Forum's Centre for Cybersecurity is a platform that brings together public and private sector stakeholders to collaborate on addressing cyber challenges[2]. On the other hand, we can also see that there are many gaps and challenges that remain to be addressed. There is a shortage of skilled cyber talent, a lack of common standards and frameworks, a disparity in cyber capabilities among different regions and sectors[2]. Therefore, I would say that we are neither winning nor losing the cyber war. We are in a state of constant competition and cooperation with various actors in cyberspace. We need to be vigilant, adaptive, and collaborative to face the current and future cyber challenges."*

Great response! I wish I had tried this about 300 pages ago. And yes, generative AI will likely prove to be all of those things that its advocates, detractors and doomsday predictors are saying. Maybe we'll see terminators roaming the streets, but more likely, we'll work out the kinks, develop the needed controls, align our laws, and then it's just business. We will need to work through issues of use, ethics, fairness, and economics, develop policies, strategies, and frameworks, and learn to detect, integrate, leverage, secure and mature AI in operations. Generative, analytic, and predictive AI and other synthetic conceptualization, behavioral, or simulation technologies will only accelerate from here, not restrained by fears, but fueled by the potential to innovate. We'll need to work through issues. Model training. Privacy. Content ownership. The scarcity of new ideas. That new uses for prior thinking are not infinite. And most difficult, monitoring our own behavior to avoid the misuse or malicious exploitation of AI and violation of the rights, safety, and interests of others. But we have survived the precipice before. Mainframes to minicomputers to distributed networks, consumerization of technologies, cloud, and globalization. Technology and regulations are tools. They will always go where business leads. We just need to watch out for that giant foot.

Privacy and security are in focus everywhere. An FTC (Federal Trade Commission) post states that "security begins with the board of directors". The message is clear and is embodied in law. Corporate leadership is accountable. Their success is tied to the effectiveness of their security programs. And the success of their security programs, to the appointment of a competent Chief Information Security Officer.

The CISO role is changing but law and accountability are not the only drivers of the redefined CISO role.

Changing business, digital transformation, new markets, and new consumers, have produced a voracious demand for the collection, aggregation, and consumption of data. Executives and operating boards recognize that disruption and innovation will be the incubators of new ideas and market success but are challenged as to how to move forward and achieve a path to disruption without damage, and without excessive risk. They recognize that the opportunities to participate in new markets and adopt transformational approaches, or to be 'disruptive', is not possible without a secure operating environment, and without a risk management strategy that enables new opportunity.

Amongst the greatest barriers to success in the digital transformation of business, cloud adoption, and mobility, and in better engaging and increasing proximity to consumers in the tools they use, physical and virtual spaces they converge, and the information they consume, are the concern for the security and privacy of data, and confidence in traditional structures for protection. Still, a recent survey found that only 19% of CISOs were confident in cyber security preparedness and protections. Cyber remains a virulent threat and an administrative priority, in the US, and across the globe, as governments in response press for greater public-private partnership, critical infrastructure protection, security investments, and an increasing emphasis on the accountability of corporate leadership.

If innovation is the path to transformation, and new models of competitiveness, then awareness and management of risk is necessary to effectively clear that path. If technology and business are to bring out the best of each, and if risk is to be managed through transformation, we will need an empowered and engaged CISO. If as Frank Wander in Transforming IT Culture suggests "we need to learn to transform knowledge into opportunity," then to succeed, we need to recognize risk without halting innovation, and the demand again is for an empowered and engaged CISO.

Business leaders know that success demands innovation but change also breeds risk. Change also moves and transforms risk. Traditional operating models and structures within Information Technology have been changing for some time. As more services leave the confines of the data center for the cloud, and more companies increasingly explore server-less architectures, infrastructure on-demand, and other emerging models, risk has moved from operations and systems management to security and privacy, less the purview of data center management, and more that of the CISO and other security specialists. This is exacerbated by the mobile / virtual client device model and increasingly so with work at home in the age of Covid-19.

## "We need to recognize risk without halting innovation" – Frank Wander

New business paradigms, an increasing and expanding environment of complex threats, mobility, the Internet of Things, new operating models, and a continually evolving body of law and regulation, all demand more in the protection of business. The surge of AI onto the corporate landscape brings challenges of adoption, management, use, privacy, new risk, and potential liability. It brings questions of trust, data reliability, quality deterioration, and model training. Of hallucinations and fatigue infiltration to the decisions we make. And it brings new HR issues. But it is the way forward, an important door, but also a door to new risk. Change breeds new areas of exposure, and breeds opportunities for compromise by malicious actors. The CISO, the Chief Information Security Officer, is recognized by leadership, and by law, as the executive to confront complex threat, guide leadership, and to enable business transformation and success.

There are new rules. We live in strange times where individuals manufacture disaster. Most of us live or work in or near locations where every disaster wants to be. And we have enemies we have never met. This is the technical reality of cyberattacks, assaults on personal privacy and the degradation of truth and quality in the information we consume. It is the reality for reputation and brand disparagement in digital social space, and the physical reality of riots, protest, terrorism, and active assailants on personnel and premises. And it is a reality of horrific natural events, pandemic disease, massive fires across the west, tornados, earthquakes, and storms like Katrina, Sandy, Irma, Maria, and so many others.

We live not just with changing climates, but in a climate of change. Threats are everywhere, they are technical, social, physical, legal, natural, regulatory, man-made, financial, and yes, the climate in which we do business. And it is diligence, prudence, a focus on quality management, effective peer partnership and information sharing, and an effective program of review that will get us through. And it is continual monitoring, testing and remediation that assures that amidst all distractions and inherent risk we stay on course.

## Leadership and the CISO Role

*Business leaders are stepping up.* The most competitive and mature businesses recognize that the demands of business protection are increasing and that the traditional role and expectations of the CISO need to change. I think most CISOs would agree. Almost every CISO, regardless of background and experience, irrespective of company size or industry, whether in the public or private sector, and whether domestic or global, has seen the position of CISO and the challenges they face grow and transform. As responsibilities for security, risk management, regulatory compliance, reputation management, privacy, and the continuity of business increase, management expectations of the CISO, and demand for those ready to inform, guide and to participate in strategy and leadership have also increased. These are roles and capabilities for which the CISO developed through traditional career trajectories has often not been well prepared.

*Business leaders need more.* The CISO increasingly is the executive called upon not just to protect, but to provide confidence, interpretation of risk, and measured response to threat. The CISO is also the executive called to provide the understanding, guidance, and leadership that enables the execution of complex business strategy within a context of risk. The growing importance of the CISO in leadership is a recognition of the new realities of business. It is a complicated world. The sub-title of this book is Protecting Business. It is exactly the ability to assume leadership and an overarching role of protection in all aspects of business and business change that has redefined the CISO.

*Business leaders are under pressure.* They are accountable not just to provide oversight, but to prove cyber program competence. In a 2016 Harvard Business Review, Bill Sweeney stated that as many as 40% of executives lacked a 'clear understanding' of cyber risks, or their preparedness for it. Nearing eight years later, I suspect that has not changed by much. It is the CISO that is being called on to provide the assurance behind the signatory responsibility of executives, and of the board, to regulators, financiers, and investors. This is not just by choice. For many, and increasingly, it is by law. And we are playing catch up.

*Executives are not just asked but mandated by law to engage with their CISO.* They mandate periodic risk assessments and reports to leadership. The CISO may define the program and communicate the risk, but it is the responsibility of the executive to understand, accept and put their signature on risk mitigating programs and efforts. Whether the CISO is part of a traditional Information Technology organization, reports through Operations, Legal, Risk, Human Resources, or to the CEO, or to the audit committee, or directly to the operating board full time, or as a periodic closed-door advisor, a practice increasing with regulatory demands, executive management is aligning to the need for a greater CISO, a more engaged CISO, and a more business focused CISO, that which I have called in this book, a CISO *Redefined*.

*This is not intended as a 'How to' book.* Despite that, you will come away with a lot of 'How to' guidance and material. I discuss some laws as models, indicators of a direction, or because they are new, or relevant, or an operational challenge, but this is not about laws. I will impart some practices that you can use, but this is not only a book on practice. It is based on years of experience, but I will not speak at length about me or what I have done, only as passing references. *It is intended as a "Why to' book* and there are increasingly a lot of reasons 'why'. It is about risk. And controls. And data. And a protective ecosystem. It is about protecting a business. Threats are changing. Laws are changing. Business is changing. The skills we need have changed. Some may not have had extensive experience in privacy, continuity, or incident response as disciplines, or may not be current with new cyber, breach, and global privacy laws. I discuss continuity at length, and a new way to approach it. I offer views on privacy, assessing and protecting it and why it needs to be matured. I address the European General Data Protection Regulation (GDPR). Also, the NYDFS Cybersecurity Regulation. And the California Consumer Privacy Act (CCPA) and the CPRA soon to replace it. I offer tools and ways to look at and better understand our business and data and to help get us out ahead of these and other emerging privacy and cyber laws. This book is intended to challenge and transform approaches, and enhance competencies, twist, ignite, and promote disruption in how we all see our roles, and how we think about risk, controls, business, and business protection overall. We need to do this because others are doing it for us. Our roles are being redefined in practice, in regulation, and in importance to the organization.

I will challenge our most entrenched of sacred security icons, beliefs, and practices, from how we approach Business Continuity Planning, to Controls, to the definition of Risk, to the CIA (Confidentiality, Integrity, Availability) Triad. This is not to disavow or degrade, not even to disagree, but to see these in new ways. We will look at technical risk and cyber. We will look at regulatory, operational, and organizational risk. Also, physical, legal, and privacy exposures. We will relook at these through a new lens of the complex world of threat and challenge, and transformative business. We will look at regulation, standards, guidelines, and proven practices. The CISO is being redefined because business is being redefined.

For some in our best companies, our most mature businesses, this is not new. The CISO, by whatever title, has attained a position of strategic participation with over-arching responsibility for business protection, and as an enabler of change. According to a recent IDG Security Priorities Study, two-thirds of enterprises have appointed a dedicated CISO or CSO. More than half of these are likely to be part of a dedicated security organization apart from IT as compared to small to medium businesses which have either not dedicated the role, and where they have, it is as an embedded IT function. It wasn't too long ago, as in the picture on the cover of this book, that the CISO was a senior technician, sitting in front of screens, interpreting, and responding to alerts. Those days for most are gone. That said, even some of our largest of name companies have not sufficiently matured the CISO role to that of a participant in strategy and executive decision. Some have limited the breadth of CISO responsibility to Cyber and other technology specific risk, a mistake.

For some new to the field, or for the many CISOs laser focused on cyber or technical risk, much of what we will cover may be new ground. And of course, we are not alone in rethinking the CISO role. Redefinition and realignments are happening everywhere in the disrupted business, from structure, to organization, to vision. Business leaders envision the path forward, but voice concern for the risk they face as they undertake investments in new means, models, views, and ideas; customer focused, business driven and digital. It is no longer a technical question the CISO is tasked to address, but strategic business differentiation and direction.

*Our best tools are as effective as their fit and our capacity to use them.*
*Our best defenses are effective until they are not.*

What we need to protect us from malware or malicious attackers remains important and the core of the security role but is now more a table stakes discussion. Increasingly, there are new questions:

- "Do we know our most severe security risks? Does business accept these? Executive leadership?
- "Can we demonstrate sufficient oversight and controls to investors and regulators?"
- "Can we mitigate the risks to adoption of a more client proximate digital business model?"
- "Can we expand globally and apply the same level of operational and technical controls?"
- "Can our protective models adapt and scale?"

These are no longer technical questions, but business questions. These require both business acumen and technical expertise to address. Business change is everywhere. It is redefining partnerships, clients, organizations, and relationships, virtual and on-demand.

Threats, physical, cyber, and reputational exacerbate with the melding of IT, Industrial Control Systems, Medical Technology, Home Automation, and the Internet of Things, and with Big Data. The CISO, by whatever title, by need, and by emerging law, has become the Chief Business Protection Executive.

And there are new concerns:

- Mobility and cloud have moved sensitive data far from the infrastructure under our control.
- Technology, cloud services, and digital communities are emerging faster than we can absorb.
- Technology and culture are changing too fast for law and policy to keep pace.
- We have ample defenses for attacks and malware, but few for human behavior.
- Security and Privacy are in a tug-of-war.
- There are far too few, with the skills we need, for the threats we face.

*Finally, a word about the structure, layout, and audience for this book.*

The drivers redefining the CISO role are risk, changes in business culture and organization, and compliance with law and regulation. Although working through a section on risk or regulation is sometimes like walking face first into a wall, I have put these sections at the start of the book - introducing my thoughts on risk, controls, discussion of the ROI of security investments, standards, and compliance. As I hope you will find I ascribe to the Mary Poppins dictum that "Just a spoonful of sugar helps the medicine go down". I have tried to deliver this in short, absorbable chapters. I do not always succeed, but you can read a chapter and then go about your day. I have also tried to keep this discussion digestible through stories or examples.

*We implement prudent controls and practices to manage our risk, and to contain the cost of risk, not to eliminate it. Security can never be pristine. People are not flawless. That alone adds dirt to the system.*

It is not unusual for concepts of corporate protection and governance to be a lot like chewing rocks – gritty, hard, and sometimes difficult to digest. I have tried to deliver each section in this book almost as a blog, a mind dump of thoughts and experience accumulated as CIO, as a business protection executive, a technical strategist, a forensic specialist, and over a four-decade career. I chaired privacy initiatives; I chaired business continuity; an executive crisis response team; I was a founding member of the CIO Executive Council; I was vice chair of an OSAC committee on media industry business protection for the U.S. State department. I will try to translate that real-world experience into a discussion focused on leadership and strategy, business protection and opportunity, and the CISO as business executive. There is a lot to cover.

We as CISO need a firm understanding of the governing aspects of business, security, and operational prudence to be meaningful voices to our colleagues, executives, and boards as emerging law increasingly requires us to be. And we need to align to company, culture, people, process, and technology, all that we as a business see or touch, to be protective of our data and to respond to both the heightened risks and increasing mandates we face as companies. Whether third party risk, red flag evaluation of our partners, contracts, or security, and for privacy, continuity, investigations, or crisis response, stay with me early on as we get through the first few sections. I am sure you will appreciate the preparation for all that follows.

*Even many of the best of companies have not undertaken, completed, or maintained an inventory of the data they collect, store or process in house, or that are held or are serviced on their behalf by third parties*

There are three types of 'callouts' to watch for.

The open palm means STOP. Attention is required.

I have single line framed specific data that I thought would be an important take away. For instance, in the section on Crisis Management, I list documents and plans that need to be kept current to enable law enforcement and other specialists to assist in response to a cyberattack.

And of course, follow the owl for 'excerpts and quotable thoughts.' Some may go down in history as linguistic gems. OK. I am pushing it, but if these are helpful to you, or you like the concepts they express, please feel free to use them, tweet them, or post them, of course as is, unaltered, in polite discourse, represented appropriately, in context, with attribution to me.

Why should you read this book?

Changing business models, continually evolving cyber threats, and emerging data protection laws challenge every company. We need to understand the risks of the new business environment and position people, process, and technology to effectively respond.

GDPR - Many of us must comply with the European Union's GDPR (General Data Protection Regulation) or similar privacy laws. I share thoughts on privacy, practical experience, and tools to help attain, maintain, and sustain conformance, not just for GDPR, but an overall privacy posture.

NYDFS - For those required to adhere to the NYDFS (Department of Financial Services) Cybersecurity Regulations 23 NYCRR 500, I provide guidance that I am certain you will find helpful.

If you are concerned about emerging U.S. federal or state breach, privacy, and cyber regulation, or are working toward SOC2 or ISO 27001, or HIPAA, GLBA, FFIEC, CPRA, SOX or other domestic or global obligations, this may be helpful. I offer thoughts on risk, controls, continuity, third party evaluation and contracts, incident management, and other areas where regulation requires that we be responsive.

Many companies are required to comply with multiple laws and regulatory structures, in the U.S. and abroad, each with specific requirements, yet with significant redundancy and overlap. Other than a few that I see as predictive of a direction I do not delve into the requirements of most regulations in depth, often only as a passing reference. But I do discuss the development of an overall ecosystem, commonalities, culture, pattern, and practice of effective oversight, security, and privacy practices. Many of the concepts are globally relevant to laws and practices from Europe to Canada, U.S., and elsewhere.

For many third-party relationships have grown more complex. I share strategies and **Red Flags**. 🚩

Engaging senior management and getting buy-in to the development of an enterprise protective program for information security and cyber defense requires the presentation of a well-structured and cogent plan they can get behind. I highlight the top ten 'High Yield Investments' that you should make for cyber and enterprise technical security. These investments will lay the groundwork in assuring the safety of your organization.

College and University students in Information Technology, Security, Law, or Business will gain real world insight and perspectives and a comprehensive view of business protection.

For those prepping for the CISSP or CIPP exams or similar credentials, either on the CISO path or working within the CISO organization, or in legal, risk, or operations, this book will provide a helpful context to your study. It provides a strong platform for new levels of understanding in many of the areas you are taking the exams to achieve. Read this and you will be a better CISSP or CIPP whatever your career goals.

I provide tools for assessing and managing security and privacy risk that will help you in identifying and understanding the risks to your data, and your enterprise; what is needed to protect it, and to become a safer company. I have targeted these to the small to medium sized business, but any business can benefit.

With BC/NT - BUSINESS CONTINUITY NEW THINKING, I introduce another way to think about crisis, and about Business Continuity, a preparedness, quality management, and business focused approach. Regardless of where you are in the development or maturity of a business continuity program this will give you fresh insights, new approaches, build on your current efforts, and help raise the visibility of your program to executive leadership. It will absolutely be worth the read!

Where possible I have conducted interviews or invited others to offer their opinions and points of view. These are area experts offering personal perspectives solely to stimulate thought and conversation.

As much as we must comply with regulation, and as much as compliance is increasingly more demanding, there is much more to governance and what a CISO needs to cover in protecting business today than simply complying with regulatory requirements. I share thoughts on privacy, continuity, organization, data protection, breach mitigation and crisis response.

I look at global laws, regulatory compliance, contracts, and investigation. I cover personnel, asset, technical and cyber security planning, incident readiness and response, and the protection practices we all need to keep business safe. I introduce sufficient topical content and vocabulary for an effective conversation on compliance with internal and specialist counsel. I'll help you to ask the right questions.

One would think that many of the most mature CISO practices in our best 'big-name' companies are already doing most or all of what I will cover. That they have established procedures, aligned organization, and have embedded an environment of prudence, care, and controls into the operating culture, and have integrated an awareness of this into the business. Some have, but many have not. Even the most mature of CISOs will find some new ideas on which to build.

If you are a CIO or other technology or business executive in a position of leadership, you will want to read this as well. This book is not just for the CISO or aspiring security executive. As a CIO in an environment of growth, innovation, and managed risk for most of my career, I address this book to all executives concerned with promoting effective leadership in the protection of business, including those from business or operations tasked to assume the role of CISO. This is not a book for technicians. It is a guide for transformational business leaders facing transformational challenges.

I have had the privilege to work with some of the best CIOs, CISOs, law enforcement, attorneys, and enlightened management. We need to engage and share information with our peers, our competitors, specialist service providers, and public safety. We need to participate in public-private partnerships and to take on challenges before they become our personal problem. This book is directed to a broad range of readers and impacted professions: lawyers, privacy specialists, compliance, IT professionals, public safety, and anyone interested in protecting business at risk. We all need to work together. `

This book captures my perspectives, ideas, understandings, and opinions, much of what I have learned, and developed as a CIO, Global Head of Business Protection, technical strategist, IANS (Institute for Applied Network Security) faculty member, Senior Privacy Consultant with TrustArc, and executive advisor, perspectives I have expanded as Cyberite LLC founder, and as an author. I have documented approaches that have served me well, in a format from which any CIO, CISO or other executive or risk specialist, regardless of company size, industry or complexity, or anyone interested in moving into the field, or simply moving the ball forward, or in changing the game in their approach to developing a program of protection for an operating business can benefit. I have tried to keep to friendly and non-technical human English, understandable by most anyone with an interest. The Table of Contents lists both chapters and blogs.

I hope you enjoy CISO *Redefined, it's subtitle renamed from Leadership, Business Protection and the Chief Information security Officer to simply Protecting Business in this third updated revision,* and come away with the concepts, competencies, and practices that in my opinion build a better CISO, the right CISO to bring confidence and stability, and to clear the path for transformative business.

*"Festina Lente" - Make Haste Slowly*

# TABLE OF CONTENTS

# TABLE OF FIGURES

# CISO REDEFINED

*Protecting Business*

Martin Gomberg, CISSP, CIPP/E

## INTRODUCTION

Who could argue with the premise that mandates for regulatory, legal, and ethical compliance have become increasingly complex? Building a program to manage this is equally complex. Almost all corporate entities, municipalities, agencies, and businesses generally, and even more so in specific industries, are affected by the increasing demands of law and business governance. This is true in the U.S., Europe, Canada, and almost everywhere cross border or overseas, from Asia, to Latin America, to the Middle East. It is a given that responsible businesses and executives need to comply with changing and emerging law and regulation. It is also a given that the scope of regulatory compliance programs and governance will continue to increase with the transformation of business to new models and as we approach new markets.

Increasingly, regulations and law have focused concern on the protection of data. And increasingly, the data we need to protect to be compliant, is global, mobile, and everywhere.

And any executive that reads a newspaper, speaks with peers, or is in tune with the challenges of the new business climate, recognizes that threats against our networks, technologies, software, and risks to theft of data have become more sophisticated, targeted, pervasive, and frequent. Increasingly they are coming to recognize vulnerability and the potential for data loss as a cost inherent to rapid innovation, increased mobility and agility, and the push for market speed and expansion. They are also recognizing that neither these drivers of transformative business, nor the risks that come with them are going away.

Breach, disruption, theft, and data loss are increasingly significant issues, but not just technology issues, and technology alone, regardless of spend, or how applied, will not fix this.

It has been said and re-quoted so often that although I am quoting, I do not know from who, or from where, that "you can have security without privacy, but you cannot have privacy without security". I would also add that without effective privacy and data protection controls, conforming to the requirements of statutory privacy regulations and laws and directives, domestic and overseas, is not possible.

So, without security you cannot have privacy, and without privacy you cannot have compliance. Unfortunately, you cannot have security without getting a lot else right in organization, operations, education, and infrastructure, also knowing what you have, why, where it is, if you need it, or have the right to have it, and how you need to protect and manage it, and that is where most fail, and downstream, privacy, and by extension, compliance suffers.

Sophisticated Cyberattacks launched by skilled attackers, criminals, and rogue nation states threaten the safety of our business. Increasingly virtual, cloud, global, and mobile business models diminish our control of data. With emerging and divergent global privacy requirements, staffing and technology challenges, natural and man-made disasters that threaten continuity, and the complexity of domestic and international law and regulation, without argument, the CISO role faces increasing pressures. These pressures are both for the oversight of regulatory compliance regarding the safety, stewardship, and proper use of data under threat, and from the changing and growing scope of responsibilities and corporate expectations.

We cannot protect everything, particularly as cloud, mobility, virtualization, and shadow IT extend the assets we are asked to protect beyond our visibility and reach. And we often get too caught up on technical defenses. There is no 'box', tool, application, or appliance that can protect us in absence of clean operations and prudence. Name companies that make this mistake are successfully breached every day despite the best of technology, staff, and budgets.

And with a focus on digital transformation, IT governance is changing. This is evident in the much discussed, changing role of the CIO or Chief Information Officer, and the emergence of new digital market focused executives. Business realignment and competitive innovation is being pursued amidst a voracious consumption of media, apps, and data, managed and not, local, mobile, cloud and virtual, all of this driven by digital communities, globalized markets, and new business models.

And many of the threats we most fear, some that put us at greatest risk, we can least influence or control. These extend beyond our perimeters, out of our reach, but are devastating in consequence to us just the same. Each of us is dependent on a web of business partners, big and small, prepared, secured, and not. Many of us depend on services and technologies that impact us in ways we cannot begin to know. Our cloud providers use cloud providers, and they in turn use others. Contracts can only minimally protect us. We, our network of partners, theirs, technologies we use, and the environment in which we operate together are a system, and one part exposed, risks others.

Our laws, culture, capabilities, and risks are out of balance. This is a fact owed to the speed of change and likely will remain so for some time. Law attempts to reconcile the protection and rights of the individual as the individual and the rights individuals demand are changing. New threats continually emerge to exploit this culture in transition, and new technologies emerge to counter these. We make investments in the security we need to protect us, but the skills and staff needed to leverage these investments are difficult to keep in pace, and are increasingly difficult to find, hire or retain. Privacy is at odds with the security that protects it. Laws are out of pace with emerging technologies, how they should be used, risks they mitigate, or introduce, and the context of continually changing threats.

To many, the cost of regulation, impact on the economy, business and competitiveness, and the ROI (Return on Investment) of the compliance spend is contentious. After all, compliance at best will only ensure a minimal standard of conscientious practice is applied, it does not assure safety or eliminate risk. If a prescriptive approach were all that was needed, we would just follow the guidelines, and we would be done - open the package, add water, shake, and do whatever else that it asked to assure complete safety for our business. That is, however, not enough. There is no magic formula or secret sauce. Many understand that each business is unique, and it is only an understanding of the business, the inherent culture, inventory of consequential risk, and the properly applied tools, technology, people, processes, budget, awareness, education, and oversight, guided by knowledge, standards, and proven best practices, that moves us forward. And we move forward tediously against an ever moving and elusive goal of operating safety, but never free of risk.

But compliance, beyond concern for penalty is important. Regulations, standards, and frameworks assure that at least a minimal competency is pursued. They address issues of privacy, security, ethical behavior, consumer safety, fairness, globalization and more. They provide a measurable baseline against which adequacy can be assessed, measured, and audited. They enforce responsibility, industry norms of professional competence and practice, and corporate policy. And despite all the arguments so many will make to the contrary, they benefit business interests, operating, growth, and transformational goals.

We do not do business alone. We are participants in a value chain of material and product sourcing, piece assemblers, wholesale distributors, manufacturing, advertisement, sales, fulfillment, legal support, and consultants, and so many others. We have markets and consumers on which we depend and competitors that help define our value. Each component of our value chain in turn participates with others in a chain of dependencies. It is all a relationship based on assumption, hope, and trust, minimally visible to us, and even less so secured by contract. That which we describe as a value chain is at best a loosely structured web constructed of trust and dependency. We build indemnification in contracts as insurance, but in fact it is an acknowledgement of the dirt in the system. There are things we cannot know.

It is our hope secured in small part by third party assurance documents that each party has done the needed diligence and all operate with prudent controls, but in the end except for the largest, closest, and most visible parts of our chain which we scrutinize, it is an exercise in the blindest of faith. Without doubt there are minor players, component contributors, niche operators, too small for detection on radar upstream, perhaps applying the resources to enforce controls, or perhaps completely open and just skirting by. Without doubt, most strive for excellence. But also, without doubt, some ineptly managed, or unscrupulous actors, making the barest of investments in protection and controls, remain elemental in contribution to the chain. We hope and trust that due diligence and good practice highlights these, that those on which each link depends have built adequate redundancies and diversity and alternate suppliers as protection, but for most of us, we cannot really know.

Regulation, mandates, and minimum investments to meet compliance help bring some truth to the system.

In almost every company regardless of size, security competes for oxygen and mindshare with other business priorities, and even other technology priorities. Business needs proximity and alignment with consumers, and the consumers are mobile, social, device agnostic, and digital. The CIO is balancing pursuit of innovation and operational effectiveness in a virtualized environment, with the management of cost through cloud, and best efforts at security against unknown threat. Except in the most mature and structured of businesses, or unless compelled by mandates and regulation, competing priorities wrestle to get attention.

Compliance protects the consumer. It provides safeguards, brings greater transparency to operating practices, and assures prudent management. Pressing regular and continued examination, cleaner operations, providing visibility to correctable exposures, and driving otherwise easily distracted spend towards protecting business and consumer interests are all tangible benefits of regulation, and each is as important as satisfying regulatory demands. Scrutiny and attention to security, privacy, ethics and more, whether mandated by regulation or other, can only be for the better if driving detection of exposures, and advocating or compelling investment, and improvement in defenses and mitigation.

I spoke briefly about the encouragement of an ecosystem of safeguards and practices broadly compatible with standards and regulations, whether government, agency, industry or professional, domestic, or global. Unfortunately, there is no one single standard that if adhered to satisfies all others but adopting and fostering an effective ecosystem of prudent controls, security, and operational practices moves us closer. The effective ecosystem implements prudent safeguards, encompasses oversight, management, and effective operations, addresses security, privacy, continuity, safety, and ethics, and manages risk and compliance. This is the realm of CISO Redefined.

Business pursues the brightest prospects of innovation, digital transformation, and global opportunity, but with that also introduces the darker forces with which modern business must contend. The CISO engages the business, assuming leadership, driving adherence, acceptance, and ownership into the fabric of the business and its operation day to day. Cultivating an effective ecosystem of prudent controls, security, and sound practices gives attention to safeguards and clean operations. Encouraging the adoption of these moves the needle towards success.

In an interview with Stan Dolberg of IANS Research posted in 'The Secrets of Top Performing Information Security Officers' by Ian Barker, Stan notes that 'three out of four high performing CISOs embrace engagement. They build alliances and adhere to a risk-based approach where the business owners 'own the risk'. These 'Top Performers' see this as the means to their effectiveness. The IANS study further states that only 10% of cyber teams have "proactive stakeholder engagement programs in place". It also notes that "88 percent have no formal, ongoing data classification practices".

In a follow-up article in Network World entitled "Secrets of successful CISOs", Stan Dolberg of IANS focused on CISO reporting channels. Having surveyed more than 1200 CISOs and security teams he finds that the most successful CISOs report into risk and business roles. He also finds that those least successful at achieving organizational engagement report into technology organizations directly.

Do not be disillusioned if that is the line in which you report, and most do. There is a barrier, it has been long standing, and the CIO role is struggling with that type casting as well. It is in part self-imposed and for us to clear. We have an opportunity in recognizing this. If we are to be seen differently wherever we report, we need to pursue a new path, and take another approach. Continuous organizational engagement at all levels will be the primary driver of success, and having a formal plan for achieving engagement, including regular periodic meetings with all business, executive, IT and operational teams is the means to make this happen. Increasingly, and now compulsory under some emerging law, even operating boards require that the CISO be engaged directly, providing reports, presentation, and guidance, defining risk and the path to navigating troubled waters. This without doubt will drive engagement and likely organizational dynamics.

In my experience, I found this to be true. Assuming the lead in Business Continuity planning and overseeing the challenge of plans presented by the BC coordinators to the department heads helped in establishing credibility and partnership. Leading privacy initiatives and helping businesses to understand privacy and compliance goals did as well. Taking a lead role in Enterprise Crisis Management, promoting confidence in InfoSec and Cyber preparedness; becoming teacher and guide, as well as advocate and enabler of new initiatives were all effective ways of achieving direct engagement.

Personal relationships are also critical. Having key executives gather in my office once or twice a month for a glass or two of wine as we talked issues established friendships, broke down barriers, and brought executives less likely to have personal contact together to share ideas. Taking deputies from finance, legal and the business units to lunch at key points in decision cycles and for planning and review also provided a setting for the business priorities to be heard by those that needed to support them and for relationships to develop. I tried to do several of these early in the year to assure we were on the same page in agenda, and then again later in the year to see how we progressed. This was an excellent opportunity to get a 'heads up' on plans and thoughts as they were being kicked around and to assure that security and protective priorities were built into projects and programs being considered.

*Most of what we need to do for any, is what is required by most*

With some variance for the culture, history, geography, economy, socio-political and business structures that make the focus of our laws and operating environments unique, there are principles and best practices in management and prudent operations and technology that we as businesses share everywhere, domestic, and global. We all face similar challenges. The same threats are everywhere. And as threats loom larger and impact more of us, it is not without good reason that the community of CISO peers and the information shared between experts in the security, legal, law enforcement, privacy, and risk communities, internal and external to the business, becomes one of our greatest assets. It is a sphere on which the CISO depends. It is the application of best practices, vigilance, and shared knowledge, as well as new technologies, and the efforts of CISOs and other security specialists and experts pushing back against the darker forces globally, that ultimately will advance a slow and sliding success.

You are still reading. With that I can assume that you either are fascinated by the topic, my writing skills, couldn't get theatre tickets, recognize the importance of this discussion, are an executive, attorney, CIO, CISO or other IT professional, a risk manager, moving into the profession, or in any one of the dozens of roles impacted by regulations and the need to manage and respond to them, or any combination of the above.

Or perhaps I would add a crisis manager, individual responsible for facilities and facilities protection, for human resources, operations, a CSO, safety architect, investigator, or in law enforcement. Thank you for staying with me. Sheer enumeration of the responsible roles and the breadth of professions and activities involved in protecting the operating business makes clear the importance of the discussion ahead.

My perspective has always been to focus on clean operations and good management first and then apply the technical defenses. Going the other way in my experience is futile. There is no technology that can fill the void of insufficient oversight and operational cleanliness. Yet that is often what is done and there is no spending regardless of how big that makes that come out right.

And so, the discussion ahead is not just about technology, but about risk and about business, pragmatic, focused, and decisive. It is about the role of the CISO, a role being redefined, in governance, privacy, security, continuity, and compliance. It is about positioning an enterprise to capitalize on opportunity and new markets.

A posture of leadership and pursuit of advantage does not come without risk and a neck exposed. Risk has a cost, but the right executive, the CISO, reduces the noise in the environment and makes that cost manageable.

*The validation of the integrity of a control, protecting an available, vulnerable, and consequential asset, defines a secured system*

# CISO REDEFINED

*Protecting Business*

Martin Gomberg, CISSP, CIPP/E

## SECTION 1.   THE CISO 'REDEFINED'

There was a palpable feeling to the right of the millennial change that things were different. Prudently managed IT was embattled with a newly emerged consumerization. It was empowered by a paradigm shift towards the commoditization of technology. A perfect storm. Corporate Information Technology standards were pushed aside by demands for new and emerging devices. This was not a ground swell. It was coming from the highest levels of our companies. There were clouds. Digital communities. New populations of consumers were born by this empowerment. They ranged from the technically savvy, to those completely bypassed by the computer age, now enabled by smart phones and tablets with global reach and access. For those completely unprepared, this was their portal to family, friends, and experience. They had nearly unlimited capability, but without the awareness of security or controls the computer age inured in the rest of us. I am reminded how much today's angst over Generative AI feels so similarly disruptive.

I recall being at a family dinner, Dinner ended, plates were cleared, and as typical I pulled my smart phone to check messages. When I looked up, everyone at the table, 3 generations of adults, each had some mobile device in hand. And on the couch, even the toddler was playing with a tablet!

Although it still seems like we are just in the midst, consumerization has been shaping and driving the digital transition, mobility, cloud, social media, online communities, virtualization, and As-a-Service platforms for the past 25 years. It has changed how we build, choose, and use technology. It has changed how we build applications and networks. And it has changed the wealth of data we produce, store, process, and expose. And again, a perfect storm; an accelerated transformation in consumers to a culture of immediacy, mobility, and expectation, and a business drive towards digital innovation, each feeding off and perpetuating the other.

Many of us who thought we knew better held firm, a mistake, 'protecting' as we lagged in keeping pace with where some in our business communities clearly wanted to go. We lagged in recognizing, understanding, and addressing the changing speed, momentum, and new business dynamics. And at the same time, we lagged in recognizing the sophistication of developing threats, from data breach to targeted phishing and social engineering, to malicious worms, denial of service, and attacks against point of sale. And there were new threats emerging. Malicious cyber threats, nation state actors, botnet attacks against IoT (internet of things), and ransomware, each feeding off the expanded risk surface of the new digital world order. It was a surface exposed by new consumers, changing technologies, less effective controls, and the speed of business innovation. Traditional defenses were stretched, and porous, 'growing thin, like too little butter, spread over too much bread' paraphrasing Bilbo Baggins in Tolkien's the Lord of the Rings. And the "Eye of Sauron" was upon us.

Many held firm to traditional defensive perimeters and anti-virus alone, insufficient for the new generation of targeted threats. For most companies, IT operations had managed security, largely treating it as a network administration function, competing for attention with other administrative tasks and business driven initiatives. Most were slow in professionalizing the practice with a dedicated specialist, a skilled and experienced Chief Information Security Officer. Even then, with the introduction of the CISO, information security was treated as an information technology issue, not a business concern. With increased mobility, virtualization, globalization and new business models, and the recognition that we are not only exposed to threat, but limiting innovation and progress and accepting unwelcome accountability, this is changing.

In this book, I have *redefined* the CISO as a new and emerging 'Business Protection' executive. I would love to take credit, but this assessment is not based on my views. The role is being interpreted in emerging law, in response to data breach and cyber threat, and the obligations of corporate leadership for business accountability. Laws which frequently lag are leading and establishing the importance of the CISO as advisor to boards and executives. Business ecosystems are emerging, expanding, and integrating, from IoT, Medical Technology, SCADA, Industrial Control, Big Data, and more, and the threat environment is converging. The CISO, as the role is being defined, will not be a cybersecurity technical specialist alone, or even a technical, or security specialist. The CISO is an executive, one with broad capability in security, privacy, continuity, risk, compliance, physical, and digital threat, and an executive's perspective. As Larry Bonfante said in Lessons in IT Transformation, "Anyone with a 'C' in the title is expected to function at an executive level and have a broad perspective of the entire organization when making decisions. Functional knowledge and experience are table stakes, not differentiators."

*This CISO as redefined is different in skills, scale, capacity, approach, and acumen for business.* Sometimes called an Executive CISO, or a Global CISO, or by other titles implying broad responsibility, this new CISO is a leader, the right fit for the transformational business, digital risk culture, and evolving threat environment.

This new CISO will assume a different posture of leadership in the organization than the CISO has before. In addition to management of threat, vulnerability and defense, corporate expectation of the 'redefined CISO' is for greater participation, executive interaction, and prudent and measured advisement.

1. *It is expected that the CISO will be an active participant in strategy, compliance, policy, and architecture;* business and technical.

2. It is expected that the CISO will assume global responsibility for the protection of data, assuring conformance with domestic law, and with international privacy statutes.

3. *The CISO promotes confidence;* advising, assuring correctness in policy, and that activities, and investments are guided by clarity, a targeted business aligned agenda, and a risk focused plan.

4. Assuming a leadership role requires that the CISO is orchestrator, facilitator, and advisor.

5. The CISO engages with leadership, and with stakeholders from Legal, Human Resources, Risk, Finance and Audit. From facilities, and business protection to IT management, technical specialists, operations, and with LOB heads (lines of business). It is a job that cannot be done alone or in isolation.

6. *The CISO will engage across the business and reach out,* leading by policy, activity, and example, embedding in the business process, not as an add-on, but in the structure and fabric of critical initiatives, providing security-by-design. Equally, the CISO must be engrained in the diligence process and in ongoing partner relationships across the *"value chain"* (Competitive Advantage, 1980, Michael Porter) assuring needed controls and regulatory conformance are in place and in practice, from 'source to production, from sale to fulfillment'.

7. *The CISO will take the lead,* with government, regulators, external auditors and counsel, law enforcement, solution providers, and with industry, and other professional security peers. Threats, laws, technology, and business are changing continually, and the CISO needs to stay current with the tools for defense, and the laws that dictate how these can be applied.

8. *The CISO provides legitimacy to statements by accountable leadership;* and is emerging as the appropriate role not only for addressing issues of security, but increasingly privacy, continuity, reputation, and other areas of business risk. The CISO mission is one of trust, relationship, and communication, called upon to deliver an often complex and uncomfortable message to managing boards, executive leadership, and operating management, in a digestible way.

New York State Department of Financial Services Cybersecurity Regulation (23 NYCRR 500) specifies that the CISO shall report at least annually to the board. It specifies that this be in writing, addressing the state of cybersecurity risk, controls, and other issues that impact the safety of the business. This mandate applies to banks, insurance companies and other financial institutions operating or licensed in New York State but is also directionally indicative of new law anticipated at the state level across the country, and across industries. Law is assigning executive accountability and setting expectations of the CISO role.

In some organizations, in addition to being an expert in technical security, the CISO assumes a corporate management role, and broader domain responsibilities. These may include IT or overall business risk. Perhaps staff, budget management, and planning. This may be unfamiliar to some CISOs that have progressed into the role as developers, lawyers, or system administrators. It may be increasingly expected that the CISO be involved with privacy, regulation, licensing, contracts, and compliance statements, and in some organizations, systems availability, application security, and protective infrastructure. The CISO is the singular cultivator of policy, practice, strategy, and oversight in some companies. In others, the CISO is a validator of policies and controls, not the architect.

Defamation and disparaging remarks against celebrities, institutions, programs, businesses, executives, and corporate personnel are often seen in online space, and they are broadcast widely through digital communities. They seek to embarrass, encourage others with similar grievances, or to do damage, or threaten harm. Increasingly this foreshadows or coincides with physical attacks, riots, assaults, disturbances, or protest. Cyberattacks are no longer just disruptive. Increasingly they are directed at causing or encouraging destruction, violence, harassment, and compromise of operational safety. As incidents increasingly blur the lines between technical and physical, the CISO assumes, along with the CSO (Chief Security Officer), a greater role in the management of incidents and crisis.

So, if a hiring manager, what should you be looking for, who is the right fit, and what is the best profile for this executive level CISO position?

The ideal CISO candidate is at the same time executive, a business presence, technical specialist, manager of risk, and of incident and crisis. The CISO joins the Chief Information Officer, Chief Digital Marketing Officer, Chief Privacy Officer, Chief Compliance Officer, and other emerging positions redefining the traditional C Suite. A curious mind, a deep thinker, a planner, a strategist, and a trusted resource. The CISO is a leader by strength of presence and confidence, a bringer of questions, soliciting more questions, and encouraging answers. The CISO is a specialist in conforming technology and operations to law and regulation, a security evangelist, a business leader, partner, advisor, and confidant.

The *CISO Redefined* is not fantasy. Leading CISO's in our most mature and progressive organizations are already there. They have assumed roles of executive partnership, as leaders, and advisors, or are steadily moving in this direction. Those who have not, soon will. Laws including the newly emergent NYDFS Cybersecurity Regulations for banking, insurance and financial businesses specifically address the CISO, how they will communicate to executive leadership, how frequently, how they will be engaged, and their contribution to executive accountability. It is what is expected, or soon will be, and we all need to be there.

*Some technologies will meet the moment. Others will last a moment.*
*Business is not static. Risk moves and needs change*

# CISO
# REDEFINED

*Protecting Business*

---

Martin Gomberg, CISSP, CIPP/E

## SECTION 2.   RISK IN SIMPLE TERMS

We live with risk in business. Risk cannot be eliminated in entirety and perhaps the positive of that is that it keeps us aware, competitive, and investing in growth, new ideas, and continued improvement. We invest in new markets and products out of concern for market saturation, obsolescence, and the emergence and success of competitors. We invest in higher performing systems because someone else will. We build Big Data Lakes and business intelligence systems to find that next opportunity before it slips away. We move apps, data, and infrastructure into the cloud, and make our workforce mobile to expand our reach, speed, and to be everywhere. We improve our privacy and security posture to address regulatory risk, and protect business, clients, and community, and to clear the path for opportunity. We infer, derive, nuance, and extrapolate new data to gain an edge.

There is no opportunity that does not come with risk. Business is not static, and all change comes with risk. The pace of business is accelerating, and with speed, risk increases. The reach of business is everywhere, and with that our risk surface expands. The potential to miss opportunity is itself a risk.

As said above, business risk cannot be eliminated. It can be avoided or deferred in specific instances by the strategic or tactical decisions we make, in each of these cases moving or shifting risk elsewhere, or later. Risk can also be transformed. A centralized manufacturing model simplifies production but concentrates risk. A distributed model, with adequate redundancy, can reduce physical risk, but may increase the cost and complexity of operation. Changing the model transforms the risk.

Business risk can also be addressed, or 'mitigated'. The purpose of good governance and most regulatory safeguards is for the recognition, understanding, and measured control of risk. Where mitigation of a risk is not prudent, whether by direct, compensating, interlaced, or layered controls, then the cost of risk can be lowered, pooling, and sharing the cost of risk through the purchase of insurance. Where the cost or impact of a given risk is absorbable, or assignable to others through price increase, or in other ways, the risk can be accepted. These are business decisions. These are decisions made by each company in accordance with its capacity, risk concerns, and risk control drivers, mandates by regulation, or by requirements or indemnifications defined in contract. The sum of these decisions shapes the risk mitigation strategy and plan for a company, and each company plan will be different. Traditionally CISOs have approached risk with strategies of "accept, reduce, transfer or mitigate." But risk is diachronic. It lives in a continuum. For any given risk, any or all of these strategies may be appropriate at different points or as context changes.

**Risk by definition**

Many of us talk about risk. If we are to understand, inventory and effectively manage our risk, we need parameters that define it. There are methodologies like FAIR, a Factor Analysis for Information Risk (http://www.fairinstitute.org/) that help analyze and quantitatively measure information risk and the factors that contribute to it, and formulaic approaches (https://www.linkedin.com/pulse/calculating-information-security-risk-scott-rosenmeier/?trackingId=QbnrWs2cnl66k8J34bMkbA%3D%3D) with much greater granularity and sophistication than the generally accepted 'risk = (impact x probability)'. Other approaches are more qualitative and subjective.

It is reasonable to interject an <u>operating definition of 'risk'</u> for most security, governance, and regulatory concerns as:

- A realizable threat where there is,
- A vulnerability that can be exploited due to the absence or insufficiency of an effective mitigating control or controls and,
- There is the potential or likelihood of impactful consequence
- Reasonable action or investment would be prudent and responsible

Many primarily focus on the first three conditions in defining risk: a realizable threat, an exploitable vulnerability in absence or insufficiency of controls, and a likelihood of consequence. Whereas this may be enough in many cases, I prefer the inclusion of the test for prudence and responsible action, and so use all four conditions inclusively in definition of what I consider 'real' risk.

Let me provide an over-the-top example as to why. In applying the outrageous test of a meteor impact, it is in fact "a realizable threat, there are no realistic controls to prevent it, and there certainly are consequences". That said, this does not satisfy the fourth consideration of whether 'reasonable action or investment would be prudent or responsible', a test of sensibility, nor does it recognize probability, or relative imminence, basic requirements for making a mitigating action reasonable.

My good friend Rich Guida has argued that 'the more traditional view of risk always builds in the concept of negligible risk, which the meteor strike would be'. Big consequences certainly, but far outweighed by the infinitesimal probability, thus producing negligible risk. In that construct, in his opinion, there is no need to consider reasonable action or investment - just decide that any negligible risk shall be ignored.

Yes, but not always. Risk is the flipside of opportunity. Risk also exists and must be evaluated in context of the environment in which it is assessed. A strictly binary assessment of risk, it is negligible, or it is not, fails to recognize the potential of even negligible risk in one context to create, facilitate, influence, or exacerbate other risk conditions, be exacerbated by other risk conditions, or assume a different level of importance in a different context, or if context or behavior changes. It also fails to recognize potential impacts or impediments to opportunities out of context to its current environment. Lastly, negligible risk may be negligible in the context of the direct or compensating controls that mitigate or constrain it but remain negligible only if controls remain sufficient. Of course, Rich might just say 'things change'. Keep it simple.

Approached either way, with an exception for the deep underground bunkers built for the 'designated survivors' or critical members of the federal government intended to assure continued operation, whether negligible and ignored, or failing the test of sensibility as unreasonable, it likely would not be prudent for most companies to invest in underground hardened facilities or other means of protecting against extinction level events. This is a risk we simply and tacitly accept (most pretty much ignore completely unless into doomsday scenarios) and go on about our lives.

In absence of these four 'inclusive' conditions, in most cases a specific risk would not likely become a focus of audit, regulation, liability, investment, or executive attention. We will use this operating definition as a test of risk throughout this book whether addressing technical risk, privacy, physical threats, or continuity.

We also use the word 'mitigation' frequently in the context of risk. From the Businessdictionary.com, mitigation is defined as the "elimination or reduction of the frequency, magnitude, or severity of exposure to risks, or minimization of the potential impact of a threat". That definition works for our purposes.

Having identified the universe of risk we as business potentially face, even having limited the definition of risk to only that risk for which reasonable action would be prudent and responsible, the enormity of the task of mitigating all potential risk even in that limited pool quickly becomes obvious. Regardless of the size of company, staff, or available resources, and regardless of commitment, mitigating all potentially realizable risk is both untenable, and if attempted, would be costly, and unmanageable.

Equally, it quickly becomes clear that addressing all potentially realizable risk is unnecessary, and that of the stock of identified potential risk, only that risk most consequential to those most important, sensitive, and exposed assets need attention.

Even having defined the pool of priority risk, it should also be clear that in the context and priorities of an operating business, not all risk, even that determined to be of highest priority, can necessarily be addressed with the same immediacy, or with the same effectiveness.

*Fish still swim in murky waters*

What risk is deemed addressable, or actionable, and in what order, is a business decision. It falls to the business to determine whether **reasonable action or investment would be prudent and responsible**. It is a decision based both on that risk which is deemed material, impactful to the core purpose and objectives of the business, and where a given response is likely to achieve a positive result, or at minimum a directionally favorable outcome. It is a judgement made based on the highest degree of confidence of success, for the potential investment a given business can make at any one time, or over a reasonable period, given the resources in dollars, time and people. It is also based on the most immediate requirements of the business, or compliance with law, regulation, and standards.

**Let me also take this opportunity to introduce that which I call 'caducous' risk** (a name based on a property in biology). This is recognized or potential risk best shed, addressed, mitigated, or compensated early or while manageable in anticipation of its development.

Risk management begins with an inventory and prioritization of risk, and specifically:

- Materiality of risk

- Relative imminence of the threat

- Severity of outcome if unaddressed

- Presence or absence of compensating controls or conditions

- Potential to create, facilitate, influence, or exacerbate other risk conditions

- Likelihood of successful mitigation

**Assessment of risk**

Risk is assessed to identify, measure, and inventory the exposure that threats or classes of threats, a country, region, political structure, economy, financial system, business, business function, or the technology, people, and processes that an operating business depends upon may face. It must be considered in terms of potential, likelihood of realization (probability), and consequence (severity of effect). An inventory of risk is needed to develop a plan for mitigation or other action, and to appropriately assign ownership of that risk to a designated individual or group so that it can be managed.

*A risk is only meaningful where a vulnerability exists to a consequential asset, in absence of effective mitigating controls, and sensibility and prudence determines that there is not only the possibility, but a probability, and imminence to realization, such that consideration of action, is reasonable, appropriate, and timely*

The assessment can simply be an acknowledgement, with actions taken or not, a simple list, or a more formalized qualitative assessment describing the risk, potential impacts, and outcomes. It may take a cost or other metric based quantitative approach. Mature multinational, multi-regulatory, multi-entity, or multi-functional businesses with complex analysis or reporting requirements will benefit from the adoption of a comprehensive governance or risk management platform, or an integrated GRC (Governance, Risk, and Compliance) system for the management of their risk inventory, as well as comprehensive frameworks (NIST, ISO, CIS, etc..), to assess their risk and control ecosystem. But these tools are not always a fit to small or medium sized businesses without the resources, skills, and budgets to manage them. Some may find a simple spreadsheet or SMB targeted platform sufficient. Several risk management resources for SMBs are listed on the NIST website. In all cases, a risk inventory starts with key stakeholders in a business focused discussion on objectives, priorities and risks, and of these, timing and critical business cycles, concerns, and opinions as to how some of these risks might be mitigated.

Regardless of threat, risk does not exist out of context of a vulnerable asset. Even so, a vulnerable asset is not actionably at risk, unless potentially, and even more, 'likely' exposable, by nature, proximity, or other, with reasonable imminence, to a given threat. Both context and imminence are important.

It is insufficient to inventory risk. It needs to be prioritized. And not all risk should be addressed, or at least not with the same urgency. Generally, efforts should be focused on risks of highest priority. Specifically, efforts should be focused on those priorities where the effort has a likelihood of success for a positive outcome with a reasonable and proportionate investment, in a reasonable timeframe. Even where a given risk is high, if not imminent, a relative term, or if no obvious means to address the risk is apparent, it may remain important, studies initiated to define potential options, but not be considered priority to fund or immediately address. At the same time, risk that is low priority in relevance, imminence, or consequence, in absence of complicating factors that might raise the need for attention, should not become a distraction.

Over the years, I have found that inexperienced advisors, auditors, or staff, engaged or tasked with the review of risk, often raise concerns about the vulnerabilities they uncover without paying attention to context. This is just inexperience. It shakes up a lot of people, bells get rung, calls come from management, meetings are called, the world goes out of balance, and clarification is painful. It also demonstrates confusion over what risk is, and when we should address it. It makes little sense to invest too much in the closing of vulnerabilities unless they create, expose, or exacerbate potentially viable and consequential risk in the presence of realizable or imminent threat, and when we act, we can achieve a successful outcome. The potential theft of the cafeteria lunch menu does not constitute consequential risk and should not drive our energies. Our financials, critical intellectual properties, and sales strategy should.

We as businesses often spend too much time, resource, and money addressing vulnerabilities to threats that are unlikely to be realized, against which existing or layered defenses are adequate, or there are adequate compensating controls. Even where controls are absent or insufficient, that attention may be misplaced where there is nothing meaningful or sensible to do or if realized the event would be limited in impact, or absorbable without consequential effect. And sometimes where risk deserves significant attention, successful mitigation is unrealistic, and the risk might be better addressed in other ways. And risk may be synergistic, a specific threat being low concern, except when exacerbated by other threats, specific vulnerabilities, context, or timing. A short-term electrical disruption is likely of less concern to a business in the wee hours than it might be during the end of quarter financial close or preparation of a corporate filing.

An effective prioritization of risk requires that we know our business. It requires that we know our physical assets, where they are, how they are configured, how they are protected, and where they are potentially exposed:

- In current state

- Through interaction with other assets

- Through change of context (when a physical asset is moved, upgraded, or altered)

- Through cyclic change or change to the business in focus, direction, priorities, or with growth over time

For much of our risk we need an understanding of our data, what it is, where it resides, its importance and sensitivity, and how it is protected. It is the exposed asset, by the significance of the data that it holds, that more than most else renders an asset, and the risk to that asset, consequential. And we need to understand our processes, how they fit and contribute to the business, and their relative importance at different times.

In a blog titled "'How to Sell Risk Assessment Benefits to IT Executives", Charles Cresson Woods states "regardless of the perceived need for security, executives and budget planners want quantitative justification for spending. A risk assessment is a definitive statement about what needs to be done to improve or correct a security program".

Risks are best modeled and explained in terms of a business consequence, not specific threats, and vulnerabilities. There is no risk to technology, only to business, and our greatest risk is in not realizing this. If it has no consequential impact to the business, it isn't a risk.

*The order in which risks are addressed is a business decision based on the priority of each risk, and the likelihood that the intended results are achievable with a reasonable degree of confidence for the investment in dollars and effort a business can make at any one time, or over a reasonable period*

Sometimes modeling affords the opportunity to reevaluate risk. If all fulfillment processing is from one location, and the risk of concern is the loss of fulfillment capability to fire, flooding, or other, the best action taken may not be to target a specific vulnerability at all (for instance, the absence of a pre-action sprinkler) but to rethink the question and arrive at a more encompassing solution (implement a redundant system at another location). This would ensure that orders can process, and that fulfillment continues unabated. While addressing the specific concern of fire by installing a pre-action system is prudent and would better protect the building, fire might still leave the business at risk. At a minimum it might interrupt the ability to process orders while damaged systems are repaired, replaced, and brought back online, and authorities inspect the damage before permitting re-occupancy. Focusing the action taken on the consequence to the business instead assures continuity. Even if there were a fire, or any other event impactful to the primary data center, or the building in which it operates, or the operator's ability to enter the building and bring it back online, or if a power loss, impact to the telecom needed to reach it, flood, hurricane, or other event local to the facility, if redundant elsewhere and active, the ability to process orders remains uninterrupted.

**ROI of risk and security**

Some executives are frustrated at the futility of attempting to identify risk, what a bad day would look like, and what the cause or impact might be. Equally, they frustrate at how much to spend to take some of that concern off the table. They are frustrated at why that answer cannot be delivered with greater clarity. Some in private moments might prefer to just take an agile or Just-In-Time approach in responding to threats as they arise. Of course, this may work if dealing with the innocuous or the completely un-anticipatable. But in most other considerations, they sit back, frustrations pass, and better judgement takes hold realizing budget realities, law, and investors would demand that prudence be applied and an assessment of risk be made.

But inventorying all possible threats, modeling scenarios for protecting against them, and then responding to the universe of threats we might encounter would be unwieldy for even the best resourced amongst us. Conversations with management absent a common vocabulary are often difficult. It is often hard to get on the same page as to priorities and where to make the investments, and it is difficult to make the case for ROI against threats we cannot measure, quantify, or predict with any certainty. Several approaches as you will see later (Adaptive BC; BC/NT) prefer to focus on outcomes over causes and prepare for these. Loss of access to a critical facility for an extended duration would be an outcome of a disaster. The impact would be the same, and preparation if focused on outcome would be the same, whether the cause was fire, building collapse, street closure, or many other potential causes.

We all look at threats. We would be crazy not to if we are to understand and assess our risks. Besides, laws, standards and professional training tell us to. But there are so many. Although the assessment of risk is a required component of many regulations, and required for certification to most standards, and for effective security, the complexity of threats in the cyber realm and increasingly elsewhere raises questions about the practicality of focusing on traditional threat inventories in assessing risk. Much the same with focusing only on vulnerabilities despite the benefit of CVSS (Common Vulnerability Scoring System) and

CVE (Common Vulnerability and Exposures). Looking at impacts and prioritizing the material outcomes we are most concerned about, may for some be time better spent. This would focus resources on the concerns for which we should prepare. Instead of 'Denial of Service Attack', 'Hurricane', or other causal agent or threat, we would instead focus on business impacts: 'clients cannot place orders', 'deliveries are interrupted', or 'cannot run payroll'. "We had a storm and now we can't take orders". 'Why' (we had a storm) is a secondary consideration and adds clarity, but the What ('we can't take orders') puts the issue in context of business and is where every executive will be focused.

Examining specific threats guides preparatory investments. A pre-action sprinkler system is installed out of concern for the threat of fire. That said, it does little in response to an explosion or a gas leak although each will render a facility unusable, and all require a mitigating response. The inability to fulfill orders, manufacture product, or to serve clients for e-commerce via our website are all outcomes of the loss of the facility. It is a risk with serious consequences regardless of cause. Examining outcomes positions for business aligned preparedness, not only incident aligned preparedness. Business risk should be examined in the context of consequential outcomes. If we sit back and think about all the threats that might cause a building to be unusable, and the defenses against or in response to them, it will clearly take far more time than to address the fact that the building is unusable and address where we go from there. That said, be pragmatic. Install the pre-action sprinkler anyway.

I mentioned 'material risk' earlier and defined it as a risk to a business purpose or objective but I did not take the time to put it in context. A malicious attacker penetrates our defenses corrupting the server that hosts the corporate lunch menu. Not to trivialize the breach of our defenses, if limited only to that impact, this would be for most an inconvenience, and other than forcing the serving of a default lunch menu, not be seen as material. The same event in context of a hospital or health facility that serves meals to patients with dietary specificity to their health needs would absolutely be a material event. Context always matters.

Risk should be described in terms of the objectives the business cares about. Focusing on business risk also simplifies and reduces the effort of the assessment as compared to evaluating the impact of hundreds of combinations of potential 'threat to vulnerability' pairs. Most importantly, it puts things in a language and perspective that eases management's ability to understand the 'ask' you are making of them. I want to protect fulfillment means more than any number of nightmare scenarios you might present.

With provisions for the management of negative outcomes, examining the line-up of potential causes and exercising scenarios to address them individually becomes a supportive exercise to a risk register that is already business aligned. Of course, for the most likely threats of concern, scenarios should be exercised anyway. We do not want our dogma to get ahead of us. But exercising the most consequential of business impacts should take priority.

*Know normal so you can better recognize that which is not*

## RISK IN CONTEXT

Gary S. Lynch in At Your Own Risk puts the understanding of corporate risk in the perspective of the individuals managing it, and their corporate responsibilities. He says that "Risk can be broad and overwhelming across a value chain; therefore, disparate views of the way risk may be managed exist."

Risk lives in context. Crisis is a condition, but sometimes also a perspective. If a major business disrupting event significantly impacts a company, and they alone have been impacted putting them at disadvantage to competitors, they would certainly from their perspective be in crisis. If at the same time all the company's competitors are equally impacted, or there is a failure or disruption of their common sources of supply, or their mutual markets, if competitors aren't doing business, and everyone is affected in the same way, and at the same time, is the company in crisis, or simply on hold until conditions clear or markets resume? This question is important in understanding what is, what should, and what in fact triggers a crisis response.

If there were a major terrorist event or devastating natural disaster all eyes would be glued to broadcast news or cable news networks. Advertisers, if and where they could, likely would pull ad spots from cable, broadcast, and online media to protect spending and wait for consumer attentions to return after the crisis has resolved. For these media networks, everyone, competitors alike, are all impacted, and put on hold in the same way. No single competitor for the ad market is impacted any greater than another so they are disadvantaged and penalized equally until markets resume. Unless there are other complicating factors, none is in crisis more, or less than another, competitors or not, but all are on hold. Of course, there is the question as to who is best positioned to pick up where they left off and reengage first and fastest when the flag goes up.

Similarly, following a major attack at a theme park, attendance at theme parks, zoos, and other entertainment facilities, parks, and malls might be disrupted, but equally for all until calm returns or caution wanes. Again, unless there are additional factors, none are in crisis more, or less than any other.

Differentiation matters. A blight impacting bananas from one country or region in Latin America impacts all fruit importers that are limited by restrictive supplier contracts or insufficient business infrastructure to importing bananas solely from that region. They are all equally disadvantaged by the dwindling or halted supply, and distributors with whom they have established relationships would be left waiting. If one or more importers have the capacity to import bananas from Africa or elsewhere, and to sell them to the same distributors taking market share and client relationships, they would be advantaged, and those that are unable to participate would be in crisis. If the duration of that crisis were sufficiently long lasting, and if their business inadequately diversified, faced with the loss of clients and markets to better positioned competitors, they would potentially face a crisis of continuity.

*Our reaction to a potential threat can be as lethal to an operating business as the threat itself.*

Crisis is not solely about an event, but a function of the context and duration of the event, and of the resources and reserves in place. We need to not only understand our risk, but also interpret risk in context. Business may be disrupted. If sufficiently, this itself is a crisis, but perhaps not a crisis that threatens continuity, or at least not immediately. The continuity of an operating business is most often threatened when the 'Burn Rate', the rate of consumption of resources for the duration of the event, exceeds the tolerance and capacity of resources and reserves of a company before markets resume and normalcy returns.

Financial resources and hard assets are not the only consumable resources. Soft assets like trust, confidence, brand loyalty, and employee morale are equally consumable commodities. These can be depleted in crisis, or simply by neglect, poor management, or behavior. These are in themselves a major risk factor to consider. Soft asset deficiencies are too often a self-induced symptom of a poorly managed company. They deplete rapidly in crisis if given inadequate attention by weak leaders during normal operations. The company that does not focus on encouraging the morale of staff when things are good should not count on loyalty when they are not. The company that does not monitor, challenge, and manage reputational insults and grievances, or focus on developing a positive relationship with its clients and markets, should not be surprised by fickle commitment to brand when confronted by a reputational crisis. Newton's Third Law of Motion dictates that 'Every action has an equal, but opposite reaction'. Every response to perceived risk introduces risk. It is important that we understand this. Our reaction to a potential threat can be as lethal to an operating business as the threat itself.

The company that chooses not to blemish its proudly flaunted and very marketable 100% record of achievement in maintaining a 'never closed' policy, and demands that employees show up for work, despite an approaching hurricane, or immediately after, while roads are still hazardous, learns quickly that forced to choose between personal and family safety, and employer, for some, it is an easy and obvious choice.

Companies that position for the risk by adopting flexible HR policies enabling remote work, and that invest in the provision of adequate and effective technology supporting these policies, accommodates the needs of employees and their concerns for family safety, demonstrate that employees are important to the business, and to the leaders making the decisions, stays productive, and will lose less and do better.

Neither are irreconcilable extremes. The prudent and innovative company would protect its 'never closed' record by allowing for an open and operational company supported by workers who choose to be there, or for operational or personal reasons need to be there, and others working remotely from home. A Sheriff's department on the east coast, with which I have worked in the past, manages jail facilities. They need their officers and so provide accommodations on site for families during major storms, removing concern for the safety of family. This allows deputies when called upon to 'serve and protect', and to focus their attention on public safety through the storm, knowing families are safe.

The natural inclination of most in a health threatening outbreak and probably the best defense against exposure to pandemic disease is to avoid aggregating with others. Most, if required to work by employers, would be reticent to commute to jobs, or intermingle with crowds at the busiest times of the day. In pandemic disease, as in the prior examples, work from home, or flexible work shifts, are provisions that support employee safety. These encourage employee loyalty and business stability. The employer that demands business as usual, forcing presence and a normal commutation, converts business operational risk, to employee safety risk, which amplifies the problem, not mitigating either. A private bus dispatched to pick up key workers might address both the need for specific employees to continue critical operations and lessen commutation concerns, or better still, the infrastructure and policies to support work from home.

The assessment of risk is complex, time-consuming, and expensive to perform, and many small to medium sized businesses are inadequately resourced to do it properly or to any great effect. On the other extreme, a very large domestic or multi-national company is not only likely to afford and be capable of an effective assessment, but also by its size, diversity of markets, suppliers, locations, and resources, be inherently resistant to much of the risk it encounters, or capable of absorbing it.

Equally, a well-resourced company may invest in a one-time mitigation to take a given risk off the table (move facilities to another location for instance) or may have adequate reserves and liquidity to fund a crisis event 'just-in-time'. In this case, they may neither plan for it, nor bake it into the budget year over year.

'Just in Time' risk management may be attractive to some that can afford it, but investors and regulators might feel uncomfortable. I suspect to reduce the annually carried burden in time, resource, and budget of risk planning and management, some companies would welcome that position, and if not for investors, auditors, and regulators, and the dictates of the laws to which they must comply, more might consider it.

*The continuity of an operating business is threatened when the consumption of resources for the duration of an event, exceeds the tolerance and capacity of the resources and reserves of that business, before markets resume and normalcy returns*

## THE ROI OF RISK INVESTMENTS

Some of the largest companies rightly ask for justification of the spend for risk assessment projects. This includes risk assessment staffing, and risk-based investments in security and other areas. Some press for quantitative justification of ROI, a return on investment.

Anthony Czarnik, a security expert states "If my business had an IT leader … I would hold my IT Director's feet to the fire while they justify their information security investments and prove that their information security initiatives address the most significant risks to the organization's assets."
http://www.tripwire.com/state-of-security/featured/justifying-security-investments/

It is a frustration for so many IT leaders that we continue to make investments, yet vulnerabilities persist in the face of evolving and emerging threats, and we cannot get a solid level set of where we are, and why despite investment, the stock of risk does not seem to diminish.

Quoting from Czarnik, "from a high level, the risk assessment process is simple and unconditionally consistent. By determining gaps in our security coverage, probability of exploitation and impact of loss, we can calculate risk. The findings from our risk assessment will lead to our development of a custom implementation roadmap, which will be based on risk, effort, and resources".

Bruce Schneier, a well-known security expert discusses the difficulties in applying ROI and loss metrics to the current threat environment on his blog site stating that "ROI as used in a security context is inaccurate. Security is not an investment that provides a return, like a new factory or a financial instrument… security is about loss prevention, not about earnings. The term just does not make sense in this context."
https://www.schneier.com/blog/archives/2008/09/security_roi_1.html

This perspective is understandable but frustrates leaders that need to manage investments and balance priorities. They do so by recognizing a need, prioritizing that need, and then investing sufficiently (preferably not excessively) for either an expected successful outcome, a perceived and measurable improvement, or simply a demonstrable achievement of tangible and directional progress.

They need to know how far they have come in taking some of the pain off the table. They would like to know how much remains. At a minimum, they want to know if they are making progress in the right direction, if they have moved the needle; some satisfaction that there has been a benefit derived of the investment.

*Absent a plan when asking leadership to fund investments, please note that facial contortions and that gagging sound are not usually a good sign.*

Equally frustrating is the sizing of investments. How much do we take on at once? Are we spending enough? Will investments made be sufficient? How will we know if for the 'spend' we were successful? What is the saying – 'you do not get credit for jumping 95% of the way across a chasm, but that last missed 5% gives you something to ponder on your way down'. Is our cyber spending like that? If we protect ourselves, but insufficiently, isn't that the same as not at all, making anything spent wasted?

The relationship of the CISO to those in executive leadership approving the disbursement, and the support of the CISO by other leaders, corporate stake holders, enterprise security, or corporate investment committees, is often the only basis for trust and confidence in the investment. The development and nurturing of those relationships are a success factor for the CISO and the corporate security or business protection program overall.

There is also the question of structure. Can we budget a multi-year program of investment and progress toward a better state, or do we need to take this on at once? We hear the message that the risk can be managed, but it will never go away. If that is so, most would be comfortable if we could bake some prudence into the budget and plan a predictable and reasonable spend against a prioritized inventory of risk, and at least manage it, and at best take it down over time.

We cannot easily calculate the cost of a cyber event without knowing what it is likely to be, what it will impact, how long that impact will last, and the resources needed to address it. History is not a very helpful guide as the nature, mode, mechanics, and characteristics of attacks adapt and change.

We look at scenarios, but they are limited in what they can forecast. We cannot easily assess the cost implications of a so called Zero Day attack, undetected malware not identified by traditional means and defenses. Unchallenged, this could attack systems and network infrastructure, exfiltrating, wiping or corrupting data, and potentially destroying hardware. It could propagate as an attack launched from our network against business partners or clients. It could establish an encrypted tunnel back to a criminal source, an undetectable pipeline for stealing our stores of sensitive and confidential data.

*Our accountability and risks have increased even as the technologies and our most consequential data are further distanced from our control*

**What are the cost implications of an attack?**

- Identifying and mitigating the attack, finding the deposited malware, and identifying the damage done
- Replacement and restoration
- Loss of productivity, business disruption and reputation cost
- There may be litigation for disrupting other businesses, or the failure to deliver on contract commitments
- Order cancellations, manufacturing, shipping, and other product delays would be likely
- Regulatory penalties could be imposed if controls are deemed to have been insufficient

The implications of the exfiltration of data in a massive breach against any large company with extensive stores of personal data are considerable. This could impact the personal data of employees or clients across the country and abroad. The loss, theft, or exposure of personal data in a successful breach can require the notification of customers in every state in which the business operates, require credit monitoring or other service offerings to all potentially impacted clients to make good, and more if there is demonstrable harm. There would likely be a requirement to retain counsel to parse the varied laws for federal agencies, and for each state, and there would likely be reporting requirements to state attorneys, regulatory penalties, and litigation.

Mandatory remediation, regulatory oversight and a period of continual scrutiny and reporting might be imposed. Investors would be uncomfortable, and the attention and press unwelcome. Evolving domestic laws and statutes are increasing accountabilities and penalties for failure to provide effective technical, operational, and administrative safeguards and stewardship. Privacy and data protection laws in much of Europe and countries elsewhere overseas, can make this cost concerning, in some cases as much as four percent of a company's annual revenue. How would we begin to budget for the loss and damage? We would turn to insurance to offset some. It would be a bad day.

And although less recently, there are threats beyond cyber. Name companies, landmarks, tourist attractions, transportation hubs, and other alluring targets in major cities plan for the possibility of a terrorist attack. Those near the roads, trains, airways, and waterways leading to major cities, or popular destinations face the same concerns. They plan for terrorism impacting them directly, or the geographic areas or business markets on which they depend, or simply disruption in customer focus and behaviors. Crisis events from active assailants to privacy breach, digital assaults on reputation, riots, and protests all have amplified as recent threats to business. None are predictable or of a nature that we can easily gauge.

*A community that believes in the mission, internalizes the goal,*

*and understands their role and how they participate advances a culture.*

*Inclusion, advocacy, and education encourage its success*

So, regardless of the source of threat, in some of these areas there is some risk that we simply cannot know. All reasonable business planners accept this. That being the case, let's return to our definition of risk and the requirement for testing prudence and responsibility to justify investments. And so, the dilemma of management.

- There is still the case that we cannot say when
- Explain why without the requested defense in place it has not happened so far
- Why we should assume it will happen now
- That all the investments made so far have not sufficiently addressed the problem
- That an investment proposed now will make us any safer

In short, when is investment in security to deal with perceived risk enough, and are we investing in and protecting the right things?

- Are the newest tools needed?
- Are we getting the most out of security investments we have already made?
- Are we just chasing shooting stars, glittery objects, and the latest trends?

In recent days, some forward-thinking companies have been focused on developing a taxonomy of risk factors to attempt to better understand risk and using factor analysis and other statistical methods to determine the probability of occurrence.

An effective risk taxonomy is an advancement but faced with so broad a universe of changing threats and derived risk, even then, exactly what to spend on, and exactly what we get for that spend still eludes us. Without diminishing the importance of an accurate taxonomy in understanding risk, and a methodology for determining the probability of occurrence, there remains the more fundamental underlying operating issues which determine consequence and limit our ability to manage our risk exposure effectively. It comes down to how well we know our data and assets. That is a first step towards making any assessment of risk useful.

Many companies, even well-known name companies, have not undertaken, completed, or maintained an inventory and catalog of the location, and classification of the data in their environment, and therefore have not assessed the value and sensitivity or the business confidentiality of the data assets they collect, process, or store in house, or are held or serviced by third parties. Many simply do not know where their greatest data asset risk lives, or where it lives at any specific time. This lack of understanding as to that which is consequential creates risk. Shadow IT increases this; lack of clarity and consistency in laws and regulations increase this further; and risk moves. We need to understand the impact on priority assets for protective or responsive action to be both prudent and sensible, and therefore reasonable.

*The potential to miss opportunity is itself a risk.*

Many also do not have a handle on the infrastructure that houses these data assets. Many do not know where or on which devices, network segments, or storage arrays or media, the most consequential data resides. Without knowing what is of consequence and where, it is difficult to determine the appropriateness and effectiveness of the protective mechanisms that secure them. They cannot determine if the systems are properly configured or hardened against intrusion or if administration and access is sufficiently granular. They cannot determine if events are adequately recorded at these systems so that incidents can be investigated properly. This even more with data moved into the cloud and virtualized across systems, storage, networks, and geographies. Cloud providers that use other cloud providers and system operators for services exacerbate this, expanding our pool of risk. And then of course there is mobility and BYOD.

Faced with the sheer number of assets, many make judgement calls as to what to document and what logs to keep. This is particularly true in smaller to mid-sized companies with limited staff and resources. It is equally a problem though for some large and multi-national enterprises simply overwhelmed by scope and complexity. They selectively or inadequately capture, retain, aggregate, or review anomalies recorded in system logs and other archives. Even when these logs are reviewed, many inadequately correlate events. There is often just too much data, data of too many types, in too many locations, or the premature disposal or cycling of that data due to storage insufficiency is such that a full picture of corresponding events across systems at a given time can be difficult to establish.

And of course, there is no better proof than proof. Penetration testing, ethical hacking, white team social engineering (intended to expose weakness, not to cause us harm), and simulated assaults, the tools of red teams, provide specific demonstration of vulnerability. They demonstrate the potential or possibility of compromise. This is valid data but needs to be presented in context. The presence of a vulnerability to a potentially exploitive threat is meaningless in absence of that threat, and even if realized, means less, unless that which is compromised is of consequence. And, successful penetration is a test, but it tests a condition, and only at a point in time. These tests are most effective when repeated regularly.

Risk assessment needs to be a program, not a task. Risk changes as the environment changes. New threats develop. Vulnerabilities are closed, or new ones emerge. New controls are put in place as existing controls are rendered ineffective by change, and as the business, business cycle, and overall needs of the business change. We launch new products, move into new markets, develop new applications, and take on new partners. We open new facilities, add, and retire technology, upgrade systems, and operate a business. Markets expand, markets contract. People leave, new people are hired. Competitors emerge, others close. We maintain accounts. We change credentials and passwords.

Assessments are a statement in time. Validity of the assessment changes because things move and risk changes. With a threat landscape that is complex, making predictions, projections or attempting to effectively measure or assure ROI of control investments against known risk will never be trivial. This is even more true for risk that varies in manifestation or magnitude or morphs over time. And that will likely remain the case and accelerate. Expectations of shelf life for risk assessments are short.

Clearly, we cannot make decisions in the dark, there are risks, because if there were not, we would not concern ourselves with security investments, and we cannot and should not protect everything, or at least we should not protect everything in the same way. In fact, if we were to protect everything the same, why do the risk assessments at all when we could just deploy the protection. Risk assessment focuses on, and targets spend where we think exposure lives, to reduce cost, or at a minimum, to correctly apply spend. We come back to the refrain heard repeatedly throughout this book. We need to know our data, what we have, where, and why we have it, if we still need it, and if so, how does it need to be protected. That is the basis of understanding ROI of any risk-based investments in security, privacy, continuity, or compliance. It is about protecting prioritized assets, an inventory of what we care about, valuable, and vulnerable to threat.

There are only so many threats we can track, and only so many holes we can close. Assessment and risk mitigation planning is less about identifying risk and more about identifying where in our business realized risk produces consequence. In short, where can we be hurt or impacted, and how do we protect our most consequential business assets.

Security is a slide switch. We can slide it all the way to the right, nothing will get in, nothing will get out, and nothing will get done. We can slide it all the way to the left, we will all do what we want, have a great day, but only one, and then watch everything melt. The risk assessment helps us to find the correct setting for the switch, so we do not over-spend and protect too much, or under spend and expose too much, or for that matter spend insufficiently so that needed protection is ineffective, making anything spent wasteful.

I will discuss security maturity assessment throughout and introduce the Security Maturity Model, or Matrix. The Security Maturity Matrix is an effective tool, an important tool. Controls are defined with the expectation that if importance and consequence of impact differs for specific data or systems, controls should differ. These may vary from robust and sophisticated to none. The cost of control investments should be fit to the need, and not more than the need, for a given class of data and systems. The matrix defines needed controls based on the specific data or systems the controls are intended to protect. Where inadequate controls are in place there is a control deficit or gap. Knowing the control deficits help in developing a forecast or proposal of recommended spend, and the priority for that spend, first against data and systems of highest importance, sensitivity, and confidentiality, and then successively diminishing classes of data risk until the risk is deemed too inconsequential to invest in further mitigation. A security matrix can both describe and map the controls in place to address the risks for a class of data or systems.

*Financial resources and hard assets are not the only consumable resources*
*Soft assets like trust, confidence, brand loyalty, and employee morale are equally consumable commodities and can be depleted rapidly in crisis, or simply by presumption, neglect, abuse, or poor management over time*

# Zero Trust Your Zero Trust Program

Business has always looked to trusted IT for its safety, and we depended on our defense model of high walls, moats and drawbridge, everything inside trusted as safe and separated by our DMZ or demilitarized zone, from the wilds of the internet, protected by routers and firewalls and antivirus. And it worked until it didn't.

For ten or so years both to the left and right of the millennium we were in a continual and increasing strain to allow our employees the use of newer, friendlier, non-corporate desktops and devices, and less restrictive services. They were using MACs and others at home, for fun, entertainment, and personal productivity. They used AOL mail and Hotmail for messaging. And then of course, social media had expanded including anonymous chat rooms where employees could meet, chat, and behave or misbehave as they liked in total anonymity. They were untraceable, unmonitorable, and could communicate, exchange, or share data, music, pictures, and content with anyone, friends, family, those they knew, and individuals just met. Their home based devices were often the same devices shared with their children or other family members. I remember going nose to nose with our CEO in a very heated exchange and telling him that he could not use his AOL mail for corporate business because we couldn't secure or monitor it. And he was bigger than me, a Marine, and he was our CEO. Not the position where you want to be as the head of IT.

And with the introduction of Gmail and other online services, the pressure came from everywhere. Not only ground up, but sales teams, department heads and executives. They wanted the ease of use and the ability to connect from wherever they were without first passing through our proxy servers to gain access to our closely monitored email and other systems. And then smart phones, and work from home, and BYOD. Employees, leadership on down, like other non-monitorable or trustable 3rd parties, had emerged a source of risk, and it was clear, it was a risk that we could not effectively contain.

The term Zero Trust is attributed to John Kindervag, an analyst at Forrester Research, in a paper published in 2010. The paper explained how traditional network security models fail to provide adequate protection because they all require an element of trust. I and others agreed, and I published a paper with similar conclusions in Computerworld (2012) lamenting the loss of prudent IT. I also contributed to a book co-authored with 8 other CIOs that same year saying much the same. But we had lost the battle. We trusted our safety and we trusted our defenses, even as our business moved to the cloud, social media, digital communities, and wherever the new consumer base empowered by phones, tablets, shadow IT, and other digital devices led them, and where our high walls were of no value.

Zero Trust is conceptually a mature security architecture for the redefined enterprise, global, cloud based, remote, mobile, and in a continued state of change. The Zero Trust model assumes no trust for any user or device inside or outside the network perimeter. It is built on the assumption of never trust, always verify, minimize access and rights, enforce least privilege, maximize monitoring and observability, and assume the worst and prepare for it.

These governing principles are interpreted and implemented differently within companies, but adherence to the principles is a requirement. Building as if you're going to be breached, segmenting your networks, hardening your servers, encrypting your data, increasing your monitoring, limiting access and privilege, and maximizing visibility of how things move through your network are all tools of Zero Trust.

But Zero Trust is defined, architected, and implemented in platform differently by varied solution and platform providers. And expectedly, there isn't a singular roadmap to achieving Zero Trust for a business to follow. Adoption and implementation likely differ for a cloud vs. premises-based company, and for an enterprise with centralized control over technology vs a federated model, and for companies of different size, structure, governance, and for those operating globally. The question of Zero Trust success falls to how we define adoption and the metrics used to measure success.

In privacy we also have some concepts like Privacy by Design and DPIA's (data protection impact assessments). They effectively are to privacy a Zero Trust model. We look at all aspects of a process requiring proof that we satisfy the privacy expectations of individuals and the requirements of the law, and where that proof fails or is inadequate, we work to resolve for conformance or disallow the process.

**In business, privilege is trust, and trust is the cost of doing business.**

There is a challenge to Zero Trust. For business to operate, grow and flourish we have to be open, collect data, expand to new places, compete in new markets, and extend our reach. We leverage tools in the cloud, through third parties, contracted platforms, services and technologies, N-Tier providers, all lessening our visibility and expanding our risk. There is a tension between Zero Trust, which demands observability, and continuous monitoring that is misaligned to the motivations of business, that we have to be out there, taking the risks that we need to compete and to do business.

I see Zero Trust as a directional improvement, an important one, but not a panacea. It is a means to provide better management of the technology and process that we can see and control. But much of our business involves that which we cannot see and control.

- We adopt new systems and approaches, collect data, enter new markets, introduce new products, we process in the cloud.

- We expand to new jurisdictions under new regulation and imposed obligations. We do business in new ways, adopting AI, IOT and other new business models. We partner with other businesses.

- Our workforces are increasingly mobile, their activities less visible. There is Shadow IT.

- There are parts of our business and supply chain touching things that we don't necessarily know about and so create defects in visibility and process minimization.

- Our third-party relationships buy components from other providers, and they from theirs, perhaps from places or providers we might not prefer, or have been sanctioned, or do not uphold our quality, ethical, cultural, or legal expectations. This risk remains invisible to us.

And perhaps the greatest challenge to Zero Trust is that our protection is now in large part just paper, the contracts, agreements, and terms of service offered by the provider. We build indemnifications into our contracts as an acknowledgement of the dirt in the system.

Irrespective of any controls that we may think we have in place, and despite that they may be better than that we could do if self-managed, there are things that we simply cannot know.

**The nature of business is that we are forced to trust**

Business increasingly involves more parties, spans more technologies, more geographies, more regulations, more legal jurisdictions. And for us to effectively do business out there, go global, do things, we're going to touch more and more privacy laws. There's now some 200 of them. Add to that cyber regulations, AI and then specific area regulations like healthcare, genetics, and children's safety and data protection laws. It's a very complicated picture.

Third party risk is inherent in all business operations. And whether a provider or a receiver of products or services, there's no business that operates independent of others, internally, or externally. Our products introduce risk. Our value chain involves a lot of parties, and practices, many of which we can't know or possibly identify. Nor can we ever fully assure the cleanliness of the third parties with whom we engage, and with whom they engage.

We make best efforts at due diligence. Yet most make a risk based decision, dictated by tolerance and the materiality of the risk, the industry in which we operate, and our governing mandates, and in absence of negative findings or inferences, buy products, establish markets, and sell. Risk does not stand still and there are a lot of moving components. Businesses are growing, changing, and exploiting opportunities. Threats are everywhere.

And wherever there are people involved, and differing company cultures, Zero Trust, as will any protective model, faces challenges. There is no magic bullet. But Zero Trust, pursued in a comprehensive program of resistance, resilience, operational prudence, proper staffing, sound administration, continual testing and monitoring, effective access management and data hygiene, and adequate budgetary commitment, matures and moves our security posture forward.

So, in my opinion:

- In business all privilege is risk. But risk is the cost of doing business.
- Treat both internal and remote employees the same as any 3rd party, not trustable, as a source of risk
- Zero trust is a direction. It is not the same for all of us. It is not easy to achieve, and not a panacea.
- You can't just buy Zero Trust for your business. There is no Zero Trust solution. But numerous solution providers offer excellent technologies that will advance your program or implement features.
- Nobody can build it for you. Many can help, on site, or in the cloud. For Zero Trust to be effective it needs to be integrated to the business and the culture of the business, it needs internal adoption and knowledge, and leadership behind it. Business, operations, and technology need to work together.

- There isn't a playbook or map that you can follow in entirety. Some can guide. There are checklists. Vendor architectures for part of the solution. But no two businesses, risk profiles, or business needs are the same.

- Zero Trust will look different to those in companies of different size, structure, industry, culture, risk level, if operating globally, and whether under federated vs. central governance.

- Zero Trust is not just a direction, but a directional improvement. Continual monitoring and least privilege improve our security programs maturity.

The title of this blog was Zero Trust Your Zero Trust Program. We shouldn't limit our monitoring and distrust to transactions and access, Zero Trust as a program itself should never be trusted. It should always be treated as insufficient. This will prove its greatest strength. Business changes, technology changes, risks change. If the programs that defend us are static, we fail. I have coined the phrase 'Zero trust your Zero Trust program', to recognize that every company that pursues this path should continually monitor, and improve it, never accept that their work is done, or that they are fully protected, and if so, despite any limitations, Zero Trust will prove one of the most important increments to our ecosystem of safeguards and defense.

*It is often said that*
*you can have security without privacy,*
*but you cannot have privacy without security*

*Unfortunately, you cannot have security*
*without getting a lot else right in organization, operations, education, and*
*infrastructure, also knowing what you have, why, where it is, if you need it,*
*or have the right to have it, and how you need to protect, and manage it,*
*and that is where most fail, and downstream, privacy, and by extension,*
*compliance and the rights of individuals suffer*

Figure 1 Security Maturity Matrix

| | Classified Vital Systems, Apps, Data | High Risk Systems, Apps, Data | Moderate High-Risk Systems, Apps, Data | Moderate Risk Systems, Apps, Data | Low Risk Systems, Apps, Data | Negligible Risk And/or Public Data |
|---|---|---|---|---|---|---|
| Validated Secure Controls | ▓ | | | | | |
| High Risk Controls | | ▓ | | | | |
| Moderate High Risk Controls | | | ▓ | | | |
| Moderate Risk Controls | | | | ▓ | | |
| Low Risk Controls | | | | | ▓ | |
| Open Systems | | | | | | |

In a maturity framework, controls are fit to the tolerances of a class of risk, understanding that risk is not static and may vary at different points in a business cycle. The determination that data is of negligible risk and can be made available to the public without imposed controls is itself a risk-based control investment decision, an acknowledgement of risk, not a determination or tacit assumption of its absence.

*Budget is the primary protective control of a secured system.*

*It assures that despite components, exposures and approaches in flux, business can anticipate and accept that change is a given, ongoing governance of that change is a given, and investment in security as a program does not end*

# TOP TEN 'HIGH YIELD' INVESTMENTS IN SECURITY

There will always be projects that need doing or are being requested by business and IT constituents, and in information security specifically, and always a demand for a finite set of people, dollars, attention, and time to take these on. Every CIO knows this and understands competing and business driven priorities. CISOs know this too. There are however some projects that stand out from the others in delivering a benefit well more than the spend. Projects that represent a transformational change to the business and how it is done, not just an incremental improvement. Every improvement of course is important. That said, you get an immediate feel for a project or product providing geometric expansion of potential over simple addition of capability. A project that enables the launch of a new business or opens a new market clearly to most feels different than an improvement in the speed or format of management reports as important as the latter may be. They are simply of different scale.

Metrics and the calculus of ROI can sometimes be blinding and misdirecting. To me, they are the follow up question. As CIO I preferred to first get a feel for the importance of proposals in front of me, and the passion and sincerity of those doing the ask. Without engagement, commitment comes to question, and without passion, success. However, anyone can sense it when they are in the presence of a great idea. And when the hairs at the back of your neck stand on end in response to what is being asked, you can feel that too.

I famously used what I called the 'nickel test' when challenging the benefit of requests made, evaluating projects, and listening to proposals for new initiatives. I would ask, 'Does it make a nickel, save a nickel, help me to do something I couldn't do before, or help me to do something I could do before, but better'.

If none of these boxes were ticked it was a short conversation. Those that enabled something that could not be done before, and sometimes those that improved on something existing, needed a bit of special attention. Somewhere in that category sits the gems that transform the business in magnitude for the better. A good senior executive learns to recognize these, and even without extensive data, can sense when something on the table for discussion is particularly important that merits getting behind and making the needed investments.

Of course, nobody will argue with the benefit of 'does it make or save a nickel' either.

We have these transformational initiatives in information security. They may feel less familiar to leaders outside of the security space, but if you think of them in terms of what they bring to the capability, stability and protection of employees, assets, business relationships, and revenue producing activities, and in fact all aspects of an operating business, or if they clear the path for new and transformative business, the importance and scale can immediately be seen by even the least technical amongst us.

Compliance with most security regulations, and the establishment of an effective and sensible security posture both need an understanding of risk against which to make prudent decisions. I have compiled a list of ten initiatives that in my opinion above all should be given priority in addressing risk, and which if accomplished, are transformational in protecting the security, integrity and availability of our data and the operating business. For almost every household name company failure I can recall, had these been fully undertaken, the news story might have been quite different.

This is not about buying another box that beeps at the bad guys, although many of those are important as well. I certainly do not want to diminish the need for technical defenses or minimize what they contribute to detection, defense, and response. The activities I am talking about are transformational. When they are presented anyone regardless of technical sophistication should recognize the importance immediately. They are foundational to any attempt at a protective program. They drill deep into what assets we have, where they are, who has access to what, what data is important and consequential if lost, taken or damaged, and what we are doing as a business for protection, and where. Without these understandings, and the proper foundation in place, there is nothing you can do in security that is not underserving your business. Without these questions answered, a nickel spent on security is a nickel spent too much. There are not enough boxes and appliances that you can lay onto a business to protect it if the basic cleanliness and sensible operations fall short.

These foundational initiatives help us discern what is important and needs to be put in place now, from what is also important, but can perhaps be planned in subsequent budgets. These initiatives provide a structure and purpose to our investments in security, target our efforts, people, dollars, attention, and time in the right direction, and to the right degree.

These are "High yield investments in security'. They are synergistic. They enable risk-based thinking about security. One builds upon another such that the sum of their parts is far greater than each initiative alone. They make our strategic roadmap clear and further supporting investments obvious and easy to understand by the exposures the initiatives reveal.

Continual reexamination, assessment and reinvestment of budget and focus on each of these 'high yield categories of security' will benefit any company, of any size, in any industry, at all points in their business lifecycle, and any CISO will recognize their importance.

*There are only so many holes you can plug, and only so many threats you can detect, track, or correlate, postulate, investigate, or model, before chasing ghosts, the irrelevant, the impractical or the unachievable*

The majority of incidents that cause damage, disruption, or loss, and often those most severe, require physical access to desktops, systems, infrastructure, applications, or people, directly or remotely, whether by the hands of a malicious attacker, a disgruntled insider, a hapless victim influenced or manipulated by another, a careless, cavalier, or undertrained employee, an over stretched or over privileged administrator, or by malware. In any of these the best and first line of defense is training.

To avoid the errant, the inadvertent, careless, or offhand click that releases malware, to recognize the phishing or spoofing attempts that lure you in, or the social engineering that tricks and manipulates, or simply to sense the poorly or abnormally behaving system or application impacted by malware or other technical attack, in fact for so many classes of attack, its often less about technical defenses, but rather, training and awareness that is our most important defense. In the majority of attacks that we as companies experience, as you can see by the chart below, training and awareness, whether of employees, developers, or administrators, and even of our executives and clients, plays a major part in our defense.

I would go out on a limb and say that training and awareness, along with clean and prudent operations, proper patching, good network segmentation and access management, end point controls, knowing your assets and data, malware detection, vulnerability testing, and the whitelisting of all software and products installed, though not a guarantee of safety, is most of the battle, and at least a baseline for a good security program. I have attended numerous law enforcement and other briefings in follow up to some of the largest and most devastating of attacks, and in many to most, had these been in place, the outcomes would certainly have been much less dire. (The chart below leverages CrowdStrike, Darktrace, Rapid7 and other reference sources)

| Attack | Mode of Action | Primary Defenses | | |
|---|---|---|---|---|
| | | Technical Defenses | Operational | Training & Awareness |
| Insider Threat | Malicious or accidental, physical or remote | | x | x |
| Malware | Viruses, Trojans, Worms, and Rootkits | x | | x |
| Spyware | Records or tracks online activity and behavior | x | | x |
| Ransomware | Locks or encrypts data until payment is made | x | x | x |
| Social Engineering | Manipulation through trickery and psychology | | | x |
| Phishing (Trust) | Deception to encourage revealing data or credentials | | | x |
| Spoofing (Trust) | Misspelling or misrepresenting a legitimate site or entity | | | x |
| Identity / Password | Targets. breaks, or usurps credentials to gain access | x | | x |
| Man in the Middle | Intercept or interfere between two points or endpoints | x | | |
| Supply Chain | Infiltration or corruption of or by 3rd party or trusted partner | x | x | x |
| Drive by Download | Delivers malware by site visit or message open | x | | x |
| Code | Injection into legitimate apps, hardware, X-site | x | | |
| DNS | Compromises normal DNS functionality | x | | |
| DoS and DDoS | Malicious traffic overwhelms site resources | x | x | |
| Zero Day | Previously unseen compromise of vulnerability | x | | x |

## Top Ten High Yield Investments in Security

Whatever else you do in security, make the case to do the assessments, planning, and needed procurements to implement these 'Ten High Yield Initiatives' as investments in business protection and test them to the 'Four Conditions of Effectiveness'. They provide a solid foundation on which to build a security program. Completed, any investment made in security or privacy, compliance will be far more effective.

Some of these Ten High Yield initiatives are accomplishable simply with operational steps. These are bulleted. Where there is recommendation for the procurement of a system or tool, these have been marked. I have indicated tools by type, not specific products, not just to remain vendor neutral which I try to be, but because they all (or at least a short list) deserve attention at the time a project is under consideration. Each is continually building and evolving, listening to their clients, adding new functionality, and year to year leapfrog each other. It is generally not a question of which is best, they all are at one time or another, and almost all are very good all the time. It is more a question of which fits better, integrates better, is easier to learn and adopt, and is in look and feel experientially closer to other tools being used by staff, enabling them to get up to speed faster. Price of course, capability, services, references, relationship, trust, and comfort with sales and support teams, and terms are all considerations.

> *U.S. Cybersecurity and Infrastructure Security (CISA) provides expertise, certification, and cyber testing and assessments to federal, state, local, tribal, and territorial governments, and public and private sector critical infrastructure (https://www.cisa.gov/cyber-hygiene-services)*

## Four Conditions of Effectiveness

The 'Four Conditions of Effectiveness' provide a means for ongoing examination. Efforts and investments in each of the Ten High Yield categories should be reviewed for effectiveness against these four conditions.

1. <u>Presence of activity</u> – are you currently doing these activities in some manner?

2. <u>Adequacy of implementation</u> – is that which is currently in place adequate?

3. <u>Frequency of activity</u> – how frequently is it done or tested?

4. <u>Validation of success</u> – does it provide the level of protection or meet the goals expected?

*Figure 2 Four Conditions of Effectiveness*

*Security is a slide switch. We can slide it all the way to the right, nothing will get in, nothing will get out, and nothing will get done. We can slide it all the way to the left, we can all do what we want, have a great day, but after that, watch everything melt*

<u>Four Conditions of Effectiveness</u> evaluates the availability and effectiveness of one, some or all deployed control(s) currently in place, and for performance over time, for one business entity, or comparing one to others. They are an availability test, (i.e., is the control present, functional, adequate, and scalable to the need), an integrity control, testing state at any one time, and a validation control, testing state over time.

| | PRESENCE | ADEQUACY | FREQUENCY | SUCCESS |
|---|---|---|---|---|
| CONTROL 1 | | | | |
| CONTROL 2 | | | | |
| CONTROL 3 | | | | |

How effectively a given control has been applied and is being used will likely vary across an organization and so evaluating these control parameters against different lines of business, departments or processes is highly effective for comparison and to identify barriers. This tells you not only that these controls are in place, but where, and the effectiveness of their uptake. A Specific Tested Control can be evaluated across an enterprise

| | PRESENCE | ADEQUACY | FREQUENCY | SUCCESS |
|---|---|---|---|---|
| DEPT 1 | | | | |
| DEPT 2 | | | | |
| DEPT 3 | | | | |

I have also used these effectively in comparing the current state of a control to its performance over time. This assesses improvement or deterioration of its effectiveness. In this use, a specific tested control is evaluated against prior performance by department. It allows the comparison of results from multiple tests to assess the state of the control over time.

Prior Performance

TESTED CONTROL _____

| | PRESENCE | ADEQUACY | FREQUENCY | SUCCESS |
|---|---|---|---|---|
| DEPT 1 | | | | |
| DEPT 2 | | | | |
| DEPT 3 | | | | |

*Without engagement commitment comes to question, and without passion, success. However, anyone can sense when they are in the presence of a great idea. And when the hairs at the back of your neck stand on end in response to what is being asked, you can feel that too.*

# 1. Inventory Physical, Virtual, and As-a-Service Assets

Whether a physical system asset, virtual, or as a service, and whether implemented with traditional structures, containers, micro services, or other, if it touches, or permits access or transit to data of consequence, it is important, and you need to know what it is, where, what it is used for, who uses it, and how it is protected. It should be classified as to risk / importance and documented. Identify:

- Physical or virtual devices including servers, security, network, fixed, and mobile endpoints
- Storage whether local, remote, in cloud, centralized, distributed, virtual, or shared tenancy
- As-a-Service implementations of hardware, software, platform, security, authentication
- Cloud services providing hosting or processing, public, private and hybrid
- Software and services installed or provided, who owns it, contracts in place, and how licensed.
- Containers, clusters, micro services, and other virtual and transient structures
- All domains, wireless networks, access, and egress points. Maintain configuration plans, segmentation maps, device maps and architectural diagrams of LAN, WAN, WI-FI, VOIP systems
- Catalogs of backups, logs, and logged events

Knowing your assets will inform design decisions in creating a risk mitigating architecture, allow better segmentation, and more effective defensive barriers. Most importantly, it is the first step in identifying where critical data is held, how it moves, and where it is processed.

> *U.S. Cybersecurity and Infrastructure Security Agency (CISA) maintains a catalog of known vulnerabilities (https://www.cisa.gov/known-exploited-vulnerabilities-catalog)*

# 2. Locate, Inventory, and Classify Data

Inventory and classify critical data, digital and other, personal, and not, collected, stored or in any way processed. Know why it is important (risk/criticality), how much you have, and where the most consequential data is collected, processed, transported, or stored, on site, at other company locations, with specific individuals, in cloud, or with any other party.

- Knowing why data is consequential enables the right control decisions for protection, data access and use to be made.
- Implementing protection fit to the consequence of the data should be considered the most primary of controls needed for data protection.
- Document how data moves through applications, processes, workflows, and business cycles, internal and external, and when in its lifecycle it is most important, and when most at risk.

*Data Management and Data Loss Protection systems* can assist in mapping the flow of data, automated discovery of data, track its movement, enforce protective policies, and aid reporting.

*Figure 3 Top Ten High Yield Investments in Security*

## 3. Manage Privileged Accounts

Privilege is trust and trust is the cost of doing business. We must trust and grant privilege for systems and accounts to be used and managed and for the business to derive benefit. Risk increases with privilege, whether granted to trusted individuals, services, or application processes, granted unintentionally or through poor management practices where unneeded, or is obtained or escalated by any means for malicious intent. Risk is often inversely proportional to cost. Minimizing the number of systems each administrator supports lowers risk but requires more staff or time.

- Adopt a least privilege strategy whether on premises or in the cloud
- Use privileged credentials only where they are needed and limit privilege to only that needed
- Require unique credentials and where practical biometrics or other means to assure identity
- Require multi-factor authentication for privileged accounts
- Where most sensitive or risk is greatest consider multi-party authorization

*Privileged Access Management (PAM) Systems* assist in restricting and controlling privileged accounts, limit exposure of privileged account IDs and passwords, assist in auditing and archiving history, and in reporting. These controls also reduce the potential impact of rogue administrators.

## 4. Identity and Access

Clean account management, prudent and sensible access policies, and operational controls, whether on earth or in cloud, are the most overlooked and mishandled of primary defenses. For the best and worst of justifications, businesses mis-manage employee and guest accounts (temps, consultants, external partners), whether account adds, deletes, changes or temporary reassignments, providing greater access privileges, and leaving them in place and active for well longer than needed. Terminate and remove or suspend unneeded accounts. Routinely review directory services and access logs.

- People are consistent. Know normal so you can better recognize that which is not.
- Control credentials, temp access and 3rd party application rights and permissions
- Enforce physical and online authentication, least privilege access and multi factor controls

An *Access Management System* can automate discovery of rights and permission, aid reporting, and keep access policies current. Implement granular identity, authentication, permissioning and access controls with logging. Consider cloud-based authentication or the use of an intermediary cloud access broker (CASB)

*If security is a slide switch, risk assessment helps us to find the correct setting for the switch, so we do not overspend and protect too much, or under spend and expose too much, or for that matter spend insufficiently so that needed protection is ineffective, making anything spent wasteful.*

# 5. Defense in Depth – Cloud to Network to Endpoint

Protect network, servers, services, and infrastructure from unauthorized access and changes.

Photo compliments of John Cool

Whether for traditional implementations, or for service architectures and microservices, on premises or in cloud, implement diverse detective, preventive, and restoration controls. For each model the technologies and approaches will differ, but the need is the same. Whether you do all or some of it, or a cloud or other provider contract assures it, properly configure infrastructure and protective controls, local and cloud, and consider these and other specific environment targeted controls:

- Harden components (servers, routers, etc.) and disable unneeded services
- Segment networks, control traffic and access, layer architectures
- Close unneeded ports, inbound and outbound
- Stay current with vulnerability patches and security updates
- Maintain malware defenses, heuristic and other means of detection and protection
- Monitor and secure communications, inbound, outbound and between processes
- Protect DNS
- Whitelist to permit only trusted installs
- Maintain VM configs or restorable 'golden images' (clean copies) of all principal systems
- Secure mobile and removable media
- Effective use of encryption and inactivity timeouts for endpoints

*Cyberattacks are not always sophisticated. The most common vectors of attack are people, and the technologies, services, and protocols we have used for years*

# 6. Protect Data and Data Availability

Limiting what you collect, keep, and for how long, and minimizing its value if taken, will make protecting what you have easier, and render any successful breach less rewarding. Data you do not have cannot be taken from you.

- Identify and rank potential enterprise, cyber, privacy, or other risk to your most consequential data
- Using the Four Conditions of Effectiveness (above) review, document and assess your controls
- Adhere to a documented policy for retention and disposal of data, media rotation and destruction
- Encrypt consequential data at rest and in transit (including backup media)
- Employ a diverse and comprehensive resiliency strategy of back-up and tested recovery, and provisions for legacy restores. How you approach this will vary with your environment but should consider online, offline, offsite, and high availability options.
- A routinely tested plan for technical disaster recovery and a plan for continuity of operation

# 7. Educate Employees

The first line of defense is an educated employee. Impart an awareness of security, privacy and ethics and promote a posture of caution. If asked to take responsibility for care of company data, most will.

- Train employees and staff
- Educate developers to implement security and privacy by design
- Simply providing training is not enough. Training should be planned, continuous, verified, its effectiveness tested against the objectives of training, documented, and should adapt with change

*Phishing and Awareness Elevation Systems* can sensitize staff to phishing, targeted spear phishing, and social engineering, identifying gaps in awareness requiring further training. Many penetration testers assess the ability to trick employees through familiarization and social engineering.

# 8. Security Team

Build a strong team. Keep skills current. Assess and certify.

- Provide adequate coverage for sufficiency and at diverse locations for continuity
- Provide for movement, reach and advancement through opportunity, continued training, peer interaction, professional networking
- Challenge, motivate, stimulate, compensate, and encourage intellectual curiosity
- Provide access to specialist resources as needed and allow the autonomy to act decisively
- Maximize remote effectiveness and security
- Build business and support team relationships
- Build relationships in the security community and public sector (law enforcement)

# 9. Scan and Test Frequently

Actively test, monitor, and historically review routers, firewalls, and intrusion system logs, specific servers, email gateways, and endpoints for detective purposes, and if needed, forensic examination.

- Scan systems, networks, and applications for vulnerabilities offline and actively online
- Test penetration of defenses. Do it routinely and make it a program
- Simulate attacks and train response
- Operationalize threat hunting
- Peer review and other code assurance strategies
- Monitor intrusion, anomalous additions, removals, and atypical behavior
- Assure adequate space for event log retention and alert correlation

# 10.  Understand How Data Moves

Do not limit thinking to technical controls. Know where the data you hold flows, goes, and is shared, between processes, systems, business partners, across the value chain, and at different points in the business cycle.

- Know the locations of your business, the processes they perform at each, and the type of data they collect, hold or process. Particularly for personal data, document its source, specific data elements collected, purpose and legal authorization for use, how long it will be retained, how protected, and obligations to be exercised when the data is no longer needed
- Establish a risk-based behavioral policy that describes the controls and permissions needed for specific data movement and usage by type, for instance for specific data to be taken off site.
- If the data was purchased from another party, will it be subsequently resold or shared?
- Document the movement, replication, and exchange of consequential data between sites, systems, companies, and countries
- Are technical means like cookies or other devices used to monitor or track data or its use?
- Any 3rd parties that touch your data should be held to contract to act only as you have authorized. Contracts should dictate 3rd party and forward party roles, obligations and needed controls
- Revisit contracts, organizational measures, and operational safeguards routinely

*Understanding risks in context of assets in a control environment with a focus on people, place, and culture, allows the targeting of proper solutions, and better and more defensible investments.*

# CISO REDEFINED

*Protecting Business*

Martin Gomberg, CISSP, CIPP/E

## SECTION 3.    CIA UNCLOAKED AND THE ACIV MODEL FOR OPERATIONAL PRIVACY ENABLEMENT

It is not clear who first coined the acronym, CIA, as in the CIA Triad of 'Confidentiality, Integrity, Availability'.

What is clear is that the acronym, and the concepts it embodies, has been the corner stone of information security, and driven the intentions, efforts, goals, and job descriptions of security professionals going back seemingly forever. In an article entitled the <u>Parkerian Hexad vs the CIA Triad</u> (Study Tiger), the acronym is attributed to a glossary reference in the CNSS Instruction No. 4009 of the Committee on National Security Systems established in 2001. I cannot say with any certainty that this is the first use of the CIA acronym.

This instruction, according to the reference, defined the purpose of 'Information Systems Security' as the "protection of information from unauthorized use, access, disclosure, disruption, modification or destruction" providing "Confidentiality, Integrity and Availability" of that information, or information system.

HIPAA and other regulations site and define CIA requirements specifically (i.e., HIPAA Security Rule 164.304).

The Parkerian Hexad is attributed to Donn Parker (1998) and includes the terms 'confidentiality, integrity and availability', or CIA, but adds three additional terms, 'authenticity, utility and possession' in defining information security. This is an enhancement which deserves its own discussion but would for our purposes take us off into the weeds, so I will avoid digging further.

Still, some authors have raised concern about using the acronym CIA in defining information security given the intelligence organization of that name. For purposes of clarity, some have proposed an alternative, flipping the acronym to read AIC, instead of CIA. If that is in fact the only purpose, and there are no functional or structural corrections or enhancements involved, I would leave that alone. There is adequate justification in my opinion in reordering of the terms, but these are not suggested by the acronym they derive.

*If asked to take responsibility for the care of company data, most will.*

Besides, who would not want to be able to say loudly, 'I WORK FOR THE CIA' (and then cover their mouth and whisper *of my business*'). Their date books would fill up quickly. Thugs and tough guys would give them plenty of room.

It is much the same as when I say, "MY SON AND I BOTH WENT TO YALE". Of course, it was on the weekend, and all the buildings were closed, but there was a decent 24-hour Diner not too far from there.

But we were discussing the acronym of CIA.

If at home you have installed a door, you know it needs a doorknob to be functional, to make the door 'available' for use by people, allowing them to open and shut the door. Without the knob, I think we would agree that the investment in the door would be underserved, and you would have less functionality than intended.

If the door faces the street, and what is inside your home is important, and there is potential consequence in allowing anyone entering who should not, then the installation of a door lock on the newly installed door is sensible, understandable, and should be expected if we are to provide the home security. There is a cost to this, but if the cost is right, knowing the risk, the spending is both reasonable and defensible.

Well, we could preferentially put in an alarm system and defer the lock, but though it would be of great value in support of a locked door, in absence of the lock, an alarm is ineffective, too little, too late. All bad actors would have had full access unrestricted. An alarm is a protective control, but absent other controls addressing the more primary needs of securing the entrance (a gate, a lit front yard, a door lock), the wrong control. So too is a peek hole to see who is on the other side of the door. So too would be a light over the door so that the peek hole is still usable after dark. These are obvious and mutually supportive of the decision to put in a locked door, although on their own, insufficient.

And so, as introduced above, there are three fundamentals often called the protective triad – Confidentiality, Integrity and Availability, or CIA. Every CISSP learns this. Confidentiality used in this manner subsumes privacy and security. I will for this discussion just use the term Security, which in purpose is analogous, in that you cannot have privacy without security. That leaves us free to discuss confidentiality and anonymity as distinct elements of privacy, and privacy and secrecy as specific goals of data protection, the latter subsuming trade, military, governmental and doctrinal secrets. Of course, having security does not assure privacy, but I do not want to ruin my argument before I even get it started. Do not be overly concerned, you do not need to retake the CISSP exam. This twisting of terms and usage is only for the purposes of this section, an exercise in rethinking controls. When we are done, the world will be put right again.

*Success demands innovation but change also breeds risk*

*Change also moves and transforms risk.*

I also will prefer to look at the CIA elements in a different logical order. Instead of Confidentiality (security), Integrity and Availability, for this chapter I prefer Availability, Security, and Integrity. This again is just for purpose of the exercise. We do not need to add another acronym and confuse things. We will still refer to this despite the substitution of term, and change in order, as the CIA triad so that we all share a common frame of reference. As you read on, I believe you will understand whether you agree with my reasons for these few mental manipulations or not.

For a system to be well protected typically it needs all three qualities, Confidentiality, Integrity, and Availability (CIA), or in our case, Availability, Security, and Integrity. Sometimes that is not possible, or practical given time and resources, or budgets are insufficient, and we need to prioritize or implement in the most effective or expeditious order. In most cases the priority is self-evident. Let us return to the door.

If the door has no knob and cannot be opened, it has no AVAILABILITY for use as a door. It cannot be opened, so there is little need to secure it. Comparably, in our world if we have no data or assets, or they are of no consequence, there is no reason to secure what is not available to lose, steal or damage. You can imagine the headlines. 'Bank robbers break into major bank, nothing taken, but locksmith was called.' That might make page 13.

The same could be said if the assets are generally and freely available where the loss would be of little consequence. We generally do not secure the leaflets and brochures at a public information center to any great extent. We might encourage visitors to take only one, but they are meant to be taken, and so do not require a significant investment in protection. That all said, clearly for that which has been made available, if it is important, it must be secured.

But forget data, banks, and information centers for a moment, we were talking about a door. If a knob is installed, the door is now available for use, and having made the door AVAILABLE, if we are to protect against unwanted access, the lock now becomes particularly important. We need to implement SECURITY for the door against unwanted entry. Additional SECURITY can be layered on by installing a peek hole and an entrance light. These, as stated above, would be insufficient on their own but add considerably in use together with the locked door. The primary protection is the installation of the lock. The peek hole and light, secondary and supportive.

But how do we know that in our absence that the lock was not picked, and the house entered? INTEGRITY is an assurance in our world that the secured conditions have not been altered, security thwarted, or that which the security protects, for instance data, has not been touched, disturbed, or damaged. A bank will need to know that the security they implement has held firm and nobody has stolen money, tampered with numbers, or altered balances. A medical researcher needs to know that the protection of their clinical data has not been breached to assure the validity of their data and have confidence that it has not been changed.

This is INTEGRITY, a trust or proof in the stability and effectiveness of the security controls that have been put in place assuring the safety, availability, and pristine quality of the data that security was implemented to protect. In our example of the door, installing an alarm provides integrity to the system. We know that the door has not been opened despite being available, and that the security of the door has not been breached, or the door alarm would have sounded. The fact that the door alarm did not sound assures that the security of the home was effective, that of importance inside was thereby protected, and that the integrity of the home has not been compromised.

Well, how do we know that the batteries in the alarm were good and that the alarm would have sounded, and that we can trust the integrity assurance of the system providing the alarm? We could test the system. We could shake the doorknob and the alarm would sound verifying that it is working, and that integrity is intact, or at least intact at that moment. But what if you stop turning and shaking the knob, did the alarm stop because you stopped, or did the batteries fail? The only way to assure that the alarm continues to provide integrity would be to shake the knob continuously. Besides being very noisy and impractical that would likely be very expensive. We would have to hire people seven days a week, all day and night to validate the integrity of our alarms. Neighbors would complain. Most would not consider that spend reasonable or defensible and would prefer and accept periodic testing as a reasonable measure of validation. Most regulation takes that approach to validation. They accept the minimized risk.

Again, revisiting some of the earlier discussion, if secured, we need to be sure of the integrity of the secured system we have provided, or we cannot make any claims as to the effectiveness of the security implemented, or the safety of that we had set out to protect. If not secured, attempts at integrity are futile, since there is no primary or compensating control to assure.

And you cannot have true security without verification of integrity. Security unconfirmed as to integrity, may perhaps be, but cannot be said with any confidence to be secure. At best, they can only be described as having the application of a 'recommended or best practice' control in place. We have all heard others say, "we are well protected – we have implemented best practice controls". Unless there is some measure of integrity to assure the sufficiency of the best practice control in an environment or context, that is a meaningless statement, as the control cannot be verified effective and therefore trusted. Integrity is a statement of condition at a point in time. A penetration test is an 'integrity' control. It quickly tells you how successfully your 'best practices' protect you and whether they need to do better. It is a measure of the success of the practices in place, but only at the time of the test.

I share this because it is easy to be lulled into complacency having worked through a checklist of controls for one standard or another and believe security is in place. It might be. Unless tested, and integrity verified, you cannot know. Swearing before the judge that the door was locked means little if you have no answer when the prosecutor says, 'how do you know that the door was locked?' Standing in one place for an extended period makes your knees tired. It is a function of fatigue, a weakening of performance over time. Security is also a function of performance over time, and conditions that once were secure may weaken, or become insufficient with the strengthening of threats or changes in context. The light was enough to light the yard when installed, but since the size of the yard was increased it no longer is so. Integrity needs to be affirmed over time for any security control once sufficient to remain sufficient, and the practice of making this assurance routine and correcting deficiencies is a function of good security governance (see Compensating Controls as defined under PCI DSS). Some writers have smartly proposed an additional control beyond integrity, 'non-repudiation', which in intent I agree with. I prefer to call the control 'validation', a function that I derive of risk tolerance, and frequency of sampling. I will introduce the model I use below and return to it again later. The model describes the 'intelligence' behind the CIA Uncloaked.

| A | Controls | | | | I | V | | |
|---|---|---|---|---|---|---|---|---|
| Availability | | | Privacy / Security / Confidentiality / Ethics | | | Integrity | Validation | |
| Presence | Functionality | Adequacy | Primary | Supporting | Compensating | Proof | Risk Tolerance | Frequency of Sampling |
| Quality / Performance / Effectiveness | | | Direct / Layered | Interlaced | | Point in Time Tests | Review and Testing Programs | |

DESIGN CONTROLS
.....

DEVELOPMENT CONTROLS
.....

OPERATIONAL CONTROLS
.....

PRIVACY CONTROLS
- consent
- transparency
- data minimization
- purpose limitation
- data quality
- accountability
- privacy by design

SECURITY CONTROLS
- detective
- preventive
- corrective
- process
- administrative
- monitoring
- security by design

ASSURANCE CONTROLS
- data currency
- correctness
- completeness
- stability
- sanctity

VALIDATION CONTROLS
- oversight
- testing
- audit
- QA
- Benchmarks

*Figure 4 Intelligence behind the CIA*

So, availability is a yes or no condition, security is a statement of condition, in a context, over time, and integrity, a statement of condition affirming security at a given time. Validation (the unnamed control I ascribe to the CIA Triad) is an accepted proxy for proof of integrity, through sampling, at points in time, the frequency of that sampling agreed upon for convenience. So, validation is a control, the effectiveness of which is determined by the frequency of sampling. The more secure the system, lower its tolerance of risk, or consequential the asset it protects, the more frequent sampling would be applied to assure that integrity of the secured controls remains intact for whatever diminished risk remains. Risk can never reach zero but can be minimized to effectively zero through adequate validation of the integrity of the controls. Where risk tolerance is low, frequency of sampling must be high for effective validation. Where risk tolerance is high, if frequency of sampling is also high, you are spending too much. This brings me back to an incident early in my career.

I managed an IT department, helpdesk, and a data center housed together on a floor secured by locked doors. Except for IT staff that worked on the floor, for purposes of maintaining security and control of the movement of people in a sensitive area, everyone else needed escort. A senior executive came to the floor unexpectedly to ask a question of the helpdesk and was incensed beyond reason that someone at his level would need to be escorted, and that he did not have access. He went to the 'high ups' enraged and demanded that this injustice be put right, and the edict came to the facilities director to unlock the floor to employee access. The facilities director clearly was concerned with that demand, knowing the sensitivity of the activities on the floor, and asked me what he should do. My reply was that he should unlock the door. I said that I would rather know that the door was unlocked and behave accordingly, than think that the door was secured, knowing the demand to unlock the door could be acted upon at any time. The security of the locked door had lost any integrity since it could no longer be trusted, and lacking integrity there would be no reason to leave the locked doors in place. Of course, all thought better of it, and the doors remained locked, but it makes for a good story, outrageously good drama, and the principle still holds.

In summary, assurance of the integrity of a security control protecting an available, vulnerable, and consequential asset defines a secured system. Understanding availability, security, and integrity and how they might be prioritized helps to understand and evaluate the business protection initiatives put before us.

Let me take us back for just a moment to availability and the applicability of CIA in the broader context of business protection.

Availability is a statement of condition, it either is, or it is not. In fact, availability subsumes three inclusive conditional tests, presence, functionality, and adequacy. A door by its presence and function provides access and egress from a house. Without the door, there is no access. If the door is damaged, or blocked, that access is denied. The function is not available. Securing the availability of that function requires redundancy, the addition of a second entrance. Redundancy is a 'security' control. It secures the availability of a function, a provision of the Disaster Recovery Plan. DR testing is an integrity control that assures that the DR provisions (security controls) in the DR Plan are working. So, the door must be both present and functioning to be available. It must also be adequate to the function it is required to perform. A doggie door may be present and functioning, enough for most dogs and an occasional hobbit, but inadequate as a means of access to the rest of us. This would fail the test for adequacy, and therefore availability.

Business Continuity is also an integrity control, but it tests the integrity of a different control. It does not test whether DR provisions work. Instead, it affirms that there is a DR plan, it is tested, it is tested with sufficient frequency to comply with company policy, all requirements of the plan are met, and that all conditions of consequence requiring availability are tested. Both the DR test and the BC assessment are integrity controls and so each make a statement about a condition that is only valid for a specific moment in time. A program of recurrent DR tests or recurrent BC assessments would provide validation of the integrity of the condition over time. The frequency of sampling would be dictated by the degree of risk tolerance. The determination of risk tolerance is deliberative and a judgement call that can only be made by the business.

If a system required 100% availability it would require continuous testing to assure it was available, or that the mechanisms that would ensure it remained available were present and functioning. It would be insufficient to verify that a standby system that could activate in failure was working (test the integrity of the control). It would need to verify that it is always and continuously working (validation of the integrity of the control). Active-active applications and many high availability routers, firewalls, systems, and databases do that by continually checking for a heartbeat from their partnered peer.

We live in a less than perfect world. Little stays as it was for long, and we need to manage change. There is a practical order that emerges which dictates how security is often considered, approved, constructed, and funded, and is applied through budget cycles over time. Systems are built typically with security as defined by design and requirements. With time, threats may be detected to which the system is determined potentially vulnerable, and we request investment in additional security controls. These are budgeted, approved, and implemented. Confidence in the applied controls requires that we verify the integrity with studies, scans, penetration testing and other means. If subsequently found deficient, or insufficient, or if new threats emerge, or if the data held is determined to be, or have grown, in importance or sensitivity, and so its loss of availability, breach or damage would be consequential, we budget for additional controls, and so on it goes.

If systems never changed from that implemented, confidentiality or sensitivity of the data stored or processed was not impacted by changes in what laws and emerging regulations define as sensitive, or what businesses consider confidential, and if the security applied closed all vulnerability to threats and threats never changed, we would build once and test once and report to management that we are done. That is not our world. Systems installed do change. Data risk changes. Security that worked before grows obsolete and we try new approaches. Even the installation of new security by itself changes the context of the system introducing new risk. How many of us have brought down systems or watched them behave in unpredictable ways after applying an update or security patch?


Let me now restate what to some may seem a very strange concept, not a technical control, but a business control:

## *'The budget is the primary protective control of a secured system'*

The budget is the primary protective control of a secured system. It needs to provide that as all components, exposures, and approaches are in flux, the business can anticipate that change is a given, ongoing governance of that change is a given, and investment in security does not end. It should remain, despite competing priorities from business growth and new opportunities, a commitment from management, if we are, to whatever degree we can, to stay protected.

*Encryption is an important piece of a protective strategy, but one piece, which along with other tools, means, and processes, comprise a strategy, not a guarantee of sufficiency*

# CISO REDEFINED

*Protecting Business*

Martin Gomberg, CISSP, CIPP/E

## SECTION 4.   WHAT'S WHERE AND WHY DO WE CARE

In the past, asset management was a matter of accounting for the proper capture of the value of assets, depreciation, management of equipment lifecycles, and to budget for replacement costs as needed.

Typically, a responsible business would track tangible hard assets with a depreciable life, whether technical, furnishing, or other, and enterprise software license costs exceeding the threshold allowing for capitalization. All other software and small components were typically treated as an operating expense. It was not unusual for capital assets to be managed by the finance department and the deployment and usage of operating software by information technology or within operating units. Increasingly now, asset management and transparency of asset ownership is governed by regulation and audited. Asset management is critical to the management of risk and assurance of security and privacy.

What's Where and Why Do We Care is such a basic question and yet most companies struggle with it. They struggle because the tracking of hardware, software, applications, storage, licensing, and data on premises, or with SAAS (software as a service), and applications on our remote or mobile endpoints, or deployed with IAAS (infrastructure as a service) and PAAS (platform as a service) contracts, and all the things we need to look at as technical assets now, has become exceedingly difficult.

Even where we effectively centralize as much as we can in the approval, procurement standards, and contract management process, shadow IT, an enabled consumer technology, social media, a digital community, pay as you go licensing for cloud consumption models, and the ease of spawning virtual environments, or using ready-made services, assures that we can never be fully confident of where our data is and what that means to us from a perspective of risk and regulatory conformance.

Businesses trying to maximize the value of asset management programs struggle, because it is hard to even define an asset in a physical sense. Often the cloud providers we engage to host our assets may use other cloud providers to lower their costs and supplement their capabilities, and as such our assets may be virtualized not only across technologies, but also business entities, operating environments, support communities, and geographies.

So, when we talk about asset management are we responsible to manage only hard technical assets at the desktop, and in the data center, or also virtual instances of servers, storage, and operating platforms onto which our license software have been propagated, and data migrated, each needing controls and protection? The answer is likely dictated by the terms of licenses, contracts and in the expectations of law.

Even a transient asset like a web page might need to be managed. Unless instructed in the header of the page to not allow caching or saving, a cached remnant of a page can exist exposed and readable at multiple points between a server and browser, at gateways, security devices, proxies, and at the client browser itself. This is a question of privacy and ultimately could expose PII, PHI or PCI data in potentially violate law.

Still, we involve stakeholders in a continual round robin of audits and inventories as we try to get a handle on assets and asset ownership across the organization. We try to determine whether there is a need for the asset anymore, a financial life, and if the assets are sufficient in license or capacity or configured in the way they need to bring value to the organization. You are the CISO. About now you are saying, that's very nice. What has this got to do with me? Don't go away, there is more.

Why do we go through the effort of inventory and management of assets? We do it for a few reasons really:

- Accounting
- Regulatory compliance
- Control of risk
- The belief that there is an ROI to our efforts

**ROI of Asset Management**

Assets that are no longer needed in most cases probably should not be insured or kept under maintenance. Surprisingly, for many this slips under the radar. We insure and pay maintenance on assets that are sitting on the shelf, or in storage undeployed, not needed, that are under expired license, mismatched to upgraded technology and operating systems, on obsolete versions, or are duplicate services. In the worst of cases, we may continue to protect products replaced by other products on which maintenance is also being paid.

There may also be a tax impact. Deployed equipment in some states may be all that is required to demonstrate that a business is operational in that state and might incur tax on operating revenues. If a tangible operation can be demonstrated based on the presence and activities of a company's material, structural, or technical assets, that company may be said to be operating in that state, and subject to State income tax, and perhaps other taxes and licenses based on State law and regulations. Removing dead assets can reduce the tax impact on companies in jurisdictions where assets are no longer functional or needed.

Some companies look to better pricing or bundled discounts and over buy, or assume licenses no longer needed can be redeployed if needed elsewhere and are less prudent than needed in purchasing. Some are simply oversold unneeded products and services. In most cases unless tightly managed and there is a need, I would question the strategy of holding unused licenses for potential future use and paying the maintenance as opposed to buying what we need when we need it. Often, by the time the need is there, the product needs upgrade, or replacement, and the maintenance spent on shelved licenses was wasted.

## Accounting and Oversight

Sometimes the main reason we inventory what we have, is simply to know what we have. We need to know what our assets cost, how long they will be useful, and on what schedule and at what cost they will be retired and replaced.

We need to know where our assets are, and the impact they have on storage and desktop requirements, on the cost of care, handling and management, and environmental needs. What we have deployed determines the staff count needed in place for support. It may influence shift coverage and rotation, specific skills required and where to place them. It impacts requirements for power, power protection, lighting, air conditioning, humidity controls, fire detection and suppression systems, security, and the lease of physical space. We also need to know the cost and means of disposition at end of usefulness and when that sunset date is going to be. This allows us to budget the removal of the asset, and if needed, to plan, select, test, design and procure, and position the needed space, power, environment, staff, and training required of a replacement system, and to solicit proposals, compare pricing, partner capabilities, and to negotiate contracts.

And of course, even if only after the fact, we need to know if the asset provided value and whether it was a good spend. That information should guide future asset procurement and deployment. However, after the fact does not suggest a mature process. The company that employs a process of continued assessment, client communication and awareness, training, and engagement, and a process of quality management, will know earlier, and if there are deficiencies or opportunities for improvement can better utilize the asset and increase client satisfaction. OK, this is operations, not you. Almost there.

## Asset inventory and compliance

A major driver of funding and momentum for IT asset inventory, classification and management programs is regulatory compliance. Regulations increasingly require that companies apply the same oversight, accountability, and transparency to hard assets as they do finances, report on what we own and what we have in service, and apply all needed safeguards to their confidentiality, integrity, and availability. We need to know what we have where, who needs it, who owns it, whether it is operational, what it requires, its importance, predictable operational life, and the consequence of failure, corruption, interruption, or compromise. We need to provide effective protection, care, and oversight, because to not do so would be impactful and irresponsible.

And who would want to see negative audit exceptions raised to management, be penalized for non-compliance with regulation, be sued, harmed reputationally, or be on the wrong side of other negative aspersions against the company for breach of license or contract, or be in violation of internal policy? So, knowing what we have and 'how it is being used and by whom' is all important to assure that we are in conformance with the rules we need to live by.

Many regulations encourage or require an inventory of assets as a means of identifying risk to those assets. Conversely, it is also to identify the vulnerable assets that might by their exposure put the enterprise at risk or cause the inadequately protected enterprise to be a source of harm to others.

Few regulations speak specifically or prescriptively to methodology, put limits on timeframes or set targets for completion. Most recognize inventory or classification of assets as reiterative. It is an ongoing process of query, monitoring, examination, and documentation. The goal of a complete inventory of assets, and a risk or value prioritized classification of the data that resides with those assets all kept current is vital to protect our systems and consequential data, and regardless of whether mandated, should be the intent.

From a risk perspective, we cannot know where we are exposed if we do not know where we are in the process and can assess what remains to inventory. From a license use perspective, or if there is a mandate in company policy requiring full visibility to corporate assets, the answer is the same.

- We should know where our assets are to know what to monitor and protect

- We must know what data is there and consequential to know what assets require further safeguards

- We should know what our baseline of installed software looks like to detect any deviation possibly suggesting malicious infiltration or malware

- We should know where our data resides and moves and how it is accessed, configured, and protected.

*We, our network of partners, theirs, the technologies we use, and the environment in which we operate together are a system, and one part exposed, risks others*

And we should remain cognizant of our normal data movement, sensitive to uncharacteristic behavior and traffic patterns for and between our assets. The more complete and the more current the inventory, whether for regulatory compliance, or simply effective operational prudence, the better we are, and the more effective our ability to manage risk. By example of the tone being set as excerpted from the FFIEC Handbook

*"Management should maintain and keep updated an inventory of technology assets that classifies the sensitivity and criticality of those assets, including hardware, software, information, and connections".*

## Paraphrasing a requirement from PCI DSS ...

*"Identify all locations of cardholder data, taking an inventory of IT assets -- and analyze them for vulnerabilities that could expose cardholder data".*

Asset inventory, prioritization, and effective management are all critical to a risk-based strategy.

Often it will be the meeting of a regulatory requirement that drives an effort or gets funding. If this were a perfect world, the mitigation of consequential risk, more than compliance, would be the driver for why we take asset management seriously, and why we invest in programs to recognize risk to assets and data of greatest importance. That said, management of risk requires an understanding of the business, factors that influence business success, and how they can be impacted, and that a case be made, communicated, and sometimes ROI demonstrated to get needed resources. The need for compliance with specific regulatory mandates for risk management, and efforts to avoid sanctions or penalties for non-conformance are easily justifiable and obvious, and as such getting support and funding is often simpler.

An inventory of assets and the development of an asset map are first steps in inventory of sensitive data (PII, PCI and PHI), crown jewel IP, privileged, regulated, and business confidential material. I treat these two efforts, inventory of assets, and a mapping of consequential data, as among the most important efforts in securing a business and limiting risk. We need to take a 'maturity' approach to security, and many of the largest companies do so to determine how assets and the data they hold are secured and protected.

A maturity approach should be implemented to define and track the required state of assets. This dictates that we classify data and protect that most sensitive more stringently than other data. This requires that we not only know what data is most important and have classified it as such, but we know where it resides. We know who is touching it and how, that it is appropriately protected, that protection has been affirmed, and that this has been documented for confirmation by audit, continually revisited per plan, and protection is maintained over time. A complete inventory of physical assets, location of sensitive, confidential, or high-risk data, and a mapping of physical and data assets to 'controls' appropriate to risk should be done by every responsible company.

Of course, businesses do not stand still, individuals do not always follow the rules, or they do unexpected things with systems and data, and we never have a complete picture of where we are. Data is in the cloud, on as-a-service platforms, in home spun applications, and elsewhere. Monitoring and managing change, continual inspection and inventory, and a baseline and ongoing process for classification of data at risk is a requirement, but a challenge even for the mature enterprise. The composition of our asset environment and the tuning of the safeguards we put around it needs to be a process of continual maturation and refinement.

And so CISO, my apologies, it took a while, but as I am sure you can see, for a wide range of reasons, we do own or at least must stay on top of this.

*Availability is a condition.*

*Security is a statement of condition, in context, over time.*

*Integrity is an affirmation of that condition at a specific time.*

*Validation is an accepted proxy for proof of integrity, sampled at points in time, the frequency of which is dictated by risk tolerance, and agreed upon for convenience.*

# CISO
# REDEFINED

*Protecting Business*

Martin Gomberg, CISSP, CIPP/E

## SECTION 5.   VENDOR AND THIRD-PARTY RISK

Modern business thrives through an inter relationship of businesses.

Each business is unique in capabilities, culture, and risk. A successful partnership aligns on capability, fits to culture, and approaches the risk open eyed through careful evaluation and due diligence. And with an evaluation completed, potential partners make a choice to part friends, or proceed in partnership, prudently, circumspect, and to contractually assure protection.

The concerns of third-party risk management are broad in scope. Each company has an investment of time, money, resources, attention, and reputation at stake. Each need confidence in the relationship, and a sense of mutual benefit. Each need to respect the other's commitment to brand, clients, and shareholders. Each need to respect the other's obligations to regulation, operational stability, data protection, human interests, and adherence to ethical and lawful behavior. Successful partnership extends the reach, visibility, potential, capability, and expertise of a company in ways it might not achieve alone.

However, modern business is complex, and more so when global, virtual, a network of partnerships, distributed, and mobile. When engaging with business partners and entrusting to them the care of client relationships, reputation, and the safety and privacy of corporate data, a business is exposed. Prudent business provides the best assurance for a successful relationship by understanding the risk it is accepting in partnering by examination and assuring it has selected the best fit partner. This is due diligence.

But as business and the operating and regulatory environment has become more complex, so too has the needed diligence for responsible partnering between companies to assure they are not accepting undue risk, and are operating in accordance with law, customer expectations, and the best interests of their brand. This demands more strenuous scrutiny when considering the extension of one operating company to another.

*Nobody can ever take from you that which you do not have*

## Due diligence

A thorough investigation uses all the tools at its disposal to evaluate the solvency, capacity, and effectiveness of an entrusted partner's business. It will look at management and oversight, focus on technology and safety, and exposure to risk. It will examine the environment in which the partner operates, and the environmental practices it employs in operation. It will look at the partner's ability to attract, develop and retain the best people and how employees of the company are treated.

It will look at the company's reputation, its competition, and its place in the market amongst others providing similar service. It will look at who is making use of their services and how happy they are with that choice. They will use traditional means of assessment, meetings, presentations, questionnaires, long lunches, and audits, but they will also use social media, digital communities, business reviews and in some cases, engage firms and specialists to investigate technology effectiveness, financial history, key employees and criminal history and behavior.

Red flags are often raised in examining a company before establishing a business-to-business relationship. Before pen to paper and contracts are signed is the time to assure that the partnership is a fit, and that the raised red flags are not sufficient to obviate the business benefit in taking on the risk of partnership.

As much as evaluating the positives of a relationship, in due diligence companies look for indicators of poor performance, inadequate practice and insufficient safeguards and controls.

Where stakes are high, or information is sensitive, and as a requirement in most relationships with government entities, they will also look for indicators that are suspicious of criminality, theft, corruption and bribery, coercion, money laundering, terrorist financing, identity theft, executive misbehavior, and the improper management and treatment of human resources. Of course, most often none are found, and this is not surprising. With few exceptions, most companies are in business to do the right thing. They are in business to bring value to ownership, employees, investors, and clients. The success of the relationship is as important to the provider of services for whom this is core business, as it is to the client engaging them, or the business considering partnership with them. Most businesses are focused on success, work hard for a successful outcome, and to assure client satisfaction and retention.

Still, not all partnerships are a fit, not all priorities align, and not all operating styles and cultures mesh. These are the areas where relationships and partnership break down. And regardless of all best intent, failure or poor performance by a partner reflects less on the partner, but on the reputation, client satisfaction and legal responsibility of the business that engaged them. So, it falls to every company to make best efforts at assessing the future of a proposed partnership with a prospective provider before contracts lock them together. Up front is the best time to exercise care.

Due diligence and the management of third-party risk helps to assure that the engaging company is protected from ethical, legal, and operational issues. They do this through revealing questionnaires, client and bank references, proof of insurance and credit, direct and independent audit, inquiries and investigations, evaluation of history and reputation, and by the strength, enforceability, and clarity of the agreement and specific provisions put in place with the third party. Letters from the provider attesting compliance to law, regulation, privacy statutes, internal policies, and prudent and acceptable practices as well as both industry and professional standards have become critical to assuring that internal and audited external controls are in place governing the third party.

Often, we attempt to stipulate the right to perform on-site inspections. Except for the largest of companies, in the most attractive of deals to a provider these requests are typically re-buffed. Review of independent audit results and the attentiveness demonstrated to clearing past audit exceptions are often the only means, even if indirect, to examine a company. In fairness, if each client requested and exercised the right to perform on-site audits of a business the impact would be overwhelming. However, independent audits are a reasonable measure.

All this said, risk can only be reduced, and any assessment is true only for conditions as of a snapshot of time. The best assessment has a freshness date and short shelf life. It needs to be continually managed.

When is a vendor, provider or other third-party risk assessment required? A disciplined assessment is applicable whenever there is the establishment of new partner relationships or a substantial change to an existing relationship of importance. This may be when evaluating or provisioning for a significant product, resource, or service, in leasing, licensing, or procurement deals, for proprietary development and sponsorship initiatives, with the outsourcing or offshoring of functions, and in merger or acquisition. The success of the assessment is dependent on the capabilities and credentials of those performing the oversight and investigation. It is also a matter of the cooperation of the prospective partner. It requires effective audit, written assurances, and diligent review of operations, financials, human resources, security, and the demonstrable compliance with law, regulation, policy, and standards. Shared Assessment Program / Standardized Information Gathering (SIG) questionnaires help companies to review and share their vendor experiences.

Due diligence does not stop once contracts have been signed and an engagement or relationship is in progress. All relationships should be nurtured continually and all contracts, relationships, and performance against agreements in place at least annually reviewed. Monitoring of adherence to agreements and challenge of performance should be ongoing, and performance should be measurable.

**Managing Contracts**

Without doubt, leverage decreases once a contract is in place and payments are made if adequate safeguards are not built into contracts for satisfaction. These include provisions in a longer-term agreement for exit with cause, exit at review points, or missed milestones, or exit for convenience, or as sometimes called, at pleasure.

Alternatively, if the contract term is sufficiently short, the client's discretion at the end of term often provides the leverage needed. Partners do not opt to invest the effort of negotiating a relationship that will be short lived. The shorter term affords a client opportunity for more frequent review of available competing choices, better priced alternatives, and consideration of continually emerging technologies and operating models. It also affords an opportunity for renegotiation at advantage and assures continued pressure to maintain consistent and acceptable performance.

Recognizing this, providers are less compelled to be accommodating in overly one-sided agreements. Shorter terms are less financially beneficial and provide less opportunity to develop a committed relationship. With that a provider frequently provides greater incentives for a longer-term contract. These incentives can be attractive and often the longer-term commitment allows the partner more flexibility in accommodating the client with favorable terms. Negotiating an agreement is time-consuming and often discounts and better terms are easier to sell upstream for a longer lock-in of a perspective client. Agreements that are overly porous and easily terminated (as with exits for convenience) also are less compelling for incentives. Contracts are most successful when both parties feel satisfied with that which they have accepted and agreed.

In any agreement, price caps, protection of pricing on renewal, and other protection of price and terms are often sought client-side protections. We negotiate hard for these and should. We also fight hard for adequate indemnifications, uncapped, or with sufficiently high ceilings to protect against liabilities and exposures that engaging with a partner for product or services may bring. These seemingly one-sided protections also benefit the service provider. A well-structured contract with beneficial terms and protections provides comfort, encouraging renewal and the longevity of a relationship. These provisions do not prevent renegotiation of terms at renewal to improve pricing and terms, and I think that is healthy. It assures both parties are incented to refresh and continually reexamine their relationship.

Transferability and provisions for changes of ownership, or changes in company structure should be anticipated in an agreement to assure that a contract does not penalize a company pursuing strategic objectives, whether merging, acquiring, being sold, spinning off a new entity or starting a subsidiary business. These provisions recognize that businesses are not stagnant, entities morph over time, and prevent unexpected changes in structure from impacting pricing or terms greater than anticipated in the agreement, hindering, or inhibiting business options. This enables the client to predict cost, parties being pulled in through strategic changes to have clarity and enjoy the contract benefits. It allows the provider to continue to forecast revenue and longevity, and for all parties to know what is expected of the relationship. Relationships are better than contracts, and good contracts protect and make relationships better. The best relationship is expressed in an agreement that clearly defines needed protection, anticipates growth and transformation, unifies objectives, and satisfies the goals of all parties.

Even the best of relationships end. When they do it is important that the agreement in place provides protection against forced dependency. When entering an agreement or partnership with a partner, process or technology that is proprietary, protection needs to be in place against limitations or obstruction to the guaranteed return, assistance in return, and assurance of portability of accumulated client data in a usable format. This is particularly true in the use of SAAS services where the data held may only be of use in the SAAS application or on the platform or technology that supports it.

The same is true as to the transferability of knowledge or process. Contracts should provide for knowledge support on exit from the relationship. This support should be sufficient to establish independence and restore operations. Of course, this likely comes at a cost, but is a sensible insurance.

Equally, contracts should identify the use of proprietary technology, formats and approaches, and stipulate avoidance of arbitrary or intentional approaches that hinder exit from the use of the product, service or provision, or limit migration to an alternate product for continuity of operation. Transition should be assured by contract, assisted till complete and successful, and neither impeded, nor delayed.

If a license there should be provisions made for uses apart from day-to-day production, for instance in disaster recovery testing, and in stand-by or active parallel operation in disaster. Terms should permit usage that are neither restrictive, limiting in duration, or onerous in costs if any, and this should stipulate an allowance for periodic testing that does not increment a usage or deployment instance count or impose limits on scope, participants, or frequency.

Lastly, in this context where data is stored by a SAAS or platform provider, contracts afford some minimal protection of the dispersion of company data across geographies, facilities, structural elements, virtual systems, and operating partners. They also may provide provisions that assure data is properly encrypted in transit, and at rest, protected with suitable controls and geographic access or transfer limitations when administered, and dictate the holder of the encryption credentials. It determines if as a client, a separate and unique key (layered encryption) could be used to assure confidentiality. Provisions can also to some degree dictate or at least bring visibility to the policies or likely response process to law enforcement or government 'Demand Letters' for access to the stored data, and the timeframes and procedures in which notification or other responses must be provided on breach, damage, or data loss by the service.

*We live not just with changing climates, but in a climate of change. Threats are everywhere, they are technical, social, physical, legal, natural, regulatory, man-made, financial, and yes, the climate in which we do business*

*And it is diligence, prudence, a focus on quality management, effective peer partnership and information sharing, and an effective program of review, continual monitoring, testing, and remediation that assures that amidst all distractions and inherent risk, we stay on course*

## RED FLAGS

In engaging with a potential partner often there are glaring inadequacies or misfits that arise as RED Flags. These Red Flags might dissuade the client or raise concerns about proceeding into a potential relationship with an external party or provider of products or services. Sometimes, these are less than glaring, and only revealed through research and investigation.

What is considered a Red Flag by one company may not be a concern, or as great a concern, to another. Third party risk and concerns vary by industry, size, and resources of the company, whether domestic or multinational, localized or decentralized, public sector or private, and the proprietary nature of the service. They are dictated by laws under which the company is regulated, and stipulations in major client agreements, particularly in government or municipal contracts. The need for the product or service offered, and availability of competitive alternatives also are factors in the risk a company is willing to accept.

Some of these red flags will arise from answers to a provided questionnaire, others to due diligence, research through contacts, inquiries made to other clients, and references of the provider, and online sources. Red Flags as to reputation, ethics, performance, and stability of the company may suggest caution, raise specific questions, prompt additional scrutiny, dictate terms to be included or stressed in the agreement if it goes forward, dissuade moving forward with a third-party relationship under consideration, or require termination of a relationship in process. Red flags may arise up front in due diligence or over the course of the agreement.

Increasingly the need for a contracted relationship between parties that dictates the collection, management and disclosure of data is a mandate of privacy regulation. So too are the specific terms stipulated in the agreement. Amongst other specifications these may include:

- Data control and limits on disclosure
- Limits on data use to only that specified by the controller of the relationship
- Audit rights
- Support in the event of breach
- Adherence to commitments made by the data controller to the data owner

*As much as due diligence evaluates the positives of a relationship, companies also look for indicators of poor performance, inadequate practice, and insufficient safeguards and controls*

*Most often only little is found, and this is not surprising. With few exceptions, most companies are in business to do the right thing*

These 10 categories of potential **Red Flags** should be considered in assessing Third Party Relationships. Others may be appropriate specific to a business, industry, mode of operation or purpose for evaluation:

### 1. Inability to demonstrate solvency, financial and operating health of the company

- Insufficiency or non-disclosure of financials and inadequacy of credit and unwillingness to provide supporting bank or reference clients
- Poor narrative as to business plan, market penetration, potential markets, and competitive landscape
- Inadequacy of insurance either for direct compensation on failure to provide services, or to assure the ability and resources to continue provision of services.
- Poor reputation for services or performance and negative comments by other users

### 2. Inadequacy of contract terms and inflexibility in the modification of terms

- Unwillingness to provide indemnification and protection from claims against the provider, technologies, processes, or patents, for ownership, infringement, licensing, or use
- Unwillingness to provide adequate price protection and lock in caps with growth, renewal, or change in entity size, structure, or ownership (spinoffs, sale, merger, or acquisition)
- Lack of an acceptable SLA (Service Level Agreement) for provision of services, upgrades, replacements, or support

### 3. Concerns about culture, staffing, capacity, and skill sets

- Questions of ethics, professionalism, or standards
- Layoffs, turnover and poor longevity of provider staff, account representatives and specialists
- Team credentials, experience, and knowledge in projects of comparable type, scope, and size
- Lack of key team engagement, enthusiasm, and motivation
- Inadequate process for recruitment of new talent and training for new and existing staff
- Neither commit key resources to your project nor assure they will not be diverted
- Unrealistic portrayal of experience, capabilities, competencies, and timeframes

### 4. Oversight and Management

- Insufficiency of executive attention to product or program
- Lack of alignment of product or program to core mission of company
- Company has acquired product but has not integrated it into core offerings or provided adequate promotion or support

*Figure 5 Third Party and Service Contract Red Flags*

## 5. Poor Administrative and Operational Controls

- Does not perform effective identity management or use adequate means of authentication
- Does not provide effective permissions, access controls or authorization
- Does not implement a program of end user awareness or responsible behavior
- Ineffective account administration (add, modify, suspend, terminate)
- Does not have a program for administrative segregation of system responsibilities

## 6. Proprietary or Misaligned Technical, Cloud or SAAS Design

- Poor alignment of technology or service to data or requirements (i.e., inability to provide PCI compliant infrastructure and controls for PCI data)
- Uses other cloud providers or hosts in the delivery of its services, and these may additionally use others (n-tier), but does not accept responsibility for their performance and risk
- Does not assure return of data on exit from the contracted engagement in a timely manner or format usable outside of the context of the application service

## 7. Inadequate Recovery and Continuity

- Provider does not have an effective backup strategy including periodic snapshots, backup to alternate media or locations, and encryption and protection of archived data. Does not have a means to rapidly restore data that has been compromised.
- Provider does not have an effective means, facility, and strategy in place to rapidly restore systems and applications or data centers lost to crisis events.
- Provider does not have an established business continuity program and does not perform scheduled recovery tests or continuity exercises

## 8. Inadequate Demonstration of Compliance to Regulatory or Risk Evaluation Programs

- Responses to risk evaluation letters are not forthcoming, inadequate, unsatisfying, untrusted
- Failure to conform to obligations as required by standards, policy, agreement, convention, or law
- Failure to meet regulatory requirements for oversight, reporting or controls
- Unresolved significant audit exceptions
- Disciplinary or regulatory sanctions

*When breached we often conclude we were the helpless victims of unstoppable malicious expertise. Where brilliance is in short supply, carelessness is not, and most often is the explanation*

## 9. Inadequate Data Safety and Privacy

- Provider does not perform effective data access and entitlement reviews
- Provider does not have a privacy policy that assures data with specific sensitivity (PCI, PII) appropriate levels of protection in keeping with regulatory requirements or standards.
- Provider is insensitive to the location of data and may move active data or backups to storage or virtual storage as needs demand or to lower cost irrespective of location including crossing national borders.
- Provider takes no responsibility for the breach and loss of sensitive data entrusted to their care and has no policy requiring notification in such an event.

## 10. Inadequate Technical Security and Controls

- Absence of system segregation and production controls; change controls including OS updates and patch management; hardened systems; or protected build images
- Is not in compliance with specific regulation if required
- Is not effectively guided by or working towards any recognized standard or guidelines
- Lacks endpoint controls including appropriate use of malware detection, whitelisting, encryption of consequential data, and heuristic protection
- Lacks adequate, redundant, and diverse perimeter, virtual and extended perimeter controls and defenses including firewalls, intrusion detection/prevention
- Inadequate application and system vulnerability assessment, penetration testing and remediation process
- Insufficient capability in threat detection / management / awareness
- Inadequately trained teams for monitoring, response, and coverage
- Does not regularly examine logs or view real time alerts to systems and infrastructure or aggregate or correlate these for intelligent management and response
- Inadequate management and protection of highly consequential system and data inventory
- Has not formalized crisis response team and procedures and there are insufficient formalized breach response procedures and notification provisions

*Controls mean little out of context to a business objective and a defined risk*

# WWW.CISORedefined.com

## for updates, error corrections and more

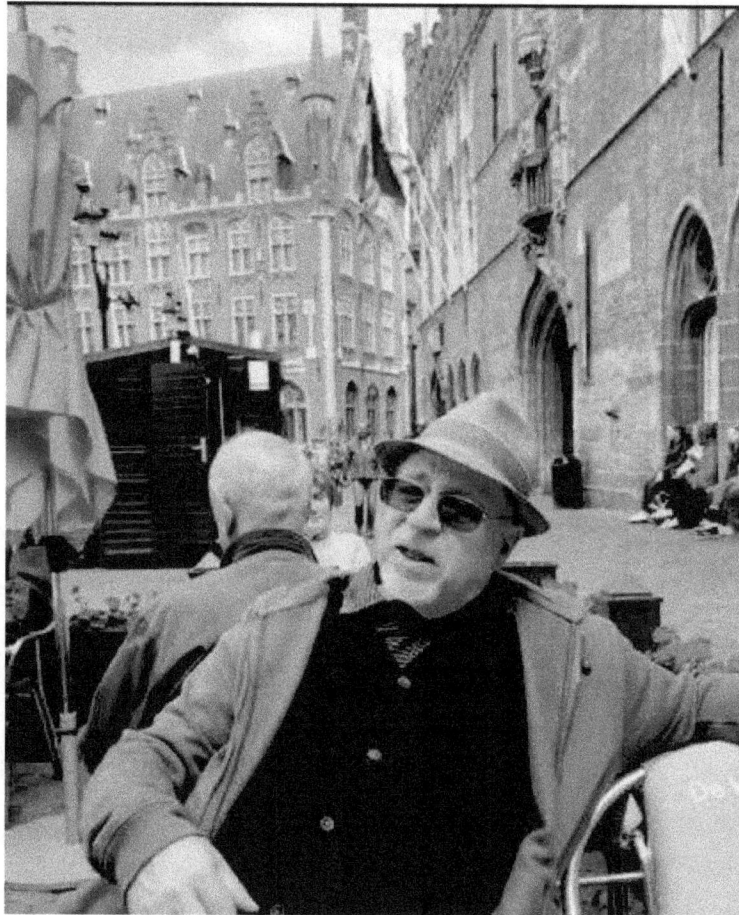

An Ad in a
Book?
What's next?

Privacy and security are constantly changing.

It is exhausting trying to keep up.

If you have a question, an opinion, have found an error (I'll send you a free corrected electronic copy for letting me know), or would like to discuss consulting, speaking engagements, or to see if there has been an updated version of the book released since you purchased your copy, I am happy to hear from you.

I can be reached at:

**mgomberg@cyberite.com**

or visit my website

**www.cisoredefined.com**

or reach out to me or any of the members of The Privacy Panel

**info@ThePrivacyPanel.com**

# CISO
# REDEFINED

*Protecting Business*

---

Martin Gomberg, CISSP, CIPP/E

## SECTION 6.   LEADERSHIP, LANGUAGE, CULTURE AND CONTROLS

Over my career, I had the opportunity to work for, and with, many very good people. I had the privilege to lead a very great team. When discussing culture, one CEO, Nick Davatzes, stands out more than any other in his efforts to foster a community, a culture, and as an exceptional leader. He led a company based on strength of character and concern for people.

He made this paramount. It was simple things. He would start each day by walking every floor to say good morning. It was a small thing, and a small company at that time, so covering the floors in an hour was certainly doable. But it was the message being sent, the signals, and the response from the staff that were telling. He cultivated a sense of belonging. A sense of shared interests. Of accessibility. His message was one of ethics. He would say, and I paraphrase, 'I'd rather that we walk away from business, than do business in a way that we wouldn't be proud of'. It was a tone that he wanted more from us than just productive business, he wanted business we could respect. Whatever any other did, he wanted us to stand apart and above in that way. He wanted a company of leaders. He would deliver a message of individual importance and shared contribution. All roles were important, and all roles were respected and valued. He would periodically stop at an office or desk at random and strike up a conversation. He wanted a feeling of openness and community and conveyed an importance and value in his employees. He was establishing a culture, and it was immediately felt in how individuals worked with each other, and how departments worked together, and how we were perceived by the industry and business partners. And as the company grew globally, of course there were no more walks, but that culture of contribution and pride in belonging persisted. So, did the message of ethics. So, did the pride in leadership and participation that he instilled. It was a privilege and an education to have worked for him.

There are many excellent leaders in business. More than any adopted platform or approach, it is a tangible corporate vision, and a commitment by leadership to a culture that embraces excellence and common interest that defines success in corporate governance. A culture of ethics, and a concern for people and their interests as individuals. A commitment to responsibility, accountability, oversight, and management, and prudent controls and practices. The tone set at the top, messages sent, and clarity of signals. Each alone are attributes worth pursuing, and together the building blocks of a better protected and more effective business. This is true regardless of size of company, industry, name recognition, or any other parameter. These are signs of maturity in a well-run company. The best of companies strives to attain these qualities. Some may achieve exceptionalism in a few of these, few in all, but most would likely confess to the want and willingness to do better.

In this chapter, I will talk about the 'House Rules'. I developed the 'House Rules' early in my career as a CIO to define operational parameters and help promote a service, value, performance, and ethics-oriented IT culture. I wanted a culture defined by quality management, continuous improvement, and effective business protection. Even within IT, it was clear that there was a language gap. Engineers spoke a different language than did developers, or analysts. Desktop specialists from those that supported the network. I wanted a common language established so that we each heard the same things. The House Rules proved to be effective even beyond the needs of the department. They codified our mission and helped others across the business and third parties with which we engaged to both understand, and to take part. It established what we considered important. It removed ambiguity. It helped engage the company to assume responsibility and participate as an informed first line of defense. It removed fear and embarrassment in reporting problems and mistakes, encouraging and incentivizing participation and personal accountability. It encouraged participation in committees and working groups with a sense of common goal.

What rules do we live by? How do we define the culture and values we want in our IT department, security group, or business overall? Each of us as leaders will confront the questions of language, and culture and grapple with what that means regarding controls, which we select to implement, and how we implement them. Where does ethics sit in governing our actions? How do we balance oversight and trust, or the interests of security and privacy? These will set our priorities as we define our teams and establish relationships across the enterprise. We are an integral part of the business. But how do we ensure that we are targeting those most important elements that we as CIOs, CISOs, IT or other executives, believe brings out our best, and delivers the greatest value to our companies?

We each hire the best talent. We all embrace diversity in people, skills, and ideas. We each come from different backgrounds and experiences, face different corporate, budget, market, and industry challenges, and have our own ideas of what construes excellence. We each in common face the constant challenge of technology change, new threats, market demands and consumer empowerment. We are challenged to find the best people, to engage them, and to keep them. We engage in new markets and approaches to business. We face the ever-shortening shelf life of opportunity. These are all pressures with which we must contend, adapt to, or embrace, and which continually redefines our approach to business, the use of information, and its protection.

Prudent IT has always been about balancing operational effectiveness, innovation and advantage, risk management, and cost control. It has always been the safety net to the decisions we make. It is precisely the grounding of "prudent" IT and effective security controls that empowers "innovators" to play safely on the busy streets of this new, exciting, but less than friendly world.

There has been a shift over past years that relegated much of what used to be an extremely important focus, operational effectiveness, cost control, and management of risks, to being 'table stakes' for a CIO, the minimum requirement of the job, while innovation and digital transformation, and the disruptive elements we call upon and that define us as 'change agents' has become the basis on which grades are given, and careers flourish, or jobs are lost.

Much the same is happening with the CISO, but paradoxically it is the technical capabilities that have become table stakes, and the ability to engage, lead, and address transformative risk in all aspects of the business that has become the metric for the high performing CISO.

Every company assumes the responsibility of developing and enforcing safeguards, processes, and policies to protect the consequential data they collect, store, or steward on behalf of others, particularly so if sensitive or confidential. If we are to protect our data or ask our employees to share in the responsibility of protecting our data, a culture of care and responsibility needs to be fostered.

Business leaders know the formula. Success requires that we find, hire, grow, and support the best talent, use that talent in new ways, build the right organizations, motivate, and encourage success, and foster contribution of ideas. We need to properly structure investments, leverage innovative approaches, and adopt the best of emerging technology. We need to participate in new communities, media and means to engage our clients and markets. We need to pursue proximity to our consumers wherever they are, on whatever platform, and will partner globally to achieve this. We will need an innovative and forward-thinking executive tier, bold steps, and new ideas.

Our rules define us. They are the framework that defines our culture, but in a sense our culture is being redefined for us with the speed of new expectations. Changing markets, demanding business, digital communities, and rabid technology adoption is now the price of entry.

.

Culture is based on a common set of values clearly communicated. A lexicon of shared interests. The CISO needs to be a master of language and will be called upon to speak many on any given day communicating with executives, developers, engineers, line of business, attorneys, regulators, and law enforcement. A common vocabulary assures a clear understanding of goals and expectations. Establishing a 'vocabulary' of commonly accepted concepts and technical terms is remarkably difficult, even amongst highly technical people. They often see and hear the same words differently and approach problems from very different points of vantage.

By example, if you bring two lines of code to the attention of a developer and say that these are redundant, they will recognize it as a problem, an inefficiency, or at the very least unneeded and correct the problem. If you review the architectural designs of a network with an engineer and point out the redundant telecom lines, firewalls, and high-performance servers, it will be a point of pride that the redundancy of critical components provides for a high availability design. Redundancy to an executive distant to the needs might suggest duplication, that somebody is not minding the shop, in either case might inure negative connotations.

A common language of threat, vulnerabilities, risk, and defenses is critical if involving disparate disciplines and stake holders in threat modeling, threat hunting and assessment of vulnerabilities, and advancing a culture sensitive to risk. In this regard, there are considerable resources technical communities, tools, and guidelines can offer. But it comes down to language.

---

These are useful resources and help define terms and establish common language:
- OWASP (Open Web Application Security Project)
- CWE (Common Weakness Enumeration)
- NIST NVD (National Vulnerability Database)
- Center for Internet Security (CIS; SANS) Critical Security Controls
- UCF (Unified Compliance Framework)
- DISA STIGs (Defense Information systems Agency - Security Technical Implementation Guides)
- NIST 800-53

---

It is also about establishing culture, a shared interest. A culture and community that believes in the mission, internalizes the goal, and understands their purpose. A community understands that their participation advances the culture and that inclusion, advocacy and education encourage its success.

So, where the goal is a culture of excellence, an ecosystem of controls and practices can assure that the business is protected while helping to meet corporate obligations under the law. It is about a culture of respect, responsibility for our decisions and actions, and a concern for the company and each other. A clear message from leadership that wherever we are now, we are going to be better, focused on excellence, our people, what we do, and the way we do it. On making business safer, cleaner, and assuring our continuity.

There are no security investments. There are only business investments. The ROI of security is business. And an ecosystem of excellence and best practices, of prudence and effectiveness is vital to a healthy business, vital to its participation in the community of businesses, and in the receptivity of clients and markets. They derive from leadership, ownership, oversight, and accountability and from an encouragement of shared purpose across the company, with partners, and in the markets we serve.

The rules as illustrated in the list below and their associated defined vocabulary have evolved, changing, reissued, and presented with celebration year after year. I expect as technology, law, and the environment of threat changes, the rules will continue to do so too.

# TABLE: House Rules for Quality Management and Effective Business Protection

| | | |
|---|---|---|
| **1** | Availability | Are data, applications, systems, and connectivity servicing business needs? |
| **2** | Scalability | Do we have sufficient capacity to store, process, deliver and grow? |
| **3** | Operability | Do we have the skills, documentation, and readiness for support? |
| **4** | Redundancy | Do we have alternatives on loss of storage, processing, delivery, or service? |
| **5** | Diversity | Do we leverage difference in technology, paths, methods, access, people, and skills? |
| **6** | Recovery | If one or more critical components fail is there a means to restore functionality? |
| **7** | Privacy | Is collection verifiably limited to that which is required, and processing to that consented, for the term and use intended, respecting the rights and intentions of individuals? |
| **8** | Compliance | Do we adhere to standards of practice, law, and regulation, domestic and global? |
| **9** | Security | Are all physical, technical, contractual, continuity, identity, access limits and integrity safeguards in place? |
| **10** | Policy | Have we communicated expected and mandated behavior and practice? |
| **11** | Inclusivity | Does security, privacy, compliance, and quality govern both internal and external relations? |
| **12** | Integrity | Can we affirm all systems are secure, managed diligently with operational cleanliness and prudent controls? |
| **13** | Liability | Can our licensing, use, ethics, actions, practices, or intentions ever be questioned? |
| **14** | Accountability | Are actions that affect us visible, traceable, measurable, ascribable, and consequential? |
| **15** | Continuity | Can contracts, relationships, technologies, process, and entities endure crisis and change? |
| **16** | Quality | In all aspects of planning, procurement, execution, and operation is excellence our goal? |
| **17** | Ingenuity | Are we leveraging the best new ideas, information, innovation, and approaches? |
| **18** | Reliability | Are we there when needed, ready, consistent, skilled, current, and capable? |
| **19** | Visibility | Do we demonstrate value that is business focused, goal directed and measurable? |
| **20** | Adaptability | Do we meet business need and change with ideas, innovation, speed, service, and effectiveness? |
| **21** | Community | Are we leaders, improving, guiding, enabling, and contributing to team, business, and community? |

*Figure 6 House Rules*

*I recall being on a computer networking panel with a colleague from Britain, discussing the limitations of building 'Trusted Networks', a technical term for connecting networks that allow the flow of data between partners and companies as if one company.*

*I commented that even if business partners, given the lack of visibility as to where else they might be connected, our policies will not allow a trust between our networks.*

*It was not long before I came across an article in a publication attributing to me the comment,*

*"We Cannot Trust Our British partners!"*

*Words last forever, but truths it seems are in short supply*

The CISO lives in a world of controls. Whether laws, regulation, standards, guidelines, advice, example, management, or policies, it is always about controls. I searched for a definition of controls, and of course there are thousands, but I chanced upon and lifted this directly from a University of Toronto document of Sept 3, 2016, that was posted on the internet, in that I thought it was as nicely put, appropriate, and as succinct a definition of controls as any I have come across:

> A control is "any policy, procedure, practice, or mechanism designed to provide reasonable assurance that the organization's objectives will be achieved. This includes controls designed to safeguard assets, ensure the timeliness, accuracy, and reliability of financial and management reporting, and to promote operational efficiency, effectiveness and compliance with all applicable laws, regulations, policies, and procedures."

Whether wholly or in part home-crafted, or pulled in entirety from an authoritative source, it could not have been said better. Hovering on the first sentence, I feel it is worth repeating:

**"A control is "any policy, procedure, practice, or mechanism designed to provide reasonable assurance that the organization's objectives will be achieved."**

I would add that controls can be:

> 'any technical, operational, organizational or administrative mechanism, policy, procedure, process, product, or practice, that acts to reveal, safeguard, enhance, or provide a measure or counter measure, in defense or response, for the detection, prevention, correction or other mitigation of specific risk to any potentially exploitable vulnerability, or for the improvement of a function, or the steering or provision of guidance (signs, instruction books, policies, education and training) that effect results or dictate or encourage appropriate actions or behaviors'

*Security and business are not different or apart. Considering them as separate does not take us to where leadership needs business to go*

**Controls come in all flavors:**

- An enlightened manager walking the floor to assure people are comfortable, engaged, and happy.

- A less astute manager walking the floor to assure everyone is hard at work.

- A guard trying the doorknobs of offices to assure they are locked.

- A secure data center facility on a hill, unmarked, separated from the road by a ravine.

- A security system, router, or anti-virus program.

- Employee policy and handbook.

- The network shut down for scheduled routine maintenance.

- A review of a developer's application code by a second developer.

- A recurring budget entry for investment in a security program.

- A bug bounty.

## Controls in context

In a prior position, I oversaw a small, localized, high availability data center with redundancy and replication processes in place and extensive monitoring and alerts. Still, I asked a team of network engineers to do a walk-through of the data center each morning before start of day.

They worked through a checklist physically looking at machines, and the color of LED lights, status of backup jobs, lifting tiles to check the water levels in the drip pans under the air conditioners, and to get a feel for the general conditions in the room. (OK. It's old school, but I'm like that).

This was effective, if not efficient, and for most not possible today, but it served a purpose much greater than the task being performed. I wanted to encourage a perception of ownership, care, and importance.

- The data center was important in that It supported everything.

- The task was important in that people perceive differently than systems, and intuition, senses, and observation see what online monitoring and diagnostics may not.

- The engineers doing the work were important for the success of the effort, improving the quality of the inspection as they learned more and added creativity to the approach, adding tasks to the checklist, modifying, or removing others, enhancing the protection of the room and its systems. Creativity is a control only people can add. For example, the engineers added a scheduled test call to an 'emergency message hotline' to confirm it was active, and that the default message was current and correct. This was a distinctly 'human' test.

Practicality would dictate that I rely on automated monitoring and alerts. That certainly would be more efficient and would make better use of staff time, some might argue. And they would not be wrong. Given the size, complexity, globalization, and virtualization of the modern data center, and that so much of our systems are in the cloud, we all are dependent on automation, diagnostics, and alerts. We live by predictive analytics and heuristic feedback. Our interaction is with dashboards, SIEM consoles and queried data lakes. Physical examination is anything from not practical to impossible. Many of our security organizations have never seen the systems they protect. But if I leave it at that it will ruin my story, which in fact is not intended to be about managing data centers and systems at all, or about security, but instead, subterfuge in introducing the relationship between controls. So, my secret is out, and with that said, I continue.

It was an established policy of mine, in line with the House Rules introduced earlier in this section, that despite an automated inspection, a manual inspection be conducted daily.

Most controls are classified as process (production), administrative, detective, preventive, deceptive, corrective, enhancing or steering. The list is not constrained to these (offensive or harassing controls come to mind as two more), but these do subsume most we consider that are lawful. Controls can be primary or supportive. They can be technical, operational, administrative, physical, legal, or other in origin. Controls can be applied as direct controls, compensating, layered, or interlaced. I will get into the definitions of these a little further down.

My policy was a 'steering control', (a guiding direction, rule, plan, advocated approach, vision, or attitude), a policy that in this case encouraged both human attention to an otherwise automatable process, and redundant inspections, each bringing different capabilities and benefits.

The walk-through process was an 'operational detective control', operationally examining the data center and systems to detect potential, pending, or recognizable weaknesses, exposures, or failures. Of course, all the automated monitoring and alerts were 'technical detective controls', probably more effective, and infinitely more efficient, but you do not get to touch stuff directly by looking at a report, a dashboard, or a screen, and you do not get that same feeling of engagement and ownership. When you get a new car, what do you marvel at, that new car smell, looks of admiration from people passing, and how it feels taking corners, or the odometer reading and measured depth of your tire tread?

Engendering and reinforcing that feeling of engagement and ownership in people and elevating the importance of the people in the roles they perform itself is a 'motivational control', improving the organization and engendering a sense of personal responsibility, in this case bettering an already exceptional team that had been tasked with detecting technical risk. In any case, those two needs, inspect the data center, and improve the team responsible for inspecting the data center, were interlaced controls. Together they had the synergistic effect of detecting technical problems, and having a better and more engaged team, with a greater affinity to the systems they were tasked to safeguard, detecting technical problems, creating that much better a control overall.

It was rare that the walkthrough would uncover a failure impactful to the start of day in that so much was invested in high availability, (a preventive control). And should something be uncovered, it could be quickly 'corrected' before start of day, a mitigating (corrective) control for technical risk.

**Types of controls**

Some controls are 'direct' in covering a specific need. High availability systems for example are a one-to-one relationship between two or more systems where if one became vulnerable or failed, another could assume its function.

Some controls are supportive, 'layered' on top of others to enhance them, like setting an alarm clock for a time to assure that you get out of bed, and then using the snooze feature to assure you get out of bed. Or having a well-defined coding policy, training developers in secure coding practices, but still doing two party code reviews, or automated code scans, to assure the viability of the code produced.

Some controls are 'interlaced' and provide a greater added value when used together. This was my objective in sharing the story. Supplementation of automated monitoring with a human element, motivating and elevating already good people, engaging them further with a sense of responsibility, and encouraging a human perspective and the introduction of learning and creativity to an otherwise automatable technical task, is an interlaced control process, the whole being greater than the sum of its parts. We use firewalls in front of intrusion prevention systems. That would be a technical example of interlaced controls. Dogs patrolling a well-lit, fenced yard would be a physical example.

I am a strong believer in people. If you have not read it already, Transforming IT Culture by Frank Wander is worth seeking out. The sub-title is How to Use Social Intelligence, Human Factors, and Collaboration to Create an IT Department that Outperforms. That pretty much says it all. Some controls work to address the deficiency, insufficiency, or absence of others as 'compensating' controls. Those familiar with PCI DSS may recognize the term. It is explored in greater depth below.

*Controls are often classified as administrative, detective, preventive, deceptive, corrective, enhancing or steering. The list is not constrained to these (offensive or harassing controls come to mind), but these do subsume most we consider legal*

## Categories of controls

**Direct** – Direct control is a risk mitigating measure whether detective, preventive or other, that specifically targets a given risk or exposure. A low light CCTV camera is a direct detective control focused on detecting intrusions.

The effectiveness of any direct control should be clearly demonstrable at introduction. It also should continue to provide that protection with the same effectiveness with change over time. That test failing, in this example, if the area it was intended to cover is expanded such that visibility is incomplete, the control ceases to be sufficiently effective to remain a direct control (although it may still be a primary control), and needs upgrade, replacement, or the support of compensating controls to address the deficiency.

In the CCTV example, the camera might still be used as a primary detective control in the expanded yard, with those areas uncovered by camera addressed by compensating controls including enhanced lighting, dogs, and guard patrols. The same would be true of preventive controls like walls and locked gates. They are only effective and can only be considered Direct Controls if adequate to meet the stated intention of the control.

**Compensating** – In accordance with PCI DSS appendix C, when an 'entity cannot meet a control requirement explicitly as stated', and where there exists a 'legitimate constraint' against satisfying the expected requirement for a control as dictated by the PCI DSS standard, or a direct control is impractical, infeasible or unavailable to satisfy a specific security requirement, one or more correlated controls can be applied that offset the risk left uncovered by absence of the direct or required control.

In accordance with the standard, a compensating control or controls must provide the same 'intent, rigorous protection, and defense' as required by the original PCI DSS required control for which it is compensating and be 'commensurate' to the unaddressed risk that the absence of the required control leaves in place, and neither introduce additional, or permit residual risk to remain uncovered by other direct or compensating controls. A compensating control or controls must be tested to assure it meets the objectives as intended of the required control both when introduced and maintains its effectiveness in meeting the originally stated objective over time.

**Layered** – Layered controls are redundant controls. A layered network uses mutually reinforcing *redundant control (two separate routers individuate the layers)*. A network configured in a three-tier design with one router connecting the outer network to the internet, and another router to the inner corporate network, is layered.

**Interlaced** – An interlaced control uses mutually reinforcing, and often *diverse controls,* where the interplay of supporting controls is a control greater than the sum of its parts. Two routers of different make and characteristics, or a router, and a firewall, or intrusion protection device, when used together, interlace defenses synergistically in the design of a network.

Where mitigation of a risk whether by direct, compensating, interlaced, or layered controls is not considered prudent, cost fit, or appropriate to the risk or the needs of the business, then in the judgment of the business, alternate approaches to the management of risk may be warranted. The decision to distribute the risk through purchase of insurance is an option in some cases. Reasoned acceptance of risk may also be appropriate accepting the responsibility to fund the response to risk and deal with the consequences if an event occurs, a Just-In-Time risk management model. A controls table is often used as a sub table in performing a risk assessment and constructing a risk mitigation plan.

International standards (ISO 27005) and U.S. Federal Guidelines (NIST SP 800-30) provide widely adopted guidance as to the management of risk.

| Risk | Direct Controls | Layered Controls | Interlaced Controls | Compensating Controls |
|---|---|---|---|---|
| Theft | Locked Doors | Security Lighting | Guards Patrol with Dogs | Move most valuable assets to bank vault |

*Figure 7 Simplified Example of a Controls Table*

*Controls are any technical, operational, organizational, or administrative mechanism, policy, procedure, process, product, or practice that enhances anticipation, detection, defense, or response, or acts in deterrence or counter measure*

## The 'intelligence' behind the CIA

| | CIA (Uncloaked) | | | | | | | | | |
|---|---|---|---|---|---|---|---|---|---|---|
| | Availability | | | Security | | | | Integrity | Validation | |
| | Presence | Functionality | Adequacy | Primary | Supporting | | Compensating | Proof | Risk Tolerance | Frequency of Sampling |
| | | | | Direct | Layered | Interlaced | | | | |

## Augmented CIA controls mapped to objectives

| Objective | CIA (Uncloaked) | | | | | | | | | |
|---|---|---|---|---|---|---|---|---|---|---|
| | Availability | | | Security | | | | Integrity | Validation | |
| | Presence | Functionality | Adequacy | Primary | Supporting | | Compensating | Proof | Risk Tolerance | Frequency of Sampling |
| | | | | Direct | Layered | Interlaced | | | | |
| Home Access | Install a door | Add a doorknob | Size and type of door | Install a door lock | An additional lock | Add peek hole and porch light | Neighborhood guard patrol | Install alarm system | Low tolerance for risk | Test alarm on every activation |
| Secure Perimeter | High Fence | Force access to entry gate | Gate is only entry point | Gate is guarded | Credentials or escort required | Locked after business hours | Well-lit yard, CCTV cameras, dog patrols; trench protects fence | Access logs reviewed | Secure facility – very low tolerance | Dog patrols hourly |
| Secure Network | Firewall | Next Gen | Works at line speed | High availability redundancy | Diverse firewalls | NAC / PNAC Access Controls | Hardened servers and endpoints | Pen Test | Moderate risk | Quarterly Pen Test Program is adequate |

*Figure 8 The CIA Uncloaked*

## Cyber Insurance as a control

Mitigation of risk is not always possible. The establishment of effective defenses and adequacy of detective capabilities are often beyond the resources of many companies for many reasons irrespective of size. And even where adequate attention is given to assets, risk inventory, staffing, training, assessment of third-party risk, technical defenses, operational management, testing, and other initiatives for cyber event preparedness, and even in our largest and best prepared name companies, we succumb to intrusion, breach, and attack.

Some companies recognize the need for supplementation of capabilities and turn to managed service providers. The best of these can bring considerable depth of knowledge, process maturity and experience to the defense of a company. Some companies might opt for acceptance of the risk, limiting, or taking only the most basic of precautions to mitigate exposure, with the intent of dealing with the unforeseen should it occur. Several recent Cyber events make that strategy questionable. Regardless though, we all recognize that defenses will fail, and we cannot watch everywhere or detect everything, regardless of whether managing threats internally, outsourcing support to specialists, or in any format in between. Many companies have turned to Cyber Insurance to ameliorate the cost of an event, or supplement preparedness efforts. Cyber insurance cannot remove the risk but can remove some of the financial impact of an attack or loss and has become an important part of a complete defensive strategy.

Corporate interest in the addition of insurance provisions as a component of Cyber defense (and regulatory risk protection) has increased. Actuaries and underwriters have gained experience, but some insurers are exiting the market, or increasing policy costs with the realization of changing risks. And there are substantial differences in available Cyber coverage plans, whether specifically offered as a cyber policy, or as a rider or addendum to other existing corporate coverage, or as line items within existing plans. Coverage will vary as to the types of incidents they cover, coverage thresholds for specific impacts, cost, terms, and incidents or impacts they exclude. There also may be differences in what they require of the client in terms of safeguards, requirements for notification of an event to the carrier, and may require prior authorizations for engagement of external responders and other costs. Some may have preparedness requirements including voluntary adherence or certifications to standards. There may be requirements for demonstrable or certifiable adequacy in detection and response capabilities and a well-defined crisis response plan.

Application for cyber insurance often includes detailed audit questionnaires and other due diligence. Misrepresentations, inadequate detail, and omissions may each be disqualifying, and insufficient adherence to minimal standards may be sufficient to void coverage. It is important to determine in advance what may constitute a disqualifying condition in a specific claim or event. (Corporate Counsel, Cooney, Young & Logan, Untangling the Mystery of Cybersecurity Insurance, Feb 2017)

*If a policy goes into effect, but nobody knows, is it in effect?*

There also may be differences in what is considered valid for coverage and whether this includes the cost of investigating the incident, incident response, repair and replacement costs for damaged equipment, and recovery of compromised data and applications. There also may be differences in coverage for the correction of the deficiencies or exposures that led to the breach or incident. As <u>Richard A. Guida points out in his book entitled The Entropy Police</u>, which by the way is a book I highly recommend to any serious CISO or CISO candidate, cyber insurance "does not cover the cost of damage to the brand; it just covers the costs a company incurs in responding to the breach, and possibly costs associated with subsequent litigation". This will likely vary depending on the provider and the policy.

There are other questions to be considered.

- Will it cover imposed domestic or global regulatory penalties, court mandated sanctions, notification of clients, provisions for identity protection, or other make good requirements?
- Will it provide coverage for the products, hardware, and services required to restore to required regulatory, industry, policy mandated or operating standards?
- Does the denial of a claim for one type of policy poison the well, negatively influencing the outcome of claims against other corporate policies?

There is significant variability in policies and these differences should be considered carefully. Insurance is complex. It is important to get clarity as to the cross points or overlap with other existing policies for business interruption, general liability, errors and omissions, director and officer protection, or fire, theft, and casualty. These may provide some overlap of coverage for cyber events.

These questions need to be addressed in interview of potential providers so there is clarity as to what you are buying, what they cover and will not, and to assure that you understand and meet your obligations under the contract.

When we will be attacked, whether defenses and mitigation capabilities will prove sufficient, and the cost of attack, breach or loss are all difficult to predict. Cyber insurance is an important element in a comprehensive cyber strategy.

*We need to understand where our business, processes, or critical technologies, have become too diffuse, peripheral, and marginalized, to be effectively monitored, secured, managed, or recovered*

# CISO
# REDEFINED

*Protecting Business*

Martin Gomberg, CISSP, CIPP/E

## SECTION 7.   STAFFING A CYBER ORGANIZATION

Every business has a mission. Executive vision defines the mission. Leadership establishes a defined organization, business activities and structures to assure it is supported. It falls to leadership to explicitly state and advocate and to each member of the organization to understand the mission and to do their part.

Threats will change, business priorities shift and compete, new technologies emerge, and investment opportunities vary with budget cycles. Within this context, it falls to the CISO to develop an organization appropriately fit to the challenges and priorities of business, structured, and targeted to fit the mission, while addressing the climate of threat, and of change. Businesses differ, as do their concerns, structures, and their capabilities. So, more specifically, it falls to the CISO to develop an organization targeted to the risk concerns of the specific business they have been tasked to protect, prioritized within their capacity for the most likelihood of success.

A business capturing sensitive data is concerned about breach. Those that have high value assets, theft. Those that live by online access, ecommerce, electronic fulfillment or transmission of signal or broadcast, concern for electronic interruption or denial of service (DDOS). Most or all businesses, if they are to thrive, do so by concern for reputation, and for revenue, and so by concern for image, availability, and continuity. Of course, protecting business requires attention to all threats, but the structure of the security organization and priority of staffing should reflect the stated mission and the business risk of greatest and most imminent concern. If in an active flood zone far from deserts, you probably do not need too much focus on addressing sandstorms. You can buy that knowledge should the unlikely need arise, and better focus the headcount.

Of course, most companies recognize that if undertaking the building of a security organization, it needs to be effective, staffed with the most capable people, in the right positions, with the skills fit to the roles they will perform. It needs to be the right organization to address current and future challenges. It needs to be improved through training to stay current, compliant, and motivated.

It also needs to be correctly structured and defined as to reporting lines, titles, responsibilities, job descriptions, with clear growth paths to be attractive, and to enable resourcing specialists, and available talent, to understand and seek out the roles available within the organization that need to be filled. There needs to be a commitment to its success through adequate budget and resources.

Finding qualified staff in a limited pool of talent is always difficult. So too is knowing what capabilities are needed, which positions are most important to fill, and which should be given priority against budget. Some opt to absorb cyber security within existing IT operations and augment the specializations needed or provide training to existing staff. Others choose to 'matrix manage' access to resources across the organization, perhaps from IT, Legal, Risk, Digital Communications, and other departments. Some invest in a dedicated team, and not all fall within Information Technology. As mentioned earlier, according to the 2017 IDG Security Priorities Study, two-thirds of enterprises have appointed a dedicated CISO or CSO. More than half of these are likely to be part of a dedicated security organization apart from IT. This is as compared to small to medium businesses which have either not dedicated the role, and where they have, it is as an embedded IT function.

Even where a dedicated security function and team is established some allocate the cost across the business. Others, depending on reporting structures, localize the cost within IT, or a dedicated security budget, or more granular divisions of security (Cyber, Enterprise) and manage P&L (profit and loss). Others charge back to specific risk centers (typically departments, divisions, or lines of business) and engage as a service provider.

For some the CISO is a hands-on technical specialist. For others, a non-operational advisor. For some the leader of a security function staffed with specialist engineers, analysts, educators, and project managers, each reporting through varying structures to the CISO. These may be embedded in the business, or as members of other operational support areas that have a 'dotted line' responsibility to the CISO for oversight and guidance. Still others elect to outsource the function to a 'managed service provider', or procure secured cloud based 'platform as a service', or 'application as a service', or 'content delivery networks', where security of the platform is embedded in the contracted service. For many, and increasingly, it is a mix. In each, the CISO typically assumes the lead, or at a minimum, plays a significant role in providing guidance and managing risk. Where the business model is federated, there may be numerous, semi-autonomous CISO roles, with CISO title or other (Information Security Officer for instance), and these may or not report to a global, corporate, or executive CISO responsible for over-all enterprise security direction.

And now, the elephant in the room.

There has been considerable discussion over the past few years about CISO reporting. Mostly this has been a discussion about whether the CISO should report to the CIO or elsewhere in the organization, whether the CISO should support operational security and administrative functions, and whether the CISO is a strategic role. The discussion is usually highly charged. Perspectives largely differ about the CISO role, as they do about the changing role of the CIO and where that role is going. They differ over changes in the technology deployment model to cloud and As a Service. And if the question is asked of leadership, they differ in their views about IT, technology and technical security threats, and their concerns about personal accountability in cyber issues.

I could weigh in with opinion, and likely inflame a few readers, but in fact it is likely less relevant an opinion than it was before. This discussion is being resolved in emerging law. The release of new cybersecurity regulations by NYDFS (New York Department of Financial services), has made clear that for businesses falling under this regulation, leadership is accountable for cybersecurity and business protection. They must employ a CISO dedicated to oversight of business protection, and leadership and the board must be briefed directly by the CISO, in writing, or by advisement and report at least annually as a fiduciary function of corporate leadership. Without doubt, this will be replicated and exceeded in emerging states law elsewhere in the country. 'Strengthening the Cybersecurity of Federal Networks and Critical Infrastructure' and subsequent executive orders discussed earlier hold leadership and agency heads accountable and elevates the importance of the CISO. This undoubtedly will trickle down as an expectation to the businesses that depend on federal contracts. And with the GDPR fully in place, the autonomy and obligation of the DPO or Data Protection Officer for privacy, a very compatible role, is a model.

The CIO role has been evolving for at least the past twenty years in most companies as a leader in innovation, business alignment, and digital transformation, a strategic role. Some are increasingly paired side by side with the Chief Digital Marketing Officer or other newly emerged roles and titles in digital adoption. The CIO for most has transformed to a business stewardship role. Technical operations and the management of technical security may fall under the CIO, but this is not always the case. These may fall under another role, and this will vary. Technical and technician functions likely go where those responsible for helpdesk, account administration, server and firewall configuration and similar functions are conducted, and technical security any number of paths.

The CISO is emerging in a strategic role for business protection. If the DPO model serves as an example, and rightly it should, the CISO should provide guidance and oversight to business protective policies. The CISO should also provide guidance to implementation, not direct management, assuring in oversight the effective execution of security policy. In either case this would be difficult if not independent. This of course is opinion. Others will see this differently.

Security operations and the CISO role should be separate if aligning with the direction of emerging law. The CISO establishing policy, signed off by corporate leadership, implemented in operations. As one attorney put it to me, you cannot create security policy on Monday, be the one to implement and execute it on Tuesday, and then for the rest of the week oversee its review, acceptance, and final sign off. A fox and a hen house come to mind.

I also believe that if regulations are an indicator, at least in the U.S., the CISO role will broaden in oversight of business protective responsibilities, with oversight of security, governance, privacy, continuity, and other areas of business protection. And the CISO will be responsible for the protection and advisement of an accountable leadership and corporate board.

The requirements, compensation, and optimal structure for staffing of a cyber security organization in the private sector are often unclear and organizations struggle with the priority and order in which to staff them. This is not surprising as business concerns vary, risk tolerances differ, and threats change, and the understanding of cyber by those in the position to approve staff investment is often limited. This is particularly so in less resourced companies that need to work with smaller teams, expect more of each hire, and prioritize focus.

There is a natural process for managing the threats we encounter, from establishing a process, to the vigilance and awareness where our efforts begin, to an ultimate response. Best practice recommendations for establishing an enterprise technical security function, and specifically an effective cyber security organization, with defined roles, standardized titles, and clearly detailed functions, have been published under the direction of U.S. federal agencies, largely as inter agency guidance. NIST has taken much of the lead in providing guidance, and sponsorship of the National Initiative for Cyber Education (NICE). The Department of Homeland Security has similarly sponsored the Council on Cyber Security of the Homeland Security Advisory Council 'Mission Critical Cybersecurity Functions'.

Emulating these federal agency guidelines allows companies in the private sector to define an appropriate organization, identify the roles required, and provides support in making the case to company management when staffing a team for cyber security. These set out standardized titles in attempt to push consistency and define the competencies and characteristics of the cyber roles, in the hope of gradually bringing clarity to titles and functions as each build on and reconcile to prior frameworks. Still, if you do a jobs search on LinkedIn or any online job board for 'vulnerability' or 'information risk', it is obvious that there is still considerable room for clarity in title, level, and reporting structure, and this dictates compensation, and so, budget.

Well-funded agencies and better resourced, large domestic enterprises or multinationals will find it easier to accrue benefit from these guidelines. Smaller companies face the same challenges and have the same requirements in scope, if not in magnitude, but often do not have the resources to staff all the positions defined in these best practice recommendations or need to grow into an appropriate position with investments in staffing over time. In many cases, they need to make best use of existing staff and skills by broadening roles and providing training, prioritize new hires for maximum gain, leverage operational spend on consultants and external services, and matrix access to talent elsewhere within the organization that might fill in the gaps. This in large part accounts for the variance in titles and positions.

*Boards and executives are accountable*

 Copyright Martin Gomberg All rights reserved - Do not copy reproduce or distribute without written consent v. 12/1/23

I am certain that most would not be surprised that in our largest and most capable companies, redundant roles and efforts are in place, each in different functional areas, each addressing the same or similar issues, going about it in different ways, duplicating spends, and yet often do not talk to each other. More than likely in most cases, they are only peripherally aware of each other, and minimally aware of what each other is there to do. It equally should not surprise most of you that in small to medium sized companies, and even in some major named companies with the capacity to do better, these efforts are ad-hoc, performed by far fewer staff than needed to manage them competently, and either taken on inadequately, or barely sufficient to say that they are being done at all.

If establishing a cogent and comprehensive security ecosystem to assure that the needed activities have been implemented and are performed adequately, it falls to the CISO to engage and establish relationships and begin to organize a comprehensive security fabric addressing any gaps. That said, it is common that much of the environment the CISO is tasked to protect is managed by others, and priorities and incentives do not always align.

The threat of compromise by cyber or other means increases if identity management and authentication are insufficiently managed, access to systems ineffectively controlled, and the administration of accounts and the privileges they carry are not properly addressed. Risk is reduced substantially if these issues of operational hygiene are correctly and diligently managed. However, these are typically operation issues within IT and the resources that address these typically report outside of the CISO's organization. There are often too many systems, and too few system administrators, and administrators are given access to more systems than preferable.

Often the same credentials are used across systems for convenience, and there are few controls if any securing or restricting changes to administrative passwords as part of the privileged credential control process. At the same time, employees come and go or move between departments and the process of shutting down accounts no longer needed, transitioning work to temps until a new hire replaces a departed worker, or revoking access from employees that have left one role for another in a different area is often not cleanly managed and is a significant exposure. Administrators try to address this, but volume, requests for exceptions from the business, and lack of clarity and communication makes this challenging. Privileged Account Management Systems and Access Management Systems can assist in managing much or all of this, as can increased management scrutiny and clear policies, but are not always or effectively employed.

Increasingly, management of desktops, mobile devices, servers, network infrastructure, application development, wireless, and data management, in whole or part, falls outside information technology to technical units embedded in the business. Often decisions made to benefit operational performance, (disable logging, delay patch application, allocate alert log archiving space to other needs), though typically for good reason and with the best of intent, are at odds with those required for effective security and incident forensics.

There are challenges for the CISO. Some of these are structural, some organizational, some cultural. Transformative shifts and business realignment may address some of these, advocacy some, and the shift to new operating models in the cloud and other external operating spaces will address others.

Comprehensive ITIL and COBIT frameworks and other management and governance models like Three Lines of Defense provide structure and direction and a framework on which to build and ameliorate some of the communication barriers and lack of clarity that exposes our business and increases operating risk. These structures are often pursued in larger companies, more regulated industries, and matured programs, but do require a commitment and resource, internal or procured, to implement effectively.

The most effective of CISOs recognize that engagement is the path to success. Wherever these functions' role up, it falls to the CISO to engage and align these critical performers, on earth or in cloud, and assure the controls required to establish adequate security are in place, adhered, effectively managed, verified, and are ultimately demonstrable through audit and reporting.

**Private sector**

In the table that follows I have attempted to capture the major activities that most or many in the private sector address, or need to address somewhere in the organization, or as a contracted service, and if not now, will, regularly or periodically. These are a brain dump so not necessarily an exhaustive list and describe categories of functions to be performed within a role or across roles, not necessarily dedicated roles, and not necessarily called the same thing in all organizations. Some also blend one or more roles in defining specific functions.

I have divided these in ten categories. These likely are being performed within corporate IT, a formalized security team, other risk management organizations within the enterprise (Audit, Compliance, Risk Management), operational business units (HR, Finance, Legal, Corporate Communications), by consultants, managed services, and outsourced functions, and may in some manner report to, or inform the CISO, or not.

Not all organizations will address these needs in the same roles, or in the same way, and separation of responsibilities and accountabilities are important. Obviously, the depth and scope of coverage implementable by many of our largest companies, municipalities and agencies will be beyond the capabilities of most small to medium businesses.

*Assessments are a statement in time.*

*Validity of the assessment changes because things move and risk changes*

| FUNCTIONS | AREAS OF FOCUS |
|---|---|
| 1. Information Risk Management and Oversight | 1. Provide oversight<br>2. Advocate an ecosystem of security, compliance & ethics<br>3. Promote adherence to policy<br>4. Measure effectiveness and validate success |
| 2. Detection and Response | 1. Monitor environment<br>2. View baselines, history, and alerts<br>3. Integrate and correlate<br>4. Detective strategies and corrective controls<br>5. Respond to incidents |
| 3. Vulnerability and Threat Management | 1. Inventory and mitigate asset risks<br>2. Perform vulnerability and penetration testing<br>3. Threat hunting and assessments<br>4. Respond to incidents<br>5. Evaluate impact |
| 4. Administration, Infrastructure Protection, and Configuration Management | 1. Install and configure infrastructure<br>2. Install and configure defenses<br>3. Install and configure endpoints<br>4. Install and configure systems and storage<br>5. Provide and configure access<br>6. Configure cloud and cloud defenses |
| 5. Data Management | 1. Inventory and classify system and data assets<br>2. Collection, processing, retention, controls & dataflows<br>3. Inventory apps and licenses<br>4. Assess consequential risk<br>5. Develop mitigation strategy<br>6. Manage breach |
| 6. Compliance Management | 1. Assess regulatory environment (security, privacy)<br>2. Understand obligations<br>3. Assure conformance<br>4. Reporting, documentation<br>5. Implement needed tools and platforms |
| 7. Business Protection | 1. Develop architecture<br>2. Encryption<br>3. Defensive technologies and processes<br>4. Data Protection, backup, and archives<br>5. Disaster recovery and business continuity |
| 8. Recovery | 1. Restoration<br>2. Testing<br>3. Briefings and postmortem<br>4. Post incident monitoring and management<br>5. Return to normalcy |
| 9. Education and Awareness | 1. Awareness advocacy<br>2. Formal training<br>3. Certifications |
| 10. Project Management and Improvements | 1. Research<br>2. Proposals, vendor assess, and procurement<br>3. Contract management<br>4. Project planning, analysis, and implementation |

# CISO
# REDEFINED

*Protecting Business*

Martin Gomberg, CISSP, CIPP/E

## SECTION 8.   AN ECOSYSTEM OF COMPLIANCE

The purpose and mandate of most programs of compliance is the assurance of the ability to measure, report, demonstrate and prove conformance with federal, state, professional, industry, or activity specific codes, or regulatory requirements, as well as internal corporate policy.

Most programs of compliance assure adherence to prudent operating practice. They assure oversight. They assure attention to security controls and safeguards. They address individual privacy, data protection, security, and ethics. They address product and information quality. They address integrity, incident response, fraud, and continuity of business. There is often a requirement for enhanced scrutiny and verification through internal review and audit. And for independent external validation.

Many regulations impose penalties for non-compliance. Ineffectiveness or intentional neglect in the face of increasingly high regulatory standards and law, domestic and global, can result in imposed oversight, monetary fines, sanctions, and operational cessation. In some cases, criminal penalties can be imposed for failure to implement and effectively execute, monitor, and report as regulations require.  At a minimum, failure to comply with regulations can result in a loss of investor, partner, and consumer trust.

Building an effective program of compliance is not trivial. There is no one security standard for instance, that by itself addresses the broad requirements needed to achieve compliance with the regulatory concerns for business, as well as operational effectiveness, stability, legitimacy, and safeguards across industries. Multiple regulations, laws, and requirements bind most companies and many of these are overlapping in scope. Some perhaps with cross border, or other complexities, or with conflicting interests. These mandate specific reports, impose the use of dedicated forms, command response dates, and each requires time, resources, and focus.

So, where does this leave us? Whereas the specifics of individual laws, regulatory certifications, mandated filings, and required documentation must be addressed for compliance, focusing on common concerns, in specific, ethical behavior, oversight, administrative controls, and safeguards, can help in developing an effective and protective 'ecosystem' on which to build. Most of these are common sense practices of good hygiene and effective management that whether driven by regulation, standards, or just running a sound business, we should be doing anyway.

**The need for a framework**

U.S. Federal, state laws, and governing agency regulations increasingly demand a comprehensive managed program governing risk. This is increasingly true in regulation globally. Structuring a governance program for corporate compliance with law, regulation and good policy typically requires a framework to categorize corporate goals, objectives, and risks, against which to apply standards and controls, measure success, and advocate behaviors to be encouraged. They each seek to assure engaged management, adequate oversight, responsible behavior of both executives and employees, and external partners, assure adequacy of general safeguards, and the prudent management of processes, commerce, and records.

CEOs and CFOs of public companies in the U.S. and many abroad annually attest to business health and impacting events. They are asked to detail and often externally audit the effectiveness of controls in place, and progress against concerns, mostly financial, but including those regarding information technology.

Executive accountability is critical to the success of any program of effective business protection, and this is being recognized. Boards and executive leadership define and tune the company mission. They define the organization and commit the resources available to support it. They set the priorities for company focus. They establish the tone that will be reflected in the corporate culture. If appropriate controls and safeguards are to be met, and regulatory compliance mandates this, it is the accountability of leadership that assures that they own the mandate, and that it is implemented, integrated, and maintained.

There is increasing pressure for executive accountability in legislation and regulation, from the Sarbanes Oxley Act, New York State Department of Finance Cybersecurity Regulation, to the California Consumer Privacy Act, to the GDPR mandating data protection controls across the European Union, and more.

Although this is not intended as a discussion of laws or governance frameworks, several are useful in making the case for prudence, controls, and ethics, and in defining an ecosystem of compliance.

🦉

*Relationships are better than contracts, and good contracts protect and make relationships better. The best relationship is expressed in an agreement that clearly defines needed protection, anticipates growth and transformation, unifies objectives, and satisfies the goals of all parties*

In the US the Sarbanes Oxley Act mandates accountability for public companies. It also establishes some prudent guidance, not just of importance to SOA compliance, or to public companies, but generally worth highlighting in establishing an ecosystem of controls:

- Establish an effective environment of correctness, performance, and integrity

- Adopt a framework for risk, security, and administrative controls, against which progress can be reported

- Affirm the adequacy and effectiveness of implemented controls by audit

- Designate accountable executives for oversight, establishing a clear message and an appropriate 'tone-at-the-top', advocating ethical and responsible behavior, leadership, and a 'culture of compliance'

The SOA also mandates the use of a framework of control. COSO is one such framework. Under COSO the primary objectives of the control system are defined as "ensuring effective and efficient operations, accuracy in financial reports, and regulatory and legal compliance". COSO is useful in examining the controls on business strategies and objectives. It does this by mapping business 'strategies' against 'specific control objectives' to determine whether the goals of the strategy have been achieved. It is used to examine the success of control strategies within an entity, compare divisions within an entity, and to gauge differences in success for the specific strategies being assessed. COSO helps to assure oversight, recognize risk, standardize reporting and communications, measure performance, and effect quality management and improvement. It is applicable to one, some, or all structures in an organization, for current assessment or comparatively with performance in prior years, and to determine directional progress over time. COSO lists the following goals for establishing an 'environment of control'.

- "Evaluate risks to corporate objectives, and the protection of objectives through controls".

- "Establish a format for assessment of performance within each entity or structure in a company"

- "Report results in a manner that can be 'continually monitored through internal checklists, review processes, and audit".

COSO sets as three primary objectives, Operations, Financial Reporting, and Compliance. It examines the performance of these to five categories of control: (1) Control Environment, (2) Risk Assessment, (3) Control Activities, (4) Information and Communication, and (5) Activities for Monitoring. COSO has recently been updated with 17 specific principles mapped against the categories of control, for the three primary objectives. For each principle, points of focus are identified. COSO allows corporate leadership to assess effectiveness in determining action.
- https://www.complianceweek.com/blogs/jose-tabuena/internal-auditors-are-you-ready-for-the-updated-coso-framework#.WLwfKCYo670

I am not an advocate of one platform or another, but COSO derived models I have seen and have worked with have been particularly useful in illustrating how the effectiveness of a control might be audited and evaluated. A Business Objective, in this example the 'Preparation of Annual SOA Filings', which is a Financial Reporting obligation under the SOA, can be examined against the first category of controls, a Control Environment. In this category, the first enumerated Principle to be tested is the Commitment to Integrity and Ethics. In doing so, specific Points of Focus are evaluated for that principle including 'setting tone at the top, establishing conduct standards, monitoring adherence, and addressing conduct deficiencies and deviations." These can each be evaluated and tested for effectiveness in meeting the specific business objective or detailed further. Additional principles within the category would be examined, and then again for each of the remaining categories. Strategies can then be implemented to influence the objectives based on effectiveness. The obtained results can be responsive to evaluating current years objectives, compared to effectiveness in meeting this same objective in prior years, or used to set improvement targets to be budgeted in subsequent years for identified gaps.

| FINANCIAL REPORTING | | | |
|---|---|---|---|
| BUSINESS OBJECTIVE: Preparing Annual SOA filings | | | |
| CATEGORY | PRINCIPLE | POINTS OF FOCUS | EFFECTIVNESS |
| CONTROL ENVIRONMENT | Commitment to Integrity and ethics | Setting Tone at the top | • **Effective**<br>• Partially effective<br>• Ineffective |
| | | Establishing conduct standards | • Effective<br>• Partially effective<br>• Ineffective |
| | | Monitoring Adherence | • Effective<br>• Partially effective<br>• Ineffective |

For authoritative information about COSO I refer the reader to the official website:

https://www.coso.org/Pages/default.aspx

http://www.coso.org/audit_shop.htm

*Meeting minimal requirements for protection is a compromise.*

*Even if adequate under the law, investors, creditors, insurers, consumers,*

*markets, and the employees and prospects that pursue, use, and define*

*great companies may see this differently*

## Frameworks of control

It is not uncommon for a large enterprise to employ more than one GRC (Governance, Risk, Compliance) platform, assessment framework, standard, or management process, each in different areas of the business or for different purposes. Each is as good as a company's ability to absorb them, purpose for adoption, and their ability to meet the needs of that company in context of fit, cost, usability, environment, reporting, and culture. Often it is simply a matter of comfort and familiarity, autonomy of operating divisions, or the prior experience of decision makers or key players that drives the selection. Whether COSO, COBIT, Three Lines of Defense Model, Unified Compliance Framework (UCF), internally developed tools, or other, each has adoptees, devotees, areas of excellence, and a place in addressing the needs of corporate governance and management, or technical safeguards. Testing Controls against Risks and Objectives is not limited to any one framework. In fact, it is a requirement of most regulations.

Security Technical Implementation Guides (STIGs) are at the same time framework and guide. These are most frequently developed by government agencies including the Department of Defense (DOD), Defense Information Security Agency (DISA), NIST, Homeland Security, or other, typically for government use, but support both classified and unclassified controls, the latter suitable to use by the private sector. STIGs define, organize and effect controls to meet objectives. They provide detail, prioritized listing, and explanation of controls. Included in this group would be technical frameworks like the CIS 18 (formerly CIS 20) Critical Security Controls. These STIGs are published and the UCF (Unified Compliance Framework) offers a STIG viewer that aggregates many of these.

Commercial frameworks bring maturity and manageability to assessment of controls for an enterprise. Our most mature organizations use these systems to conduct enterprise control assessment, control testing, risk alignment, and control deficit reporting. Most require some sophistication and resource to leverage effectively. But every company has the need, and any company, of any size, regardless of the framework they use, enterprise grade or internally developed spreadsheet, can incorporate the concepts of controls testing and management, and will benefit. It begins with defined objectives.

*Homogenization works well for milk products, not security.*
*Whether systems, applications, or concerns for privacy, all data are not created equally when it comes to sensitivity or risk, nor do all need the same level of vigilance and controls*

## Defined objectives

Regardless of our business or industry, success requires effective governance. We categorize our objectives based on the performance we want to test, measure, or qualitatively assess. These are parameters of importance to understanding our business, or that reflect our activities in a way that can be informing to us and scrutinized and evaluated by others. It is about understanding those qualities of importance to our business and watching how they change in state or perform over time. For the goal of establishing an ecosystem of compliance we want to assess our performance to meaningful objectives:

- Oversight and Accountability
- Environment and Culture
- Controls and Metrics
- Policies and Practices
- Technology and Infrastructure
- Compliance and Reporting
- Awareness and Education

Defined objectives are any measurable areas of performance which arguably a business cannot run without. They are used by the largest of enterprises and the smallest of shops, regardless of resources, and from the most basic cost of operation and profitability tracking to assessments of effective regulatory conformance or cultural change. We standardize the questions we ask to compare performance year over year, between one business unit or department and another or against competitors or industry benchmarks. They are useful in determining the effectiveness of controls and categorizing control deficits (gaps). They are useful in highlighting targets for improvement or to help keep goals in focus amidst changing priorities. They help manage our projects, programs, and investments, current state, progress against prior state, or establishing milestones for achievement and benchmarking in a multi-year plan. They can be equally tested to privacy, continuity, security, ethics, or other measurable goals. Achievement can be measured by:

- **Presence of Activity** - All entities have been internally evaluated for the presence of the primary controls reasonably expected to achieve enterprise and process objectives.
- **Adequacy of Implementation** - All entities have been internally evaluated for the sufficiency and adequacy of provided controls
- **Frequency of Activity** - All entities have been evaluated as to the frequency of performance to determine sufficiency in accordance with requirements or internal policies.
- **Validation of Success** - All entities have been validated for the presence, adequacy, and frequency of provided controls and have been described as sufficient by internal review and external audit

---

The CAPA" principle - (Corrective Action / Preventive Action)

– assess root cause, correct, and prevent. https://www.fda.gov/iceci/inspections/inspectionguides/ucm170612.htm.

---

**Assessment State Tables can be used to document performance and sufficiency**

Achievement to Defined Objectives

|  | Presence | Adequacy | Frequency | Validation |
|---|---|---|---|---|
| Oversight and Accountability |  |  |  |  |
| Environment and Culture |  |  |  |  |
| Controls and Metrics |  |  |  |  |
| Policies and Practices |  |  |  |  |

Classes of Controls

|  | Presence | Adequacy | Frequency | Validation |
|---|---|---|---|---|
| Monitoring |  |  |  |  |
| Detective controls |  |  |  |  |
| Preventive Controls |  |  |  |  |
| Corrective Controls |  |  |  |  |
| Privacy Controls |  |  |  |  |

Control Activities

|  | Presence | Adequacy | Frequency | Validation |
|---|---|---|---|---|
| Vulnerability Testing |  |  |  |  |
| Backup |  |  |  |  |
| Role Based Training |  |  |  |  |
| Disaster Recovery Testing |  |  |  |  |
| Business Continuity Review |  |  |  |  |

Effectiveness Table for State of Activity (by business unit, application, etc.)

| Effective, Partial, Ineffective, Verified | Business Unit 1 | Business Unit 2 | Business Unit 3 | Business Unit 4 |
|---|---|---|---|---|
| Documentation |  |  |  |  |
| Data Inventory |  |  |  |  |
| Application inventory |  |  |  |  |
| Workflows |  |  |  |  |

Prudent controls and practices for corporate ethics, business protection, asset and personnel safety, quality, integrity, privacy efforts, and technical security reflect good governance. These are measurable as parameters of success in highlighting accomplishment, defining areas of focus, or reporting status for any operating business.

I spoke earlier about establishing an 'ecosystem of security and practices' for business protection and compliance'. What does that mean? Effectively, not much if not in context of the business, or in context of the risks to the business. Without context, it is at most that some might tout as 'best practice'.

Frameworks provide the context, and a means to gauge the success and performance of controls independently, or synergistically in meeting a specific objective, or set of goals. They put objectives in context of the specific risks identified for a company and the effectiveness with which these can be addressed. A framework provides an opportunity to compare the effectiveness of the controls in one area over another, or as implemented by one group or another, or in any other comparative context. They provide the ability to assess the improvement or change in state of effectiveness from one point of measurement to another. They provide the ability to see gaps in need of correction, or direction in need of change.

Frameworks provide the opportunity to simply compare the efficacy of controls, one to another, and to examine the synergistic effect of layered or compensating controls in satisfying an objective. But all that said, how can we know that controls are adequate unless they can be tested and verified? Let us test one.

We will use a test case from the perspective of business protection or security.

---

**TEST:** Is 'Validation of Integrity' required to improve the effectiveness of 'Confidentiality + Integrity + Availability' as a protective strategy to meet this specific business objective.

- The Business Objective or strategy is to assure <u>continual protection</u> of a critical data center from breach.
- The Control Objective is to <u>determine the sufficiency of C I A controls</u> for this purpose

I spent nearly an entire chapter talking about a door. I did that to explore the validity of controls. I determined, and if we agree that 'availability is a yes or no condition, security is a statement of condition, in a context, over time, and integrity, a statement of condition *affirming security at a given time*', that will prove <u>an insufficient control</u>. Although likely secure, we <u>could not affirm the integrity of the controls except at the time they were tested</u>. This would fail to meet the business objective of 'continual protection'.

Conclusion:

Validation of Integrity is required to improve the effectiveness of C I A for this specific business objective. Even this is limited within levels of risk tolerance which determines the frequency of sampling for validation.

---

Validation, that which I called the unnamed control in the C I A Triad, I defined as an 'accepted proxy for proof of integrity, through sampling, at points in time', for which I said the 'frequency of sampling, which determines effectiveness, was agreed upon for convenience'. The frequency of validation could be from 0% to 100%. This is the degree of assurance sampled over time. It is in fact a measure of risk tolerance, how much dirt we can accept in the system, how much uncertainty about the state of our controls we are willing to accommodate.

Validation also introduces a quality management component. Frequency of testing can be adjusted to improve effectiveness immediately, or throttled over time, and this is a determination that is made by the business in satisfying their objectives. Where the tolerance of risk is low, by necessity investment in validation of the integrity of controls will increase. And if as an outcome of that testing the integrity of the controls tested are found deficient, so too might investment in control improvements or additional synergistic layered controls to compensate. Of course, the integrity of these too would require validation.

Continuous validation of the integrity of all the primary security controls protecting all parts of a system, and any supplemental layered controls, would certainly be effective, but also prohibitively expensive, and I suspect rarely would be done except by governments requiring extremely high levels of protection and perhaps the largest of companies. And even with this level of control risk will never be zero, the likelihood of attack or even successful breach will probably never approach zero, and we will never be immune.

Validation is used as a term by the FDA that requires that a system, drug, device or other behaves in predictable ways. Failure is acceptable, if consistent and predictable. Our use of the term though differing, is not incompatible and likewise assures the consistent behavior of an integrity control over time. But for us, failure invalidates the control. For an integrity control to be validated it must consistently and continually perform as is expected for its stated risk tolerance and for the frequency of sampling defined, or it fails.

For air gapped systems, computers that are completely isolated from the internet, erased, and rebuilt on demand before every use, risk might near zero, but still not be completely immune from harm. A researcher in Israel demonstrated exactly this by showing that data can be read off the flickering of the hard drive LED, like a signal in Morse code, interpreted by a spying drone hovering near the window. Similar experiments have been tried measuring power fluctuations read off building wiring synonymous with hard drive activity. http://www.computerworld.com/article/3173346/security/a-hard-drives-led-light-can-be-used-to-covertly-leak-data.html

*There is often just too much data, of too many types, in too many locations, or the premature disposal or cycling due to storage insufficiency makes correlating a full picture of corresponding events across systems at any given time difficult*

We implement prudent controls and practices to manage our risk, and to contain the cost of risk, not to eliminate it. Security can never be pristine. People are not flawless. That alone adds dirt to the system.

For a culture of compliance and adherence to prudent practices with the best interests of the company and Its employees to be established, it will need to be nurtured and encouraged. That will require examination, critical inquiry, some tough love to assure it takes hold where weakness or disinterest shows, and a bit of science. Ethics, privacy, security, acceptable inter-personal conduct, and conformance with corporate obligations for compliance are qualities to be encouraged.

Properly and consistently applied, by whatever business of any size and in whichever way, a framework for asking questions of the enterprise in a consistent format with defined objectives allows information to yield intelligence over time and permits an organization to ask:

- How effective are we at 'monitoring adherence' to 'integrity and ethics' in each of the operating units that we have examined through audit; in each that have self-reported?

- What controls are in place to assure adequate monitoring of adherence to ethical behavior?

- How well are those controls working; do we need better or more comprehensive controls?

- Which operating units need improvement and what action do we need to take?

- Have we seen improvement in adherence to these controls since last measured?

- Have we identified new, better, or additional controls that should be implemented?

- Where should we invest for maximum improvement?

And as Rich Guida points out paraphrased from personal discussions and in his book, The Entropy Police:

*'Do we thoroughly investigate our failures and learn the right lessons?'*

*The purpose and mandate of most programs of compliance is the reasonable assurance of the ability to measure, report, demonstrate, and prove conformance, with Federal, State, City or other municipality, industry, professional, or activity specific codes, or regulatory requirements, as well as internal corporate policy*

## Establishing a Roadmap for Compliance

Some time ago I met an attorney at a party and as always happens when in a relaxed setting with a glass of wine in hand, we talked about the weather, cars, and the 1999 U.S. Federal Sentencing Guidelines. I am sure this happens to most of you from time to time.

Why are the guidelines interesting to us in a discussion of a business protective ecosystem? The guidelines introduced several structural concepts that have reemerged in many current laws and regulations. They encouraged businesses, non-profit, and government entities to avoid or minimize potential penalties by demonstrating a good faith effort to reduce corporate, entity, or agency risk. They advocated demonstrating directional progress toward compliance goals, not through prescriptive steps, but through adoption of accepted 'best practices', appropriately fit to the business. They advocated self-determination in satisfying compliance goals. They encouraged a culture of compliance supported by effective safeguards. They required risk assessment and mitigation, a program of education and awareness, monitoring, and the measurement of reportable progress. They mandated background checks to assure bad actors didn't assume managerial or executive roles. The flexibility of the Guidelines in conforming compliance to the specific needs, capabilities and characteristics of a business has in large part set the tone and structure for much of the current regulatory approach in the U.S. and elsewhere. The key tenets on which they focus are:

- Encouragement of a culture of compliance and an executive tier providing oversight
- Advocacy and education
- Implementation of an established code of conduct
- Clear and documented policies
- A capable team for oversight, administration, and operations
- A community that is made aware, accepts, and supports it, and is willing and free to raise concerns of misbehavior, fraud, waste, and abuse without reprisal when reporting violations

The Guidelines established a road map. With limited exception, most bodies of current regulatory law that require implementation of safeguards are similarly risk based. They recognize that companies differ, the risks they face differ, and their capacities differ. Some regulations establish a framework of safeguard objectives to be adequately met; develop an incident response plan, establish a cybersecurity policy, or establish a data retention policy. They mandate oversight. Some specify that key administrators be named, trained, and certified, but generally not how programs are staffed or organized. Few are entirely prescriptive in the specifics of how to provide continuity, security, or privacy safeguards, or organize a program for incident response. Typically, the nature of the incident response plan or cybersecurity policy are non-specific and for the business to define. Still, some requirements might be specific, for instance defining a requirement to retain data for a specified period or report a breach of data to authorities within a specified time. There are also requirements that are absolute in some; a mandate to fill the CISO position or engage a Data Protection Officer.

How a program of safeguards meets the requirements of the law is often not spelled out. They are left to the enterprise to pursue in accordance with risks and a mandate to adequately meet objectives for compliance. They are left to the enterprise to demonstrate effectiveness in accordance with standards and practices best fit to their environment and common practice. They are left to the enterprise to pursue appropriate to its size, resources, and capabilities, such that it would be operationally effective, cost prudent, and when scrutinized by audit, would be satisfactory, and withstand external review. They often call for conformance to NIST guidelines or adherence to other professional standards or frameworks.

The U.S. Department of Health and Human Services (HHS) Office of the National Coordinator for Health Information Technology (ONC) provides extensive downloadable tools like the Security Risk Assessment tool for HIPAA against which a covered entity can test whether implemented controls are sufficient and where there might be gaps. Tools address administrative controls, technical security controls, and physical security controls. Use is voluntary, and in the end, it is up to the organization to assure adequacy of controls for compliance.

Let me take a moment to return to the Guidelines and at the risk of dwelling on what to most is history and irrelevant to your day to day, please indulge me for just a few more paragraphs. I think you will find this to contain some of the secret sauce in implementing any effective risk program or policy.

> The Guidelines advocate a means of 'incentivizing good and disciplining bad behavior', and tuning and tightening code, policies, practices, and behavioral compliance expectations in response to situations experienced and lessons learned, and as requirements change over time.

If you have not read the statement highlighted in the rectangle above, please do. This perhaps is one of the most important of the contributions of the Guidelines and to our use of it as a model for constructing an ecosystem suitable to protective needs and legal requirements, both of which continually evolve. It is adaptive. The Guidelines advocate a progressive focus on continual 'operational quality management'.

**'A progressive focus on Continual Operational Quality Management'**

Let me ask you to hover on this above statement for a moment. The tangible manifestation of the compliance auditor, the financial auditor, and even the security auditor has become the dreaded 'checklist'. This is unfortunate and a missed opportunity. As a CIO, I always welcomed the audit process as an extra set of eyes, not about satisfying a checklist, but as an assessment and affirmation of prudent management of operations and controls, and assurance of good practice. These are traits in a modern organization that are critical if we are to make continual progress toward quality as we grow, transform operations, and test new business models. We need to instill a progressive focus on continual operational QM in all we do.

*Vision, risk, quality, cost, speed, care, and capability are equally key metrics in evaluating performance or potential fit in a third-party relationship*

**'Problem is that often we are solving the wrong problem.'**

We cannot protect everything, particularly as cloud, mobility and virtualization and shadow IT extend the assets we are asked to protect beyond our visibility and reach. And we often get too caught up on technical defenses. 'There is no box or application that can be implemented that can protect us in absence of clean operations and prudence'. Name companies are successfully breached every day despite the best of technology, staff, and budgets. We need to inventory and understand our data environment, assets, and risk, and focus our capabilities on that which is most consequential, targeting our efforts and spending. The compliance audit, and the checklist, help assure us we are on track, doing the things that we need to do, in the right places, and are making the investments we need to make.

**'We cannot follow, detect or respond to enough threats or close enough holes'.**

With an increasing cyber threat, failing legacy defenses, complexity of new tools emerging, a shortage of skilled staff, increasing litigation and regulatory penalties for failure to provide effective data stewardship and care, and a concern for the growing social, geopolitical, and physical threats to business, we need to welcome all perspectives that improve effectiveness.

I would add that few companies are as effective as they need to be in knowing assets, access, whose data they have, or mapping back to where they have it. This alone puts many at risk, both from a security and a privacy perspective, exposed to litigation, and in violation of the standards of care that most regulation is pressing to achieve. Let me return to a statement I made earlier. 'Most of what we need to do for any, is what is required by most'. The requirements of many regulations overlap, and the requirements of securing most applications, networks and systems do as well. We can leverage commonalities.

**The security maturity model**

Homogenization works well for milk products, not security. Whether systems, applications, or concerns for privacy, all data are not created equally when it comes to sensitivity or risk, nor do all need the same level of vigilance and controls. Imposing the same strength of controls for all systems and data, typically dilutes that which is needed for our most critical and overspends on our least. Over control where not required inhibits data sharing, collaboration, and innovation.

A blended approach that meets in the middle neither protects the critical, nor protects against the spend on that of lesser concern. A security maturity model helps in identifying the level of applicable controls in alignment to risk classes needed to maximize safety. Some keep it as simple as two classes of data, generally accessible unsecured public data, and secured non-public data. Non-public data can be a classification to itself, or further delineated as to category of risk as in the model illustrated below. Once data is categorized and classified best fit controls can be established. Policies can be set to establish approved uses by data category and to designate required authorizations for specific data classes based on risk.

| | Classified Vital Systems, Apps, Data | High Risk Systems, Apps, Data | Moderate High-Risk Systems, Apps, Data | Moderate Risk Systems, Apps, Data | Low Risk Systems, Apps, Data | Negligible Risk Systems, Apps Public Data |
|---|---|---|---|---|---|---|
| Validated Secure Controls | | | | | | |
| High Risk Controls | | | | | | |
| Moderate High Risk Controls | | | | | | |
| Moderate Risk Controls | | | | | | |
| Low Risk Controls | | | | | | |
| Negligible Risk Controls | | | | | | |

There are some validated secure systems or processes vital to life, liberty, property, national defense, and intelligence requiring absolute protection. Most of us will never deal with these or the controls they require. Most, however, will be required to effect, implement or evaluate high risk controls. As will be discussed later, High Risk is a broad category and implemented controls will vary. Data, systems, processes, or activities may be at high risk because of the breadth of attack surface they expose, insufficiency or inadequacy of controls, attractiveness as a target, means of process or processing, vulnerabilities of the populations impacted, or the nature of the data or consequential asset exposed.

*As one attorney said, you cannot create security policy on Monday, be the one to implement and execute it on Tuesday, and then come Wednesday, certify it, and provide oversight. A fox and a hen house come to mind*

## Control Matrix Example

This example below expands on a specific entry area in the security maturity model preceding, in this case 'High Risk'. Whether focus is on asset security, information risk, privacy, or other, which will be exposed as critical areas of focus (systems, processes, data, etc.) will differ, as will controls.

Specific controls appropriate to all applications within a given class of risk would be mandated and described in the security maturity matrix. The specific controls would be dependent upon the needs and requirements of the business and its tolerance for specific risk at a given level. A good GRC system is the best way to approach this.

| Risk Level | Systems in Risk Category | Examples of Controls Designated for Risk Category |
|---|---|---|
| High Risk | General Ledger<br>Sales Planning<br>Human Resources<br>Engineering | Redundant and diverse detective and protective perimeter<br><br>Multi-tier network architecture<br><br>Hardened facilities or secure cloud service<br><br>Effective identity management and authentication.<br><br>Limits on access, rights, and privilege<br><br>Privileged and administrative access controls<br><br>High availability configurations<br><br>Application testing, scanning, and peer review<br><br>Firewalls and segmentation<br><br>Secured and diverse backup protection<br><br>Recovery provisions<br><br>Active monitoring and logging for forensics<br><br>Preventive, detective, and corrective controls<br><br>Authorization and use controls |

*Figure 9 Controls Matrix Example - High Risk Systems Controls*

*Let me take this opportunity to introduce that which I call 'caducous' risk. This is recognized or potential risk best addressed, mitigated, or compensated early in anticipation of its development*

## Industry models to follow

Health, aviation, energy, finance, chemicals, transportation, and communications amongst other industries are all considered critical infrastructure, and each are strongly regulated, and if operating globally, may be regulated under multiple authorities, and national laws. Each address compliance through comprehensive government, inter-agency or industry frameworks, certifications, use of standards, and/or industry specific workbooks. These define or identify best practices, implementable controls, and standardize forms and templates. In the U.S. examples include HIPAA, HITRUST CSF, NERC, and the Federal Financial Workbooks (FFIEC).

The regulatory framework for protecting critical infrastructure mandates effective safeguards. It recognizes the pervasiveness of risk, and pooled professional and expert knowledge spanning industries, geographies, and experiences is reflected in the safeguards and controls embedded in current regulation. Most have built on precedents in existing law and standards of practice. In some cases, these are 'codifications of the state of existing practice, or best practice' as defined in STIGS, Standards and Guidelines, and with each new law emerging much of the best of that which preceded is carried forward. Evolving law tries to keep pace with changing risk.

Without doubt there are commonalities, and this overlap contributes to the modeling and development of an ecosystem of safeguards and practices. We see it in language in common across laws spanning concerns that address:

- Oversight and operational controls

- Consumer and employee safety

- Infrastructure and asset protection

- Technical and cyber security

- Product safety and controls

- Financial stability

- Adherence to privacy

- Incident response and continuity of operations

- Audit and reporting, ethical management, and employee behavior

These can be leveraged, and an ecosystem established reflecting culture, controls, and business objectives, that helps comply with law by advancing the safety of the business.

*There are no security investments. There are only business investments*

**So many laws, so little time**

In a practicable sense, there is a lot to do, but much is simply good governance and clean operations.

An effective ecosystem of prudent controls, security, and compliance begins with appointing a capable and engaged executive for oversight, designating and certifying qualified, ethical people for required or mandated positions, segregating responsibilities, and removing conflicts of interest or authority. With that, assessing and prioritizing business risks, promoting and implementing good policies, sound procedures, and the use of best practice standards, regularly tested, addresses much of what is required to satisfy many or most regulatory safeguards.

Additional controls include conformance to a risk governance framework, inventory, and classification of assets and consequential data, performing initial baselines, and subsequent progress measures. Implementing effective controls governing external partners, regular assessment, audit, and reporting, and monitoring of performance and effectiveness also defines an effective ecosystem.

Lastly, an effective ecosystem of prudent controls and practices assures the confidentiality, integrity, and availability of data through care in the selection, access, and protection of facilities that house sensitive systems and protected data, and the application of effective technical defenses, administrative, and operational controls. With that, the prudent use of services for training, testing, external examination, and validation through audit.

I should add that not all defensive regulation concerns are for protecting data confidentiality, integrity, and availability alone. FAR, a federal procurement regulation for instance is equally protective, but focuses on process, protecting against fraud, waste, and abuse, providing standardization of the procurement and purchase process across agencies. If not already, it is anticipated that breach notification provisions for companies doing business with the government and their agents will be defined in FAR in the not too distant.

Several industries have assumed the initiative to self-regulate and lead the law. Others to be responsive to the common impacts of numerous regulations. As an example, whereas there is no single framework for the Banking and Finance industry, the FFIEC Workbooks are a formalized inter agency initiative of the Federal Reserve Bank (FRB), Federal Deposit Insurance Corporation (FDIC), Consumer Financial Protection Bureau (CFPB), and several other regulating agencies.

*Prioritizing consequential loss ahead of other data risk, limits exposure, targets investments, and reduces legal liability, while increasing the safety of the most sensitive and consequential of data assets*

As stated earlier, compliance as a discipline in the business environment is complex and developing an ecosystem advocating compliance is not trivial. The control objectives defined will need to reflect maturity, or a process of continual maturation for security, privacy, continuity of business, and other, and be responsive to numerous sources of authority. And where attestation, or audited certification of compliance to specific regulation is mandated by law, regulation, contract, or license requirement, meet these for:

- Federal, state, and agency regulations and international laws

- General guidelines, licensing, and professional competency standards

- Industry specific self-regulation standards

- Internal company policy

- Inter-agency governing and oversight councils, and trade and work councils in regulated industries, for multi nationals, and for critical infrastructure

- Regulatory environment specific to the industry for which the program is being developed

- Employment, confidentiality, and other contracts

*GDPR, CPRA, LGPD, PIPL are laws,*
*but not solely a legal issue for an operating company*


*It is about absorbing an increasingly complex and continually changing set of regulations and requirements amidst all the challenges of globalization, digital transformation, competitive differentiation, emerging threats, and changing markets, adapting to new consumer expectations, and a workforce in flux*

## Comprehensive Standards and Frameworks

For the most mature of companies, those that serve critical infrastructure or of highest risk, or those required by law or contract to demonstrate adherence and achievement to a specific standard or framework, standards like ISO 27001, NIST CSF (Cyber Security Framework), NIST 800-53 (Security Compliance Framework), and the CIS 18 Critical Security Controls are frequently adopted. Each varies in focus, sector adoption or applicability, and each has advocates favoring one over another. There are other frameworks as well not mentioned here, some favored more for their effectiveness for smaller businesses, others for their cost, industry specificities, or applicability or popularity in a specific country.

Which framework or standard is best? Well, they all are. That is to say that they all are, for some company, at some time, if they help to understand and address potential risk, meet a business objective, and align to a company's operating size, needs, environment, skills, capabilities, risk profile, maturity, timeframes, budgets, and ability to absorb and utilize them. Absent these the best of standards and frameworks, despite reputation, dominance, prevalence, recognition, and maturity and effectiveness, will underserve a company that cannot effectively use them.

From my perspective, and regardless of fit or preference as to standard or framework, any used are more effective if assuring that the control set is tested for maturity. Many, even in the best of companies, and regardless of framework, do not. By this I mean testing four conditions:

-presence of activity or control
-adequacy of its implementation
-frequency of activity, its use or testing
-validation of its success in meeting objectives

Unfortunately, many audits simply focus on the first condition, is the control present, a checklist. Despite that these may be extremely robust and comprehensive, if not leveraged to their full potential, and only concerned with the presence of controls, this is insufficient.

These four conditional tests should be applied to assess maturity of controls individually, across departments, and against prior state of testing to measure adequacy, improvement, or deterioration of controls over time, regardless of framework. Absent these, we are only preparing for an audit.

And more, it is only an audit against the implementation of a checklist of best practice controls, at the point of audit, without an assessment of context, our business environment, or the perspective of growth, time, and change.

*You can neither violate nor conform to a policy unless it exists*

# CISO REDEFINED

*Protecting Business*

Martin Gomberg, CISSP, CIPP/E

## SECTION 9.   NYDFS CYBERSECURITY RULE IN CONTEXT

**Overview:** NYDFS Cybersecurity Regulation 23 NYCRR 500  (New York State Department of Financial Services Cybersecurity Regulations), touted to be some of the most stringent in the nation took effect on March 1st, 2017. The rules have been amended twice, in December of 2017 to clarify definitions and exemptions, and again on July 29, 2022, in pre-proposal with official drafts published in November 2022 and again, June 2023. These rules set a high bar in cyber readiness for reasonably sized financial institutions, banks, and insurance companies, and other financial entities, excluding those with fewer than 10 employees, less than $5m in gross annual revenue, and less than $10m in assets. NYDFS governs all banking, insurance and many financial services firms chartered in New York. It also extends to those working with or providing services to those entities covered under the regulation, regardless of where located. This is to ensure that services provided to institutions are afforded the level of protection required. This is exceptional compared to existing law. It is not unlikely that financial regulators in other states, and regulators of other industries, will follow similarly. I have characterized some aspects of the law below.

- It mandates the board and corporate leadership be signatory parties in attesting and committing to corporate cyber security effectiveness and this will likely be emulated by emerging regulation in other states and industries.

- It defines who in the finance industry must adhere to the law; mandates a CISO role; applies to solution providers serving NY financial entities; and for in-scope providers applies 'regardless of where they are located'.

  https://www.protiviti.com/sites/default/files/unitedstates/insights/decoding-nydfs-part500-protiviti.pdf

**Applicability:** According to the Orrick Financial Industry Review, entities covered under the new regulation include "any individual or any nongovernment entity that operates under or is required to operate under a license, registration, charter, certificate, permit, accreditation or similar authorization under the New York State Banking Law, Insurance Law, or Financial Services Law. Accordingly, *covered entities* include, among others, New York branches and representative offices of foreign banks, but do not include "investment advisers" and "broker-dealers."" (Orrick Financial Industry Review Feb 21, 2017)

**Focus:** NYDFS Cybersecurity Regulation 23 NYCRR 500 of the New York State Department of Financial Services has been described as a Cybersecurity Regulation applicable to covered entities, and specifically non-public electronic data, but with proposed revisions, broader still regarding overall business protection.

- It is risk aligned to the business, but comprehensive in expectation of controls.
- It incorporates a responsibility for technical, operational, environmental, and physical safeguards.
- It requires the protection of consumer risk and privacy interests; personal, financial and health data.
- It requires a defined, focused, and scalable crisis response, crisis response exercises, and testing.
- It requires business continuity preparations including effective backup and recovery.
- Asset inventory, identity and access, multifactor authentication (MFA), encryption in transit and at rest
- Strict rules for data retention, logs, and protective controls for data safety in the context of ransomware.
- Understanding of interdependencies in transactions, data movement and data archiving for forensics
- Rigorous requirements for notification in breach or other 'triggering' events.

**Executives:** The NYDFS focuses on executive cyber competency and accountability. Specifically:

- Awareness, attention, and accountability of executives, and the board, regarding cybersecurity
- Designation of an accountable executive for oversight of the cybersecurity program
- That the board or a senior officer submit an attestation of compliance February 15th annually.
- Board and senior officers appoint and are briefed by a CISO in writing now yearly, but to increase.

**CISO:** NYDFS imposes an obligation of financial institutions to professionalize and mature their approach to cybersecurity by engaging and leveraging a skilled and competent security executive on staff, as a new hire, an affiliate, or as a retained service. The CISO, the Chief Information Security Officer, or an officer overseeing a third party performing that function, is now responsible to interpret the risk of the business in security terms, oversee the development of a cyber security program to address that risk, and to elevate leadership awareness in support of their signatory responsibilities and accountability. The CISO is also required to submit a written report at least annually. The regulations are not prescriptive, but adherence to professional standards and practices enable the CISO function to assure and demonstrate:

- An effective cybersecurity program (people, process, technology, oversight, and reporting)
- Confidentiality, integrity, and availability of information systems
- That a cybersecurity policy aligned to business cyber risk is developed
- That confidential and sensitive assets and data are identified, assessed, classified, and prioritized.
- Technical and operational safeguards meet the requirements of the cybersecurity policy.
- Proposed or implemented controls, internal and third party, are assessed for effectiveness.
- Compensating controls satisfy where implemented controls are insufficient.
- All controls are properly implemented, tested, monitored, and corrected, and periodically audited.
- Cyber risk and vulnerabilities are assessed, penetration tests performed, and reevaluated over time.

A primary responsibility of the CISO under the regulation is to brief and report to leadership addressing the cybersecurity program and material cybersecurity risks. Briefing should address the basis for prioritizing and means to assuring confidentiality of non-public information. It should assess the security of information systems, review cybersecurity policies and procedures, highlight the material cybersecurity risks that the policies and procedures defined in the cybersecurity program address, gaps, exposures, and effectiveness, and material events that occur during the period covered by the report (since prior report).

**Requirements:** NYDFS 23 NYCRR 500 rules require the development of a cybersecurity program. This program will address people, process, technology, oversight, and reporting. It will define the means, scope and frequency of review, testing, audits, internal briefings, formal reporting, and annual filings to the Superintendent. It defines how data is retained, related to events, and events investigated. An entity may choose to adopt the cybersecurity program of a conforming affiliate, or third party. As specified in the regulation (see section 500.01 for definitions and terms), NYDFS requires a covered entity to:

(https://www.dfs.ny.gov/legal/regulations/adoptions/dfsrf500txt.pdf; Sphere Technologies Webinar, other sources)

500.02  define and implement a comprehensive cybersecurity program approved by company leadership.

500.03  develop, maintain, promote, and enforce a risk-based cybersecurity policy.

500.04  designate a qualified CISO or engage a third party under the oversight of a senior staff member.

500.05  perform vulnerability assessments and annual penetration tests.

500.06  establish an audit trail of transactions and material events for investigation and forensics.

500.07  define, limit, and periodically review access privileges both for user and for privileged accounts.

500.08  implement and assure application security (code controls, static and dynamic testing, firewalls)

500.09  assess internal, third-party provider, and external cybersecurity risks, documenting results.

500.10  define, manage, and implement staffing, roles, and capabilities.

500.11  assess third party information security policies (and review / correct relationships and contracts)

500.12  use multi factor authentication in identity management (particularly for privileged accounts)

500.13  follow data retention / disposal requirements, five years for transactions, three for supporting data.

500.14  provide adequate staffing, training, testing, appropriate certification, and employee education.

500.15  encrypt non-public data in transit and at rest (data field, record, database, message, file, device)

500.16  develop an effective incident detection and response capability (testable and scalable)

500.17  comply with the obligations for reports and filing.

500.03 cybersecurity policy requirements include: (1) information security, (2) data governance and classification, (3) asset inventory, (4) device management (5) access controls (6) identity management, (7) business continuity and disaster recovery (8) system operations and availability (9) system and network security (10) monitoring (11) system and application development (12) quality assurance (production controls), (13) physical security (14) environmental controls (15) customer data privacy (16) vendor and third-party management (17) risk assessment (18) incident response. Policies are required that demonstrably protect confidentiality, integrity, and availability of information systems, and provide the ability to detect, respond, recover, and report in all cyber events.

**NYDFS 23 NYCRR 500 Cyber security regulation is not prescriptive, but it is directive:**

- A covered entity is required to develop a program fit to the risk it has identified as consequential.
- Develop a technical and operational security policy that is approved, documented and demonstrable.
- Conduct business and transactional processes that are protected, traceable and auditable.
- By April 15, 2024, and then yearly, the CEO will be required to cosign in certification of its program

**Notices:** There are three types of notice identified under the law, notices attesting compliance, exemption from applicability, and notices of events.

- A notice of compliance is submitted annually reflecting the year prior. Records, plans, certifications and evidence of remedial actions or updates including plans for correction of deficiencies that have been identified, should be maintained for a period of five years in support of this attestation.

- Exemption in whole or part may be asserted based on specific conditions defined in the law. To claim these exemptions there are timely filings that need to be made. Which, when and what actions should be taken if the required filing date is missed should be addressed by attorney or with the New York State Department of Financial Services.

- Any potentially harmful cybersecurity event, or event that would trigger notification to any regulating body, domestic or global, and regardless of why, including security, privacy, fraud, or other event, triggers the obligation to report to the NYDFS Office of the Superintendent. This must be done as soon as possible and **not later than 72 hours** from the realization that an event has taken place.

**Managing Material Risk**: 23 NYDFS 500 raises specific concerns, responsibilities, and required actions as applies to realized and potential 'material risk'. Material risk, whether potential or actual, applies to customer transactions and customer personal data. It applies to risk to affiliates of the covered entity when such risks threaten or impact the information systems or non-public data of the covered entity. It applies to the normal operations of the covered entity, whether attempts at compromise of systems, data or communications are successful and impactful, or not. It does not apply to routine or mundane events.

This requires an entity to plan, monitor, detect, assess, and respond to realized risks, when material, and invokes the obligations to report within the 72-hour window following realization that an event has taken place, regardless of whether the event was successful. The same is required if the reporting obligation under any other regulation, domestic or global, is triggered by an event. The 72-hour obligation should apply regardless of the reporting threshold allowed by any other regulation that has triggered the reporting requirement. Unsuccessful attempts, if material and of significant concern, and not routine in the judgement of the covered entity, should also be included in the annual report submission. Identified potential risks should be included as well. A data breach that succeeds, or a clever social engineering attempt whether successful or not, should be reported.

**Events likely to require reporting:**

- Risk to customers including any events that impact the performance of transactions, impedes the ability of a customer to perform or complete online transactions, or that might result in harm to the customer (identity theft), or to customer data are reportable events. This latter would include data breach, and likely would conform to the same broadened definitions of breach as is emerging in the EU under the General Data Protection Regulation. This would include breach where there is exfiltration (removal) of data, isolation (ransomware), manipulation, alteration, denial of access, or data destruction.

- Affiliate risk can also be a source of concern where an event or potential risk to the affiliate is impactful on the covered entity, or the non-public data that it captures, processes, stores, or transports. This would be the case where a third-party payment processor, an affiliate, engaged to handle credit and debit card transactions on behalf of a merchant bank is impacted, potentially threatening both the completion of customer transactions, and the personal data handled in the process. The affiliate may be engaged at the front or back end of the process, and in either event, material risks to the process or to the data due to an impactful event are reportable.

- Cyber activities that impact important transactions and functions performed by the covered entity are reportable. This would include denial of service events preventing the accepting of transactions, fulfillment of processes through affiliates, or the acquisition or retrieval of customer data and account information. It would include malware or ransomware that compromises processing. It would include all cases of breach. It likely would include successful phishing and social engineering campaigns that raise risk concerns for the safety and fidelity of information systems and non-public client data.

- Mundane events without consequence (port scans for instance) if not evidence of a rigorous attempt at compromise likely would not be reportable events.

*Every response to perceived risk introduces risk. Our reaction to a potential threat can be as lethal to an operating business as the threat itself*

## Discussion

Some years back I was engaged in the systems and operations side of a debt reconciliation and subsequent restructuring for a debtor nation in Latin America on behalf of a consortium of lender banks. We started with what the banks showed on the books and compared it to that claimed owed according to the records of the debtor country. The amounts were different, currencies different, debt instruments did not align, nor did transaction dates or the participants in the obligation on record. Debts changed hands, were broken into parts or tranches, refinanced, sold, converted into different currencies, and different instruments over time. Reconciliation took the better part of two years. That was the 'good old days. Things were relatively simple then. With electronic trading, online banking, and the internet, and now the integration of mobile banking, and with AI, things are infinitely faster, more immediate, and more complex. Without doubt, despite tremendous capabilities in detection and defense in place for the best of our financial institutions, the opportunity for compromise and the difficulty in retracing compromise is also far greater.

NYDFS 23 NYCRR 500 was introduced to protect the NY banking and digital finance system from cyber compromise and improve its transparency, traceability, and accountability. Varied aspects of the regulation were enacted with phased grace periods for adoption with full compliance to the law effective by March of 2019. For all covered entities in scope, it is now fully in force. This includes those in the finance industry that are operative or licensed in New York (with few areas of exception) or processing on behalf of NY covered entities. It is also applicable to service providers to NY covered entities and those intending to perform business services for covered entities as service providers regardless of where they may be. Some of the demands of the new regulation had been anticipated in other law, agency, and industry standards applicable to the finance industry including GLBA, FFIEC, SOA, PCI-DSS and NAIC, and there is overlap, but NYDFS 23 NYCRR 500 brings risk assessment requirements, increased territorial reach, mandates for informed executive accountability, CISO engagement requirements, broader event triggers and reporting, a structure for effective controls and investigation, and risk based control requirements for service providers and other third parties.

Some of the defining strengths of the NYDFS 23 NYCRR 500 include an emphasis on identity controls, multi factor authentication, detailed and traceable access and transactional and account management history. NYDFS requires that all non-public data should be encrypted whether at rest or in transit. This should already be in place in the largest of our banking and insurance institutions. Where this is not possible, compensating controls can be put in place, approved by the CISO, but these need to be defensible, and short term. Full encryption is due one year from updated proposal adoption, 3$^{rd}$ quarter of 2024.

Also emphasized is the mapping of processes and retention of logs needed for effective audit and end-to-end examination of completed cyber transactions or events. Five-year retention is now required of all transactional data. Also, three-years for all supporting or informational data. This is intended to maximize forensic capabilities, permit the entity or auditors to validate and certify processing and control effectiveness, and to investigate failures and events.

## Operationalizing for ongoing success

Without doubt most to all businesses in scope have made the needed investments and process accommodations to meet the requirements of the law. That alone does not assure success. Business is not static. Risk and technologies have changed as has our business environment, markets, culture, and consumer expectations. Accommodations to the law need to be continually revisited and operationalized to be sustainable and to adapt to change over time. Continuity of business provisions with change as well.

Change is constant. IANS faculty member Mark Clancy provides an example where "you might have a front-end web application that initiates transfers and includes all authentication events, source IP addresses, second authentication factors evaluated, risk-based decision values, ... etc. An action within this front-end application may have led to a back-end system conducting a batch transaction to move the funds based on a particular instruction set" ... (and to comply with section 500.06) "the ability to tie the front-end user session and instructions to the back-end transfer is what is needed" (Tackle the NYDFS Cybersecurity Regulations, Mark Clancy, IANS, AAE ANSWERS, July 20, 2017).

The NYDFS 23 NYCRR 500 regulation requires a cybersecurity program to be maintained, defined cyber policies, and a defensible, explainable, and justifiable plan and program based on an assessment of risk and changes to risk and business activities over time. This requires knowing what we have and where, gaps in protection, where the business is exposed, and where the clients of the business may be exposed. It requires building a program and specific policies that address the gaps in each. A risk-based solution is not prescriptive. There are many ways to meet the intended objectives. Frameworks are used because they help assure that the best of professional thought is being used in defining the needed controls, these have been tested elsewhere, and auditors understand them. Whether using the NIST frameworks, ISO standards, or other, they need to be fit to the environment they are applied for a meaningful and supportable result. This is important in defining the correct protection, closing any gaps, and demonstrating competency. A risk aligned program requires a continual reassessment of assets and processes. It requires prioritization of consequential data whether individuating, regulated, transactional, business confidential, privileged, keys and credentials, crown jewel creative or intellectual property. It requires a mapping of where these exist and how they are protected. It requires an understanding of potential and impactful risks and where they might be compromised. It requires continued evaluation, and where needed, investment. Over time, processes change, and program, technologies, organization, and protection must keep pace.

Technology life cycles need to be considered. Significant adoption and adaptation of process and processing is likely still required of many compliant entities to accommodate technology life cycle changes, business transformation, and for new development, and for new entrants or participants to meet the requirements of the regulation, whether as covered entities or service providers. Implementation of more effective technology, controls, accountability, and traceability may require redesign, rebuild or replacement. It will require review and ongoing audit to assure use, behavior and technical change does not impact conformance or lose integrity by failing to adapt, and as said above, keep pace over time.

Existing contracts will need periodic review, and new contracts for products and services once identified, tested, and piloted will need to be negotiated. Partners that cannot, do not have sufficient capacity, or are unwilling to conform to the new requirements within given timeframes should already have been replaced. New vendors, providers, products, and processes will need to integrate smoothly with existing programs, infrastructure, technical, and operational environments. Existing contracts should be periodically reviewed to reflect changing business and new requirements. Where the management of processes are outsourced to service providers or moved to cloud, there will be new risks introduced which will need to be evaluated and addressed and contracts put in place.

Enterprise applications and processes will need to be continually reevaluated, but so too those that are online, in digital communities, virtual, as-a-service offerings, and mobile. All companies are in transition and those in the finance industry lead, not just for competitive advantage but also to keep pace with changing markets, consumers, media, means, risks, and client capabilities. There is big data and analytics and the internet of things. Cloud spans technology and geography. Newly emerged containerized apps and micro-services. Software defined everything. And large model generative AI. Awareness programs for the business community will require advocacy, education, and resources. Each need to adapt and scale.

Divergent internal priorities and perspectives need to be managed and focused, and budgetary attentions aligned. There are active engagements, new projects and products, and business. Each introduces new risk that needs to be fit to the conformance goals of the regulation. And executives are being asked to assume accountability for an area of risk they often do not understand, is outside of their comfort zone, and is at the same time a concern, both the regulation and the cyber risk that prompted it, and a distraction from other business priorities. The opportunity to delegate accountability has been removed.

Coordination of efforts across the enterprise. It is often the case that multiple departments or individual teams are involved in the support of information technology systems and networks, from account administration to network support, to desktop, helpdesk, and more. A comprehensive cyber program requires that the efforts of varied stakeholders and support contributors be coordinated, the varied parties educated as to the regulation and their obligations, and that their compliance be assured by review and audit. This includes the assurance of backups, system, and data protection whether at the server, endpoints, mobile devices or in data bases, assurance of clean account and rights administration, effective operations and production controls, and the assurance of security, monitoring, secure development practices, and system implementation. The requirement of an annual review, testing of controls, third party assessments, and annual penetration testing are prudent practices and each a requirement under the law. For availability, continuity, and restoration of compromised data, (for instance restoration of data impacted by ransomware) an effective backup strategy is critical. Understanding assets and how risks to assets or data impact specific business objectives will satisfy much of the overall business risk assessment and prioritization process. Implementation of a risk aligned program requires stakeholder engagement. It requires a mapping of process with process interdependencies. It is important to know with which systems each interact, transactions in which they might participate, and where data travels. This is important both for documenting the process, and applying the appropriate risk measured protection in a maturity approach. It is also important for addressing the linkages between processes, maximizing traceability, and auditability.

Identified risks, control objectives, and the effectiveness of controls need to be documented and the method or framework by which risk was assessed, and specific controls applied, explainable and supportable in audit. It will be a plan for protection. And it requires that appropriate controls be implemented to mitigate identified risk, and these tested for effectiveness. It will require inventory, analysis, and management of business, operational, physical, and technical risk, particularly from threats to internet facing transactions, breach, and other cyber compromise or exposure, but not only. A cyber-attack can be as much the result of a link in an email, or malware delivered on a flash drive or other physical media, or by phone through social engineering, as from the internet. Mark Clancy, former CISO for the Depository Trust and Clearing Corporation (DTCC), and an IANS colleague says that the "challenge is (that) you must have a risk assessment process that allows you to justify the decisions that you made" and paraphrasing, "whether your assessment accurately reflects the risks, and (can) survive a 'post incident' or 'after the fact look back' in defending the decisions made and approaches taken when asked by regulators". The program of controls and safeguards must be appropriately fit and adequate to the risk. (Tackle the NYDFS Cybersecurity Regulations, Mark Clancy, IANS, AAE ANSWERS, July 20, 2017)

A comprehensive program of protection, active monitoring, detection, and response, including a forensic capability is required, and needs to be adequately staffed, trained, and managed. It requires that there be a defined and scalable response when incidents in process are detected, how that is done, how quickly, and who is involved. It requires an investigative process. There is a requirement for regular vulnerability testing including annual penetration testing. There is also a requirement for internal review, an examination of effectiveness and compliance, and external review through audit. Third party relationships and contracts need to be examined and will need a program in place that assures their compliance. Architectural decisions that have removed the business from an intimate awareness of its data, how its data is managed, or the ability to influence application of controls, or if the architecture or process interferes with required archiving, encrypted data storage requirements, provisions in contract for data portability and return, and the performance of forensic investigation will also be problematic. Needed investments are much less daunting if already maintaining a clean and secure operation, process, and an ecosystem of safeguards, controls, and prudent practice. It is also less so if in compliance with prior existing regulations and if maintaining full visibility and control of all material business processes.

*A maturity focused approach to security, privacy, continuity, ethics, compliance, and other critical domains sharpens our efforts and investments*

Under the NYDFS regulation section 500.06 the ability to reconstruct transactions is required. This is particularly important where there is a material risk of compromise, fraud, or intrusion against a consequential data asset. Accomplishing this requires knowledge of the assets which are consequential, understanding of process and data flows and the systems involved in these. It requires adequate documentation, and correlated event logs, and should broadly considered implement:

- Forensic review and reconstruction of both recent and archived transactions
- Examination of transaction failures occurring in normal operations for indicators of compromise
- Detection and analysis of suspect events
- Active monitoring, in-process controls, input, and output validations
- Dynamic fault checking of transactions in flight to identify, log and intercept compromise in real time, to respond defensively, and to reconstruct the event and assess what may have been impacted

This is not trivial.

- This will likely have an impact on infrastructure. On transactional data monitoring as well. Workflows will need to be well documented in the risk assessment to determine which is 'material'.
- Policies will need to be reviewed and updated to reflect the new requirements of the law. Where these policies have been enacted in automated processes this will need to be addressed.
- There are specific requirements for the archiving of data, and associated transactional information and instructions, and event logs, how long these are retained
- Storage, data management, and existing retention policies.
- It might include reconstruction of events passing control from front end to backend systems, involve processing partners, or processes that may not occur contemporaneously
- It will require adequate storage and the maintaining of transaction and event logs in keeping with retention rules. It will require process maps and documentation.
- NYDFS sets new ground on notification and notification triggers. Like breach notification requirements under the GDPR emerging in Europe, on breach or suspected compromise, notification must be given the NYDFS within 72 hours of becoming aware of the event, even where the event is only partially understood. It is equally likely that the expanded definitions of breach as emerging in EU law will apply broadening the incidents requiring notification.
- There is also a requirement that the NYDFS be notified regardless of any event that triggers the
- notification requirements for any other agency or law, domestic or global, regardless of basis.
- New ransomware guidance has been issued that needs to be reviewed and adopted as well as MFA and are two areas that the NYDFS has documented as areas needing focus.

*Regulation, mandates, and investments made to meet compliance, helps bring some truth to the system*

John Masserini, CSO at MIAX Options said in an interview by Techtarget, that "by understanding the revenue generation processes, which are identified and protected under the BC plan, one is able to see how various applied security controls can mitigate the greatest amount of risk with the least amount of effort". He added that he would "encourage every security executive out there to take ownership of – and understand – the business continuity plan as a foundation for their security program. This is an important statement which I have reiterated again when discussing continuity later in this book. NYDFS 23 NYCRR 500 identifies recovery and continuity as two elements of the cybersecurity plan requiring increased focus and documentation and that should be measurable and demonstrable in programs by 3rd quarter of 2024. http://searchsecurity.techtarget.com/feature/MIAX-Options-CSO-on-securitys-role-in-business-continuity?utm_content=control&utm_medium=EM&asrc=EM_ERU_75073362&utm_campaign=20170403_ERU

Proposals awaiting approval now require Class A companies (those with more than $5 billion in assets or revenue) to conduct an independent cybersecurity audit at least annually, all covered entities to implement multi-factor authentication for accessing sensitive data or systems, encrypt all nonpublic information in transit and at rest, unless infeasible, report any cybersecurity event that has a reasonable likelihood of materially harming any material part of their normal operations within 72 hours and to adopt written policies and procedures for the secure disposal of any nonpublic information that is no longer necessary for business operations or other legitimate purposes .

Although New York is leading by example with this far reaching and broadly sweeping regulation, it is likely that similar cyber security laws will emerge in other states relatively soon.

NYDFS 23 NYCRR 500 raises the bar with its specific requirement for board oversight and executive assurance and requirement for the appointment of an internal CISO or the delegation of CISO functions to other designated roles or engaged externally.

For a comparison of the new regulation to prior obligations under GLBA or FFIEC I found this reference from Delta Risk, a Chertoff Company, useful: https://deltarisk.com/blog/uncovering-the-differences-between-23-nycrr-500-glba-and-ffiec-regulations/

Perhaps one of the most important requirements of the new regulation regarding the CISO role is the mandatory reporting in writing by the CISO to the board at least once yearly, and now ad hoc, a responsibility for the CISO, but holding the board and executive management accountable.

Also, the requirement that a covered entity submit an annual written statement of compliance to the NYDFS with executive (CEO) signature, attesting to having reviewed and understood the informed advisement provided by the CISO, and acceptance of accountability for the Cyber Security program.

Full certification will require updates by companies and partners due by April 15, 2026.

# CISO
# REDEFINED

*Protecting Business*

---

Martin Gomberg, CISSP, CIPP/E

## SECTION 10.  RISK, HOLES, HUNTS, AND MODELS

I have said before and again, there are only so many holes you can plug, and only so many threats you can detect, track, or correlate, postulate, investigate, or model, before chasing ghosts or encroaching on the impractical, unlikely, or irrelevant. Understanding the consequential, focusing where these are vulnerable, on threats that will have a meaningful, likely, and imminent impact on assets and information with a potential for negative effect 'risk aligns' efforts, and guides investments in implementing mitigating controls.

Assessment of risk and vulnerabilities, threat modeling, and threat hunting are all components of an effective program of risk inventory and management and critical to a successful security program if focused where the pain is, or is likely to be, and where attack, loss or damage would be consequential.

Vulnerability assessment and threat modeling sessions are some of the best ways to drill deep into the structures in our environment, understand strengths and weaknesses, bring together disparate perspectives and areas of expertise, grow and leverage knowledge, stimulate team interaction, and get a bottom-up focus on risk and risk priorities. Threat hunting focuses our best efforts and aligns organizational interests in maintaining a clean operating environment.

Threats morph and new threats emerge. Often it is those with which we are or should be familiar that does us harm. Sometimes this is because we have been effectively targeted where it is evident that we are weak. Sometimes we are tricked into traversing old paths and revisiting old pains, but more often it is because we are either slow to learn, repeat mistakes or do not know our environment. Sometimes the threat is new. Through the course of our day to day, we change, and with change we create new paths for compromise.

*Courts, cases, and cultures decide what is valid for a given body of law.*

## Risk Soup and the Threat Hunter

A program of controls and policies, detective and protective technologies, defensive coding practices, and awareness training programs for our communities provides the best path to effective security. There are no guarantees however, security can be compromised, and the prudent business will want to assure the integrity of the program with testing. Threat hunting, bug bounty programs, peer code review and bug hunts are all integrity controls that test the effectiveness of security measures and assure that they have not been compromised. They are themselves detective controls.

On any given day, new hires begin work, new equipment is rolled out, and firewalls and systems are reconfigured to support new business needs. Developers create new applications or build on those existing or being readied for launch, often under deadlines. New network segments are created, and older equipment is shut down and retired. People work, read, write, click, visit, access, alter, and explore as business pursues new relationships. They sometimes deploy new applications, or move data to the cloud, with the awareness of in-house technical and security professionals, or sometimes not. All this is with the best of intentions, except when it is not, but in either case, dependent on that taken or moved, there is new risk and the potential for harm.

In many companies, technical operations and technical security report differently. Their interests and attentions do not always align. Security systems, new servers or services, end user rights and credentials, and administrative privilege all carry risk. In our best companies changes to these are governed closely by policy and process controls. That said, even our best companies are not at their best all the time.

Every morning newspaper highlights yet another breach and many of these are to our best companies, all names most would recognize. In some of our largest companies there may be numerous technical organizations or Infosec teams and these may not communicate effectively, may take conflicting paths, or may differ in priorities. Administrators take short cuts cloning the profiles of departing employees to set up the temps or staff that replace them. Business units engage temporary staff to cover gaps left by departing or vacationing employees using the employee's credentials. Passwords are unchanged. We procure new security and protective tools, devices, and applications with which we are less than fully familiar, and frequently there is a learning curve before we are effective. Management changes, and with that so do perspectives, knowledge, approach, areas of competence, focus, vendor relationships, interests, and preferences. We make decisions, often motivated by budget priorities or staff resources, as to which doors we will watch, where we will scan, and what tools we will use where, and what roles we will cover.

This is risk soup, most of which is normal and well-intentioned day-to-day business, but also the primordial broth from which most of our security problems emerge. Anyone who does not believe that the above is true, and is likely at every company, needs to look harder. Business is about change and movement, change and movement create or exacerbate vulnerabilities, and threats succeed. Risk evolves with the decisions we make, and with the things we touch, it is cumulative, and it is compounded, and we have been walking upright for some time. It is only continual suspicion, shared perspectives, and reiterative examination of our environment and the changes that we have made to it, in all the above, that can ferret out the threats that have compromised us or reveal the holes we have created that might make compromise possible.

Many companies narrowly define the role of the threat hunter to technical threat, and specifically, cyber incursion, data theft, and malware. Some deploy their threat hunting teams to examine their 'attack surface', examining the technical infrastructure that might be compromised, validating server and endpoint inventories and that configurations are sufficiently hardened. Some are targeted and focus on threats to the most consequential of assets, a maturity approach.

But threats to business are not just technical, and not just the result of how things have been deployed, or what may have skirted by our defenses, but equally how resources are used and how people and processes operate. For the CISO this can be an opportunity to engage the business to join in unearthing threats beyond the outbound theft of data, or the incoming nasty, beyond the technical, but those that are operational, structural, legal, physical, and cultural. So, from that perspective, tracking the footprints of the nasty things that may have come in from outside, but also all the above, is the realm of the threat hunter in the best hunt programs.

Hunters should not only be our technical best, but also our business brightest. There is opportunity and upside in establishing shared understanding and ownership of risk if we partner with the business in finding the holes, working through the scenarios of concern, the models, and in turning over the rocks together as we hunt to find hidden threats. They may be violations of policy or license limitations, improperly configured or sized systems, poorly defined functions in applications, insufficient protection, or continuity measures, inadequate or inappropriate alignment with business cycles, expiring agreements, poor understanding of the environment, third party behaviors, or they may be potential failures or attacks, and malicious or intrusive cyber threats. They are all potentially threats and the best team to expose them is drawn from technology, security and the operational lines of business and support working together, meeting together, and identifying exposures together, pooling knowledge and diverse areas of experience. And if the CISO is to be effective, it is with the recognition that threats live where the business lives, that there are no threats to technology, all threats are to the business, and the greatest threat to the business is not recognizing this.

Except in the largest of companies, dedicating resources to retrospective examination of change even where consequential, is difficult. Some companies have the resources to dedicate to threat identification and forensics, and build comprehensive programs, but many do not. Often the same team members responsible for the monitoring of the environment and current events are the ones tasked with forensics and the discerning of past events from archived data. Sometimes specialist hunt teams can be brought in from the outside with the expertise and tools to be successful. But even there, success is proportional to the information that can be provided to them based on the awareness of what is consequential in our environments, and the mapping, documentation, and inventories we have conducted in assessing risk.

That said, it is almost a given that even without direction or adequate guidance threat hunting specialists will find something, often something that has been lingering for months to years, and the investment will be worthwhile. If nothing is found it might be due to the inadequacy of the information or limited access or time provided them, selection of the wrong team, or an incredibly good day that confirms either that your defenses are fully effective, or the bad guys simply do not find you interesting, either a good outcome, both unlikely.

## Vulnerabilities and Threats

In addition to active hunting, vulnerabilities can be highlighted, and potential threats discussed and prioritized in tabletop exercises and brainstorming sessions. When done properly vulnerability assessments and threat modeling are effective components of any risk evaluation. These are opportunities to inventory weaknesses that are exploitable. It is also the opportunity to mentally walk through the attacks, hazards and conditions that maliciously exploit, or through accident or incident impact at these points of weakness. It is an opportunity to 'group think' about every possible hole in our defenses, gaping, transient, conditional, opportunistic, or other, and every threat we might encounter and to get these onto a list. It is an opportunity to bring diverse perspectives as a room full of area experts and specialists focus on potential exposures. That said, of course we will neither encounter every possible threat, nor will every threat be to an area where we are vulnerable, and even there, if the vulnerability is exploited, result in consequential impact. Threat modeling is most effective when prioritizing the effort with all of this in mind for context. For this reason, I prefer to start with an examination of possible threats to our most consequential assets, and even there focus on areas where known vulnerabilities or insufficient controls increase our risk.

So, a few things should be obvious whether for threat hunting, or for threat modeling, or looking for vulnerabilities. To be most effective we need to know our assets, our data, our access, our processes. We need to know the on ramps and off ramps where data moves. We need to understand the state of technology, both available to procure, and that already in place, where we are current, and where we are behind. We need to discern which is most exposed and that most important. We need to know our stakeholders, who know the business best, how things work, and in their opinions, where the exposures live. We need to know our business, our relationships, our business cycles. A threat or inadequate control that permits a selling season to be interrupted is always of concern, but likely is of greater concern at specific times of the year. Downtime for financial systems before the close of the quarter is completed is more impactful than it may be a few days after. A manufacturing disruption may be less immediately visible and consequential to a company after product is built and warehouses are stocked then it would be to a Just-In-Time Manufacturer. With that information, we can begin an effective risk aligned assessment.

Our businesses do not exist in a vacuum. They exist in a context of markets, competition, and objectives. Cultures vary, organizations differ and the personalities in leadership set the mission which drives our course. Our business has priorities. They vary with revenue cycles, with budgets, regulatory reporting events and requirements, and with variance in consumer demands for products and services, and the priorities of investors. The tone set at the top defines the speed at which we move and in which direction, where investments will be made, where line of business management will give focus, and the initiatives that will be funded, and how budgets will be applied. The tone set by leadership is either a breath of fresh air or depletes all the oxygen in the room.

Our overall assessment of risk lives and is conducted in that context and our analysis of threats and inventory of vulnerabilities are part of this. It is as important to look at leadership, business, and culture as it is to focus on endpoints and cyber-attacks. This should be reflected not just in the approach to assessment and modeling, but also the team assembled to participate. They should be senior, but close to the ground. They should be representative, diverse in knowledge and inclusive in role and function. They should be broadly encompassing of the technical, operational, supportive, and managerial. They should be drawn from both internal and partner, and include specialists in oversight, audit, and risk. They should have the backing of executive authority giving them the freedom to ask questions and to get answers when needed.

The CISO that pulls together management, operational lines of business, and those responsible for funding and financial approvals has moved the needle. Pulling in risk and audit, human resources, physical security, legal specialists, as well as technical engineering, development, analysis, and operations takes this further. If bringing privacy, continuity, risk, and security specialists, and engaging them all in the process of thinking risk and identifying exposure, the CISO has gone a long way towards achieving good governance, has aligned the business toward protective goals, engaged the business in security as a mutual and shared responsibility, and has succeeded where many have not.

For some time and increasingly in the past several years, house legal counsel has been responding to executive demands to identify enterprise privacy' risk and to develop comprehensive privacy policies. There has been an increased awareness and concern for breach, legal exposures, penalties, and reputational impact. Data, whether owned by business, legal, or elsewhere in the organization, ultimately is managed by technology and technical operations, and so increasingly, and sometimes predominately, the CISO has a role. That said, it is a joined trust. Sensitive personal 'PII, PHI, PCI' data, regulated data, 'company confidential' data, privileged communications, and critical 'crown jewel' intellectual property fall to IT management, security, legal, risk, business leadership and informed employees to protect and assure together.

Ultimately, any company can be breached. Reduction or mitigation of the risk of breach and data theft requires prioritization of focus, analysis of exposure, and targeted protective investments, but we as CIOs or CISOs are often not as intimate as we need to be with the data we collect and store across our lines of business, where that data resides, and how it is or needs to be protected, or for that matter, the consequences of its loss or theft. This is even more an issue as access to the cloud permits the capture and storage of data by varied lines of business without IT involvement, so called shadow IT.

For all the exceptional benefits of cloud and cloud services when used correctly, mobility, cloud and storage virtualization has moved our data beyond our physical control and challenged our ability to effectively monitor and protect our data assets.

*Complexity exacerbates risk*

Cloud providers themselves use cloud services downstream, as do their providers in turn, making contractual assurances of compliance and protection less binding and enforceable, and the ecosystem on which we depend less visible. Failure to select the appropriate cloud provider to house specific types of data (a PCI compliant provider for PCI data for example) or to activate or properly configure offered cloud security controls increases exposure. Whether ownership rests with the business, risk policy with legal, protection with the CIO, or housing and data management with the cloud service, on breach with data loss, regardless of how or where it takes place, to be sure, the company is accountable.

Again, anyone can be breached. That said, mitigating the risk in data breach also demands recognition of a weakness in the data protection strategies of too many of the large and competent organizations that have suffered breach at significant cost. They have emphasized the deployment of technologies to broadly target 'enterprise vulnerability' to threat preferentially, although probably not intentionally, over the implementation of effective administrative controls and operational hygiene. It is easier to buy a box than to fix a process. And often resources responsible for the management of administrative controls and clean operations report organizationally apart from the CISO. Monitoring tools and vulnerability mitigating technologies are a critical component in awareness of compromise and effective defense, but without the more mundane attention to operational cleanliness and prudent controls, and accountability for its assurance, a component with diminishing returns relative to the increasing and pervasive threat environment.

For some it may be more appropriate to consider a prioritized risk approach focused less on 'overall enterprise vulnerability' from the perspective of breach mitigation, which for all but the largest companies may be too broad and expensive to effectively address, and may be impossible to achieve, but instead limiting focus to the consequence of breach of specific high-risk data.

*There are transformational projects in security, the importance of which would be immediately understandable by anyone, regardless of technical sophistication. They are foundational to any protective program.*
*They drill deep into what assets we have, who has access to what, what data is important and consequential if lost, taken or damaged, and what we are doing as a business for protection, and where.*

Accomplishing this will require attention to architectural segregation, needed controls, mitigation of specific vulnerabilities, and reduction of the consequence of exposure for that data particularly considered most sensitive, whether it is regulated, or entrusted personal data stewarded with an expectation of privacy, concerns for corporate confidentiality, privileged communications, or crown jewel intellectual property assets. It requires that our most important data be made less obvious to find, harder to steal, disrupt or damage, and made less attractive to theft. Lastly, it requires diminishing the impact of the loss itself by rendering the data less exposable, vulnerable, and less exploitable using encryption, digital wrappers, etc.

Prioritizing reduction of consequential loss ahead of other data risk, limits exposure, targets investments and reduces legal liability, while increasing the safety of the most sensitive and consequential data assets.

This is not to say that investment in detection capabilities, testing, technical safeguards, investigative capabilities, threat management or threat intelligence sharing for the enterprise overall should be given any less attention where the resources are available, and the organization can leverage that investment, but not all organizations can. It requires supporting the investment in enterprise security with appropriately skilled staff, ongoing staff development, or an effective managed onsite or cloud service, but foremost for breach concerns, prioritizing and maximizing attention on the data considered most sensitive.

Risk and the prioritization of risk is an inclusive discussion with executive, legal and business stake holders, allowing the CIO and CISO to adopt a powerful and positive position owning the narrative for success, not just accountability. This will permit both the CIO and CISO to assume leadership and partnership with legal and operational executives, in defining, identifying, and codifying exposed 'consequential' data, and in communicating steps towards mitigation and shared ownership of best possible outcomes. It is a discussion on effecting a prioritized risk-based strategy, carefully defined policy on data usage and care, and data specific protective investments. Not all data is created equally. Corporate secrets deserve better protection than the lunch menu.

It cannot be repeated enough, there is no approach that eliminates all risk or the possibility of attack, breach, or compromise of systems or data, even with the best of hunt programs and vulnerability assessments. We cannot track enough, detect enough, stop enough, or close enough holes regardless of investments and diligence. Success in managing breach is measured by the minimization of consequence, and the brief and uninteresting press coverage, if any, which follows.

*We live in a data driven world. Data shapes culture*

# REQUIREMENTS FOR PROTECTING OUR MOST SENSITIVE DATA

- Executive ownership and the commitment to drive technical and operational investments

- A well-managed process, and skilled security team, are not a guarantee of safety, but absent these, failure is assured.

- Understanding of data inventory, ownership, and stewardship, what we have, its sensitivity or regulatory restriction, where it is kept, how it is used, how long it is needed and how it needs to be protected, and the process assurances that keeps this knowledge current.

- Effective operational hygiene including identification, authentication, authorization, access management and limitations, and protection of administrative credentials.

- The management of account, software, system and data life cycles, all basics, but weakly implemented by many. Do not keep what is not needed. What you do not have cannot be taken or lost. Where data is most sensitive, these need to be maximized.

- Preservation of data along with all mechanisms needed for its recovery and use – hardware, software, and operating environment.

- Fitting the best technical protections to the specific requirements of an organization or industry, and in specific, the data and assets it most needs to protect. This includes tools for detection, protection, mitigation, 'whitelisting' of technology and applications, and policy driven data loss prevention

- Effective operational controls, managed with knowledge, prudence, and expertise.

- An effective mapping of exposure to controls (a maturity model).

- Policies and approaches evidentiary of due care, that reduce liability, and enable better decisions as to spend, aligning requested security investments to budget.

- Backups, disaster recovery, and continuity safeguards for that data considered most critical

- Insurance responsive to data breach or loss liabilities and residual risk.


*'Partitioning, Containerization, Virtualization, Segmentation, Clustering, Inter Process Communication, Security, Redundancy, Performance and Scalability'*

*~*

*These are tools of architecture. Approaches and products differ, but the concepts are not new. They drive cloud innovation and microservices today just as they have desktops, networks, mobile devices, storage, and telecom for decades*

# CISO
# REDEFINED

*Protecting Business*

Martin Gomberg, CISSP, CIPP/E

## SECTION 11.  THOUGHTS ON PRIVACY

Digital footprints, virtual communities, and the pressures of security, have made privacy, or any hope for preservation of identity, and lives individuated, and in quiet, vital. The right to a quiet life is so important to us, a life without intrusion, it is legislated throughout our operating democracy, is an inherent human right under European law, and is emerging as a protected right in countries on every continent across the globe. It is a broad topic of thought and discussion and an increasing obligation in business, and for quality of life, of great importance to each of us.

### Privacy for business and individuals

Business struggles with privacy. It has been said and repeated so often that although I am quoting, I do not know who, or from where, that "you can have security without privacy, but you cannot have privacy without security". It should also be added that without effective privacy and data protection controls, conforming to the requirements of statutory privacy regulations and laws and directives, domestic and overseas, is not possible. So, without security you cannot have privacy, and without privacy you cannot have compliance with most of the bodies of law that safeguard the sanctity and respect of individuals, of workers, clients, or prospective consumers, and the right to a life in quiet without unwelcome intrusion.

Unfortunately, you cannot have security without getting a lot else right in organization, operations, education, and infrastructure, also knowing what you have, why, where it is, if you need it or have the right to have it, and how you need to protect and manage it, and that is where most fail, and downstream, privacy, and by extension, compliance suffers.

Individuals struggle with privacy as well, mostly in the tacit acceptance of its violation. In the U.S, aligned to the tenets of the Constitution and the Bill of Rights in common law, we have what is sometimes called an endowed privacy right of 'Quiet Enjoyment'. It is unenumerated in law, but implied and accepted as the right for individuals to peacefully go about life without government encroachment without cause. This is fragile, precious, and concerning, as fear of threat and harm drives us to increasingly forgive our liberties in favor of security. Europeans far less so as they struggle to preserve privacy as an individual inherent right, but this too is fragile. Our travels are scrutinized through PNR (Passenger Name Records) and 'no fly' lists. We succumb to annoying body scans at the airport and are photographed from every view as we walk along the continual turning rope line to the security scanner. Where public interests of security, safety and the effectiveness of law enforcement are a concern, the privacy of individuals, a last bastion of hope that we might maintain some semblance of individuality, dignity, and anonymity amidst the digitization of our persons and everything about us, struggles to keep hold.

People accept change and culture adapts. Increasingly, across the western world, and in fact over much of the globe, as a matter of choice and for small returns, we relinquish our privacy daily for convenience and personalization. We share contact information, likes, and preferences for a personal greeting, products customized to our tastes, and avoidance of waiting lines, and do so freely and willingly, online, and in person. We request an online price quote for an insurance product, and they ask our name. Why do they need that to quote a price? We hand over our credit cards with no concern for whether our information is photographed or recorded for subsequent misuse, offer up our social security numbers or other personal identifiers when asked, allow apps to access our location with little thought, and are compelled to discuss prior salaries on job interviews even prior to hiring commitments, in short, for nothing in return. And with each bit of privacy handed away, it gets easier. Whether out of fear, security, apathy, or convenience, as we chip away at privacy the argument for its preservation becomes increasingly difficult to make.

It is a slippery slope. Laws, regulation, and sizable penalties compel business to do the right thing and to assure privacy holds amid the forgiving and relaxing culture of convenience, and is not overly exploited for advantage, despite it being easy to do so. Successful business, good faith concern for customers, compliance with law, and avoidance of costly conflict challenges business to understand and respect all above, and continually strive to protect privacy, even at a cost, wherever we operate.

Security and privacy are in a tug of war. Who wins we will have to wait to see.

What determines that which is private, and personal, may derive from the demands of the person. It may derive from sovereign laws protecting the rights of the individual. Or it may come from concerns less for the privacy and sanctity of the person, but for the contribution of the individual to a specific activity or group, or religious doctrine.

For corporations operating globally, managing privacy can be complex. Laws differ, and what is defined as personal, and therefore private, varies. So do ownership, standards of care, and the rights of data owners. So does the basis for the need of privacy. So does what will constitute private information.

Privacy is emerging as policy around the globe, on every continent, but the drivers of concern for data protection are not the same, and privacy does not mean the same everywhere. The terms Privacy in the U.S., and Personal Data Protection in the EU, and elsewhere, are often used as synonymous, but in fact are different and often treated so globally, as is the concern for its violation, and how it is protected.

**Personal Information can mean different things in a global context.**

It may be a name, ID, or other individualizing assigned information, Information that describes, is associated with, or is about a person, A reputation, or related data or activities that would help identify an individual from behavior, custom, context, or association, or from an attribute or unique physical characteristic

The mandates and mechanisms governing the protection of individuals with respect to privacy and the rights and interests of people as citizens, as consumers, and as employees differ. They differ at work, in marriage, in transactional relationships and business disclosures, in collective rights, and in context of affinities, activities, and behaviors. They may be dictated by omnibus governing law as will be the case across much of Europe under the GDPR, or as federated regulation enforced by states, municipalities, governing agencies, and industry bodies as is the U.S. model. They can be governed under contract, policy, custom and culture, accepted practice, or under religious doctrine. In some cases, more than one of these will dictate concurrently. Privacy law is emerging across the globe. In this section we will reference specific laws and jurisdictions but are speaking to generic privacy and privacy practice, an operational privacy posture.

# What is Privacy?

*Along with anonymity, modesty, and sanctity of body and mind, privacy is a derived right. It is derived from the willingness of others, compelled or not, to grant it.*

*Privacy is a personally asserted, legally affirmed, culturally expected, or natural human right, but it may not be all at the same time, in all places, or all times, and it may not apply equally to everyone, or be appropriate to everyone in the same way, or remain so for all time.*

*It is as much a human need as it is a right. As much as it is the right of a person, it can also be the right of a group, extrapolated from the collective rights of individuals.*

*It is a fragile and precious right, but limited, recent, and untested, and survives in any form only if protected'.*

*Who we are, what we know, and what we care about is our story*
*Our consent assures that it is told only as we want it to be told*

## Privacy and Business

With considerable variance by country, as a generalized statement, and to varying degree, corporate adherence to privacy requires a respect for the rights of the individual to be informed and to consent within the context of the business relationship. It also requires operational and technical practices that conform to state and national laws protecting the interests of the individual, and their data, its use, domestic, across borders, and overseas. These practices vary widely. http://www.dlapiperdataprotection.com

Along with consumer and employee data rights, a discussion of personal data protection from a business perspective means a policy, plan, technical, and operational framework for identifying and mitigating risk to captured, stored, and stewarded data. This is the case whether sensitive and individuating personal data (PII), health (PHI), or credit information (PCI), or identifying, affinity, behavior, and affiliation data for individuals, and for social, exploitable, and vulnerable communities, including children.

Managing this requires implementation and oversight of technical and operational safeguards. It requires a sensitivity to local culture and an understanding of sovereign laws, secular and religious. It requires the limiting of data exposure and risk through prudent control practices.

In the U.S., Europe, and increasingly elsewhere, as technology advances, data protection and personal privacy will mean amongst other controls the use of encryption, or with Big Data, the anonymizing or pseudonymizing of individuating data as a prudent safeguard. In some countries, law dictates where and how that data can be held, used, managed, shared and by whom.

Corporations worry for other consequential data as well. This is data that is not associable or individuating of a person, sensitive or exposing of information about their activities or associations, or impactful to the rights and freedoms of individuals overall but is instead important to protecting the interests of the operating company. This includes company confidential, privileged communication, regulated data, keys and credentials, and crown jewel intellectual property (IP). These all need to be addressed through a process of inventory and classification, assignment of risk and priority, and appropriate protection and mitigation just as does personal data and may be protected by the same teams and technologies. But these are not an issue of concern for privacy, but for confidentiality, and the securing of material and intellectual assets.

## Business in the context of privacy

Corporate adherence to privacy establishes responsibility and accountability and requires a respect for the care, use and dissemination of the individuating information collected about us. About the products we research and consume. About the inquiries we make, and the personal information that we reveal. This is the personal information captured and retained, whether in finding and engaging us as customers, or satisfying us as consumers through personalized service, or in the provision of ordered products or through our traceable digital footprints. It is the data exposed about us, purchased, or collected from 3rd parties. The data inferred and derived from other data.

Privacy requires a respect for the wants and interests of the individual, whether customer, employee or other. It requires a respect for their interests in how we as businesses interject, and with what purpose, authority, or needed and obtained permissions into their day, or whether we do at all. This includes provisions for specific or implied consent. It also includes the means of establishing informed use, policies, privacy statements, banners, pop ups, and EULA agreements, opt-in consent for collection and use of sensitive information, opt-out for less sensitive information, and the ability to request removal from contact lists, product marketing, and promotional activities.

It includes provisions for limiting annoyance and unwanted targeted communications by phone (do not call lists), mail, email, or text message, assuring that the right to stop, limit or control intrusion is specific, respected, and can be asserted.

By extension, corporate adherence to privacy requires that any business engaged in partnership with an affiliate or third-party provider assures that the engaged partners respect and reflect its policies and interests. That they provide an equally appropriate plan, technical, and operational framework for data protection and the safeguard of personal privacy rights.

In a global context, if a U.S. company serving clients that are foreign nationals and live overseas, live domestically, but are foreign nationals, have placed employees, U.S. citizens, overseas, or are employing staff that are foreign citizens or maintain dual citizenship, there is an expectation and may be a legal requirement of adherence to the protection of privacy and labor rights in accordance to foreign and specific jurisdictional laws. This obligation differs with sovereign privacy statutes across the globe. Where U.S. citizens, and perhaps even in other cases, the protections of U.S. federal, state and municipal laws and agency regulations may apply as well.

Managing privacy globally is not a trivial matter regardless of which pond or border we cross. It requires careful consideration of unique differences in law and context and local interpretations of how these laws apply even beyond the written law. By example, Russian privacy statutes disallow anonymous access to the internet by individuals and require an authenticating 'login'. They also require data captured by foreign companies that buy or sell to Russians in Russia be localized in Russia. Local interpretations of regulation are important, and missteps impede progress, cost time and money, or can in some cases violate law. https://www.theguardian.com/world/2015/sep/01/russia-internet-privacy-laws-control-web

Michael Tan and Yang Cui of Taylor Wessing reviewed draft regulation recently introduced by the Cyberspace Administration of China which proposes restrictions on personal and other classes of critical data. It would require that such data be stored locally by Critical Information Infrastructure Operators (CIIO) and restricts unapproved outbound transfer of 'personal data where consent has not been granted, where subject interests might be compromised, or if data is considered of importance to national security or belonging to one of several classes of data barred from export by Chinese authorities.

How privacy is managed and overseen globally often differs. The rights of individuals differ. Data protection laws vary as does the stringency of their enforcement. The CISO needs to navigate carefully with the benefit of counsel in developing technical, operational, and monitoring strategies, and to protect against negative impacts to business, often severe. Commonly there are:

- Differences in rights of notice and consent to the collection, use, and retention of data
- Restrictions on how, where and what data is collected and requirements for localization of data, systems, and support
- Restrictions or prohibitions on data transfer between countries and for what purposes
- Limits on subsequent forwarding to other countries after transfers occur
- Specific restrictions on data transfer in response to foreign legal or law enforcement requests

For the CISO overseeing the applicability and appropriateness of out of country technology and operations in accordance with sovereign law, all this can have an impact on:

- The design of websites and portals established for data collection and behavioral tracking (cookies)
- Systems used for collecting, processing, and analyzing data
- Technology deployment and follow the sun models of support
- Where employee records are stored, and payroll systems are operated and maintained
- Roll up of subsidiary system data in varying countries to corporate systems out of country
- Use of cloud or distributed services

http://www.independent.ie/business/technology/data-commissioner-must-halt-transfers-to-the-us-court-told-35458076.html) – Tim Healy Published 17/02/2017

Increasingly, companies are looking to technology as a safeguard for sensitive and confidential data and for the protection of their operating environment. As cyber and other digital threats increase, and the demand by regulators for more effective data stewardship, and the penalties for inadequate safeguards also increase, more companies look to technology to anticipate, detect, identify, and mitigate threats, target misbehavior, and safeguard against data loss. Driven both by the increasing intensity and multiplicity of threat, and an expanding need and market for the use of these defenses, new technologies and capabilities continually emerge. Corporate clients welcome these and look to their potential fit to the protection of data and operations. Where operating globally, consistency in the use and application of these technologies across the global enterprise, from corporate headquarters, to manufacturing centers, to the smallest of sales offices is desirous for simplicity, and so that multiple tools and skill sets do not need to be managed and the data can integrate cleanly. But this has been and still can be problematic, and in some cases, whether physical or technical, monitoring of individual activities and personal behaviors may be illegal.

**Is it personal?**

Privacy laws vary and interpretation of them can be complex. Most would recognize personal data in its most obvious form, name, address, contact information. Other data may also be personal, data associated to an individual, contextual data such as an individual's relationships, locality, affiliations, affinities, characteristics, and behaviors. Also, referential data, keys, addresses, and IDs allowing location and association.

The ICO (UK Information Commissioner's Office) has offered a qualifier test of personal data as 1) information, 2) relating to, 3) a natural or living person, 4) directly or indirectly'. All four qualifiers must pass for data to be considered personal information. Reference to a university library named for its donor seemingly is a reference to a building not personal data about the donor it is named for. The name of a corporate shipping receiver on a delivery document would be referential, the focus of the document being the shipment, not the individual referenced. Failing to 'relate to' the individual, these per this test seemingly would not be considered personal data. That said, I have provided the link to the ICO so you can decide. https://ico.org.uk/for-organisations/guide-to-data-protection/guide-to-the-general-data-protection-regulation-gdpr/what-is-personal-data/what-is-the-meaning-of-relates-to/

Personal data is most recognizable when found in structured files, databases, and spreadsheets. Some personal data is less easy to find, particularly data in less structured environments, documents, contracts, paper, voice, and video. Also, personal communications. Search technologies and big data increasingly make data findable and content increasingly relatable. Careful interpretation in context of specific governing law may be needed to determine if it is personal, in which scenarios, and this may differ or be nuanced in interpretation by law.

1. **An individual makes a statement of fact** – Does an individual stating a fact make the fact personal data? 'Revenue numbers exceed last year by 20%'. This statement relates to a business even if stated by an identifiable person and likely would fail the 'relate to' test required for data to be personal.

2. **An individual's affiliations and beliefs are revealed** – Revealing an individual's affiliation to a group or an espoused doctrine of belief is a disclosure of personal information about them. Stating that "Jones is a member of the self-proclaimed 'growth advocates' and shares the view that ..." certainly reveals affiliation, membership, and a shared philosophy or view. It provides attribution to an individual, verifiable affiliation, and an espoused doctrine of belief.

3. **Non-personal data is used to discover personal data** – 'Revenue numbers may exceed last year by 20%' and 'Jones is a member of the self-proclaimed 'growth advocates' when collocated or technically relatable makes findable both a statement of non-personal business fact, and personalizing data discussing the opinions and affinities of an individual. Where a statement of business fact attributable to an individual can be used to discover personal data about an individual it is less obvious whether the non-personal data would remain non-individuating. This is particularly so where an electronic search of the non-personal data could be considered a referential key to the personal data.

4. **Coresident data, Big Data and AI** – Non-personal data as a referential key becomes particularly problematic in the context of data lakes, oceans, and Big Data, and in the use of sophisticated query, predictive analytics, LLM (large language models), and AI. Non-personal data, readily obtainable public data (home ownership, licenses, political contributions), and low risk personalizing data can be associated to more sensitive personal data, and perhaps used in rendering automated decisions, generating narrative, or developing contextual intelligence. Associating information provides the opportunity to enrich and develop a more intimate perspective of an individual. This also may further align an individual to others professing similar views, or expose others, associating them where views and philosophies in common serve as a referential key to their beliefs and affiliations.

5. **Monitoring** – Video, sound, web access, tracking and cookies are used for productivity management, behavioral assessments, security, theft control and traffic management amongst other uses including recognition of individuals for personalization of service. A User_ID whether obtained through login or cookie can recognize unique visits, recurrence, frequency of visits, gaps and intervals, patterns of activities, and device detail, providing individuation sometimes without actual identification. Does a clear and consistent association of behaviors without specific identification of an individual render this associable data personal information? It may be a question of likelihood of actual identification or likelihood qualified by the reasonableness of the effort required. Laws may vary on this.

6. **Derived, extrapolated, inferred, or enhanced data** – created by the association, interpretation, combination, aggregation, supplementation, or manipulation of other personal data

7. **Density, association, localization, and demographics** – Increasingly the value of relating ever more disparate data sources for advantage grows compelling. As density of data grows, incremental, recombinant, and derivative, corporate and cloud, social media, digital communities, public and private, current, and past, and the tools for assessment refine with time, increasingly localization, association, and demographics encroach on individuation. If geolocation can localize to an area, and demographics age, race or other characteristics localize to a group, with context, association and time, individuation becomes increasingly likely. With time and experience, algorithms refine, and data density increases. That which is considered personal today and that which is regulated by law to protect our fleeting privacy tomorrow undoubtedly will differ.

This exercise was not focused on applicability of specific law. It was solely intended to demonstrate the difficulty in determining what constitutes personalizing data. There are considerable differences in privacy laws and interpretations of their applicability. We are reaching deeper and mining data for relationships increasingly more and this clearly will continue. Identifying individuating data in documents, contracts, presentations, and free form media where data in context combines non-individuating, innominate, and personal data is challenging. Individuating data is interpreted differently by individuals, under specific law and varying circumstance. Codified law, courts, cases, cultures, and time decide what comprises personal data, its sensitivity, how it can be used and shared, and too, what constitutes a disclosure violation and its ramifications under a given body of law.

But where courts and regulators have not yet weighed in, we skirt grey areas between espoused opinion and assumption of risk. Source, accuracy, whether opinion or a disclosure of verifiable fact, cultural perspectives, and potential effect or harm may each be factors in determining if specific data is PII, and if protected by law. Companies will need to be cognizant of differences in domestic and global law, state, and local jurisdictional variances. Big Data and AI will only increase data access and interpretive or derivative exposures, local, cloud. and virtual, and further render unrelated data, relatable.

## Use of Technology

Many of the technologies for detection of threat and anomalous behavior, theft protection, data loss prevention, and access monitoring, tracking, or filtering, operate to scan, inspect, and interpret data. They may identify the presence of harmful or malicious content, flag inappropriate use or destinations, violations of data policy, indicators of uncharacteristic behavior by employees, or criminally suspect activities. They look for the carriage or presence of content that is deemed sensitive, confidential, or in some way generally restricted from unauthorized egress. They act to log, prevent, require authorization, or limit the performance of actions or access to specific data or websites.

In most of Europe, and increasingly many other locations around the globe, the protection of personal information is considered or is emerging in law as a fundamental right. This often and typically extends to the workplace where the thoughts, intentions, movement, affiliations, and behavior of the individual is protected under both privacy and labor laws broadly, and specifically under local and jurisdictional codes by country. This often raises questions as to the legitimacy of the use of technologies and monitoring practices that may be considered intrusive.

There is a concern for the violation of fundamental privacy through behavioral monitoring, tracking of access, and the inspection of content. Automated assessment and interpretation of individual intent, exposure of interests and affiliations, individually targeted measurement of performance, and monitoring of individual behavior, may impinge upon fundamental rights to privacy. This impingement on privacy is particularly problematic where such intrusion or monitoring has implications, such as restrictions or impact on compensation or promotion, sanctions, negative reviews, or dismissal. This is particularly the case where adequate notice of the monitoring practice has not been given. Still some laws tolerate these intrusions to personal privacy in the workplace to varying degrees where security and protection from fraud is concerned.

Considerations of privacy across the European Union and much of greater Europe and the U.K., dictate that all individuals should be informed of actions that impinge upon or limit rights of privacy. Adequate and proper notification must be provided to the individual of intentions, goals, ramifications, and purpose. When privacy is encroached, even with legal basis, it requires that the purpose be legitimate, and that any infringement with respect to the rights of the individual be minimal and proportionate to the achievement of the 'stated and legitimate purpose' for which the action is being considered. Unless informed, legitimate in purpose and application, and proportional to the need, implementation of security measures may be considered intrusive, and be considered abusive of individual privacy, and disallowed, or considered illegal.

Privacy and security often are in conflict, and naturally so, as one imposes limits, the other assures freedoms. As stated earlier, one can have security without privacy, but cannot have privacy without security. It is a challenge to the CISO operating multi-nationally to understand which is allowed as a safeguard, and that which is not, often a very local mandate, and with what imposed limitations or restrictions on use. In general, best guidance is to work closely with local attorneys, security, and privacy specialists.

I should add that even when deploying specific safeguards within the domestic United States we need to be cognizant of what these technologies do and how they operate. There are some prosecutors that have suggested for instance, that a case can be made for violation of the U.S. Wiretap Act by technologies including DLP (Data Loss Prevention) systems that scan, interpret, and identify data moving across the network, if implemented in some states without proper notifications, advisement of policy, and consent. A 'reasonableness' argument would say that of course there would be an operational exception. I do not know if ever such a case has been brought to the courts although I have not researched this extensively. At first thought, if automated scanning were not seen as different than wire-tap monitoring, I would assume that not only data loss prevention monitoring for specific terms and triggering content, but anti-virus systems that scan personal email content for the vectors of embedded code and code signatures as the message traverses the network would potentially also be in violation if tracking source as well as payload. Anti-virus software has been around for at least 40 years. I am certain that this would have been an issue challenged and addressed long before now. At any rate, again, I am not an attorney, and if for no other purposes than an interesting conversation for breaking the ice, and to establishing a relationship with your internal General Counsel, you can raise this with yours.

Risks to data privacy are present throughout the lifecycle of any data processing relationship. Technology is often complex, and complexity exacerbates risk. And the more complex the relationship, the greater the risk to individual rights and privacy. Risks are present from time of collection, processing, distribution, transfer, dissemination, or use of an individual's data. They are present in any imbalance of power and authority. They are introduced through improper use, abuse, insufficient care, or interference in the rights and freedoms of an individual by any other.

*Many security tools for monitoring, tracking, and deep traffic inspection including the use of CCTV cameras for workspace surveillance, biometric authentication, business processes that employ automated decision making, background checks and other investigative procedures, depending on the law, may be disallowed, require alteration, require specific approvals of authorities, require assessments to justify, or in some cases may simply be illegal*

**Individuating data**

That which is defined as personal data globally varies, and may change with adoption of new law, reinterpretation of existing law, reevaluation of potential harm from an exposure, or a reduction in the effectiveness of defenses typically a result of new threats that render prior protection insufficient.

A business is expected to secure confidential data. Certainly, data that is considered personal. Not all data a business collects is personal, and not all is secured in the same way, for the same reasons, and not always to the same degree. And data that is sensitive and personal is not always obvious.

When we as individuals visit a website, or use a web service, although we likely give it little thought, we often expect anonymity. We assume that providing a website with a login ID or screen name is safe enough. It would be sufficient to individuate us for interaction with the site, but still conceal our identity. We also do not get overly concerned if an IP address, machine ID, or similar data, is acquired by the website through cookies or other technical means making it more convenient for us to traverse the site or follow its links elsewhere.

Some businesses might think they are providing convenience by collecting and retaining screen names and IP addresses for recognition and improved service. Increasingly this is being questioned at least when combined with other individuating data, and these unique IDs are classed as personal data.

In a blog entitled '*Is IP address still considered non-personally identifiable information in US?*' Cliff Gilley, JD, challenged the likelihood of IP addresses being considered PII. IP addresses are often 'dynamically assigned (DHCP), weakly determinate of a source location, and publicly accessible'. Also, in his opinion, they provide insufficient specificity to 'tie an individual to an infringing activity for a preponderance of evidence' as required to meet most legal standards.

That opinion is not globally accepted. According to Mark Vincent and Brett Winterford, as defined under Australian Privacy act, PII is information or an opinion about an identified individual — or about an individual who is reasonably identifiable from the data. If data can be matched with other easily obtained data to establish an ID as is the case for a car license, an IP address or MAC ID, it would be considered PII. http://www.mondaq.com/australia/x/291476/Data+Protection+Privacy/Is+your+IP+Address+Personal+Information

And in the European Union under the GDPR (General data Protection Regulation), the ECJ (European Court of Justice) and numerous GDPR experts have reached a similar conclusion. A screen name, IP address, or similar data provided to a collector or acquired by technical means is personal data. The court concluded that an individual or data subject need not be identified by name if that individual's identity potentially can and likely would be discovered if:

- There is a relation to other data already collected that can be made
- Related data is likely to become available to the collector
- There is a likelihood of discovery from other sources given reasonable intentional effort

As a frequently used example, a website operator might contact the ISP from which the connection originated to make the association of who or what company owns the specific address.

https://www.whitecase.com/publications/alert/court-confirms-ip-addresses-are-personal-data-some-cases

Each of these require a *reasonable intentional effort*, but not a disproportionate effort, and so, an IP address would according to the ECJ be considered personal data. This will certainly be true under IPv6 where a specific machine address (MAC ID) is concatenated to an IP address, the MAC ID designating a specific machine typically used by one to few individuals. Given that, it is important to recognize that seemingly anonymous data may still be considered personal data, and the improper collection and handling by a collector (data controller or processor), can still fall afoul of the law.

## Encrypted data

There are also several categories of data that would not likely be considered individuating under the GDPR. Per a recent decision by the ECJ (European Court of Justice), data that could link to an individual, may not be considered personal data if:

- It is 'illegal to obtain'
- It would require a 'disproportionate effort or expense to obtain'
- If 'current technology would render the effort needed extraordinary'

Under the GDPR, encrypted data would be exempted. This is because a *disproportionate effort* would be required to unencrypt that data and relate it to an individual. However, technology moves at a fast pace, and this exemption only remains true until a viable means is developed to break the encryption or any other similar protection. This however forces an obligation for continual reevaluation of technology, and the law, a point raised by Giulio Coraggio. If data formerly illegal to obtain was subsequently made legal, or barriers to individuating data requiring a disproportionate effort in relating data to an individual removed, exempted data would again be considered personal data protected under the GDPR.

http://www.gamingtechlaw.com/2016/10/best-personal-data-privacy-regulation.html?utm_content=buffer0d57f&utm_medium=social&utm_source=twitter.com&utm_campaign=buffer

For the most part U.S. law has not considered encrypted personal data as PII. It has been common practice to consider encrypted data protected, or at least less exposed, even if lost or stolen. This is changing. Even now if breached, liability would likely be considered in context of other care and protective practices, a demonstration of measures, norms of competence, or at a minimum a plan or progress in that direction.

Operationally, that which can be encrypted, can be decrypted, if one has access to the decryption key legitimately, or can gain access through subterfuge, social engineering, improper care by data owners, recipients, or administrators, or the use of malware. Encryption as a means of protecting PII from exposure is only as useful as the current state of effectiveness for that mode of encryption permits it to be, and time, and context. The longer data remains in the hands of those with bad intent and the resources to invest, encrypted or not, the greater the exposure to the data they hold. And in absence of sound overall protective practices to resist breach, encrypted data may not in itself be considered sufficient to meet standards of care as defined under emerging regulations, whether here or elsewhere. Laws and standards differ globally and change over time. No truth is ever lasting. Encryption is an important piece of a protective strategy, but one piece, which along with other tools, means, and processes for breach mitigation, comprise a strategy, not a statement of sufficiency. It is also not a guarantee that if compromised it is in fact or will be considered adequately protective when evaluated for due care in court, by regulators, or for purposes of insurance.

Sovereign policy in confronting terror is also at issue. The EU is clearly averse to the inclusion of 'backdoors' to bypass encryption, protecting privacy and security. This contrasts with some governments and bodies of law enforcement, and perhaps is at odds with some of its principal members. The UK is pressing for provisions to provide counter-terror investigators access to encrypted data to facilitate investigation for security. France maintains the right to hack pre-encrypted data on suspect systems. In the United States, we have confronted this several times, primarily for mobile devices, but have not defined clear policy. As we continue to confront terror, this discussion continues.    https://euobserver.com/justice/138223

Security risk and privacy risk, or more specifically in a global context, data protection risk, are not the same. The controls for each, though often complimentary differ, and differ in respect to their concerns in protecting personal data. The emphasis on protecting privacy and data using security controls focuses on encryption and other access controls including multi factor authentication, and breach mitigation, through detection, technical defenses, and preventing data exfiltration. Privacy specific controls in a global context often focus on an informed data subject through notice, transparency, and options for choice, allowing specificity of, and minimizing the data permitted for processing, modifying data to assure accuracy, or requiring its deletion. It includes the ability to opt in, often at a very granular level, opt out, and to proceed with anonymity. In Privacy by Design (PbD), system developers should consider both notice and choice, but also when unneeded, avoid the collection of personal data. When personal data or other unique identifiers must be collected, they should avoid its persistence beyond the session during which it is used, or the communication and linkage with other systems or processes where it might be captured and retained. Privacy introduces new risk concerns including distortion, misuse, mischaracterization, impact on decision processes, exclusion from opportunities, leverage, fraud, intimidation, and more as suggested in part in the excellent IAPP Whitepaper 'Check or Mate? Strategic Privacy by Design', by R. Jason Cronk. I have opted to include this prior paragraph in discussing privacy globally and generically, rather than in a specific discussion of GDPR, despite it being GDPR centric in tone. GDPR is a model on which emerging law will be based. It is also the model to which existing law will aspire and evolve.

Earlier in this book, I devoted a chapter to the uncloaking of the CIA Triad, Confidentiality, Integrity, and Availability. The underlying CIA framework is very appropriate to questions of technology, infrastructure protection, physical security, operational performance, and business continuity. That said, although security and privacy risks differ, CIA is equally appropriate when examining privacy and the protection of personal data. In fact, I would posit that a company cannot effectively meet the requirements of the GDPR or similar regulation without an adequate reflection of CIA principles in their implementation. Not just for technology, but for process as well. This is particularly so when examined more granularly, drilling down into the often-neglected component controls that I view as comprising CIA. As an example, to say that a system is 'available' to use is less meaningful then to demonstrate that a system is not only available because it is present, but also because it is functioning fully and properly, and has been determined and vetted adequate for the need, and therefore, satisfying these three granular component controls, is 'available' to use.

### The Self-Service Data Subject Portal as an example

Let me give an example, Satisfying the GDPR requires an individual to be an informed participant, given choices, or at the very least awareness, as to the data held about them. A prudent and forward-thinking business might elect to provide the subject with a self-service portal. They would make access to that portal a feature of compliance and of good customer service. They would promote it as a customer focused service that is always available for the individual to access and use.

Ideally, this portal would enable subjects to see what data is held and affirm that it is correct and current. It informs them of the purpose for holding and duration of the need of that data, and the basis on which it is held, and whether their authorization is required.

For data requiring consent it would enable consent to be provided or to revoke any given prior. It allows each subject to make choices as to what should be changed, updated, or erased. It would allow specified data to be downloaded in a format that can be readily ported for use in other applications or brought to another service as the subject prefers. It would provide guidance as to subject rights allowing informed decisions. This portal would provide instant subject access to the data held about them, a benefit to the subject, a competitive differentiator to the company holding the data, and an effective means of satisfying the law. The use and purpose of the system would be easily demonstrated to auditors.

In many public, legal, transactional, or contractual relationships processing may be necessary and may not require authorization, or further authorization once an agreement is in place. Under the GDPR it is considered reasonable and legal for a business, utility, or public entity to process data without requiring additional or ongoing consent in specific cases. It may be for the performance of a contract. It may be to meet the legitimate business interests of the data controller where that collection, processing and retention is not data subject averse in supporting the legitimate interests of the business. It may be performed in the public interest, in the interest of the data subject, as an obligation under the law, or performed for other reasons, quite specific, and none requiring consent. That said, even where consent is not required, or a choice is not available, or is available only at specific times as in the renewal of a contract, notice of the basis for collection informs the data subject, and permits them the opportunity to assure they are being treated fairly and afforded their rights under the law for that basis of data collection. A prudent and progressive company seizes the opportunity to engage and empower their customer. Tools for self-management of personal data, awareness, and informed choice are good client service, and competitive. As said above, the prudent and forward-thinking company empowers their customers, building consumer trust, and doing so derives the benefit of the relationship with the consumer, an offload of manual effort through automation and self-service, and adheres to the requirements of the law. That is an effective strategy, but only so where the implementation of that strategy is effective. Any strategy is only as effective as the controls which assure it.

GDPR and similar laws typically require timely access to data held about a subject. This portal application provides instant access, and so would more than meet that requirement, if it is available. But being available as a service requires that all the components required for its operation are 'available'. These include not only the portal application and the technologies that host it, and the telecom needed to reach it, but the features that meet its purpose and provide the ease of use that makes for a satisfying user experience. It would include a means to provide appropriate notice to data subjects of the existence of the portal and education in its use. It would require trained customer support available when additional help is needed. It would require the marketing and promotion needed to make it an effective service ongoing. And each of these components needs to be more than just present. They must function as required, offer an intuitive and pleasing interface, and provide the full range of capabilities the subject is likely to require, accepting subject feedback for continual improvement, while keeping pace with changing regulatory, technical, and operational requirements. They must perform adequately to be effective as a means of addressing the access and data management needs of the subjects that use it, be responsive, and capable of scale to meet the volume and demands on the system, and the data subject requirements for access to it.

And the system in entirety must be designed to be secure, and if breached, it should be detectable and traceable so that damage can be limited, reporting obligations can be met, and corrections made. Where it involves external 'processors' there must be an effective means of communication and a coordinated response governed under agreements defining roles, responsibilities, and obligations in accordance with 'controller' policy and the law. These would be supported by effective capabilities for rapid detection, diagnostics, and response. And if notice is required to the community of data subjects that may be impacted by a breach, the capacity to scale sufficiently to meet those obligations, handle calls and emails from concerned subjects, coordinate with counsel, provide reporting, and update to supervisory authorities, and appropriately respond, all must be in place.

To satisfy the CIA of a system requires more than the examination of component technologies, processes, partners, agreements, or controls. It requires examination of them as a functioning system, all parts meeting the needs of the data subject and satisfying their rights under the law. Examining the 'availability' of a system looks at all parts. Whether the server hosting the portal is powered on and will load the application and run (presence), provide the services and processes needed within the portal application as expected (functionality), and perform with sufficient speed to be usable (adequacy). If not, is there a standby server (direct security control) that recognizes the failure by continuously monitoring and activating automatically, or another means to rapidly restore operation in failure? These would include data backups, hardware spares, contracts for repair services (compensating controls) or similar. And is there a means to test the operational integrity of this system end to end? A program of inspection, monitoring and ongoing validation? The same questions can also be asked of the application allowing the subject access to their personal data. Does it provide needed functionality? Is it adequate to provide access with sufficient performance and scale to be of use? And are there security mechanisms in place to assure each of these requirements, are they adequately tested, and then monitored ongoing to assure that the qualifications that defined the system as acceptable and in compliance when implemented, still do as the laws, environment, needs, usage, and context in which the system operates changes over time?

Let me close this section with a few words on GDPR which I will expand upon in the chapter following. GDPR is good law in its intentions. It is about protecting the rights of the individual from powers greater and preventing the loss of control of an individual's data through rampant data leakage, sharing and abuses. Although there is considerable angst over the potential penalties for non-adherence, not all businesses have the same risk under GDPR, and the preparation and where focus is placed will be different.

A company in the B2B space, without a direct-to-consumer involvement, and no interactions with individuals, either directly or through their information only websites, clearly has a smaller risk footprint than does a B2C business with direct consumer exposure, collecting information about data subjects through a subject aware web presence, serving targeted advertisements based on interests and demographics, and certainly if sharing individuating data with data brokers and others. And any business without an informed and consenting subject relationship that feeds itself off the valid relationship of another business to its consumer, increases the risk to both. Of course, any business that has EU resident employees has risk, and needs to assure that the employee's interests are protected under the law. But planning for the GDPR will be different for each, as is the risk we need to mitigate in seeking conformance. Our benchmark is not each other, our competitors, or our industries. The only meaningful benchmark is how we look today in comparison to our readiness posture yesterday and in days prior.

Global privacy and data protection can be complex and often the laws of more than one sovereign entity can apply. For many operating in healthcare or as healthcare business associates serving US citizens resident in Europe, or for EU based associates of US businesses, agencies, or institutions in scope for HIPAA, both GDPR data protection laws, and US HIPAA requirements for protected health information likely apply. These may interpret risk and the assignment of risk, define individuating data, records and data care, applicability of encryption and protective measures, and what constitutes reportable breach differently, and the requirements of both will need to be met. For some in the finance and banking sector based or operating in the EU and in-scope for GDPR but doing business with New York banks and other financial institutions, New York Stated Department of Financial Services cyber regulations may be applicable imposing obligations for operational process, forensics, and reporting.

*Safe harbor method of de-identifying HIPAA compliant data* requires removal or rendering the following data unusable, unreadable, or indecipherable to unauthorized persons:

- Names
- Geographic subdivisions smaller than a state
- All elements of dates (except year) related to an individual (including admission and discharge dates, birthdate, date of death, all ages over 89 years old, and elements of dates (including year) that are indicative of age)
- Telephone, cellphone, and fax numbers
- Email addresses
- IP addresses
- Social Security numbers
- Medical record numbers
- Health plan beneficiary numbers
- Device identifiers and serial numbers
- Certificate/license numbers
- Account numbers
- Vehicle identifiers and serial numbers including license plates
- Website URLs
- Full face photos and comparable images
- Biometric identifiers (including finger and voice prints)
- Any unique identifying numbers, characteristics, or codes
- First three numbers of any zip code where the population is less than 20,000 must be set to zeroes using only the last two digits as identifiers or the last three of five numbers in the zip code can be used. https://www.hhs.gov/hipaa/for-professionals/privacy/special-topics/de-identification/index.html#standard

Figure 10 Safe Harbor HIPAA De-Identification

*With time and experience, algorithms refine, and data density increases.*

*That which is considered personal today and that which is regulated by law*

*to protect our fleeting privacy tomorrow undoubtedly will differ*

## Vulnerable communities

In the United States, federated privacy and labor laws protect our citizens from exposure, abuse, and exploitation. Compliance with state privacy statutes, and federal law including COPPA, FERPA, ADA, HIPAA's Privacy Rule, and similar regulations, provide protection of vulnerable communities from exposure of personal, health, and financial information, as well as unapproved disclosure of affinity and affiliation (military, education, religious, sexual, political, criminal, and organizational) data. In Europe and elsewhere overseas these affinity and affiliation categories are often considered particularly sensitive requiring explicit controls and even greater attention often than do financial or transactional data, account numbers, bank routing numbers, or personal ID.

## Law enforcement and transparency

There is a bill before the New York City Council to increase transparency as to the tools and means for surveillance and monitoring in use by New York City police for public safety. Developed by a privacy focused group, this bill has been presented for consideration to several major cities across the United States. One aspect of this bill is a concern for data captured for the purposes of public safety, and how it is stored and protected. It is hard to contest the value of that. We all want to know that if our information, our likeness, our whereabouts, or our activities are captured for the benefit of the public good, that our data is adequately protected. According to John Miller, Deputy Commissioner of Intelligence and Counterterrorism for the New York Police Department, the bill also asks for exposure of the means and methods by which the police acquire data be exposed for transparency. The bill not only advocates disclosure of the data that is captured, but purportedly why it is captured, from where, when, and how it is used. Understandably, and importantly, it seeks transparency and proportionality in policing. We touch a fine line. If our means of surveillance are exposed, criminals, organized crime and terrorists are at advantage. If they know our defenses, they can avoid them. This is an important discussion and will be repeated from state to state, in municipalities across the country, and without doubt across all western democracies striving to protect open society. How much security do we relinquish for transparency, and what cost do we accept in loss of security and safety to enhance our privacy? Even the courts are wrestling with outdated laws given the pervasiveness of digital data available to law enforcement. I read the New York Times article 'Justices Seem Ready to Boost Protection of Digital Privacy' by Adam Liptak, November 29, 2017, and recommend it. I said it before. Security and privacy are in a tug of war.

*Encryption is an important piece of a protective strategy, but one piece, which along with other tools, means, and processes for mitigating breach impact, comprise a strategy, not a statement of sufficiency*

## Even at home

We leave a digital trail from the time we wake, and increasingly before, in digital media, social communities, email, messaging and phone. It is inescapable. We take photos revealing presence, context, time, and place. We carry addressable and locatable smart phones, watches, and increasingly other wearable technology that monitors movement, behavioral and biological activities. Some of these wearables record patterns and intensity of activity, awake and not.

*The myth of privacy aside, so much about us, correct and not, real, and fabricated, accumulates, and has a perpetual digital life, stored, repeated, misinterpreted, and translated, obscured in plain sight by sheer volume to all but the most persistent, but there for all to see*

We are recorded and tracked when we leave for work, school, or fun, and as we go about our day, and our night. Our image is captured on cameras, our presence recorded at tolls, our spending patterns are tracked. We pass through turnstiles, gain access to floors using ID badges or biometrics, sign on to networks, order products online, use our credit cards, and give our names just to buy coffee. Where we are picked up and dropped off, our behavior, and the areas we go are recorded by the car services we use to travel. We are 'rated' and 'scored' as consumers with sometimes impactful consequence.

A new camera and several apps have recently been released that help make decisions as to which outfits you choose that will look best. Innocuous enough, they will take pictures or videos when you request, and these will be uploaded to the cloud, analyzed, and an opinion offered as to the outfit most flattering. Harmless. Everyone will love it. But what of the other images captured in the photo submitted, the stuff in the background. The magazines for expecting mothers on the dresser, the pill bottle, the airline tickets, and travel brochures. Would this be considered an acceptable use or a violation of trust if captured, analyzed, and used for targeted ads and promotional calls?

Even in the privacy of our homes, when we pour a drink and sit down to watch television and talk to our families, our Smart Televisions may be listening and profiling us for services.

The sensitivity and intimacy of intrusions will only increase. Privacy is important.

*Codified law, courts, cases, cultures, and time decide what comprises personal data, its sensitivity, how it can be used and shared, and too, what constitutes a disclosure violation, and its ramifications under a given body of law.*

# CISO
# REDEFINED

*Protecting Business*

Martin Gomberg, CISSP, CIPP/E

## SECTION 12. GDPR – EU GENERAL DATA PROTECTION REGULATION

Privacy in Europe is viewed as a fundamental and inherent right. The GDPR is as much an expression of that philosophy as it is a body of law. It is a pervasive philosophy that starts with privacy and the control of personal information as a right, how it is expressed, how it is claimed, and how it is protected. It understands the need for business to succeed but obligates it to do so while protecting the rights and freedoms of the individual, designing the protection of the individual into the fabric of how business is done. It addresses the role of government in protection of the individual. It assures that adequate protection and redress for grievances is provided by other nations as a condition of open data exchange. It assures that the individual is protected from abuses of personal data and intrusions on privacy from even the largest of data acquirers and repositories, government, health systems, utilities, telecom providers, direct and mass marketers, and without doubt commercial digital communities and social spaces, and this applies globally. It assures that intrusive technology and digital communications do not undermine or outpace rights to privacy.

Doing business in the EU, whether employing, targeting, monitoring, or marketing to EU residents, requires understanding and preparation for the GDPR, the General Data Protection Regulation. As of May 25th, 2018, GDPR became enforceable EU law across the European Union, and applies to all those in-scope under the law, wherever they may be.

Companies have been actively assessing what needs to be done and preparing since the GDPR was approved in 2016, but for many companies, preparations remain incomplete. The GDPR (EU 2016/679) 'General Data Protection Regulation' replaces the EU Privacy Directive (95/46/EC), embodying much of the concepts and requirements that have established a culture of personal data protection these past 20 years. The GDPR in many ways codifies and builds upon existing practice, establishing law while recognizing new business strategies, technology, public safety concerns, and global relationships. The Directive which preceded the GDPR was not law, but a standard, locally interpreted and embedded in the privacy laws of each member State. This resulted in differences in implementation, tone, and execution, and often a lack of clarity as to allowable technology and practices, a difficulty when operating in multiple countries. GDPR is binding on all members of the EU, homogenizing, and reducing the variance in enacted in-country data protection regulation but allowing for enhancement and derogations by individual states.

The GDPR is a significant body of data protection law. It applies to personal data collected, where, why, with what authority, and how cared for and maintained. How long data is kept and the reasons, legitimacy, and legality of doing so. It applies to governments, municipalities, agencies, and utilities; EU resident and foreign business enterprises; business partnerships, affiliates, small businesses, and specifically, how each relates to the individual (described under GDPR as the data subject) and their personal data rights.

There are some aspects of the GDPR that will dictate evaluations that you will need to perform, first of which is whether the GDPR applies to your business or not. It will direct decisions that you will make, guidance and education that you will need to provide or impart to executives, employees, and operating business units. It will influence ongoing strategies for applications and processes that interface with and collect data from residents of the EU while seeking, developing, promoting, or doing business.

If it is determined that you should comply with the GDPR, you will need to know the communities you serve, your employees, customers, partners, and prospects and how you relate to each. You will need to know your role in managing their data. You will need to examine your business workflows, processes, systems, portals, and applications, finding all means and locations where personal data is solicited, captured, processed, or stored. You will need to ensure that these are required, limited, lawful, and properly implemented. You will need to understand the rights of individuals, and how these 'data subjects' are monitored, targeted, and solicited. You will need to ensure that relationships are established and serviced in a means that is fair, protective, and transparent, and demonstrate proper care of data once captured.

You will need to consider the data held about the data subject. It is important to relate all data captured about or provided by that subject in both current and prior relationships, assuring traceability, portability, and eradicability. If you do not know what data you hold about an individual, or cannot locate it with reasonable effort, you cannot respect the rights of the individual to access and control the use of their data, and you cannot comply with the law. This will prove a challenge for many companies. As I have said elsewhere, most of the systems we use have not been built to accommodate this. That said, under the GDPR, the right of the individual to assure data held is current, complete, and correct, and at their discretion can be modified, erased, or returned in a usable electronic format for portability requires ready access and availability of the data we hold about them. We can minimize exposure through hygiene, discarding what we do not need or should not have. We limit data risk by collecting data we need, not everything we want.

GDPR with minimal exception requires the ability to demonstrate compliance through documentation. A register (process inventory) of all activities that involve the processing of EU subject data should be maintained, a list of the processes, purpose of processing, type of data, degree of risk, and implemented controls. It will be necessary to determine which processes infer the greatest risk to the rights of individuals and prioritize these for examination and needed corrections. Where significant exposures are suggested, you may need to perform data protection impact studies, make corrections where deficiencies are identified, verify that risks have been addressed, and document actions. You will also need to examine the partnerships that you have in place with other companies as service providers, or more specifically 'processors', and whether the data you share and the activities they perform are controlled for GDPR risk.

# Does the GDPR apply to your business?

### GDPR applies if:

- Your company is based in or has facilities in EU
- Your company has employees in the EU
- Your company solicits, markets, or provides goods or services to EU residents
- Your company monitors behavior or tracks the activity of EU residents while in the EU
- Your company processes EU personal data on behalf of another company wherever located
- A company engages EU residents or processes their data on your behalf
- A company monitors the performance or tracks the behavior of EU residents on your behalf (polls, profiles, use of tracking cookies or beacons)
- You service EU based retirees, ex-pat employees, research associates, contractors, consultants
- In an inextricable undertaking between one or more companies processing data of EU residents

## Less obvious, GDPR and other protections will likely still apply if:

- Your company is not based in the EU, but any of the above listed conditions is true
- Your company routinely collects data or monitors behavior of EU resident individuals (data subjects) or those of other countries in the European Economic Area that visit your website
- Your company purchases data or utilizes the facilities of another company or partner to collect data about individuals from varied locations globally that may include the EU
- You do business with the outermost regions and collectivities of EU countries
- Are an Int'l org with privilege and immunities (remedies to grievances may still be sought in court)
- EU data collected for statistical purposes is inadequately de-identified to protect data subjects
- EU data archived for journalistic purpose is injurious, and incorrect, out of date or irrelevant
- You process the data of self-promoted celebrities and public personas from EU
- Your household business periodically processes sensitive EU data or data in high volume
- You maintain a stable facility, full or part time, or a local phone number or PO Box in the EU

## GDPR likely does not apply if:

- A non-EU company providing services to non-EU residents or an EU national not resident in EU
- You collect limited, low sensitivity data infrequently for use by a household business
- You collect personal data for personal household use only (maintain lists to send out holiday cards, send meeting announcements and group invitations to social club members)
- You collect or process data for the purposes of law enforcement or national security (other specific laws apply)

*Figure 11 Does GDPR Apply to Your Business?*

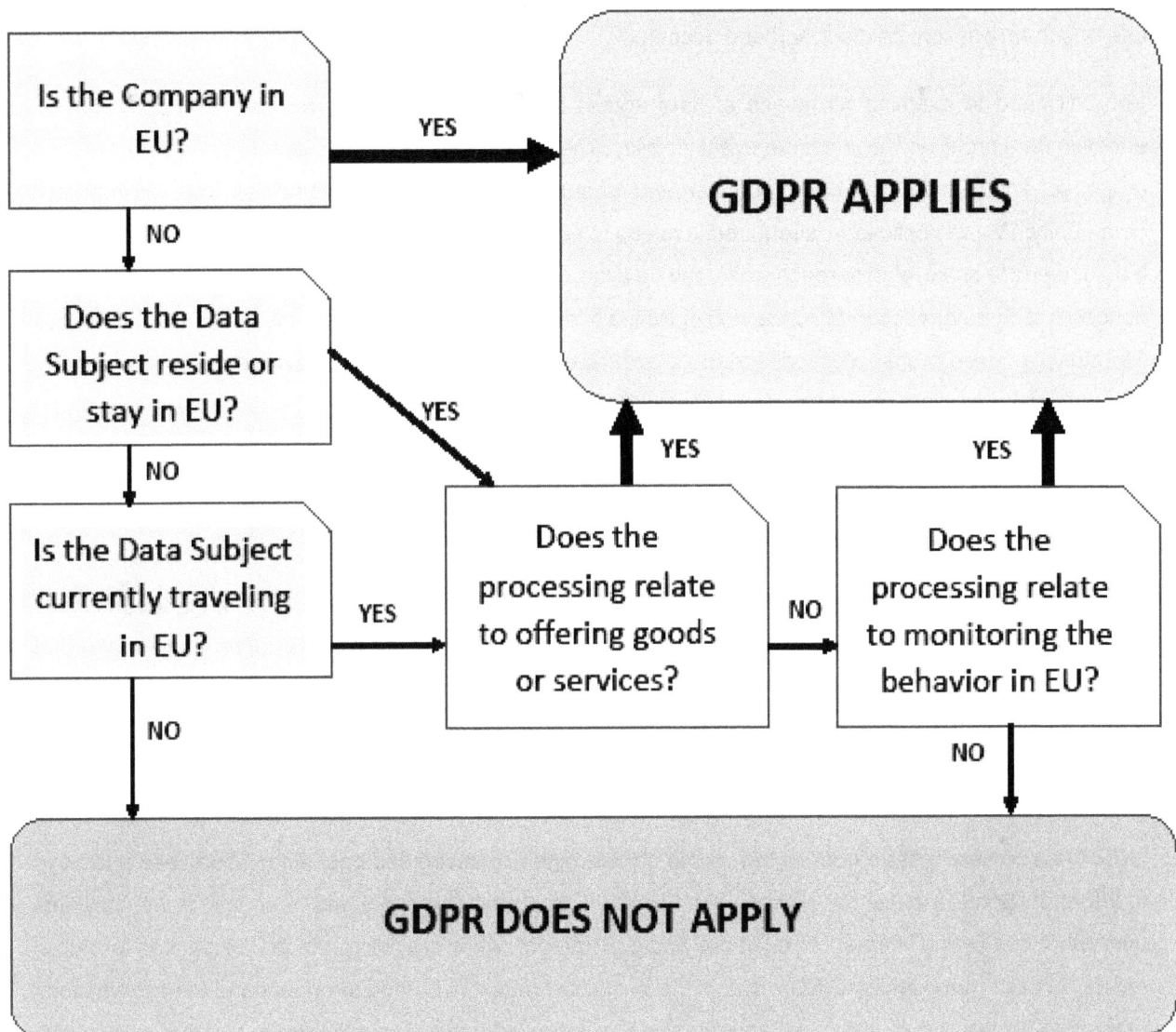

**Is the Company in EU?** → YES → **GDPR APPLIES**

NO ↓

**Does the Data Subject reside or stay in EU?** → YES → (toward GDPR APPLIES)

NO ↓

**Is the Data Subject currently traveling in EU?** → YES → **Does the processing relate to offering goods or services?**

NO ↓

**Does the processing relate to offering goods or services?** → YES (↑ to GDPR APPLIES) → NO → **Does the processing relate to monitoring the behavior in EU?** → YES (↑ to GDPR APPLIES)

NO ↓

**GDPR DOES NOT APPLY**

---

**Territorial Scope of the GDPR Flowchart**

*Published under Creative Commons CC BY-SA 4.0 license*

Siarhei Varankevich

*Figure 12 Territorial Scope of the GDPR Flowchart*

Processors of personal data working on your behalf will be bound to process only as you dictate in signed contract. This is the case even if these partners do not directly deal with Europe or European clients, but simply process on your behalf. Sub-processors they engage will similarly be bound, as will theirs, and the use of sub-processors be disclosed and accepted.

You will need to examine all means of data egress and provide adequate resistance to compromise, effective data protection, and assure event visibility. The latter is needed both to assure rapid detection and response, and to meet notification requirements to supervisory authorities, and if required, an impacted community. Where notification is required, it needs to be timely to meet reporting obligations under the law. It also needs to scale, able to reach what may be a large, impacted community, and manage the questions, concerns, and irate reaction of concerned individuals, as well as partners, press, investors, and authorities for multiple jurisdictions. You will need to examine all means by which personal data is shared, communicated and where it is transferred or forwarded to assure that exchange of data is permitted under the law. Appointment of a DPO or Data Protection Officer may be required.

Stewart Room, Global Head of Cyber Security and Data Protection Legal Services and UK Data Protection Practice Lead at PwC cautioned that 'many companies lack a clear plan for adoption of the obligations under the GDPR. They also lack understanding of the risks they will undertake or accept in the process'. He stresses that 'it is important to consider vision, strategy and structure and the targeted end state that would be considered success. He also advises avoidance of compliance focused efforts without a clear understanding of why these are being pursued.
http://www.computerweekly.com/news/450417764/Many-companies-lack-GDPR-plan-PwC-data-shows

GDPR is a comprehensive body of law, some articles highly nuanced and best left to courts and attorneys to interpret. Some aspects are patently clear in intent, to protect the rights and freedoms of the individual over other competing interests of business and government, while providing needed exceptions for public safety. For our purposes as CISOs, and in the business context, we need to understand the expectations of the GDPR, the culture it defines, and our role and expected behaviors in the context of that culture. We also need to understand the changes that need to be made to conform to the law, and then operate within it, for competitiveness, EU market access, and avoidance of penalties.

GDPR is an omnibus law, applicable across the EU with little to no difference in implementation, but with provisions for local enhancement or derogations. This differs from the federated design employed in the U.S. allowing each state self-determination in the privacy laws they develop and how they are applied, with few alike. That which we call Privacy or Breach Reporting Law in the US falls under the broader heading of Data Protection Law in the EU and EEA. In Europe it is less about protecting specific sensitive data elements and combinations of private data from exposure, and more about context. It is about maintaining a culture of privacy, rights and freedoms, and respect for the concerns of the individual. This applies particularly in the context of individuating physical, social, mental, economic, or other identifying characteristics, affinities, affiliations, and behaviors.

*Figure 13 Developing a Data Protection Program*

| GOALS | DEVELOPING A GDPR OR SIMILAR DATA PROTECTION PROGRAM |
|---|---|
| **EVALUATE** | **Assess the business**<br>• understand the business and its data needs, plans and strategies for growth, new markets, globalization<br>• know your clients, employees, territorial footprint - current and planned, physical, affiliate, and virtual<br>• entities that comprise your business, what they do, where, who they employ; your role: controller, processor<br>• define goals; risk level and basis; determine if a DPO or other Data Protection specialist may be required<br>• nature and volume of data collected and used, its sensitivity, movement, and risk<br>• reason for collection and use of data (statistical; goods, services, monitoring) how acquired; shared; transfers<br>• know the laws; rights of data subjects you employ, solicit, or serve, directly or through partners<br>• determine if the law is applicable and why |
| **ADVOCATE** | **Build awareness - explain the purpose - develop the message – secure the budget**<br>• executive awareness and ownership – oversight, accountability, tone from the top<br>• assure business partner awareness, attestation to strategies, efforts, progress, and status |
| **EDUCATE** | **Educate key participants; stake holders; partners**<br>• educate, motivate, and inform employees / data subjects / B2B Partners (clients and processors)<br>• train designers, developers, testers, assessors, community |
| **PLAN** | **Consider timeframes and set reasonable expectations and goals**<br>• develop a prioritized plan based on risk aligned objectives<br>• Select tools; methodologies; specialist partners, legal advisors, consultants<br>• determine needed resources and identify business SMEs (subject matter experts)<br>• build teams; train the trainers; oversee, evaluate, and document the progress and success of training programs |
| **IMPLEMENT** | **Do the research; engage experts**<br>• identify the data subject communities you serve, who they are, where they are, how you interact<br>• inventory personal and sensitive data, what you have, where, why, if you need it, and how it is protected<br>**Assess readiness and find gaps**<br>• assess legitimate basis for activities; adequacy and appropriateness of consent (opt/in, opt/out)<br>• assess marketing, tracking and communications practices to assure they are proper (B2B / B2C)<br>• assess data use and care disclosures and policies (privacy, TOS, cookies) for form, content, and adequacy<br>• assess data collection limitations, retention practices and protection effectiveness<br>• examine security, organizational readiness, and conformance to protective standards<br>• analyze processing / processes / what data moves, how, and the processes it moves between<br>• assess processing partners / contracts / required EU representative presence<br>• assess mechanisms for transfer and EU / International operation, data protection adequacy, safeguards<br>**Perform remediation – conformance must not only be attained, but engrained and sustained**<br>• assure practices promote transparency, minimization, proportionality, disclosure, choice<br>• assure data subject rights are protected – subjects, children, vulnerable populations<br>• assure processes, applications, workflows adhere to law, policies, and principles<br>• evaluate, correct, or implement systems to enable a 'subject to data' linkage<br>• assure (SAR) subjects access rights for awareness, access, correction, portability, erasure<br>• implement controls to mitigate technical, cyber, operational and privacy risk; a DPIA process<br>• implement technical defenses - encryption, hashing, anonymization and pseudonymization<br>• consent and legitimate processing, processor agreements, legal basis for transfer<br>• implement 'Privacy by Design' in approval, planning, development, and production |
| **OPERATE** | **Document systems, processes, controls, incidents, actions, data flows – build a repeatable compliant process**<br>• Obligatory reporting to authorities; Breach notification to scale; Call handling<br>• Audit, assess, test, tune, detect, correct, map and document for ongoing compliance through change |

In the U.S., data protection concerns are embodied in federal agency regulations, protecting veterans, children, elderly, disabled, and other vulnerable communities, and state breach protection laws. The California Consumer Privacy Act in effect as of January 2020 is the first US state privacy statute to address privacy contextually and comprehensively as in the EU model.

As introduced before, there are new terms that describe the roles and relationships of businesses and agencies to each other, and to individuals, with which you may not be familiar. These are *Data Subject, Data Controller, Data Processor*, and *Personal Data*. There are also derived relations such *as co-controllers* and *sub processors*. There is also a new position defined, that of *Data Protection Officer* or DPO, and a responsibility, the *Data Protection Impact Assessment*.

*Data Controllers* dictate the means and purpose by which *Personal Data* is captured, processed, used, or stored, whether on their own, or partnered with a *Processor* acting on their behalf and under their direction in the performance of services. Personal data is any data related to an identified or identifiable individual, or *Data Subject*. Data Subjects are the natural owners of the personal data related to them. GDPR assures Data Subjects specific rights as to how and if that data is used by others.

In-scope companies, wherever from, are required to have a *formalized presence* in the EU. The same for Post Brexit UK. It may be an affiliate, or even a single employee or representative, under contract. Most EU member states will not require businesses to register with the governing supervisory authorities for data protection. Some will. The UK requires a fee to be paid. Internal oversight, and for many an internal privacy specialist, the DPO (Data Protection Officer) will be responsible to assure the business is executing its obligations to privacy, the protection of Personal Data, and the communities of Data Subjects they serve as clients appropriately under the law. As will be discussed further, a DPO is not mandatory for all companies, need not be an employee, can be an affiliate, consultant, or contract service. Sensitivity and volume of processing dictates whether a DPO is needed, but in some specific industries, or cases, it is required. Where processing performed is overly sensitive or impactful there is a need for a Data Protection Impact Assessment, a comprehensive analysis of risk with documented results and remediation guidance.

**Data Inventory and Identification**

Not all data carries the same level of risk, requires the same degree of protection or controls, or is likely to be governed under the same regulation or mandated obligations for reporting if breached. Where all data to varying degrees is important, not all data is confidential, or consequential, and of that which is, not all data is individuating, or personal, and governed under privacy regulations. A specific application or system may manage varying classes and types of data, domestic and global, some private, some not, and reporting and data management obligations can be in-scope under the mandates of multiple regulations. It falls to each business to identify and also to inventory the data that they hold, know where it is and why they have it, what controls are in place to protect it and to which regulations they must be responsive. The GDPR is a data protection regulation and as such a GDPR data inventory should consider in-scope all classes of data risk that may expose personal data of varying levels of sensitivity.

# Identifying In-Scope Data Under the GDPR

### In Scope Individuating Data

- Personal Data (data that identifies, describes, is associated with, or individuates a person)
- Sensitive Personal Data (and special category data governed under GDPR articles 6 and 9)
- High-Risk Personal Data (defined by the sensitivity, volume, risk, and exposure of personal data)

## In Scope Contextual and Prosopographic Data

- Family and Family Attributions
- Individual Affiliations (church, military, team, union, club membership)
- Individual Affinities (sports, political opinions, philosophies, religious beliefs)
- Self-Definition and Behaviors (gender identity, sexual orientation, sexual activity)
- Identifying Characteristics (appearance, genetics, biometrics, morphology)
- Pseudonymous associations (user_ID, device_ID, IP address, individuating or tracking cookies)
- Referential Keys and Credentials (email address, login ID, screen name, pin, passwords)
- Individuating Technologies (x-rays, machine ID, addressable or serialized body implants)
- Associated Tangible Assets (financials, investments, auto, home)

## Business Consequential Data That Likely Does Not Fall Under GDPR

- Business Confidential Data (not associated with individuals)
- Crown Jewel IP (corporate intellectual property, designs, and operating intelligence)
- Company Financial Data (aggregate, not associated with individuals)
- Corporate Vision and Strategies
- GDPR plans themselves are business data as are involved systems, processes, data elements, reports, and project status, a business risk if exposed, but without associated PII, not a GDPR risk

## Data Typically Rendered Out-Of-Scope Through Law or Protective Controls

- Encrypted Data (with some limitations)
- One-Way Hashed Data
- Anonymized or statistically represented Data
- Pseudonymized Data (with some limitations)
- Some data revealed or processed in the public interest (historic, scientific, journalistic exceptions)
- Data that is exposable only by extraordinary means
- Data exposed or shared for reasons of law enforcement or public safety
- Personal data collected or processed purely for personal or limited household business use

*Figure 13 Identifying In-Scope Data Under the GDPR*

# Assigning Risk to Personal, Regulated and Business Data

## Low to Moderate Risk Data

- Data that is generally shared, publicly available or of limited consequence if disclosed
- Data that is adequately protected (encrypted, hashed, obfuscated) such that disclosure is minimal risk. If loss is due to malicious breach, potential risk increases with time until recovered or resolved, and with the sophistication and intent of the attackers, even if the data is protected.

## High-Risk Data

- Data that is sensitive, impactful, or discriminating in nature (genetics, race, affiliations, orientation)
- Special vulnerable population categories (children, disabled, medical afflictions, criminal records)
- Accounts, keys, and credentials (login ID, passwords, domain memberships, application group)
- Privileged communications (what is considered legally privileged is not the same everywhere)
- Data and disclosures damaging to personal reputation by itself or paired with other data
- Results of impactful automation, prejudicial processing and artificial intelligence in decision making
- Voluminous loss of individuating data (PII) irrespective of sensitivity
- Protected data classes including health (PHI) or financial and credit (PCI) information
- Consequential data that has or can be breached, compromised, disrupted, or lost through inadequacy or insufficiency of controls, lack of compensating controls, vulnerability of the attack surface. This is an issue of high risk for company confidential data, proprietary intellectual property, technical specifications, or trade secrets as well as individuating personal data.

## Very High-Risk Data

- Data which if exposed would be impactful to life, health, property, or the rights and freedom of individuals (high-worth executive travel, critical asset plans, security threat intervention strategies)
- National and military secrets

*Figure 16 Assigning Risk to Business Data*

*The chart above is not specific to GDPR. It applies to overall data risk.*

Not all data falls under the GDPR, only personal data, but all data is at risk and laws vary globally. Data should be secured, managed, or discarded appropriate to its risk. Cleanup of data is good hygiene. It should be done irrespective of the GDPR. The retention cycle for archived data and data backups should be visited and data stored should be deleted in accordance with company policy or law. A documented policy reduces the opportunity that stored personal information lingers longer than it should or persists on media and in places not obvious or is erased for reasons that are unexplainable. GDPR and member state labor, contract, and other civil law, each may have specific requirements for retention or erasure. The legal basis and appropriateness of retaining personal or individuating data should be determined, and if the conditions for holding that data are suspect then the basis for its retention should be reevaluated and addressed, or that data purged. Backups and data archives should be stored and transported, protected, and encrypted reducing the opportunity that compromised storage can expose personal information.

| Profiling Corporate Data Risk | | Classes of Consequential Enterprise Data | | | | | |
|---|---|---|---|---|---|---|---|
| **CHARACTERIZATION OF RISK**<br><br>Figure 14 Profiling Corporate Data Risk | | Personal Data | Company Confidential Data | Crown Jewel Intellectual Property | Privileged Data | Technical Configs and Specs | Keys and Credentials |
| *Very High Risk* | Impactful to life, health, liberty, or property - Individual rights and freedoms | | | | | | |
| *High Risk* | Inadequate controls or vulnerable attack surface | | | | | | |
| *High Risk* | Attractive target (High worth - high profile) | | | | | | |
| *High Risk* | Data has not been inventoried | | | | | | |
| *High Risk* | Voluminous or complex data | | | | | | |
| *High Risk* | Sensitive, regulated, derivative data | | | | | | |
| *High Risk* | Impactful or discriminating data (Health, affiliations, race, orientation) | | | | | | |
| *High Risk* | Nature of processing (Monitoring, profiling, automated scoring) | | | | | | |
| *High Risk* | Exposes vulnerable population (Children) | | | | | | |
| *High Risk* | Undeclared or unauthorized uses | | | | | | |
| *High Risk* | Improper disclosures, transfers, disposition | | | | | | |
| **Moderate Risk** | Limited consequence data but controls in place have not been tested or validated | | | | | | |
| *Limited Risk* | Adequately protected by tested and validated controls aligned to risk | | | | | | |
| Negligible Risk | Data is generally shared data of limited to no consequence | | | | | | |

This chart is not specific to GDPR. It does not reflect all areas of risk. It can be used to visually map or assess systems, processes, or classes of consequential data and characterize them appropriately as to areas of exposure.

## Sensitive and other Special Category Personal Data

Not all data are created equally when it comes to sensitivity or risk and not all law will necessarily designate which is sensitive or attribute the same level of risk to the same types of data. For example, much of the information below is considered generally to be sensitive:

- Account Login with password
- Social Security Number
- Financial Account
- Driver's License
- Debit or Credit Card Number
- State ID
- Passport Number
- Racial or Ethnic origin
- Sexual Orientation
- Religion
- Location and movement
- Health Data
- Biometric Data
- Private Communication (non-commercial)

Similarly, the California Breach Protection Act considers a breach actionable if the disclosed includes First Name or Initial and Last Name along with any of the following 'sensitive' elements:

- Social security number
- Driver's License / ID card number
- Account or Card number if combined with a security access code
- Medical information
- Health Insurance Information
- Data collected from an automated license plate recognition system
- Username or email address with password or security question and answer

Data of children is treated as a special class of data requiring specific controls and consents in most laws.

Article 9 of the GDPR (Processing of special categories of personal data) and Article 10 (Processing of personal data relating to criminal convictions and offences) with varying conditions and limitations includes:

- Racial or ethnic origin
- Political opinions
- Religious or philosophical beliefs
- Trade union membership
- Genetic data
- Biometric data (for the purpose of uniquely identifying a natural person)
- Health data
- Sex life or sexual orientation
- Criminal Convictions or offences

Wealth, credit, financial history, and monetary transactions vary in attribution of sensitivity with regulation.

European Data Protection Board is comprised of one member of each of the 27 individual member state data protection authorities and provides guidance in application of the GDPR. The EDPB defined Ten Categories of High-Risk Processing for GDPR.

- Evaluation or scoring
- Automated Decision Making with legal or similar effect
- Systemic Monitoring
- Sensitive data or data of a highly personal nature
- Data concerning vulnerable subjects
- Data processed on a large scale
- Data sets that have been matched or combined
- Innovative use of new technologies
- Interference with rights or opportunities
- Other likely high risks to the fundamental rights or freedoms of individuals

Every business is different. How and where these ten categories of processing are conducted may not immediately be obvious and may require broad thinking about the scope and distribution of the business and the manner in which it is done. This includes any data processing that may in any manner be impactful to an individual's life, health, liberty, safety, property, prosperity, image, or the persona of any individual the business employs or serves, or any data collected, obtained, or in use about them. Also, processing performed impactful to the rights and freedoms to grow, attain, move freely, achieve, be included, or accepted, be offered, or considered for opportunity, be treated fairly and equitably, and to be informed, to consent, or to object to the collection of data about them, or any aspect of the use of their personal data, to the extent that is within their rights to do so.

Generally, high risk processing would include processing that is rendered high risk through its delicacy or intimacy, data that is sensitive, impactful, or discriminating whether for conditions of health, race, financial status, affiliations, orientation, behaviors, genetics, or morphology. It may be rendered high risk through its visibility, a target made attractive through its high worth, high profile, symbolic value, reputation, associated image, or disruptive value. Or it may be the vulnerability of the population to the impacts of their exposure, children, persons with disabilities, disadvantaged persons, those of specific national origin or with criminal records, or who may be stigmatized for their medical conditions or handicaps.

It may be the complexity of the processing, impactful automation, profiling, scoring, transformation of data, inference, extrapolation, derivation, combination, enhancement, enrichment, technical innovations, or artificial intelligence. Or it may be in the inadequacy of the protections attributable to a location or regime, its laws, risk mitigation measures and safeguards, or legal protections and recourse. Also, the deficiency inherent in the processing of any data of consequence whether put at risk through inadequate oversight, overly expansive distribution, vulnerable attack surface, volume of exposable data, inadequate controls, inconsistency of controls, inadequate scrutiny, systematic or clandestine monitoring.

## GDPR and the Rights of the Individual

GDPR is law that exists to protect the individual from abusive and intrusive practices, both in the information targeted to them, and in the information solicited and collected from them. GDPR assures that transactions involving the exchange or collection of personal information are fair, transparent, and lawful, and defines remedies and recourse to protect individuals in the privacy they relinquish, and the information they share.

Whether being solicited by phone, shopping on the internet, at a job interview, doctor's office, or applying for a loan, people surrender data when asked. Without this exchange of data, individuals could not get the conveniences, services, and products they want, or succeed in transacting for the opportunities they pursue. The GDPR protects individuals from excesses, annoyances, and abuses of privacy, and affords these protections towards any individual that is EU resident, irrespective of whether the affected data subject is an EU citizen. All data subjects within the EU, regardless of nationality, permanence of residency, or status of citizenship, are afforded the same privacy protections under the law. GDPR does not apply in most cases to citizens of the EU if located or are travelling outside of the EU geographically. In this sense, the GDPR applies based on EU residence, not specifically on citizenship.

GDPR (and supporting laws and directives on electronic communications) recognize that there is a life cycle to each transaction and that there is a requirement to assure the individual is protected throughout.

First, it prevents aggressive marketing without recourse. It ensures that individuals are not inappropriately targeted with unwanted solicitation. It prevents the installation of cookies or other means of 'profiling', determining, or tracking the individual's interests and behavior without specific, informed, and unambiguous consent, whether that capture is performed either by the collector, or in third-party processing.

It assures individuals have the right to enjoy and participate in online activities, purchases, and activities with the knowledge that the collection of their personal information is fair, transparent, and lawful, limited by what under the law is termed *data minimization* to only that data required for the completion of the transaction or establishment of relationship. It also assures that the information surrendered is properly cared for and protected. It prohibits use beyond that which was specified, and beyond the term for which the data is needed, or apart from the purpose for which approval for use was given. It assures the data provided will not be shared except for agreed processing by partners or be subsequently sold or misused.

Lastly, amongst other rights, it assures the rights of individuals to see, change, be guaranteed accuracy, erasure, and revocation of relationship in entirety (right to be forgotten), and to conveniently port (right to portability) their personal data elsewhere. These latter operationally will present the greatest difficulties for compliance, the Right to Be Forgotten requiring an awareness of data, participants, and permissions, in house and not, and the Right to Portability a potential obligation for transition support as well as delivery in a format allowing the data to be moved and reused. In protecting each of the above, the GDPR provides that there needs to be a legitimate basis for the collection of an individual's personal data, and one of those most basic is consent. There are some issues with consent which I will discuss later in this section. Suffice it for now to say that the GDPR assures that consent is informed, and unambiguous when granted, and consent and personal data exchanged are both revocable on request. Also, consent must be given freely, and so can only be granted in a balanced relationship where the party seeking consent is not in a position of leverage or authority. Consent as a legal basis for requesting personal data in an employer to employee relationship would be suspect. It might be coercive, and balance would be questioned. Children under the age of sixteen are provided additional protection and cannot be targeted or grant consent in absence of a parent or guardian. There may be some variance in age of consent in different member States. There is also a process by which subject access rights or SAR, are expressed and respected.

---

# ⚖ Data Subject Access Requests (DSAR)

Data subjects have the right to request of a controller, and to be informed in a reasonable timeframe and at minimal cost if any:

- Whether their personal data is being held and processed
- Type or category of data about them being processed
- Purpose of the processing
- To whom the data is being disclosed
- If their data has been subject to automated processing in any decisions rendered pertaining to them
- If the data held is current, complete, and correct
- If their data has been transferred cross border

And to:

- Revoke previously granted consent to processing
- Request restrictions be applied, or that data be modified or corrected
- Request that data be erased or if appropriate returned in a usable electronic format

The data subject also has the right to have that information provided to them in an easily accessible and understandable manner. There is some variability country to country as to request methods and formats, whether confirmation of identity is required, how that confirmation is provided, and the time limits allowable for the controller response. Controllers are generally subject to penalties for inadequate response or excessive delays. Minimal age of consent varies across member states. SAR requests may be issued by parents of minor children, guardians of those incapacitated, legal proxies, and courts or as an indirect exercise of individual rights by supervisory authorities. https://gdpr-info.eu/art-15-gdpr/

*Figure 17 Subject Access Requests (SAR) Requirements*

---

*We limit data risk by collecting the data we need, not everything we want*

The fundamental obligation of any company in-scope for GDPR is transparency and disclosure. That disclosure is the obligation of every data controller to the data subjects it serves. It binds every processor and all related parties to perform in accordance with the disclosures made by controller to subject, and this is set in contract. It is the first line disclosure offering tangible assurance of compliance with the law.

**Privacy Policy**

The fundamental principle underlying the GDPR is 'Informed Choice', allowing the individual to be informed by transparency and full disclosure in support of the decisions they make. And there are decisions to be made. Under the GDPR a company does not have the right to an individual's data. It is a privilege granted by the individual or in satisfaction of an interest granted by the law. Full disclosure and transparency include clearly worded and easily found terms of service, notices, pop-ups and banners, data retention policies, data handling and care policies, but most importantly, the Privacy Policy, describing how we obtain their data, why we need it and what we plan to do with that data if permitted. It details their rights in allowing the use of their data. If fully disclosed, all decisions made regarding the use of system and services, and the provision and ongoing use of an individual's personal data are clear and deliberate, an informed choice.

## PRIVACY POLICY

There is not one standard defining what to include or a specific format required for the privacy policy. In simplest terms and in the clearest non-legalese language, minimally most should address:

- *Who we are (business name, ownership, corporate headquarters, EU locations, DPO)*
- *What we do as a company*
- *Who (by type) are our clients*
- *The type and specifics of data we collect*
- *How we obtain data, why we need it, and for how long*
- *Processing and the legal basis that permits it*
- *Security and protection of your data*
- *Third parties with whom we share your data and why*
- *Personal data disclosed, how and how frequently*
- *Data transfers to locations outside of EU or EEA*
- *Opt-in, Opt-out and setting preferences*
- *Use of cookies and other digital tracking*
- *Rights as granted by the law*
- *How policy changes are handled and communicated*
- *Who to contact for requests, concerns, or complaints and how to reach them*
  - *Within the company*
  - *Data Protection Authorities*

*Figure 18 Elements of the Privacy Policy*

## GDPR and the Obligations of Business

In protecting the rights of individuals, GDPR defines the responsibilities of data controllers. For our purposes, and as commonly defined, that is any business, agency, municipality, or other entity defining the purpose, or controlling the collection, use or processing of personal data. It also requires the data controller to provide oversight and accountability of processors (business or operational partners) that are engaged to provide supporting services on their behalf. Any ambiguity as to processor responsibilities to the controller under the law that exists in agreements will need to be revisited.

Under the GDPR, data controllers are required to engage individuals through practices that are fair, legal, and transparent. That is the basis of the law. They commit to respecting the rights of the individual. They assume responsibility for the care of the data they steward on their behalf. They assure that while in their custody, all employees, systems, processes, and partners that may perform services responsible for that data do the same.

The agreements put in place between data controller and processor regarding the performance of data protection functions should clearly stipulate the responsibility of the processor in performing the functions for which they have been contracted. These should include data care, privacy controls, data deletion or provisions for data portability and return. These should also include business continuity, incident response, and breach notification. Likely, the controller will demand GDPR compliance of all processors they engage, or specific stipulations in the agreements between them, whether directly involved in the management of personal data, or not. Processors can be fined for violating the law. Under the GDPR, data processors cannot subcontract processing to other processors without the approval of the data controller. (*Ten Implications of the New EU General Data Protection Regulation, Daniel Solove, Teach Privacy, December 2015*). This includes processor use of cloud for storage or processing not directly addressed in disclosures to or agreements with the controller. Processors may require a representative presence in the EU.

According to Siarhei Varankevich, (Author of the Territorial Scope of the GDPR Flowchart that has been included with his permission in this chapter), under the GDPR, "companies must be 'accountable', and adhere to the provisions embodied in the GDPR when soliciting, collecting, processing data about, or targeting data subjects in the EU, specifically with the intent to offer goods or services, or to monitor the behavior of EU located data subjects".

The above is true if the company (data controller) is an EU resident company, partners with an EU affiliate acting as a data processor for facilitation or has operating facilities within the EU. This according to Varankevich may apply if the company has a business representative or has established basic operating infrastructure including bank accounts, postal address, or phone. It also would apply to any ecommerce service or website that collects personally ascribable data. This would be true for direct-to-consumer marketers or promoters, subscription media firms, or any other business that acts as a data controller and uses individuating data to target EU resident data subjects. This would also apply to any company, service or agent acting as a processor on behalf of these entities in procuring, analyzing, or handling this data, providing data storage, data backup, purchased demographic analysis, telemarketing, or customer mailing lists, or similar.

GDPR is 'technology neutral' (recital 15). It addresses non-electronic repositories (except unstructured paper), and also digital modes as does the current Privacy and Electronic Communications Directive 2003 (Directive 2002/58/EC), and as do numerous local member state electronic privacy directives, and the ePrivacy Regulation, omnibus law governing direct electronic marketing. In addition to targeted electronic marketing the new ePR regulation should address the use of cookies or other means of behavioral tracking or electronic influence, and the sharing or sale of 'identifiers, likes, follows, location, links and preferences'.

---

### Marketing and Sales Contact in a B2C Context

- Where an existing relationship exists with consumers (those that have unambiguously and freely subscribed to a service, requested to be on mailing list or be contacted regularly with coupons or notice of specials or events, or are active purchasing consumers with existing accounts):
    - Ongoing contact should be related to the services requested and identified areas of interest for which consent had been given for contact and/or preferences had been established.
    - Provide a means to opt-in expressly for additional services or to opt-out of some or all of the relationship at any time as well as the ability to easily review and update preference settings.
    - Information should not be shared with business partners or affiliates unless the consumer was informed and agreed by acceptance of the privacy policy and/or has specifically agreed through the provision of consent and/or setting of preferences elsewhere.
- Where an existing relationship does not exist, unsolicited B2C communication is disallowed under the GDPR, a protection to consumers from unwanted intrusion. New consumers must be attracted by an engaging website, through bulk or mass media marketing, and social media, not solicited directly.
- For new clients, an unambiguous and documented 'opt-in' establishes a relationship, the terms of which are dictated by the preferences they elect, and by the privacy policy. Processing and data held is limited to that required unless further consent is obtained. Local law may require double opt-in, a confirmation of consent. A means of opting-out of some or all subscribed services should always be available.

(Author opinion may not apply in all circumstance. There may be a legitimate interest in direct marketing. Check with attorneys before proceeding).

*Figure 15 Marketing in a B2C Context*

The rules for B2C marketing and solicitation apply to individuals, but also may apply to sole proprietors. https://www.sonovate.com/blog/key-differences-b2b-b2c-gdpr/. There are often questions asked as to whether a charity reaching out to a high-worth donor, or a business soliciting a celebrity for paid endorsement, or for the guidance of a self-promoted expert that frequently appears on television talk shows or as a speaker at conferences are B2C or B2B contacts. These are public persona without doubt and as such these are B2C contacts. Without a prior relationship they cannot be solicited directly but better through an agent where a relationship governing contact does exist. Newsletters to existing donors informing them of the good that their contributions have done are appropriate if they have agreed to receive them. Unexpected contact for further solicitation is not.

The rules for B2C also apply to the recruitment of talent by HR departments. Unsolicited contact of individuals is disallowed, as is the 'clandestine surveillance' required to investigate the fit of targeted prospects without their knowledge and consent. Social media, job boards and electronic posts are viable, but care should be taken in the use of unvalidated prospect lists. Some may use inadequate means for capturing or expressing consent or include individuals that had requested opt-out of further contact.

---

## Marketing and Sales Contact in a B2B Context

- Where an existing B2B relationship exists, operate on that basis. Otherwise, with legitimate interest.
- Targeted contact lists, business contact repositories, business card catalogs, clean purchased lists, consenting event participant lists, or online research may be appropriate in a B2B context
- Where prospecting for new business a few conditions must be met:
- It is reasonable to identify potential business contacts in an appropriate role (purchaser, buyer, etc.) And to reach out to them for legitimate business interests.
- The individual contacted should be in a position that should expect to receive such contact
- Any contact made should be regarding information and business offers that the individual should normally expect to be contacted about
- Allow opt-out of current and future contact and request to be removed from contact lists
- Assure they had not opted-out prior in which case they should not have been contacted at all
- Adhere to electronic marketing directives and local member state laws

(Author opinion may or may not be appropriate to all or in all circumstance. Check with attorneys before proceeding with B2B contact or processing)

---

*Figure 20 Marketing and Sales in a B2B Context*

Cookies are often used, and in some cases required by websites to establish a structure or communication, shape an experience, or as a means of monitoring the interests, activities, frequency, and purchasing habits of website visitors. They may be implemented by the website directly or by third parties for their own use, purposes not directly controlled by the website visited. Privacy policies should disclose the type and use of all cookies. Tracking cookies and beacons and other means of behavioral monitoring requires unambiguous consent before these should be deposited or used. There may be discretion as to infrastructural cookies, or those implemented for security (session management), but safest practice is to provide notice and obtain consent prior to depositing any code, of any type, for any purpose, to the client device or browser.

Data accuracy is the responsibility of the data controller. Where and how data is captured is important to its integrity, currency, and accuracy. Data input directly by an individual filling an online form would be expected to be more accurate than data pulled from public records or purchased from a third party. And it is the responsibility of the data controller to correct the accuracy and integrity of the data they hold about any individual if an inaccuracy is detected, or reported, and it is the right of the individual to confirm this. Additionally, it is important that the data held, however it is received, be documented to reflect the consent of the individual if that is the basis on which it is used. This is being operationalized by many companies allowing individuals to manage the accuracy and quality of their own data through self-service portals.

It is also important that all the data captured and kept about an individual can be readily linked to the individual to whom the data belongs. As mentioned earlier, this is perhaps one of the greater challenges' companies will have in conforming to the GDPR. Portability and the Right to be Forgotten assures a subject the ability to request all personal data about them be reviewed, returned, or that it be deleted, and that proof is provided. To meet this requirement a company needs to know and track what it has and where it is. This is true for personal data held locally by the controller, with a processor, virtualized in the cloud, or elsewhere. It may be a URL linked to data that is incorrect or no longer relevant. It may be data remotely carried on laptops or flash drives. It also may restrict the use of proprietary technologies or formats for storing data if these inhibit the ease by which data is returned, or potentially infer a requirement to perform needed conversions and to provide transfer support. This may be an added complexity for controllers contracting SaaS (Software as a Service) platforms as processors. If the applications are proprietary, or linked to a specific operating environment, data portability may be difficult or not possible, or require a disproportionate effort to accommodate.

*If performing a ROPA or Records of Processing Assessment, a Data Inventory, or Assessment of Data Workflows for one or more businesses, or under one or more regulations, see chapter 14 (Inventory, Classification and Data Risk) for useful guidance.*

In a blog hosted by Veritas it was rightly pointed out that both structured and unstructured data should be evaluated and purged of records or files that are no longer needed. These would include accumulated ROT (redundant, obsolete, trivial data) whether held by the controller, or by a processor, and whether active or archived. This will help to reduce the scope of the data that will need to be assessed for risk in preparing for compliance with the law and going forward.

In a webinar by Coalfire, a cyber risk management and compliance specialty firm, a presenter cautioned that records of the disposition of personal data determined to no longer be needed, or that had been purged as part of the normal data retention and deletion policy, should still be maintained. He posed the interesting scenario of a 'Right to be Forgotten' claim being made asking that held personal data be returned or destroyed, and the complexities that might arise if that data had already been destroyed as part of normal data retention and disposition policies and practices, and no record kept of the history.

The GDPR also designates the SA or Supervising Authority for Data Protection assuming jurisdiction based on location. Under the GDPR, a company that operates in multiple EU member States, falls under the jurisdiction of the SA at its primary or main location or facility, or in a state where it has representation, and that SA coordinates with authorities in other jurisdictions.

*Data protection laws are only in part about the protection of personal data. They are more about protecting the rights of individuals regarding their personal data.*

## GDPR and How We Do Business

Many of the companies that had worked under the prior Directive implemented practices, imbued awareness within their corporate culture, and built applications compatible with much of the requirements of GDPR. Even so, some of the newly introduced or redefined concepts under GDPR require considerable work to conform. I have already mentioned a few of these.

Amongst others, including record keeping and documented processes, several areas require focus:

- Consent
- Right to be Forgotten
- Right to Data Portability
- Privacy by Design

Consent is not a trivial matter under the GDPR. It must be an affirmative act, unambiguous, informed, freely given and revocable. Consent cannot be inferred or by default. It is also not easy to apply. It needs to be received, handled properly, managed, and documented. This might require altering the design of systems or business processes to make that possible. For this reason, where a legitimate basis for the collection and processing of data apart from consent is feasible, many opt to use it. Processing required for the execution of a contract, conformance with legal obligations, public interests, interests of the data subject, or the exercise of other defensible legitimate interests would be examples of an alternate basis.

An individual from whom data is requested, or solicited, for any use other than the gathering of 'en masse' statistics where the individual is unidentified, must freely give informed and specific consent to have their personal data collected, processed, and used, or there must be another legitimate (and defensible) basis for the acceptance and handling of that data. There are special considerations afforded historic, scientific, journalistic, and health research, and these often do not require consent for anonymous processing.

https://ico.org.uk/for-organisations/data-protection-reform/overview-of-the-gdpr/key-areas-to-consider/

Specific rules govern consent under the GDPR. Consent cannot be inferred from absence of a needed action. It is insufficient for a website to post a banner stating that by using the website consent is deemed granted. It is inappropriate to set acceptance and consent as a default condition using ticked boxes, approval granting language, or other means that require action to revoke (an opt-out).

The right to freely given, informed, and unambiguous consent should not be obscured or buried within EULAs, Terms of Use, or other legal text requiring significant effort to find. There must be an unambiguous 'opt-in', or other clear and undisputable indicator of acceptance that is recorded and can be tracked. That information should be easy to locate. A means to revoke prior consent and opt out is also needed, equally easy to find and access. Use of a service cannot be conditional on consent being granted or it cannot be said to have been freely given. Consent must be clearly informed. There should be an obvious pop up, link or policy page provided that explains the basis for collection, rights of the individual, and provisions of care for the data collected. And it must be unambiguous for what consent was granted and intended.

# Generic example of a SAR (Subject Access Request) Workflow

| ACTION | Group | Flow | Procedure |
|---|---|---|---|
| Notify | | Notify | Notify requestor of status or completion |
| Document and Track | | Document actions | Document action taken, by what authority, and when |
| Act | | Satisfy request | Perform needed actions to satisfy or deny the request |
| Approve | | Not all requests can be satisfied. Some may need approval. Some will be denied or delayed. A reasonable explanation must be provided for the delay or rejection of the request as permitted based on applicable law. | SARs may be rejected if the request is not reasonable, or the effort is not proportional. They may be rejected if data processing is based on a valid means other than consent and the request would be inappropriate. Provide subjects a path for complaint escalation internally and to the supervisory data protection authorities with contact information. |
| Review | | Compile results | Aggregate findings and if needed get authorization to take the requested action |
| Investigate | | Research the data being held or processed | Data may be held on internal systems, partner (service provider) systems, or in the cloud. |
| Acknowledge, Validate and Assess | | The clock starts on receipt of the request and response must be timely as dictated by law. | **Acknowledge request, validate the individual's identity and standing.** Verify requirements, response format, and time to respond per law. |
| Receive | | Prospective, new, and existing clients have the right to know the data that is being held about them or being processed and to opt/In, opt/out, make corrections or otherwise express their intentions, submitting a request called SAR. | Prepare to accept these SARs by phone, email, text, paper, or other means and to document actions taken. Allow data subjects to verify, view, request data held, modify, delete, port, erase, change preferences and to update consent. **Subjects making requests must validate their identity and their right to request if for a child or another party.** |
| Describe | | Build the policy documents and notices that inform individuals of their rights | Use the privacy policy and other GDPR notices to inform individuals of their rights and help them exercise them. Provide access to the policies through all online interfaces and communications. Provide contact information. |
| Define | | Internally define how Subject Access Requests (SARs) will be received, addressed, and documented. This can be a manual process, a portal, use an existing system, or a purpose-built commercial platform. | Have a means of addressing client requests, to accept subject requests, acknowledge them, validate identities and standards, forward for needed approvals, and to report status. A dedicated platform is not required but many are available and some also simplify and manage correspondence. |

*Figure 21 Subject Access Request – A Process Example*

Once consent or other legitimate basis of approval for the processing of data is provided, a data controller is responsible to assure that data is collected only for specified and legitimate purposes, collects only the data that is needed, it is kept accurate and up to date, held for no longer than needed for the purpose collected, and that the reason for the collection of the data be lawful, fair, and transparent. It is also the responsibility of the controller to assure that the integrity and confidentiality of that data be protected against error, unlawful processing, theft, loss, or damage.

Right to be Forgotten is a comprehensive right, new to the EU.

The Right to be Forgotten is often directed at websites for the removal of URLs and digitally persistent documents, stories, purchasing records, and images. An individual can demand that links to information held about them be deleted, and the removal of that data be proven on completion, all in a reasonable and timely manner. This is a challenge to even the largest of digital service providers in balancing the rights of an individual with the public interest. It is a challenge to validate the legitimacy and basis for the request. And it is a challenge technically as sites are crawled, cached, content scraped, and links propagated across the web.

The Right to be Forgotten is generally less applicable to data held by a company with legitimate interests (contracts, applications, tax records, loan records, pensions, security, and system access logs), an employer, or to academic institutions that keep student records.

Businesses often collect data numerous times from the same individuals. It is used in numerous systems, participates in varied workflows and processes, some under direct control, some through partners or affiliates (processors). It may be stored on site or in cloud, distributed across an array of virtual servers and storage, and incorporated in backups and archives. Few companies have systems in place that map an individual to all data about them and where that might be located. This is particularly true when the complete relationship of the subject to the controller is not obvious. Companies must respond to inquiries about the data held about them and subject requests within 30 days and in most member states do so at no cost.

There is a close relationship between a company and an employee. An employee of a company expectedly will have information stored about them in the human resource system, payroll system, perhaps in a system tracking retirement investment, or benefits, in facilities and building records that list where they are located, and in an asset register if they have been given equipment to use. Some employees may elect to take part in some services, but not in others. Some may sign up for voluntary programs, company sports teams, or other activities sponsored by the company. They may have opted to get the company magazine, promotional materials, discount announcements, or not, some as an employee, some as a consumer. They may take part in the company fitness program and health, medical release, and emergency contact information provided to do so. They may be listed in an incident response system, so they can be contacted in crisis, and then of course, in the phone system. The basis for held data will span consent, legitimate interests, processing on behalf of the data subject, and the execution of the employer / employee contract. An employee providing health data to participate in a sponsored sports team does so with consent, not often as a stipulation of the employee contract.

Despite the intimate relationship between employer and employee, few companies link an employee to all the potential personal data that may be held about them in any comprehensive way because information held, particularly with older or legacy systems or resources, is in context of systems that grant rights to individuals through accounts, and not always the other way around where individuals adopt systems or programs as objects associated to them. Sometimes, it is both.

And when an employee leaves the company, some internally stored data will be more locatable and easily addressed, but some would need to be researched. Where the data is externally stored or managed, requests will need to be made of third parties. And of course, some information cannot be removed, or there may be legal requirements for its retention. There may be disputes as to data ownership between company and departing employee that will need to be resolved. And there may be some services or benefits that the departing employee does not want terminated or transferred elsewhere, insurances, managed investments, or services subscribed as a consumer, magazines, discount programs, so each case may require some manual processing to assure individuals rights are protected. Generally, the right to be forgotten won't apply to most employee data beyond removing references or pictures from online marketing materials or use of their name in promotional or representation activities with or without consent.

If the relationships to a data subject with which there is as close a relationship as with an employee is difficult to track, one can imagine the difficulty of tracking and mapping relationships with a more removed subject, a consumer, across all the possible businesses and systems that may have touched them in a complex business enterprise over several years. A publisher might find a specific consumer with numerous magazine subscriptions, some subscribed directly, some through channel partners, be found in different loyalty programs, as a participant in sweepstakes, in the marketing data bases, having submitted letters of complaint, or even as a job applicant, former employee, or more. They may track the consumer through installed cookies or other electronic means. This exacerbates the already considerable difficulty of tracking consent, a revocable right, and is one reason why consent is not the preferred mechanism for approved use. The Right to be Forgotten as introduced with the GDPR, is a broad reaching provision, and technically and operationally perhaps one of the more significant challenges to companies in complying with the new law. For many of the same reasons, and the potential requirement for system modifications and the need for a company to provide transfer support, I see the Right to Data Portability similarly, an operational challenge.

Privacy by Design (PbD) is a commitment to quality management in the development practices for applications and websites, mobile apps, portals, and operational processes. I spoke about this earlier. It commits to an evaluation of privacy and controls for informed choice and exercise of preferences at the start. It considers obfuscation through technology, and minimization in data collection, processing, retention, and transfer. It associates data captured, stored, and processed to the data owner, not a system orientation, and is not the design of most traditional systems. It allows individuals to exercise decisions about their data and its use. Although this is very likely a change in process for many businesses and will require investment and thinking, it is needed on a go-forward basis. R. Jason Cronk is well known for expertise in this area and has written numerous articles, and a brilliant book, Strategic Privacy by Design.

## RIGHT TO BE FORGOTTEN

<u>Basis for exercise of the Right to be Forgotten</u>

- Data collected is no longer needed or applicable to the purpose for which it was collected
- Consent for its use is withdrawn
- Legitimate basis argument is insufficient to override data subject's objection
- Processing was unlawful and should not have been conducted
- Data has been improperly used, sold, marketed, represented, or transferred
- Agreed term of use has expired
- There is a legal requirement or court mandate that the data be removed

<u>Exemptions to the Right to Erasure</u>

- Where it unfairly restricts or conflicts with the rights of expression of another
- Impedes archiving of data in the public interest (i.e., journalistic purposes)
- Impedes archiving performed in the interest of historic or scientific research
- Held for legal purpose or if it interferes with the ability of another in filing or exercising a legal claim

*Extrapolated from a very excellent article by Mark O'Halloran:*
*GDPR and the right to erasure, ComputerWeekly.Com*

*Figure 16 Right to be forgotten*

## GDPR in the Cloud

It is increasingly the case that software, storage, platform, security, and services reside in the cloud with any of numerous providers. These can be public, private, or hybrid clouds by design, or a multi-cloud strategy involving more than one provider, the distinction being where and how assets, processing and storage are owned and shared between enterprise and provider, in this discussion most often, controller and one or more processors. It is also about how structural elements like physical segmentation, virtualization, containers, micro services, and other mechanisms are used, impacting how and where systems for processing are established, and where and how data is processed, stored, managed, and supported, and where risk lives. Any of these elements may be globally distributed by cloud providers allowing them to leverage time zones for continuity of service coverage, to achieve overall efficiencies, and reduce costs, a follow the sun, and follow the cost of labor business strategy. Data, data access and data support may span servers and storage systems, diverse infrastructure, differing support organizations, and varied providers working in partnership, crossing borders, sovereign, and legal entities. This has obvious ramifications as to locating and tracking the data we hold. It also has implications as to conformance with GDPR and imposes challenges in achieving and demonstrating compliance and offering credible disclosures to data subjects.

Processing data in the cloud moves and distributes

processing, not accountability. Respect for the rights of data subjects, effective data management, and legal obligations for conformance to GDPR remain the responsibilities and a commitment of the controller. Effective data processing contracts obligate processors and third parties in the performance of their defined roles in support of the controller. So does the law.

Territorial scope dictates who are impacted by the GDPR, and this applies everywhere in the world, and applies virtually in the cloud. Any company soliciting, marketing to, monitoring the behavior of, or providing products or services to EU residents, operates in the EU or employs EU residents is in scope for the GDPR wherever located, through whatever relationship, and for the most part, however implemented. Typically, businesses engage cloud providers as processors, each providing specialized services, or providing rapidity of establishment or deployment, often on demand and at scale, for consumption of technical resources.

Under the dictates of GDPR, a processor requires instructions from the controller as to what processing to perform. For some that 'instruction' is limited to the specific service option selected off a menu of services. There may not be provisions to control localization of processing or storage, cross border data movement, or to define specific arrangements for support. There may not be the specific required levels of security and data protection or the appropriate implementation of controls for data privacy in the offerings by default, or at all, or require specific additional services be selected, purchased, or enabled. There may not be the commitments to notification on breach and disruption or the mechanisms to assure availability that GDPR requires. These cannot be assumed. That all said, some of the best of providers have certified to numerous protective and security standards. These processors comply with the most stringent of regulations, operate hardened and tested facilities, and have the resources and capabilities to support compliance with GDPR and other law allowing clients to focus specifically on other areas of their business processing knowing their processing in the cloud is conforming and effective.

Actual use of platform and infrastructure may be self-service, through contracted hands offered by the provider as a service, or though engagement of third parties to perform specific functions including administration, support, operations, security monitoring or development. Where several parties are engaged in different roles, each is performing an individual processor function. Data Processor Agreements between controller and the processors on which they depend for provision of services may be negotiated agreements with specific and defined terms, or detailed compliance addendums to individual enterprise contracts, or they may be offered as 'pay-as-you-go' just in time services with any needed commitments defined in the terms of service and privacy disclosures. GDPR requires a binding processing agreement. Not all cloud providers are appropriate to GDPR, and some are inadequate in the privacy and security commitments that are made in the online terms of service or privacy policies published, with little or no opportunity for revision or modification. Others are fully compliant with GDPR and conformance capabilities in their service offerings exceed that which many companies can attain in-house. It falls to the controller to evaluate capabilities, commitments, credentials, and resources in assuring the selection of an appropriate processing partner. This is particularly so in a multi-cloud strategy.

As stated above, GDPR requires that a business engage cloud providers or any processor under a 'Data Processing Agreement' or other binding mechanism dictating the terms of processing and controller instructions. Of course, with large providers offering a specific business or technical function and acting in the capacity of processor on behalf of multitudes of controller clients, variance from standard offerings or customizations may be limited or constrained by the underlying infrastructure, deployable micro services, and the demands of support. The cloud business model depends on the shared use of services and support capabilities across multiple tenants.

Compliance offerings are good business for the cloud. They are compatible with the shared use model, all in scope clients having similar needs. As such, compliance is not just a minimal price of entry, or an inconvenient must, it is a competitive differentiator for cloud providers. Those making the smartest investment in capabilities, resources, and knowledge can provide richer services including extensive controls and features, controller selectable options, comprehensive contractual assurances and addendums, and the provisions and capabilities to provide a competent GDPR offering to those that have that requirement.

With the benefit of a competent processing partner or partners in the cloud, compliance can be achieved for specific processor managed functions. But there is much more to GDPR success than outsourcing processing and managing third party relationships. It remains for every in-scope controller to assure it is compliant in all other aspects of its operation and business functions, understands its data, and is meeting the expectations of the law regarding data subject rights.

---

*Figure 17 Controller / Processor Relationship*

**CONTROLLER – PROCESSOR RELATIONSHIP** under the GDPR (See Article 28) Requires:

- Processor must process data in accordance with the dictates of the controller
- A processor does not dictate the 'means and purpose' of processing
- A binding agreement should be implemented between controller and processor
- Processor should attest to GDPR compliance for each of the services for which it is performing
- Processor must provide assurance of technical and organizational protective measures
- Processor should provide transparency for approval regarding types of sub-processors used
- Processor should obligate staff and third parties to confidentiality and controller intentions
- Processor should provide notice to controller where processing would be in violation of law
- The processor will promptly notify the controller if breached to support reporting obligations
- The processor will assist the controller in meeting its data subject obligations (i.e. SAR)
- The processor will comply with requests for audit or provide the results of third-party audit
- Assure that a legitimate and legal basis for transfer is implemented
- Assure complete erasure or port of data back to controller if requested

**GDPR SECURITY CONTROLS**, though generally not prescriptive, amongst other requirements, are discussed in articles 32-36 of the GDPR. A few are characterized below:

- The controller will engage processors capable of providing needed protections
- Will assure the confidentiality, integrity, availability, and resilience of processing systems / services
- Make risk-based decisions in implementing encryption, pseudonymization, controls
- Assure that there is a mechanism to restore data availability in the event of an incident
- Assure that the integrity of the controls in place are regularly tested to verify effectiveness of technical and organizational measures
- Is advised to demonstrate conformance through adherence to a professional standard
- Assure effective testing, monitoring and breach response
- Provide adequate protection and management of electronic and printed personal data and records

*Figure 18 GDPR security controls*

Breach is very broadly defined under the GDPR to include malicious data exfiltration, data loss, data isolation (ransomware) and impactful loss of access and availability. Not all security breaches impact personal data. Not all breaches are significant reportable events (i.e., port scans). These do not impact personal data. The GDPR has mandated a **72-hour breach notification requirement** for all those subject to GDPR for reporting to Data Protection Authorities on awareness that a significant event has taken place and it has impacted personal data. There may be a requirement to notify the impacted community where the public is significantly impacted (a high risk to the rights and freedoms of natural persons), or at risk of potential harm. In accordance with guidance from the Article 29 Working Party, that notice is triggered on a reasonable degree of certainty that a breach impacting personal data has occurred.

**72 HOUR BREACH NOTIFICATION REQUIREMENT (article 33)**

GDPR (and stipulations under local law) dictate the reporting to Data Protection Authorities (and in some states other jurisdictions or impacted individuals), what needs to be reported, how frequently, and under what circumstances. A standardized template should be used for consistency, records maintained of all events, and prompt notice provided to supervisory data authorities with jurisdiction including:

- what happened (breach laws may vary by country – consult local counsel)
- what data and how much data has been affected
- who (type of subject) and how many were impacted and where they are located
- severity, likely consequences, measures taken, or actions planned
- name and contact details of the DPO or other party in authority that can provide updates and information
- if necessary, provide partial information as it is known to avoid reporting delays

*Figure 19 Breach Notification Requirement*

## Any strategy is only as effective as the controls which assure it

# Some thoughts for Data Processing Agreements (DPA) and Use of Cloud

*Figure 20 Data protection agreements and cloud*

A third party or cloud engagement can vary with purpose, size, services procured, role of parties, operating model, and whether addressing new GDPR legal requirements (SCCs), within this agreement or elsewhere, or other law. This list focuses in no specific order on some of the business, technical and operating safeguards that may be considered in constructing a cloud or other vendor processing agreement, GDPR or not, and varying with the engagement including:

- Accountability and oversight. Description and purpose of the engagement, duration, expectations, renewals, terms.
- Under the GDPR, language in the agreement to conform to Article 28 mandates.
- Establish defined walls of responsibility. Services, roles, participants. Controller instructions, processor commitments.
- Processor assurances of confidentiality, expertise, and training to meet service commitments.
- Attestation to standards, regulations, and security frameworks to which the processor has conformed or certified.
- Data types to be collected or processed. Frequency, sensitivity, care, protection, and special handling (children's data).
- Processing of personal data, by whom, for what purpose, what is done, where, how, care and security controls in place.
- How data will be captured, where it will be stored, processed, and accessed, by whom, and from where.

- How is support performed, parties involved in providing support, remote access, transfer, required authorization.
- Downstream parties, disclosure, types, roles, vetting, controls (providers of services, support, admin, backups, etc.).
- User access controls, authentication, identity management, application, and assurance of least privilege.
- Localization, transfer, and onward forwarding of data. Adequacy, safeguards, legal basis, instrument (i.e., SCC).
- Backups, snapshots, offsite data storage, media rotation and data disposal. Database protection (active, standby, etc.).
- The means and frequency by which security testing and update takes place, and privacy and security are reviewed.
- Regularly scheduled security training, penetration, table-top exercises, and recovery testing as a program.
- Handling of in-country legal, policy and surveillance risk. Audited assurances, risk indemnification and insurance.

- Staff resources to be committed if any, why, how often, in what role, skillset, level of capability, additional costs.
- Roles and obligations of controller and processor in account setup, administration, and privilege management.
- Roles and obligations of controller and processor in assuring security and controls (direct and third party).
- Roles and obligations of controller and processor in data entry, access, update, delete, care, quality, and correctness.
- Roles of parties in presenting privacy and collection disclosures, handling rights requests, consent, or any other basis.
- Roles of controller and processor in notification, management and reporting of security incident or breach.
- Audits and assessments. Maintenance plans and schedules. Uptime assurances. Performance reporting.
- Encryption and key management (who holds keys and where, multi key configurations). Data protection / obfuscation.
- Systems, resources, tools to be provided by the processor for the controller's benefit (API, interfaces, portals).
- Code escrow for change of ownership. Transitional 3rd party continuity assurances. Costs and limits if any for end of engagement support, conversions, replication, transport, and end of use return, deletion, data portability and transfer.

- Conformance with CISPE (Code of Conduct for Cloud Infrastructure Service Providers) or other professional, industry, or emerging guidance, oversight, or standard setting organization.
- Risk aligned protective, detective, corrective, and continuity controls and validations in place.
- Policies and practices - data retention and secure disposal / security / privacy / security testing / n-tier party mgmt.
- Incident response and disaster recovery plans are documented, reviewed and appropriate.
- Handling of digital data capture (cookies, tracking, IP address, electronic IDs, cached data, logs).
- Adequate storage for performance and event logging. Assistance provided for forensic investigation.

**GDPR, Adequacy, Transfers and Transfers Forward**

The EU grants the right to data transfer by a finding of 'adequacy' following review of the data protection principles, practices, and assurances of a country. These findings are reviewed and typically renewed every four years to assure adequacy remains unchanged. It enables the exchange of data based on the native levels of privacy protection inherent in the laws of a country, or the commitments it has made in fostering privacy protection. A finding of adequacy means that safeguards are appropriate and data transfers can occur between the EU and an adequately protected country without further concerns.
http://ec.europa.eu/justice/data-protection/international-ransfers/adequacy/index_en.htm

Adequacy is conferred to all EU member states permitting the free flow of personal data between companies and individuals without the need for special mechanisms to allow it. Norway, Iceland, Lichtenstein, Andorra, Argentina, Faroe Islands, Guernsey, Israel, Isle of Man, Jersey, New Zealand, Switzerland, and Uruguay have been listed as countries found adequate in implementations of protection sufficient to support data transfer. Adequacy is a process of periodic review and current state should be verified before establishing transfer policies or practices. Canada has been determined adequate in commercial applications. A mutual adequacy decision has been reached with Japan. Korea is in active negotiation for commercial adequacy. The UK was deemed adequate post Brexit. Lacking effective controls over access and seizure of EU resident data and offering little means for redress or access to the courts in complaint, the US has not been deemed adequate to permit the free exchange of personal data with EU.
https://ec.europa.eu/info/law/law-topic/data-protection/data-transfers-outside-eu/adequacy-protection-personal-data-non-eu-countries_en

Absent adequacy at the country level, there remained for US companies three legal means for EU - US data transfer under the GDPR, an entity certification mechanism like the US Privacy Shield that had been overturned by the Schrems II decision finding it offered inadequate protections, contractual safeguards (SCCs or BCRs) supported by additional technical measures including a TIA or Transfer Impact Assessment to evaluate the 'risks and effective equivalency to EU protections' provided to EU residents, and Article 49 derogations. The legitimacy of some standard contractual clauses had been challenged (primarily those governing transfers to non-EU processors), and pressured by the absence of a certification mechanism, new SCCs better fitting risk and needs, along with required supplemental safeguards were adopted.
https://www.mwe.com/en/thought-leadership/publications/2017/10/irish-court-casts-serious-doubt-eu-model-clauses.

There are two new SCCs, one intended for data processing agreements (as defined under article 28), and the other out of country and onward transfers. These better anticipate new business models and are structurally comprehensive, addressing EU and non-EU/EEA controllers, EU controller and non-EU/EEA processors, processor to sub-processor, and processor to controller relationships. They apply as a single agreement across relationships and are also extensible permitting all the entities in an undertaking to sign on to the same contract, anticipating and permitting the adjoinment of new participant entities to the agreement over time. They address both data importers and exporters.

Where both parties are already subject to the articles of the GDPR, Territorial Scope governs, and the new SCCS are unneeded and inappropriate to be used. Where the SCCs are used, the controller is still required to interpret the needs and risks of transfer through a Transfer Risk Assessment, assess contractual, operating, and technical controls, and to implement them through the new SCCs. Post Brexit the UK has implemented two SCCs, one an EU replacement for companies conducting transfers with the UK, but not the EU, the other an addendum where an SCC for EU transfers is already in place. Where both entities are operating under GDPR, processing is defined in contract under Data Processing Agreements without the need for supportive safeguards. Even with the adoption of the new and anticipated Data Protection Frameworks as a transfer certification method, companies not certifying through the program still require safeguard mechanisms like SCCs and BCCs. Also, TIAs to assess the sufficiency and adherence to Supplementary Transfer Safeguard guidance. (EDPB, June 18, 2021).

1. Know your transfers (where they go, how protected, need, relevancy, minimization, and limitation)
2. Verify the transfer tool (GDPR articles 45, 46, 49) that your transfers will rely upon
3. Assess the laws / practices in the 3rd country that may impact needed safeguards
4. Identify supplementary measures that will elevate data protections
5. Take any formal procedural steps needed to adopt the supplemental measures
6. Monitor and periodically re-evaluate your safeguards (their effectiveness and any impactful changes or developments that may impact their ongoing sufficiency)

*Figure 21 Supplementary Transfer Safeguards*

## EU–US Data Privacy Framework (DPF)

Lacking protections for EU residents equivalent to those provided under EU law, and access to the courts or other redress mechanisms, the U.S. had been designated inadequate for transfers of personal data at the country level by the EU. Absent a mechanism to permit it, transfers between the EU and US had been disallowed without one or more compensating mechanisms like SCC's, and needed TIAs. A new proposed EU-US Data Privacy Framework has now been adopted filling the void left by the Privacy Shield program vacated some 3 years ago by the Schrems II decision. The DPF provides US companies that elect to self-certify to the program administered by the International Trade Authority (ITA) of the Department of Commerce, effective adequacy, sufficient to exchange personal data freely with the EU irrespective of and without the need for additional safeguards like the presence of SCCs (Standard Contractual Clauses), BCCs (Binding Corporate Rules), and without a TIA (Transfer Impact Assessment. Data bridges to the UK and to Switzerland are expected through this agreement.

The program will be enforced by the FCC assuring that safeguards limit US intelligence authorities access to only data necessary and proportionate to protect US national security, that there is enhanced oversight to ensure compliance with limitations on surveillance activities, an independent dispute resolution, arbitration and impartial redress mechanism including a Civil Liberties Protection Officer, a process to enlist the aid of an EU residents own national data protection authority to transmit the complaint and assure its handling, and an appeals process before a newly created Data Protection Review Court to investigate and resolve complaints about the collection and use of their data by US intelligence agencies.

## PIA (Privacy Impact Assessment)

DPIA is an active instrument. It is specifically mandated by EU law, introduced, and defined under GDPR article 35, and aligned to Article 8 of the European Charter of Fundamental Rights. It is a 'drill down' assessment of one or similar processes, asking questions specifically to evaluate 'data protection' risk, and weigh harm to the rights and freedoms of individuals. The terms DPIA and PIA are often used indiscriminately or interchangeably even in the EU. But some see PIA as a management tool, a higher-level risk review, assessing organizational more than individual privacy impacts, involving different skills and stakeholders, organizational levels, and invoked at different points in the privacy assessment lifecycle.

In the US, Privacy Impact Assessment or PIA is the preferred term for the formalized process of evaluating data risk and its impacts to a business. PIA templates are used widely by federal agencies including Health and Human Services, Government Accounting Office, and the Department of Homeland Security amongst others. These are formalized and standardized templates. Most generally include an overview of the initiative, project, or undertaking, sponsorship, legal authorities, accountabilities, funding, data and more.

In a business context, PIA is often employed at a high level for initiatives where people or communities are involved or touched, and employment, deployment, geographical expansion, human rights, health, or other impactful legal, ethical, cultural, or practical considerations are weighed, examining the risks and the value of the undertaking. It addresses what the proposed initiative is called, its goals, who has requested and sponsored it, costs, laws, and environmental, social, and governance considerations, as much as who is impacted and how. It assures principal stakeholders are aligned on intentions, risks, and impacts involving consequential business activities before they are pursued, money spent, or a substantial change is put in effect. It assures that accountable parties are aligned, controls are in place, and management can weigh in on business purpose, benefit, and risk to business, impacts to markets, communities, or individuals. Where DPIA is an active assessment of individual rights and protections, PIA evaluates a business decision risk.

PIA identifies populations affected and where, any risk they might incur, and how they will benefit or be otherwise impacted by an undertaking. Will it displace people, deny services, or raise their costs? It addresses goals, importance of the initiative, how effectively it will meet objectives, implications of not taking on the effort or its deferral, and the criteria or metrics that will determine effectiveness or success. PIA also defines the needed teams, tools and methodology that will be used and what is in place or additionally required for effectiveness, security and adherence to privacy and proper and legal operations. It describes how they will be tested, maintained, and validated effective, and the locations involved. It provides basic descriptive information, stakeholders, data collected, where and how processed, retention, backups, risk, and controls, and identifies the needs and costs in people, technology, space, dollars, and operational care.

PIA informs leadership and aligns stakeholders. PIA is not a legal process; it is a formalized business process designed to obtain buy-in and approvals, define objectives and expected outcomes, reduce unintended consequences, and highlight risk in privacy, security, ethics and reach a risk-based decision.

*All initiatives in business address a risk or pursue an opportunity*

**PTT (Privacy Threshold Testing)**

A PTT is a threshold test. In planning or examining the processing of personal data there are often risk triggers exposed that indicate a threshold has been exceeded and a DPIA, a detailed data protection impact assessment, is needed or required. Examples of these risk triggers are:

- The volume or sensitivity of the data or the vulnerability of those impacted
- Processing performed inures greater risk to one population than it does another
- There are questions about process or transparency in collecting, holding, or using personal data
- Processing is for a new purpose or has been collected or derived from new sources or in new ways
- There are questions about sharing or overseas transfer, legal and adequate safeguards, potential for individual harm and whether the rights of the individual have been sufficiently considered and protected

**DPIA (GDPR Article 35 Data Protection Impact Assessments)**

The DPIA is a targeted tool invoked by the GDPR and similar laws in specific conditions of identified risk. In accordance with the European Commission, DPIA, a Data Protection Impact Assessment is a process intended to evaluate risks to the rights and freedoms of individuals. Specifically, it is intended to assess 'the risks, their origin, nature, particularity and severity', and assesses the sufficiency of the 'measures, safeguards, controls, and mechanisms' that are in place to address these risks in protection of individual rights and personal data. The assessment is intended to describe the processing and its purpose, necessity of the processing, and proportionality of the risk introduced to achieve the intended purpose served by the processing. The means for mitigation of the risk if indicated is then defined and detailed.

If determined that high risk is introduced without clear mitigation, consultation with the DPO and/or supervisory authority is required before the processing evaluated can be performed.

The DPIA is a carefully considered process. It is used to examine process risk through thoughtful evaluation, serves to demonstrate that a process is not harmful to individual rights, and that the process complies with the law. It is not intended to be a checklist, but a well-developed risk-based assessment.

Where more than one of nine High Risk Processing categories are impactful, or one is likely to produce consequential impact to the rights and freedoms of individuals, a DPIA should be performed.

Risk should be continually monitored and periodically reassessed with change in the risk profile, business concerns, or on advisement by the DPO, or by the CISO. It is typical that the DPO and CISO would assist in defining the methodology of the assessment to be performed by the process owner and participate in evaluation of the outcome. The outcome of a DPIA informs an action, cease a process, or seek direction.

*Executives 'execute', and if pulled together for less than that is a missed opportunity. The PIA should succinctly inform and enable decision makers to either reject an investment or accept the risks and approve*

## HIGH RISK PROCESSING AND DPIA

The following are categorized as high-risk processing. They are likely to impose significant risk to individuals and trigger the need to conduct a DPIA (see GDPR art. 35). Local law defines others:

1. Scoring, profiling, or predictions based on personal aspects
2. Automatic decisions which lead to legal consequences for those impacted
3. Systematic monitoring
4. Sensitive data, special category personal data and data that potentiates harm (financial, location)
5. Data which is processed in a large scale
6. The merging or combining of data which was gathered by various processes
7. Data about children, convictions, incapacitated persons, or those with limited ability to act
8. Use of newer technologies or biometric procedures
9. Data processing which hinders those exercising their rights, using a service, or entering a contract

*Figure 22 High risk processing and DPIA*

A DPIA is an assessment. There are often numerous stakeholders, a questionnaire at some level of detail, and a meaningful evaluation. And it is often an evaluation of a specific risk, or area of risk, not a general determination that a process or program introduces risk. It is data subject and impact focused. It is tasked under law to be examined at depth, be performed as needed, as an on-demand or on-going process of assessment and risk review. A DPIA is also a process for compiling the 'proof of test' documentation appropriate to present to auditors and for consulting the DPO or supervisory authorities. It demonstrates deliberation in conformance to proper practice and adherence to the protective requirements of the law.

Specific conditions may suggest the need for a DPIA to be performed and findings may require further inspection or suggest additional examinations need to be done. DPIA is effectively a Zero Trust process. It is a risk unearthing process that needs to be followed until the risks are fully exposed and understood or can be mitigated.

ICO, CNIL and other privacy bodies offer guidance and commercial tools to address DPIA. There isn't a standard DPIA format or methodology required, and it rests with the business to include executive sign off or not. The DPIA will require at least these four elements be adequately exposed:

- A description of the processing being performed (defining why the personal data is being processed)
- The proportionality or necessity of the data processing being performed to the purpose intended
- Who will be impacted and how (risks and potential impacts to individuals and data subject rights)
- Measures and safeguards in place (and an assessment of their sufficiency to address the risk)

DPIA questions should be granular, probing, and deliberative asking for example:
- Have the communities or individuals likely to be impacted or benefitted been identified?
- Is there a disproportionate impact to specific communities, vulnerable individuals, or children?
- Can introduced risk be mitigated through existing security, legal or operational controls?

The ICO offers detailed guidance and provides a template with questions useful for conducting a DPIA at an effective level of granularity. (DPIA template 20180209 v0.3 or subsequent updates)

**GDPR and the Data Protection Officer**

Notification of processing to the supervisory authorities as previously required under the Directive is not a requirement under the GDPR (Recital 89) in most cases and has been replaced by the requirement to provide effective procedures and mechanisms where processing is "likely to result in 'high risk' to the rights and freedoms of natural persons". There are member state exceptions to this. Finland for instance requires advanced notice to the Office of the Data Protection Ombudsman when automated processing is planned and launched and in debt or credit processing and other specific instances. Bosnia & Herzegovina requires notice to the AZLP on compilation of personal data filing systems. Iceland requires prior notice when electronic technology will be used in the processing of personal data or in the processing of data for genetic research. Companies must implement appropriate safeguards to assure that the privacy of individuals is maintained and there is oversight. For many companies and particularly public authorities or public or private entities that monitor or process data on individuals in large scale (phone companies, hospitals, banks, utilities, etc.), this will require the appointment of a DPO, or Data Protection Officer.

This appointment is particularly required if a company collects, stores, or processes personal data considered sensitive, in specific, individual characteristic, affinity, affiliation, and behavior data. This would include physical, mental, religious affiliations, sexual preference, philosophic beliefs, and political alignment. It would also include information regarding criminal offenses, charges, convictions, or records of incarceration. Whether the DPO is an employee, or the function is performed by an external service, or an advisor, and whether the function is performed by an individual or team, anyone designated to perform the function of DPO needs authority, direct executive access, and should not be encumbered by distracting or conflicting interests. EU employee status is required to hold the title of DPO, although the function can be performed by others. As a non-employee of our Italian affiliate operating remotely in management of privacy and security, I had the title of DPSA or Data Protection System Administrator to reflect my responsibility to perform these functions. The appointment of the DPO affords a company some leeway. Decisions that had required the approval of Data Protection Authorities can more often be made locally under watch and direction of the DPO. There has been considerable discussion as to whether the CISO can assume the role of DPO or whether one could report to the other. Some feel a dual role would present a conflict of interests. Others, a unique blend of competencies.

The DPO will weigh in as to whether a Privacy Impact Assessment (Data Protection Impact Assessment) needs to be performed before introducing new technologies or new business processes to determine if they 'run a high risk of interference or impingement upon the rights and freedoms of individuals. http://www.gamingtechlaw.com/2016/04/privacy-impact-assessment.html.

*Business is about change and movement. Change and movement create or exacerbate risk*

Penalties for non-adherence with the GDPR or failure to provide adequate safeguards and protection of stewarded data are severe. Fines, the greater of Euro 20,000,000 or 4% of annual turnover for an operating company are possible for performing activities in defiance of the law, as well as enduring significant events resulting from poor conformance. These fines are enough to get the attention of companies that want to engage or provide services to EU residents, while anywhere in the EU, whoever they are, and wherever they may be. Engaging a DPO is a protective decision for a company. Guidance, advisement, and education, and appropriate monitoring of compliance, responsibilities of the DPO, can help avoid costly missteps and failures. The DPO is not an implementor, but will serve an audit and check role, advise, monitor data protection impact assessments, cooperate and liaison to supervisory authorities, workers unions, and other jurisdictional authorities, and assess the overall risk of processing operations. The role would include liaison with those managing internal corporate risk and security functions, human resources, processes and policies, breach notice obligations, and review of processor contracts for conformance.

Questions have been raised about whether the DPO may be liable for failure, negligence, inadequate guidance, or performance or if the DPO may be fined if too operational and so a 'conflict of interest', prompting one writer to suggest the need for officer insurance, (https://www.linkedin.com/groups/1243587, Jose Belo). In accordance with the European Data Protection Supervisor, it falls to organizations, not Data Protection Authorities, (and not the DPO), to demonstrate that an organization is compliant with the law.

DPO is a reviewer, not responsible for the program, and not liable for the company under the GDPR. https://edps.europa.eu/data-protection/our-work/subjects/accountability_en .

**Technical Monitoring and the Workplace**

In past years, there has been considerable confusion as to what technology might be deployed in different states across the EU in accordance with law for the purposes of assuring information security, and what would be disallowed. Whereas under the Directive laws varied by interpretation for each EU member state, GDPR acknowledges legitimate interests in processing personal data for prevention of fraud, and for purposes of maintaining information security. This clarification and its application across the EU certainly ease some of the decisions that need to be made as to technology deployment for the purposes of security, and reduces the cost and research required in developing a deployment plan that spans more than one EU member, or the EU in entirety. That said, any monitoring performed must be informed, typically by information provided at time of hire, time of deployment, or by information provided on the employee website, privacy policy, or in the employee handbook, and if needed, assessed by DPIA, and approved by the DPO. In all cases the benefit needs to be proportionate to the stated purpose or concern for which it has been deployed. When informed of the use of monitoring technologies, and advised as to the purpose for its use, employees also need to be informed of potential consequences.

*And it is diligence, a focus on quality management, and an effective program of review, that assures that amidst all distractions we stay on track*

200 | P a g e   Copyright Martin Gomberg All rights reserved - Do not copy reproduce or distribute without written consent v. 12/1/23

## PETS (Privacy Enhanced Technologies)

PETS, Privacy Enhanced Technologies, have become a major topic of conversation in privacy circles. That said, they don't seem to mean the same thing to all people, in all cases, all the time. They are alluded to in law but not well defined, identified, or their use dictated or in any manner specifically prescribed to the best of my knowledge in any regulation. GDPR article 25 which is the genesis of PETS for many, and the supporting recitals 28 and 29, dictates the use of 'reasonable technical and organizational measures'. GDPR recital 78 goes a bit further and roughly extrapolated adds that 'to demonstrate compliance the controller should implement internal policies and measures which meet the principles of data protection by design and by default'. This includes minimizing processing, pseudonymization of data, transparency of practices, enabling self-monitoring by the data subject, and controller creation or application of security measures. Producers of products, services and applications should be encouraged to take into consideration these principles to permit controllers and processors to fulfill data protection obligations.

But what qualifies technology as 'privacy enhanced' is not entirely clear. A word processing system or spreadsheet that allows a document to be encrypted and password protected is certainly privacy enhanced. Pseudonymization, data collection minimization, and retention limitations are certainly operationally effective privacy principles and are used in many technologies and internally developed applications. Most technologies can in fact be said to embody some specific privacy or data protection enhancements in some manner. So how can we categorize these to clarify the taxonomy so that the term does not lose relevancy? This topic is a book unto itself.

I see PETS as falling in two categories. Although this categorization is solely mine, I differentiate them as:

PETS 1 - Privacy Enabling Technologies, and PETS 2 - Privacy Enabled Technologies.

There are excellent companies in the PETS 1, Privacy Enabling space. These are purpose-built platforms provided by many of the companies we would recognize as best of class today. They are designed to assist businesses in their data protection posture through automation and process facilitation, inventories of data, assessments, data discovery, expression of individual rights, incident response, and regulatory alignment. These I consider privacy enabling, they can be purchased, contracted, and leveraged now, are in use by businesses of all sizes and in all industries globally, and are continually improving and helping businesses to meet corporate data protection objectives.

Privacy Enabled Technologies, PETS 2, I see as something different. At the risk of minimizing the importance of the category, many are still concepts and capabilities explored in universities, discussed in scholarly dissertations and by AI and privacy experts. I suspect that we as consumers will not be the purchasers of the best of these enabled technologies but get the benefit of them as features or services in the enabling platforms, the PETS 1 companies and platforms that will be their market, and with which we contract. And although some features have been adopted already in commercial 'enabling' products, many are still only available for the benefit of companies to limited degree. But these are the future of data protection, privacy enabled operations, process, organization, and technology.

## Operationalizing GDPR

Most executives will be acutely aware of the GDPR by now. Some may still only peripherally be aware of the impacts of the law in breadth and scope, and in the investments in reengineering that likely will need to be made. Others are exhausted by privacy regulation and will need to be coaxed to designate leadership, mandate cooperation, and align budget. The GDPR will impact people, technology, process, controls, and agreements. It will impact culture and fundamental business practice. This is often understated.

**As the CISO**, it is not unlikely that you will be tasked to put the GDPR in context for executive leadership, business, and operational divisions, and for staff. This requires clarification of obligations, and setting of expectations, regarding preparation, alignment of organization, and business impact. It requires fitting the GDPR in context of other legal obligations and technical standards, particularly those that define safeguards for data protection. This will include data retention policies, backups, and business continuity provisions.

**It will require targeted education** for specific groups including human resources and finance, as both are intimate with the personal information of employees. Processes may need alteration for compliance, background checks and maintenance of recruitment files for instance, or at a minimum, specific procedures and policies enacted.

**Representatives of each business** unit should be engaged to assure that the impacts on their business are understood and accommodated, and that needed information is brought back to their teams. These should be advocates and ensure that department obligations to the process are met. The specific competencies of each area should also be leveraged. Marketing will be invaluable in communicating to the customer community. The legal department for working with processor contracts. And if a processor business to business relationship is in place, can assure that appropriate and required attestation of compliance is made.

**IT application developers and database teams** will also need to be educated to understand and recognize personal data, identify repositories that exist, and the places and means by which processing or collecting occurs in existing systems. They also need to be taught to incorporate proper handling of personal data when retrofitting existing systems and processes, and in building new. Service tickets should be adapted to capture privacy issues and concerns, so these can be investigated and properly resolved while maintaining a record of the activity.

**Expectations of business partners** that participate in data processing (processors) requires a process and it be monitored. There should be an assessment or attestation of compliance, demonstrable and effective policy governing compliance, and expectation set that all contracts will be revisited to satisfy GDPR. And there are specific obligations and agreements required of them by law.

**The employee community** will **also need to be informed about the GDPR**, and specifically how it may affect the way they work and what is expected of them. They need to understand their obligations of confidentiality and duty of care in support of data subjects and how processes and policies in an employee context should be structured to meet the expectations of the law. Lastly, where business process is changing, and customer information handling is being changed, the customer community, data subjects, should be informed. They are all aware to be sure, at least we should hope, but should be informed of their rights through adequate and appropriate disclosure, and your responsibilities to them under the law, and how you plan to achieve compliance. Keeping clients informed minimizes incidents, reduces complaints and confusions, and engages the customer in the process.

**Fines and Penalties**

Beyond the egregious potential for fines of 20 million euro or 4% of total annual worldwide turnover for major infractions, half that for lesser infractions, or judicial remedies for harm (Daniel Solove), GDPR will have a massive impact on business, corporate governance, interaction between companies and individuals, and the exchange of data across borders. Although not limited by them, Dutch authorities have issued tiered guidance on the basis for fines, these influenced by the duration of the event, number of individuals impacted, type of data, and speed to address (https://thenextweb.com/eu/2019/03/14/the-netherlands-premieres-the-first-gdpr-fining-policy-in-the-eu/). The enormity and breadth of the law seems staggering. From executives to legal, finance, risk and compliance, IT, marketing, and human resources, how to respond to GDPR will be viewed with as many different perspectives as there are constituencies within an impacted business. It addresses the borders we traverse and information we share, processors with which we partner, markets in which we operate, data we collect and use, and consumers that drive our business. It will drive the focus of IT analysts, engineers, system administrators, database specialists, helpdesk, and application developers. Project managers, privacy specialists, security experts, continuity teams, and business operations. Its impact will be felt by almost every employee regardless of line of business activities.

**Compliance**

It is not uncommon to see articles talking about a number of steps to GDPR compliance. There is nothing wrong with that. There are areas of focus in the law, and we all need a framework. But it is often from a perspective, an area of expertise. And an expert in one area is not typically an expert in all areas touched by the law. I am certain that when an attorney, or a privacy specialist talks about protecting data, the breadth of that statement, though easily made, eludes them. As much so when the CISO talks to the changes in marketing and customer interaction. As much when any outside of legal discusses the intricacies and problems with establishing a legal basis for data collection or global transfer. The CISO faces different challenges than does the GC and the head of corporate risk, will see the problem differently, will approach it differently, and needs to view it from a unique perspective to succeed. Of course, ultimately the plans will need to come together, not likely as a super plan, but as an achievement of coordinated, but disparate efforts, a set of swimmers each in lanes, each headed in a common direction. Sometimes one will cross another's path, sometimes one or some spurt ahead of the rest, sometimes lag, but all working toward a collective vision of success. GDPR conformance for every company will be an adaptive, uniquely individualized, and reiterate process, working towards a common set of goals, but with a finish line that differs for each of us. For many companies, compliance is a target still ahead, and for some the work has not even started.

Businesses often invest their energies with a short-term focus. A tremendous amount of energy has and is being expended. There will be very few that will fail to achieve some measure of success in compliance with GDPR. That said, there will be equally few that successfully internalize a privacy focused culture and sustain the focus and energy to operationalize GDPR compliance, to attain, engrain, and sustain, and that is where without care many will fail.

Despite being law, and in a global context, GDPR, and the adoption of the multitude of other emerging privacy laws generally, is fundamentally not a legal problem. It is also to most astute corporate leadership not only an issue of penalties and fines. It is an issue of internalizing a pervasive and complex regulation into an operating business amidst a digital transition, globalization, an environment of cyber risk, competing agendas of personal privacy and security, other regulation, and the pursuit of competitive innovation. It is about oversight, culture, education, practice modification, technology, staffing, aligning the business interests, systems, and operations of a company, utility, or municipality with those of our markets, and the consumer, in a way we have not before. GDPR is about business. The CISO should view it in that context.

The ICO or UK Information Commissioners Office is an independent authority mandated to protect and uphold public rights and interests in individual privacy. Although no longer in the EU post Brexit they have provided a 12-step guidance for GDPR. https://ico.org.uk/media/1624219/preparing-for-the-gdpr-12-steps.pdf. Also look to the tools for self-assessment provided at the following link. https://ico.org.uk/for-organisations/resources-and-support/data-protection-self-assessment/data-protection-assurance/.
And for a compilation of the articles another useful resource is https://gdpr-info.eu/. Out of country transfer is an area of complexity and high-risk processing, not just in the EU but globally and should be evaluated with guidance of legal and in-country specific counsel (see GDPR articles 45-49) and new guidance from EDPB on data transfers.

---

*DATA TRANSFER EXEMPTIONS (Art. 49 DEROGATIONS) UNDER THE GDPR*

There may be allowances for transfers of data to countries outside of the European Economic Area even if not deemed adequate if for limited activity in specific conditions as derogations including:

- explicit consent has been provided by the data subject for the transfer
- the subject has been informed of the risks of transfer
- it is required in preparation, execution or in conclusion of a contract between the controller and data subject (transfer is made at the request of the data subject)
- public interest
- establishment or defense of legal claims
- protecting the vital interests of the data subject (if incapable of providing consent directly)
- legitimate interests of the controller if not impactful to the rights and freedoms of the data subject

---

Countries monitor communications and the flow of data as a means of securing borders and protecting the citizenry from the threat of terror. Sharing of law enforcement data to provide intelligence in counter terror operations, fraud, and crime is not governed by GDPR, but by the EU Law Enforcement Directive, ensuring that there are no impediments to needed public safety information between allies and cooperating sovereign entities. Security or law enforcement transfers of data are governed and addressed under PNR (Passenger Name Records) and TFTP (Terrorist Financial Tracking Program) agreements and similar law elsewhere.

## A Framework for Sustainable Privacy Program Maturity

<u>Leadership advocates conformance</u> and cultural adoption through appropriate tone, message, example, and resources.

<u>Line of business management has established the needed governance,</u> oversight, training, and means to evaluate and report effectiveness for their areas of responsibility.

<u>Staffing is adequate</u>, adequately resourced, and adequately trained, and is provided the needed access to leadership and line of business management to be successful

<u>Entities have been identified, mapped, and evaluated across the enterprise</u> for exposure, conformance, and controls, and to identify undertakings, entities that participate in their activities, and their governance

<u>There is a process to assess relative progress</u>, both within and comparatively between areas.

<u>An assessment and closure of exposed gaps</u> has been completed.

<u>An inventory of processes and data</u> has been undertaken and is maintained. Processes are in place for evaluating and continual assessment of change

<u>Data and process risk are examined and addressed,</u> internal, 3$^{rd}$ party, and shared risk within the organization

<u>Privacy and security are aligned</u> and reiteratively tested and reviewed for the presence, adequacy, and validation of controls.

<u>Contracts, licenses, and processing agreements are adequately protective</u>, operationally effective, in place with all required parties, address transfers, changes of ownership, and meet the tenets of the law

<u>Policies, disclosures, support, infrastructure, and safeguards</u> are sufficient to meet objectives

<u>Collection, purpose, processing, and retention limits</u> conform to the reasonable and rightful expectations of individuals. Basis for processing, data localization agreements, contracts and legal mechanisms for transfer are each in adherence to law and individual rights.

<u>An operationalized program</u> of security, quality, ethics, and privacy by design are inherent in all processes throughout the business and process lifecycle.

<u>There is a means to detect and respond to incidents, a technical response, and a regulatory response.</u> Preparation has been done, resources identified and aligned, agreements and NDA's put in place with critical response partners, and there is a process to determine needed actions and to document, assess risk patterns, trends, and vulnerabilities, and to learn from failure.

<u>Programs are in place</u> and have been institutionalized for risk assessment, continuous inventory, controls testing, vulnerability assessment, a process of audit and validation, and documentation

<u>Business owns the process.</u> Enterprise shares accountability for success.

*Figure 23 Framework for Sustainable Program Maturity*

# POST BREXIT DATA TRANSFERS: A BRIEF INTERVIEW WITH RALPH T. O'BRIEN

On June 28, 2021, almost surprisingly, adequacy was granted to the UK enabling unrestricted data exchange with the EU. This was surprising as this came amidst critique of UK adequacy, and proposals in the UK for a less European privacy stance, a more business friendly and less onerous privacy regulation, and a softening towards UK-US data transfers. I had the opportunity to ask Ralph T. O'Brien then for some comments. <u>Now a year later this is once again all up in the air. Ralph's comments below are a year old.</u>

*Ralph, prior to Brexit the UK was a member of the EU and in large part shared a cultural, economic, and historic context in shared institutions and agreements. Brexit had muddied the waters regarding EU-UK adequacy in data transfer. The EDPB (European Data Protection Board) recently found EU-UK law alignment strong but expressed concerns, these now apparently resolved. This is determinative for the UK, but does it have implications for the UK-US going forward? We are wrestling with EU data transfer following the Schrems II decision that resulted in dissolution of the US Privacy Shield and now the direction of UK-US transfers lacks clarity. How would you characterize the relationships and structures that despite Brexit align the EU and UK and what should we expect regarding data protection?*

Though the UK has left the EU, it remains part of the Council of Europe. It remains a signatory to Convention 108 and the European Convention of Human Rights. The UK still acknowledges the jurisdiction of the European Court of Human Rights in Strasbourg. So, core values and some important institutions and agreements remain intact. However, the ICO (UK Information Commissioner's Office) is no longer an EU supervisory body. Anything approved by the ICO prior may need to be re-approved by an EU supervisor. This might be the case for instance if you are still relying on ICO approved BCRs, etc. as a transfer mechanism. CJEU decisions no longer are binding, however data processed before 1st January 2021 is still subject to the "Frozen EU GDPR". That means that prior processing is still subject to CJEU decisions and the rules in force at that time.

The UK has been committed to viewing the EU as an adequate place for data export and had grandfathered EU adequacy decisions as being adequate for UK data exports. The EU commitment was less clearly defined but had granted temporary adequacy for up to six months conditional on the UK not changing anything including creating its own adequacy determinations or standard contract clauses etc. during this period. This is now behind us granted adequacy as of 18th June 2021. But a declaration of adequacy does not mean we are back to a pre-Brexit posture. Data is free to transfer without supplementary measures, but the UK is an external entity with its own legal, legislative, law enforcement, data transfer and trade interests including data exchange with the US and other trade deals like the Australian – UK deal.

*If it has no consequential impact to the business, it isn't a risk. Threats are only of concern if they impact a business objective.*

The Queens last speech for her government included "Data Reform". This takes the view that human rights may "get in their way" of asserting sovereignty and making the UK more "business friendly" by "EU removing red tape" are all stated Brexit goals, so how far we drift from the EU law remains a question. As at July 2023 we now have a new proposed "Data Protection and Digital Innovation Bill (no2)" - that looks at adding a layer of exemption and softening of some requirements, making minor modification and changes, whilst strengthening the PECR/ePrivacy fines to match GDPR, and to reshape the Information Commissioner's office to an Information Commission. Whilst basics stay the same, DPOs, DPIAs, PbD and ROPAs and UK representatives are all targets for change, even if just renamed and softened in terms of their scope and applicability.

As a bill anything can still change, but the proposed changes are not bold, trying to toe the line between keeping EU adequacy and adding flexibility for UK businesses. Sadly, it's my conclusion that it achieves neither - instead creating further "track changes" to an already complex legislative state.

*What about companies conducting in scope activities in both the EU and in the UK?*
The GDPR requires an EU representative. Now organisations may have to appoint a UK representative in addition to an EU representative even if they do not have an establishment here but are targeting products and services at the territory. For companies performing in scope activities in the UK after the 1st of January 2021, data processing is subject to the UK GDPR and the UK Courts. The UK implementation of the GDPR is now the UK Data Protection Regulation as amended by the Data Protection, Privacy and Electronic Communications and EU Exit regulations of 2019 and 2020. The ICO is the supervisory body.

*Was the determination of adequacy for the UK conditional and what does the UK data protection future look like in your opinion?*
Is adequacy conditional? If we choose to change the law, what effect might this have? Prior to the adequacy decision the UK has had two draft adequacy statements released by the EC for the purposes of GDPR and LED *(General Data Protection Regulation, Law Enforcement Directive)*. These contained conditions such as a 4-year review cycle and were contingent on assuring no onward transfers to "inadequate" countries. This clearly would impose difficulties on any UK-US trade agreement. These conditions persist and may be at odds with ongoing UK interests where the UK wants to add data transfer to new trade deals.

Given UK interests what do you see as next steps and things to watch?
The UK government commissioned a project to "review Data Protection law". Reducing human rights that may "get in their way", asserting sovereignty and making the UK more "business friendly" by "EU removing red tape" are all stated Brexit goals, so how far we drift from the EU law remains a question.

How the UK courts interpret the UK GDPR/DPA2018, and how these judgements will differ in approach from the CJEU approach remains to be seen. Also, any further amendments to EU law may not be paralleled in UK law, and the future will likely see increasing divergence.

There are many questions remaining. If the EU passes the new ePrivacy Regulation, for example, will the UK follow?  Similarly, will the UK take the same direction with EU-US adequacy or create its own "data bridges"? The biggest question had been one of the adequacy agreements and most organisation had planned for the worst, putting in place mechanisms like SCCs with post Schrems II additional safeguards to deal with importing EU personal data, at least for now, unneeded.  In seeking Trade deals with the US and others, data transfer is very much on the table as a bargaining chip, so if the UK wishes to create its own deals such as a "UK-US Privacy Shield" equivalent, what will this mean for the EU transfers?  The UK public sector also has adopted largely a "UK Cloud first" strategy, causing non-UK providers headaches in how it manages, supports, and stores data accordingly.

The future is a book yet unwritten, and so in the absence of a crystal ball, even with adequacy affirmed, 2023 and beyond will continue to be an uncertain time for UK Data Protection and global data transfers.  As the UK and EU regimes begin to diverge, we will all have to pay close attention to the changes as the ground rules turn beneath our feet!

*Ralph T. O'Brien is Principal, REINBO Consulting, Ltd., a UK based consulting firm specializing in privacy and data protection regulation. www.reinboconsulting.com.*

*Increasingly, regulations and law have focused concern on the protection of data. And increasingly, the data we need to protect to be compliant, is global, mobile, and everywhere*

# CISO
# REDEFINED

*Protecting Business*

Martin Gomberg, CISSP, CIPP/E

## SECTION 13.  CCPA - CPRA – CALIFORNIA PRIVACY RIGHTS ACT

The CCPA or California Consumer Privacy Act, or the CCPA as amended by the CPRA, the California Privacy Rights Act, was the first comprehensive 'contextually cognizant' privacy law to emerge in the US. Like GDPR, the CCPA considers not just personal information specific to an individual such as name, contact information, health, financial, employment or educational records, but the entire 'personal context' of an individual, behaviors, traits, affinities, affiliations, purchasing patterns, browsing histories, biology, and other information permitting association, individuation, and attachment to household.

There is a reasonableness test as to whether data is associated to an individual in language that reads 'is *reasonably* capable of being associated with, or could *reasonably* be linked, directly or indirectly, with an identified or identifiable individual, and in the case of the CPRA, broadened to include households that purchase or use products/services jointly'.

An earlier exemption expired as of 1/1/23 so that individual rights protections now extend to all California consumers including full and part time employees, job applicants, independent contractors, remote workers in CA., temps, former employees, corporate officers, executives, franchise owners, licensees, business to business contacts, and 3rd party employees. There is a newly defined category of 3rd party, an independent contractor, with specific requirements for annual reviews, contracts, and disclosures.

 The CCPA went into effect January 2020, amended by CPRA, January 2023 with substantial changes. The amended CCPA provides a broader set of rights (including the right to request correction of personal data), defines a new category of sensitive data with specific protections, emphasizes data collection minimization, purpose limitation, and limits on retention, and that processing be relevant and necessary. It implements a more granular and specific definition of consent. It requires verification of identity for access requests but recognizes that verification may be different for employees with whom a business is more intimately familiar than other consumers.

The amended CCPA also sets new obligations for companies including more complete disclosures, adds new contract, risk and security audits, reporting requirements, and requires opt-out notices and links both for sale and sharing. Disclosures and a means for individuals to limit sensitive data use is required of companies that collect sensitive data and use it for the inference of characteristics about an individual. Generally, this excludes services like HR, IT, payroll, emergency contacts, and similar. Whether financial incentives are offered for the collection and use of data must be disclosed.

CPRA further departs from CCPA in that it distinguishes 'sharing' as its own category of transaction. It is defined differently than the 'sale' of data. Each requires its own notices and opt-out processes. CPRA mandates support of global opt-out from electronic tracking through cookies and other means through browser controls.

The CPRA removes the 30-day cure period which had allowed businesses under CCPA the opportunity to correct deficiencies and address compliance issues before fines were imposed. Legal actions formerly handled in state court are now addressed in administrative Law Court, and oversight is through a newly defined governing body, CPPA (CA Privacy Protection Agency), no longer the California Attorney General's Office. The CCPA and many of its requirements remain in effect alongside many of the CPRA changes until CPRA is fully implemented.

CCPA applies to for profit companies. Most information generally available to the public is not considered personal information under CCPA if lawfully available from federal, state, or local records. Also excluded from CCPA are commercial processing activities involving an individual's data collected outside of California even if collected from California resident consumers while outside of California. Data collected in California maintains its protection under CCPA even if the consumer no longer resides in California. Personal data is protected if used for commercial purposes within California regardless of where it is acquired. There is a one year look back period for DSAR (Data Subject Access Requests) requests by consumers for information held about them. This requires that companies focus on the linkage of individuals to their contributed data, or any procured data about them. CPRA extends the lookout to be as long as feasible.

There is inheritance language in the CCPA which may extend obligations to corporate parents, entities that share common branding if they share CA personal data, and partnerships and autonomous entities in joint ventures. Companies are obligated to comply to the CCPA if they directly, or through an entity they control, or are controlled by, directly or indirectly, in whole or part, wherever located, collects, receives, or processes the personal information of California residents.

Data that has been de-identified in a manner that is not reversable is not PI. But encryption, and any other key based or reversable de-identification are only defensive arguments to claims. They may not mitigate risk or liability. In event of breach the California Breach Protection Act applies.

There is no cap to penalties under the CCPA. They range from $2500 per impacted individual per violation to $7500 if the violation is willful. There is also a private right of action granted under the CCPA. This private right of action allows additional potential penalties of up to $750 per individual or actual damages for disclosed, stolen, or inappropriately accessed information that had not been encrypted or rendered de-identifiable or had not been adequately protected by security measures.

**To fall in scope to the CCPA as amended by CPRA** companies must meet any of three litmus test conditions. I have labeled these a size test, a volume of activity test, and a derived benefit test:

| Size Test | Gross revenue of $25 million or greater in prior 12 months |
|---|---|
| **Volume of Activity Test** | Buys, sells, or shares the personal information of 100,000 or more California households or individual residents. |
| **Derived Benefit Test** | 50% of its revenues is from the sale of the personal information of or about California consumers |

## Discussion

The CCPA grants the consumer specific rights, rights to know, access, correct, delete, opt-out of sale or sharing, limit use and disclosure of sensitive data, incur no retaliation for exercise of rights, and an expanded look back. An authenticated consumer may without fear or concern for discrimination, unfavorable treatment, terms, pricing, or denial of goods or services, twice in a twelve-month period request disclosure of the categories and specific information collected about them, categories of sources and third parties or types of third parties with whom it is shared, and the business or commercial purpose for its collection. They may request information held about them be deleted, or returned to them, and if returned electronically, in a usable format permitting its reuse elsewhere.

Data collection notices follow the formats defined for CPPA but should now also address sensitive data. Where that data is collected for sale, the verified consumer may request disclosure of the categories of information that are sold, and at their discretion exercise the means provided to opt out, limit or disallow the sale of their data. A third-party receiving data, whether purchased or shared with them, may not re-sell that data unless the consumer has been provided an explicit notice of that intent and an opportunity to disallow resale by opting out. Data purchased from brokers by acquirers with the intent of sale for purposes of commercial gain by any party requires broker registration. There is increased protection for children. Verified parental approval is required for the collection or sale of children's data if age 13 or less.

### Data Sale vs Data Sharing

Under CCPA a data sale is any exchange of information for monetary or other valuable consideration including sale, lease, rent, transfer, disclosure or sharing and similar activities. A consumer must be provided proper notice and means to accept, limit or opt-out of the sale of their data. If there is a financial incentive to allowing the sale of their data, they need to be informed.

Under CPRA sale and data sharing are differentiated and each requires notices and an opportunity to opt out. Sharing is redefined to include cross context behavioral advertising, the enabling of 3rd parties to target ads to consumers using data obtained from cookies and other devices that expose a consumers interests tracked from patterns of activities across different sites. If a company shares data through the targeting of advertising to a consumer based on data obtained from the consumer's activity across businesses, distinctly-branded websites, applications, or services, other than the business, distinctly-branded website, application, or service with which the consumer intentionally interacts, a Do Not Share link is required. A notice and a means for a consumer to opt out of cookie collection or specifically 3rd party cookie collection is required as part of a more granular consent. Sites should disclose the use of cookies and permit individuals to elect to allow all cookies and permit 3$^{rd}$ party cross contextual uses, limit to only essential requirements for the operations of the site, or disallow all cookies. Global browser preferences should be respected if provided

(California Lawyers Association) - https://calawyers.org/business-law/digital-trackersdata-protection-how-the-cpra-closes-ccpa-gaps-in-addressing-cross-contextual-behavioral-tracking/.

If a request to opt out of sale or sharing is made, it is binding until retracted, but reauthorization may not be requested by the business for at least 12 months following an opt-out. Transfers of data to a service provider for processing governed by a contract does not constitute a sale under CCPA.

CCPA is not limited to electronically collected data, but any consumer data. CCPA generally will not apply to data collected, disclosed, or sold for purposes of credit assessment, protected under the Confidentiality of Medical Information Act, HIPAA, or comparable laws, although the exemption may be limited to only specific data and activities for companies operating under those laws. CCPA should not apply to medical provider data or to data collected in conducting a clinical trial. Most charities and non-profit organizations are exempt.

The CPRA lists specific data collection and sharing activities that can be considered a "business purpose." These include auditing, data security, debugging, internal research and maintaining quality and safety, as well as "advertising and marketing services (non-personalized advertising)" that do not target individuals, and therefore do not constitute "cross-context behavioral advertising.

CCPA requires annually updated privacy policies and consumer facing notices. It requires consumers to be provided multiple means to request information or express their intentions and preferences, a website, toll-free number, etc., and requirements for this differ by business type. Once verified, data requests about data collected over the prior 12-months activity should be addressed within 45 days. Deletion requests should also be communicated to service providers. CCPA defines 11 specific categories of data considered individuating and any disclosure of collected data should reflect these.

CPRA is relatively new law, and we can expect that there will be changes and additions for some time to come. It would be prudent to verify current status of all previsions or work with professionals when implementing a program of compliance.

The Office of the California AG offers this link: https://www.oag.ca.gov/privacy/ccpa#sectionb

# Some Sources by Which Personal Data is Acquired or Enters a Business (Not CCPA specific)

## Employee Related

1. As an employer personal information is collected from/about individuals. Data is gathered through interviews, resumes, from references and in background checks or investigations. It is used in prospecting, recruitment, onboarding, administration, retirement, separation, and post-employment communication.
2. An employee is given systems and data access, creates a user ID and password, is added to directory groups.
3. On premise CCTV, building access cards, biometric scanners and logins capture identity, time, and activity.

## Consumer Related

4. A person shops at a physical store location or visits a restaurant and pays with credit.
5. Individual establishes non-commerce online account for downloads, support, event registration.
6. Individual establishes eCommerce account for online shopping, obtaining products or services.
7. An individual shares personal data directly, though corporate email, blog, post, webform, chat or application.
8. An individual uses a common interest site, social community, dating site, or subscription membership service.
9. An individual uses an enrollment, referral or service matching app for social services, clinical trials, etc.
10. Procured consumer contact lists are used in prospecting for customers or for other company uses.
11. Data is purchased with the intent to disclose, transfer, or sell for commercial benefit or gain.
12. Consumers visiting a website are referred to a business or service; a visitor referral is tracked for shared gain.
13. Data is shared under contract for the provision of consumer services or to better consumer services.
14. Links and referrals from external sites or services.
15. Data is captured or transferred using cookies and other technical devices or cached to network devices.
16. Validated identity for rights requests or validated parental consent for the processing of children's data.
17. Manufacturer or service receives identifiable data when validated consumer uses IOT device (i.e., monitoring).

## Business to Business

18. Representatives of a business interact online through email, CRM, sales system or other B2B activities.
19. Representative of a business establish eCommerce accounts or shop for products or services.
20. Using obtained or procured client contact lists for prospecting and targeting corporate buyers or similar.
21. Business cards, event participant lists, cold calls. or prospect research on behalf of an organization.
22. As a processor or collector of personal data on behalf of governments, agencies, or int'l organizations.
23. As a processor or collector for charities and non-government organizations.
24. As a service provider that receives data directly from consumers on behalf of other companies.
25. As a service provider receiving data about consumers from other companies for processing.
26. From data exchange agreement between companies or affiliates, data exchanged by an interstitial app, third party cookies and trackers, or through referral programs from other consumers for commercial benefit.
27. Data transferred in relation to acquisition or merger.

## Other Processing

28. Data provided in legal privilege, contracts, medical examinations, public safety inquiries or clinical trials.
29. Impactful automated processing of data
30. Digital tracking of behavior including unique visitation, recurrence, frequency, gaps, time spent, interests.
31. Data inferred, derived, or enhanced from other data or sources.
32. Publicly available information.

# Categories of Personal Data as Defined under CCPA

| | | |
|---|---|---|
| 1 | (Personal) Identifiers | Name, Address, Alias. Unique ID, Email, IP Address, Accounts, SS#, License or Similar |
| 2 | CA 1798.80(e) Categories | Information that identifies, relates to, describes, or is capable of being associated with a particular individual. This does not include publicly available information lawfully made available by federal, state, or local governments. |
| 3 | Protected classification Under California or Federal Law | Age, Minors, Health, etc.. |
| 4 | Commercial Information | Records of Personal Property or Products Purchased or Considered |
| 5 | Biometric Information | Fingerprints, Retinal Scans, DNA |
| 6 | Network Activity | Browsing History, Search, Online Behavior, Cookies & Tracking |
| 7 | Geolocation Data | Location, Telemetric, Travel Patterns, Travel History, Demographic |
| 8 | Sense and Perception | Audio, Electronic, Visual, Thermal, Olfactory Data or Similar |
| 9 | Professional / Employment | Job history, Recruitment, Onboarding, Benefits, Compensation |
| 10 | Education Information | Not Publicly Available; Educational Information as Defined In FERPA |
| 11 | Inferences and profiling | Information derived through algorithms, subjective inference, examination of patterns or by enhancement of data through combination or comparison to other data that individuates, associates, or provides a deeper insight to characteristics, attitudes, predispositions, behavior, or aptitudes of an individual |

Note: There is also a category of probable identifiers, a qualifier which adds relevance and reasonableness to the association

# WHERE IS US PRIVACY HEADING?  JANALYN SCHREIBER, DATA PRIVACY & SECURITY ADVISORS

While the United States is not yet at the point of adopting cohesive federal-level legislation on privacy, the ongoing flurry of state-level activity gives us insight into the trends that are beginning to define the US's stance on privacy, and the rights of individuals with respect to their data. It is likely unsurprising to many that we are seeing business-friendly, weaker regulations advancing.

The California Privacy Rights Act of 2020 (CPRA) seemed to usher in a new opportunity for the US (or at least the States) to align our regulation more closely to the EU/UK's General Data Protection Regulations (GDPR). This would have explicit requirements for necessity and proportionality, data minimization, use limitations on sensitive personal information (and that as a distinct category), and processing risk assessments submitted regularly to the California Privacy Protection Agency (CPPA). And these enhanced obligations (or Rights, depending on your perspective!), coupled with a Private Right of Action (PRA) in the event of a breach would create a foundation that moves the needle closer to the GDPR's concept of data privacy and protections as a human right.

However, the US has always been one to go its own way.  We see echoes of and variations on these requirements in newer state regulations that have passed or been proposed. Led by Virginia's Consumer Data Protection Act (VCDPA), which passed in March 2021, there are over a dozen state privacy bills in process that have diverged from the CPRA with twists that arguably make them weaker and less favoring of the individual data subject.

First is the narrower definition of "consumer" which explicitly excludes individuals representing a business in a B2B relationship. Next the exclusion of employees where personal information is collected or processed by an employer in an employment context. This narrowly limits the protection of privacy rights to only consumers, and only in the context of in-state B2C commercial transactions.

Next, there is the narrower inclusion of data associated in the context of "sale,". The VCDPA excludes from a sale personal information that the consumer "intentionally made available to the public via a channel of mass media and did not restrict to a specific audience" (§ 59.1-571.). These limitations dramatically increase the volume of data by us or about us that businesses can disclose, transfer, and sell without either our consent or ability to prevent. The modification to the definition of "consumer" also has a dramatic impact on the scope of newer regulations. The exclusion of B2B and Employment Data Subjects means fewer businesses will hit the volume thresholds of in-state Consumer (B2C) Data Subjects to be subject to the act at all.

Still another area where we are seeing divergence in the US from more ubiquitous practices globally is in consent.

Opt-in consent allows consumers to exercise their rights to the privacy of their personal data, its collection and use. Without a specific and informed opt-in consent that expresses an individual's permission for a business to collect or use their data and use it in the way the consumer intends for it to be used, collection would be disallowed. Most privacy regimes in place globally and those emerging seemingly everywhere have adopted opt-in consent to protect the consumer's interests, assure that businesses provide a means for the consumer to easily give their consent if they choose, and to be informed about what it is to which they are consenting. The states appear to be leaning towards a more business-friendly 'opt-out' approach, some permitting businesses to collect personal data perhaps with notice but without obtaining consent and to continue unabated until the consumer takes active steps to determine where their data is being held, to navigate the sites, request their data be erased or returned, and to opt-out of further collection.

The balance tips heavily in favor of business here. And even though the CPRA goes the furthest by creating the "global opt out," where CA residents can use internet browsers and extensions that automatically notify every website that the user is opting out of the sale of their personal data or the use of it for targeted advertising, it is still opt-out consent; it applies only to CA residents; and it does not into effect until 2023.

Business is pressing to prevent the Private Right of Action currently in the California Consumer Privacy Act (CCPA), which allows consumers to sue for security violations, from making it into other state acts. They argue that the cost of litigation could be extinction-level for many. Consumer advocates argue the watered-down versions of privacy bills allow companies to continue with business-as-usual operations under the guise of privacy protections, which offer little by way of actual protection.

The VCDPA does not include a PRA. It was struck from draft acts in Washington, Florida, and Connecticut. Business lobbying efforts have been so successful in Oklahoma and North Dakota that the bills died in committee. In Texas there is neither an opt-out nor opt-in requirement and no PRA. And Arizona, Hawaii, Illinois, and Minnesota have acts inspired by the VCDPA, a much less robust role model than the CPRA would have been.

But to be fair, Virginia's CDPA is another step forward, offering significant new rights for consumers. It draws on global regulations for several key data and risk management requirements demonstrating the ongoing interest of Americans in protecting their data. Taken together and when viewed in combination with other states with proposed acts, this may put pressure on Congress to pass a federal data privacy law.

It is also not the only path forward - Massachusetts, New York, and New Jersey are considering bills that include opt-in frameworks, a private right of action, and other provisions that strengthen consumer protections. So even as trends are emerging, the patchwork nature of privacy law in the US will continue and continue to keep businesses on their toes.

*Janalyn Schreiber is Partner, Data Protection & Security Advisors, a US consulting firm specializing in privacy, data protection regulation and security -* janalyn@TheDPSA.com / www.TheDPSA.com

# CISO REDEFINED

*Protecting Business*

Martin Gomberg, CISSP, CIPP/E

## SECTION 14.  INVENTORY, CLASSIFICATION AND DATA RISK

As stated earlier, where you cannot have privacy without security, implementation of any effective program of privacy or data protection is dependent on understanding areas of consequential risk so that an effective plan can be developed to address it. Compliance reviews should assure that an effective program of identification, inventory and classification is in place for consequential data, an assessment and alignment of risk to data, and tested controls. It should ensure that there is appropriate prioritization, directed spend, and adequate risk mitigation efforts. An understanding of risk and an appropriate classification of data also permits the establishment of a policy governing acceptable use and needed controls for specific data types.

Technology is continually improving for the search, inventory, cataloging, and protection of specific classes of data, and the automation of privacy studies. Some of these couple the capability to locate sensitive data stored at rest, with the ability to detect, apply policy and take appropriate actions when sensitive data is in transit, encrypting PII on the fly, or perhaps requiring authorization for that data to be used at all. Ironically, some that monitor access and activity to predict the malicious intent of insiders, or Data Loss Prevention or DLP technologies that 'read, inspect and monitor' the movement of private data 'across the wire' in attempt to protect against exfiltration may themselves raise privacy concerns under worker's rights and federal and state wiretap acts and similar laws globally. Healthy skepticism in the application of controls is appropriate. Those that impinge on privacy should be scrutinized and not tacitly accepted. Security is critical to business success and effective operations. So are people and their privacy.

### Sensitive data elements

In the United States, privacy, and obligations to report detected incidents of privacy breach are embedded in federal laws, agency regulations, and in state privacy statutes. Definition as to what constitutes sensitive 'personally identifiable information' or PII varies from state to state and changes over time. In Europe privacy is less tied to data elements, and more to the context in which data is collected, cared for, used and exposed, so a list approach is even less relevant there. California has introduced contextual privacy law like that in the EU and other states are exploring or legislating variations of that model.

*The CISO is a factor of maturity for the quality business*

# MANAGING MULTIPLE DATA PROTECTION AND PRIVACY REGULATIONS

Business, Data and Relationship Analysis

Process Description and Documentation (PIA)

Risk Testing and Assessments (DPIA)

Authorized Use

Training and Adoption

Security and Change Management

Planning and Design

Respect of Individual Rights

Obligations and Reporting

## Establish a Privacy Program

- Executive Oversight and Advocacy

- Documented Policies and Practices

- A Capable Team for Planning, Administration, Development, And Operations

- Adherence to Regulation, Standards, And Practices

- Culture of Compliance

- Inventory, Classification and Assessment

> Privacy regulations may differ but for most there are core principles. Each requires a commitment to embedding conforming practices and the rights of individuals in the planning, intent, and operation of all entities of a business, its relationships, workflows, applications, processes, and data protection controls.

Transparency

Data Minimization

Purpose Limitations

Consent

Individual Rights

Retention Limits or Regulation

Security controls

Operational controls

Incident Response

## Reiterative Testing and Correction

- Define Privacy Objectives

- Assess and Inventory Risks to Objectives

- Protect Objectives Through Controls

- Test Performance of Controls

- Gauge Success at Achieving Privacy Objectives

> Despite the best of intent and diligence in implementation, business changes, new products are released, new deals are done, new data assets are acquired, and risk moves. Effective data protection requires continual reevaluation through testing to identify data at risk and assess the effectiveness of the controls in place to mitigate that risk.

*We are only as secure, and effective, and our efforts only as clean and complete, as the greatest of our residual exposure, or as the saying goes, our weakest link in the chain.*

Corporate data including compensation plans, client lists, sales plans, and financials, privileged and confidential attorney communications and work products, and crown jewel IP including designs, art, formulas, and patentable works, all of which make a company competitive, from a corporate sense are all highly confidential. These are the secrets of a company, protected at great effort, the exposure or loss of which would be critically impactful, but to businesses, less so people. In that sense, these are treated more as matters of business protection and less as matters of privacy. These exposures though often protected in much the same way technically, organizationally are treated separately from that considered personally sensitive, matters managed by Human Resources and Legal Departments and protected by law, insurance, and statute.

Sensitive data is typically a special category of PII (personal information), PHI (health related information) or PCI (credit and financials) data that exposes specific aspects of private and personal matters of health, wealth, or behavior for individuals or that may be discriminatory or impactful to vulnerable communities. Sensitive data as a source of risk and potential harm is protected by US federal regulation (HIPAA, COPPA, ADA, FERPA), numerous global laws, labor acts, unions, medical, and employment contracts and releases.

The data collected, processed, transported, and stored by a business application determines the confidentiality and sensitivity classification of that application, not its exposure. More specifically, the confidentiality and sensitivity of an application is as high as the most confidential or sensitive data elements it contains. If a data element is sensitive, the application that holds or processes it is sensitive. If the highest risk data element in an application is of moderate risk, the application is moderate risk. Exposure is a factor of the placement of the application, and appropriateness and effectiveness of controls, whether encrypted or deidentified for example, whether behind multiple firewalls accessible to a limited group, protected by source controls and other access restrictions or placed in the DMZ at the periphery of corporate defenses. Equally, it might be in the cloud, configured for ease of access and availability to a community at large. Confidentiality, sensitivity, and exposure are important and should be considered in any review of data protection and privacy.

Assessing data risk requires us to understand the processes we perform, why they are important, and how they are exposed. This requires us to know our business as an enterprise, constituent entities, operating divisions, the processes each performs, sub processes and component tasks, and if automated, the applications involved in the process. It requires us to know the sensitivity of the data and how it is exposed. If applications and operational processes inherit risk from the data they process, where applications and processes are high risk, the workflows in which they participate are high risk. Businesses inherit risk from the communities they serve, business they do, means by which it is performed and the data they collect. Rationalizing this for conformance begins with an inventory.

In the lists that follow I offer some thoughts on privacy assessment, necessary data, and process to be inventoried, information to be collected and documented by inventory, documentation of workflow, some thoughts on data classification and how these all contribute to an operationalized privacy program.

**Records of Processing Assessment or ROPA - what you need to know about the business**

- Profile the business, its structure, entities, business units and brands, where it operates, has customers or employees, and collects, processes, or stores personal data
- Where and how that collection or processing is done for each process and where and how data is stored or used, on premises or in cloud, domestic or out of country
- Parental entities, sub entities, peers, partners, and vendors that provide guidance or participate together in joint undertakings or derive benefit in that processing wherever located

**Data Inventory - information to gather and document for each process – (a new hire example)**

- Business unit or department that owns the process (example: Human Resources)
- The name of the process (example: New Hire Process)
- Executive ownership of the process (example: EVP HR Finance Division)
- Name and contact information for the owner(s)
- Is there a legal basis and / or authorization established for the collection or processing?
- Source of data – (example: Directly obtained from prospect in interview, indirectly via references)
- Purpose of the collection or processing – (identifying, assessing, and hiring an employee)
- Categories of data collected – (identifying information, education, professional background, banking)
- Data elements collected – (name. contact information, degree earned, prior employer, bank, etc.)
- Disclosed to categories) – i.e... Internal (IT and facilities), Service Providers (benefits provider, payroll administration services, bank for direct deposit), Commercial Providers (sells services to new hires)
- Vendor(s) systems participating in process – (i.e., an online candidate search website and service)
- Internal technical / Cloud or other operational systems participating in process - (HR, IT, Payroll)
- Where is this data held?
- How long is the data collected in this process retained?
- Is there a legal or operational basis to the retention period?
- How is this data protected?

**Data Workflows (expose and visualize data touch points, internal handoffs, external transfers, or the flow of guidance from or benefits received by parental entities.**

- **A basic workflow map - (continuing with the New Hire process example)**

  o *Candidate is identified using a candidate search service.*
  - o *Interviewed by search committee using remote video.*
    - ▪ *Hire recommendation made by email for management approval.*
      - • *Offer approved by management.*
        - o *Offer letter created using Offer Letter Template.*
          - ▪ *Offer letter sent via email.*
            - • *Acceptance contract sent using online system.*
              - o *Digitally signed acceptance returned*

**An effective data classification should:**

- Apply equally to data, applications that engage that data, and the systems and infrastructure that participate in that process.

- Define and govern access to data through a trust and privilege model.

- Identify applications, supporting systems and infrastructure specific to a given class or data set

- Utilize a recognizable risk classification – high, medium, low risk; red, yellow, green; a means or codification system easily communicated and understandable by end users.

- Designate a pseudonymous classification for tagging, recognizable by internal users, systems, and policies, but obfuscates the significance from intruders.

- Identify the basis for the classification – confidential, regulated, sensitive, privileged, asset (crown jewel intellectual property).

- Assess the impact of compromise to a specific class.

- Designate the protective mechanisms required for that class.

- Designate the privilege and credentials required for administration and care.

- Designate the access privileges.

- Activation, duration, and predicted variance over lifecycle of the classification.

- A mechanism for elevation, demotion, or change of classification or ownership.

- Designate required authorizations, care, and approved use by class.

- Define approved mechanisms, times, and sources in a governing usage policy.

*Excellence and quality in governance should be the goal, compliance should be just one outcome*

## Data Localization and Transfer Risk

Data transfer violations, along with use of data collected for purposes other, and breach due to ineffective controls are commonly three areas along with the violation of informed individual rights granted under law that are likely to draw the scrutiny of authorities and regulators. This statement as regards transfers of data is in large part true irrespective of the body of law if data localization is a governing precept, and localization of storage, processing, restrictions of transfers for specific classes of data, some form of localized retention, non-anonymity, approvals authority, adequacy, specific transfer mechanisms or safeguards, or forward transfer rules in one form or another have been put in place as a sovereign mandate as to how data is allowed to move and under what controls or controlling bodies. This is true under Europe's GDPR, China, Russia, Vietnam and for the privacy and data protection mandates of numerous other regimes. The US has largely avoided data transfer restrictions.

The question of US adequacy and onward transfer of EU, UK and also Swiss data to the US is for the post Schrems II and post Brexit time complex, bridges established or in process to be tested, and despite the recent announcement and enactment of the Trans Atlantic Data Privacy Framework likely to remain unresolved until proven to withstand legal challenge. As an intermediary measure improved contractual clauses, approved language and disclosures, documented assessments, and additional technical and operational safeguards to minimize data transfer risk are being implemented by companies. These safeguards are contracts, encryption with key management protection, strong security measures at perimeter, server, and endpoints, effective records of processing, clear documentation, and record of how the information captured is used and categories of recipients with which shared. Minimization of the data collected, and policies that dictate its retention and explain its participation in data sharing work-flows are all secondary safeguards or compensating controls. None of these fully eliminate transfer risk liabilities, but as to overall risk, all of these controls are prudent. defensive and reasonable.

## Data Inheritance Risk

Parent companies inherit risk. CCPA applies to any for profit business entity, or an entity it controls, or is controlled by, directly or indirectly, in whole or in part, or with whom there is common branding that conducts commercial activities in California, and collects the personal information of individuals in California, and passes the size, activity or derived benefit tests. Parent and subsidiary companies that share common branding with a CA in-scope business can be in-scope even if not established in CA themselves. (1798.40)

GDPR is silent on risk inheritance, but EU trade and competition laws may be turned to in absence of clarity in the articles. An entity may be considered a participant in a larger undertaking, for our purposes a commercial activity performed for the common gain or benefit of multiple entities, based on the degree of direct exercise or influence over its business activities by a parental or controlling business, and whether itself conducting activities in scope to GDPR or exercising direct influence over the activities (ownership, voting, strategy, board participation, direction) of an in-scope entity under the GDPR, wherever located, and could be considered in assessment of global turnover penalties.
http://www.marsh.com/in/insights/risk-in-context/GDPR-for-parent-companies-and-their-subsidiaries.html

## Aligning Controls to Risk

Maturity attestation permits a company or department to demonstrate that for a defined risk or risks, entities and activities have been evaluated for the maturity of controls. I prefer to represent this in a chart that examines the presence of controls, their adequacy, how frequently a needed activity is performed, tested, or reviewed, and whether it is validated through internal or external assessment, identifying residual deficiencies. At a minimum describe or develop as a checklist:

| Presence of Activity | Adequacy of Implementation | Frequency of Activity | Validation of Success |
|---|---|---|---|
| The entity or activity has been internally evaluated for the presence of the controls reasonably required to address this defined risk. | The entity or activity has been internally evaluated for adequacy in the function and performance of provided controls for the assessed risk. | The entity or activity has been internally evaluated to affirm sufficient frequency of the performed activity, testing or review | The entity or activity has been externally reviewed for validation of controls and processes |

Figure 24 Alignment of controls and why privacy projects fail

---

## Why Do Privacy Projects Fail?
### (The Non-Compliance Dirty Dozen)

1. Data protection projects are undertaken but not completed

2. Data protection projects are completed but not maintained or operationalized

3. Initiatives lack leadership sponsorship or support

4. Insufficient resources or authority

5. Poor understanding of goals – assessment of progress

6. Laws are complex and still in flux – businesses stall in absence of directional clarity

7. Efforts are de-prioritized as other projects and priorities take focus

8. There is no mechanism in place to stay current with business activities

9. Costs overwhelm budgets

10. Gains made are lost to business change and growth

11. Unaware if laws apply

12. Emerging laws have overwhelmed the capacity of the business to absorb them

---

In its simplest form in a green, yellow, red world, where red elements produce our greatest exposure, and green our least, whether from the perspective of mapping cyber exposures, continuity, or data protection risks, we are only as secure, and effective, and our efforts only as clean and complete, as the greatest of our residual exposure, or as the saying goes, our weakest link in the chain.

Where one application or process in a workflow is at risk, the workflow is at risk. If all the endpoints in a company are protected against malware except one, if exposed, the risk of compromise to the company may be high, despite all other mitigation efforts elsewhere. If one gate is left open, the locks and chains on the others may not matter. If one laptop carrying sensitive data unencrypted is lost, the impact is high regardless of how well all others were protected. Of course, most protected is better than none protected, but try explaining to the judge if it is the unprotected asset that is compromised.

Every deed will need, feed, lead, or breed another. As much as this is true for individual behaviors, this is true of applications, processes, defensive investments, and of business workflows. Just as an application or process is as sensitive as its most sensitive element, a workflow derived of sensitive applications or processes is a sensitive workflow, and all component processes should be examined and protected as such. A payroll system is both sensitive for the financial information it holds, and the personal and sensitive data it derives from the Human Resources System that feeds it. Tax, Pension, and Investment Systems are each sensitive, and participate with Human Resources and Payroll in a sensitive workflow. Each is sensitive because they are, and because they participate in a workflow that is. Examining one part of a workflow is insufficient. A workflow that moves data or guidance between entities is an undertaking

**Approved Use**

Policies that dictate approved use and required authorizations in the access and use of data should not be overlooked. These behavioral controls, as much as any technology, are protective controls, whether applied to personal data, or any other class of consequential data assets.

This format permits authorizations and uses to be defined in a maturity format, such that specific categories of data risk require specific controls. These might include technical controls, authorizations for use, permissions, access and transport restrictions and other limitations. Numeric behavior codes can be used in the diagram above. A sampling of Behavior Codes is listed on the page following.

*Whether Cyber, Enterprise, Point of Sale, or Industrial Control Systems, data breach and other attacks can be difficult to detect or recognize, devastate swiftly, and sometimes, wherever they have gained access, irreparably, and if uncontrolled or unimpeded, completely*

## Data Protection and Approved Use Matrix

| | Onsite Use Only | Authorization Required | Approved Device Required | Specific Controls Required | Low Risk or Discretional Use |
|---|---|---|---|---|---|
| Corporate Confidential | | | | | |
| Regulated | | | | | |
| Privileged | | | | | |
| PII Sensitive | | | | | |
| High Risk Data | | | | | |
| Moderate Risk Data | | | | | |
| Low Risk Data | | | | | |

*Figure 25 Example of a data protection and approved use matrix*

### Coding behavioral policies for the Data Protection and Approved Use Matrix

The list below increases the usability of the Approved Use Matrix. The categories should include all the needed approvals, authorization of behaviors and required protections for a given class of exposure for a given business, process, or application. This list is just for example. Each business should fit appropriate controls as dictated by internal policy and the nature of the data.

1. Onsite use only.
2. Requires password protected media or system.
3. Requires encrypted disk media or system.
4. Requires encryption, password protection for specific file.
5. Requires encryption in transmission.
6. DRM and Watermark.
7. Log activity for tracking
8. Remote digital tracking is required
9. Remote wipe capability required.
10. Executive authorization required.
11. Business data owner approval required.
12. IT approval required.
13. Legal written approval required.
14. Approved for public transport, disclosure, and distribution.

*Figure 266 Coding categories for approved use matrix*

As example, personal data participates in numerous workflows, internal and external

*Figure 26b*

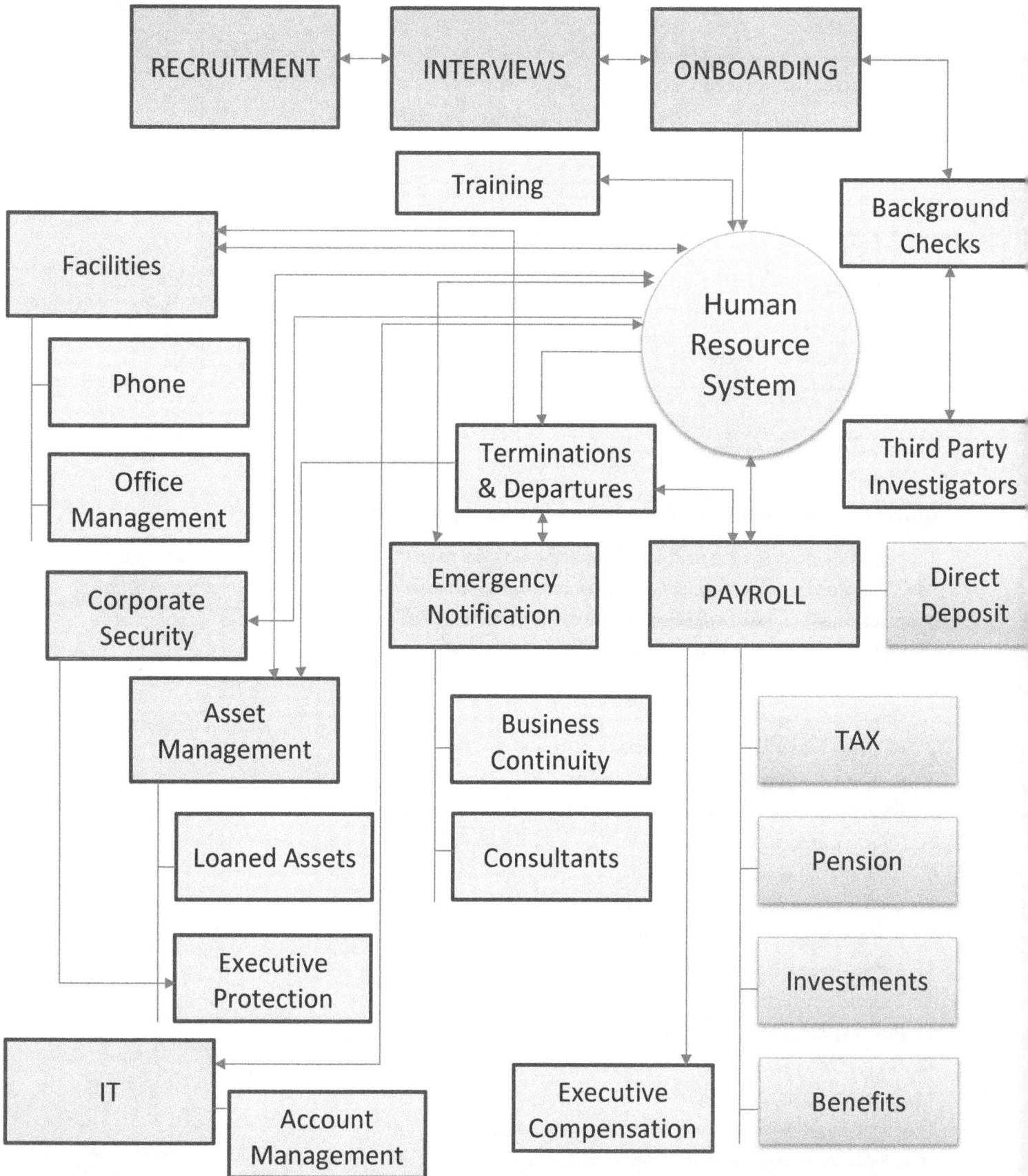

# INVENTORY, MAPPING, AND CLASSIFICATION - NOTES FROM THE FIELD - CHRIS SUMNER

We cannot have a meaningful discussion of security, privacy or even customer service without knowing our data. Companies often raise this as their greatest challenge. We spoke a bit about inventory and classification above. Recently, I had the opportunity to ask Chris Sumner to put this in practical terms.

*Chris, why has understanding their data footprint been so difficult for so many companies?*

Organizations are faced with constantly growing amounts of data, stored in a variety of locations, often with little or no control oversight. Knowing what data an organization has and where it is stored has always been a challenge. With the recent explosion of cloud services, this challenge has become much harder. However, there is great value in having visibility and control of the data held with an organization. A data mapping exercise can identify problematic practices, security risks, and uncover duplication of effort and other operational inefficiencies.

And establishing an inventory and mapping capability does not need to involve a big-bang initiative. It is often beneficial to adopt a more agile and iterative approach; starting at a high level and, if required, filling in the detail over time. For example, an organization might start by understanding the high-level flows of information in a group such as Human Resources, that is likely to handle sensitive data and have relatively well-defined processes. Starting with one team will provide a feel for how to roll a process out more broadly. Approaching a project in this agile manner enables an organization to continuously modify its approach to ensure that it is appropriately tailored to business needs.

*Do you have any guidance as to how a company should proceed and where they should begin?*

To simplify the inventory and mapping process, an organization may apply classifications to broad categories of data. For example, all personnel files may be classified as 'Confidential', even if some of the files, are not. This is often referred to as the high-water mark concept. Similarly, data may attract a higher classification rating once it is aggregated with other data. An employee's email address is unlikely to be considered as highly confidential, yet a list of every employee's email address might well be.

An inventory should establish the flow of data throughout an organization. Before embarking on an inventory and mapping exercise it is beneficial to consider teams with overlapping needs. Depending on the organization, legal, privacy, cybersecurity, data governance, information management, and records management teams may all need to have a clearer understanding of data within the company. Cross organizational collaboration and planning at this stage is time well spent, not least because each team may already have some documented knowledge of organizational data. We would want to know (1) where the data came from; (2) what categories of data are being collected; (3) the data elements within those categories, e.g., last name and social security number; (4) the purpose of data collection; (5) where the data is processed and stored, both from a systems perspective and geographically; (6) whether data is disclosed to a third party; and (7) any data retention obligations. There are mapping and inventory tools and services available from a variety of vendors, but smaller organizations may manage perfectly adequately with well-maintained spreadsheets. This is a good time to ensure that the organization also maintains an inventory of the systems, applications, and other services that store or process data. This is especially important considering the myriad of "Shadow IT" cloud services that teams now use.

The organization may choose to maintain its data inventory and mapping at a relatively high business process level or may desire to obtain a more granular view. They might take this as an opportunity to understand the data flow between systems and system components. They may choose to link to directory services, configuration management databases (CMDBs) and other inventories. They may opt to undertake a labeling initiative for data types and need to provide specific labeling guidance. Labels can provide a bridge between the inherent properties of a data asset, and its handling requirements, such as "Confidential – Do Not Print". Regardless of the approach to data mapping, it is likely that themes or categories will emerge. Classification is the process of logically grouping these different data assets based on their attributes. And as an outcome, classification should enable an organization to define how it expects personnel to handle and protect different types of data with different usage and protection requirements.

*Is this one of those endeavors that you need to get spot on or is the perfect the enemy of the good?*

A welcome trend seems to be towards keeping classification schemes simple. As such, a reasonable place to start is with a three-tier classification scheme which can be extended or further reduced. A common approach is to classify data as data intended for the public or a third party, data intended for widespread distribution within the organization, and data intended for a limited, non-public, audience. While data assets are typically grouped according to their sensitivity and importance to the business, it does not need to end there. Organizations can use the inventory and mapping process to collect additional metadata to enable personnel to locate the data sets that meet their needs. An example of this metadata might be the flagging of retention requirements. NIST 800-60 and FIPS 199 outline a more nuanced view of classification, which some organizations may prefer.

When considering how many levels of classification are necessary, a good rule of thumb is to think about how different types of data will be handled. For example, if an organization handles its 'secret' data in the same way that it handles its 'top secret' data, then the tiers can be collapsed and simplified. Once a data classification scheme has been established, it is useful to provide some handling guidelines for employees. A data handling matrix can be used in conjunction with a data classification scheme as a guide to applying and implementing the classifications in commonly occurring scenarios, such as sending an invoice to a client or collecting identification documents during onboarding. However, it is important to note that sharing of data, regardless of classification, must not violate any non-disclosure agreements, and must comply with applicable copyright and other laws.

*What do you see as the challenges in undertaking a classification effort?*

Getting a classification scheme ingrained in company culture can take time, but its adoption can be aided by providing simple guides, updating company document and presentation templates, and ensuring that terminology is used consistently. Rolling out a classification scheme and handling guidelines is not without pitfalls. For example, data must be properly defined, and data collection, use, management, and retention policies must be worded appropriately to limit the organization's potential legal liability. Often, having bad documentation is worse than having no documentation at all. If the organization has a legal team, it is recommended that they are involved in policy creation. The classification scheme acts as a foundation stone for other policies and activities and is frequently referenced in guidelines from access controls to media sanitization. Considered together, classification, data inventories, and data mapping enable a company to not only understand where their data flows, but also to reduce blind spots, and improve the data protection and data loss prevention capabilities.

As with all processes, inventory and mapping processes must be routinely reviewed, and inventories and maps must be kept up to date. It is often useful to continuously compare data ownership with employee directory information, to ensure that data is not left without an owner if someone changes roles or leaves the organization. Data owners and data custodians should routinely review data to ensure its classification is still appropriate, based on changes to legal and contractual obligations, as well as changes in the use of the data or its value to the company.

*Any final thoughts?*

Data inventory and mapping processes may first appear as unachievable, futile, or even wasteful endeavors, but even a simple, high-level inventory can enable an organization to wrestle back control of its data and ensure that the right people have access to the right data and at the right time.

*Chris Sumner is Co- Founder, The Online Privacy Foundation – Chris@onlineprivacyfoundation.org*

*It is the responsibility of any solvent business to operate, survive and optimally thrive, delivering on its mission in meeting the needs of clients, partners, employees, owners, and investors at the best of times, in adversity, and through change.*

Martin Gomberg, CISSP, CIPP/E

## SECTION 15.  INCIDENT / CRISIS MANAGEMENT

Calamity periodically disrupts every operating business, from the inconvenient nuisance event, to the catastrophic. From weather, building fires, and cyberattacks, to crisis of credit, currency, sovereign seizure of assets, or market or supply disruption. From employee abduction, product related crisis, active assailants, suicide, or implication in fraud, crime, or executive misbehavior. Increasingly, we need to detect, track, and manage disparagement and assaults on reputation and incitement in digital media and social communities that can escalate to protest, riot, boycott, intimidation, threats, or violence.

Malicious breach, data destruction, disruption, alteration, unauthorized access, disclosure, exfiltration, or isolation for demands (ransomware), are each a constant threat. So is accidental data loss or unintentional exposure. Where protective efforts are shown inadequate, or data is improperly exposed, we violate trust, risk tarnish of brand, and falling afoul of data protection and consumer privacy laws, some imposing egregious penalties. The same where technical defenses or operational practices are insufficient to protect identifying credentials, or the intimate personal, health, affinity and affiliation privacy of consumers, employees, and others with which we engage and for whom we steward information.

Private, consequential, and confidential data will likely at some point be exposed, whether in data loss or compromise events that impact us directly, or that impact our partners, here, overseas, or in cloud. We are at risk to services or resources we procure where we are protected only by contract. Breach and loss of client data in the cloud is data lost by us, not by the cloud provider, and this will be true in the perception of those whose entrusted data may have been compromised and is true under every law and every statute without any exception of which I am aware. Regulation is increasingly broadening the definition of breach to encompass all the above, particularly in Europe, but also elsewhere, and expanding the circumstances that might trigger reporting, penalties, and obligations for compensation and reparations for harm.

Cyber raises the stakes as phishing, social engineering, hacking, and malware permit intrusion, access, theft, and destruction. Denial of service attacks cripple business, ransomware holds data hostage for payment, and social disinformation campaigns distort perspectives.

Modern business does not operate in a vacuum. We are the sum of employees, consultants, and partner relationships. We do business, local, global, and virtual. We confront and manage business impacting incidents and events. Some of these may be external or adversary inflicted. Others will be internal, some malicious, some not, but damaging just the same. These will come from trusted executives, employees, and contractors, through exploits, intentional misbehavior, careless acts, or accidents, or through the actions or vulnerabilities of partners. When considering enterprise crisis management, it should be in the context of all of this.

There is often debate about the differences between events, incidents, and crisis. I prefer not to get off track with that discussion so will spend just a few moments here to clarify my perspective. Consistency in the use of terminology is important, but I think we often get too caught up with the categorization. What we call any specific situation may be less a function of precision in communication, and more purposeful management of perception through crafted language in accordance with the messaging plan.

- From the technical perspective, some view an <u>event</u> as a system recordable activity of significance. It can vary from the starting of a device or process, to the logging of an interruption, anomaly, or failure.

- Jim Mitchell, a BRP (Business Response Planning) specialist describes an <u>incident</u> as a "disruption in operation that starts with the reporting of the incident and ends when operation is returned to its original state".

- Mitchell also notes that a <u>crisis</u> could be a result of rumors, product defects, adverse publicity, negative social media activities, or any actions of employees, distributors or suppliers which reflect poorly upon the organization.". He defines crisis management as the "plans for and actions taken to protect and defend the reputation of the organization, its brand and its products / services."

  https://www.ebrp.net/incident-management-crisis-management-very-different-often-confused/

*There are those that hate us, and those we hate, and the math for that leaves that condition true for at least the next two generations, and likely beyond. Terror has gone digital.*

I understand why the concern for accuracy in terminology. Accuracy and precision in terms though is not always easy and may be a matter of perspective.

- Often, lines seem blurred in what flows from seemingly minor technical events to the failure incidents and missteps that follow, to the inevitable operational crisis that impacts business. The speed from one to another is often much faster than one could imagine in what seems to be just a miserable day with a lot of moving parts, one flowing inexorably into the other, limiting clarity to a jaw dropping blur.

- An incident to a company of one size, with given resources, expertise, and operational maturity, without doubt, is a crisis to another that lacks them.

- Equally, the language used, whether event, incident, or crisis, will depend on the audience. Prudent management often avoids use of terms like crisis when communicating to the press or investors, to prevent exacerbation of the event, and to manage perceptions.

How an event is managed and by whom is typically a function of the severity and nature of the event and the size and maturity of the company. A large or multinational company will undoubtedly have a formalized crisis response team that takes the lead in all but the most sensitive of events.

An Incident Management group assesses and manages the incident and communication and information flow to executive leadership as dictated, and the mobilization and coordination of operational, technical, legal, and business response. A smaller company may not have the resources to dedicate to an incident response program and will designate an individual, conscript a LOB (line of business) representative as they need, or respond to crisis as they arise ad hoc. Many treat managed incident responses as a component of the business continuity program along with disaster recovery.

In line with the definitions of incident and crisis offered by Jim Mitchell on the previous page, some treat enterprise impacting crisis, that commanding executive attention, as something different and apart from the interruptive, but non-existential 'incidents' they can delegate. An executive or executive crisis management team addresses those issues that threaten significant revenue, investor confidence, executive safety, or brand and reputation. Or at a minimum will make their presence and expectations known.

In highly regulated companies, or for critical infrastructure, the mandates for an incident management program are broad, encompassing physical, technical, and operational threats. They need to meet the requirements of compliance with most regulations and adopted standards or certifications. Boards expect competence and coverage, as do investors, partners, and clients, and increasingly, laws. At a minimum, these designate an executive to provide oversight, team leads, key internal members and needed external parties, service vendors, and specialists. They define roles, testing, training and rehearsal, and communication between team members, within the company, and externally. They leverage an understanding of assessed and prioritized risk to define a plan for response.

The response to an incident will vary. The approach, participants involved, level of authority, and area specific specialists required, are largely situation dependent. They are dependent on whether authority and area governance are centralized or federated, whether localized or geographically distributed, whether multinational, multi-jurisdictional in terms of law and regulations, and the responsible authorities applicable to the event. Where executives, law enforcement, legal, insurers, area specialists, negotiators and extrication specialists will be mobilized in an executive abduction, and where human resources, facilities management, communications, and public health officials will be engaged on a health matter, the response to a cyber-attack on a manufacturing facility will require very different resources and expertise.

The approach to an incident is dependent on the visibility and duration of the event, company culture, and the potential for negative or criminal implications and outcomes. It may differ if chronic, whether the company is operating under mandate for oversight by a managing board, court or regulating body, presence of a formalized crisis response group, and the specific personalities of the executives in control. The nature of the event likely will dictate the inclusion and degree of involvement of the CISO, CIO and other executives. Incident response is not one size fits all. All incident response should be managed with oversight, default authority granted to the specialists, with adequate access to the tools and resources for response. Default authority should permit responders to leverage external expertise as it is needed, while communicating status, obstacles, and outcomes through the oversight executive to leadership.

Management of enterprise crisis will involve multiple crisis planning, response bodies, and teams. These may be comprised of internal resources at the executive level providing oversight, authority, and approvals for disbursement of funds. They will also include internal resources at the operational level for implementation, coordination with insurers, and engaging external resources for advice and specialist expertise. Both formalized and ad hoc communication between oversight and implementation teams is required for coordination and effective implementation.

Delegated or default authorities are often required to respond to fast moving or highly technical events like cyber, or active assailant events where there is little time for discussion or consensus opinions. Briefing may be after the fact, with the executive body providing review and management of issues secondary to the event. This is often the coordination and delivery of message within the company, to business partners and investors, press, and civil authorities.

An incident response program requires capable response teams, under an effective structure of governance, assessing risks and preparing for them, educating the community, and effectively detecting and responding to events that unfold, providing communications properly and timely with a clear message to all concerned parties. It will address incident assessment, mobilization of response, post response secondary events which may occur, and post incident evaluations of response performance.

*It is normal and well-intentioned day to day business that is the primordial broth from which most of our security problems emerge*

There are some aspects of an incident response that are required irrespective of the event. These are the characteristics that provide structure to the program and ultimately, to the actions, speed and effectiveness of actions taken. These are accountable executive oversight, permission to act, prior approved spend caps or budgetary authority, and preparation to the extent possible. This may simply be having the best people adequately trained, access to needed resources, a clearly defined message for line of business and operational heads, employees, and for external reporting, and a protocol for how it is communicated.

It will include identifying critical partners, negotiating terms and costs in contract, and implementing Master Services Agreements and Non-Disclosure Agreements in advance of an incident occurring. Specialist counsel, investigators, hostage negotiation and extrication specialists, digital media investigators, cyber specialists, facilities, and data restoration companies should be identified. These should be included in the response planning and preparation along with standard utilities (electrical, plumbing, air conditioning and environmental), law enforcement and public safety relationships.

Other aspects of incident response will be specific to the event and require expertise. Destructive malware infiltration will require IT and technical security specialists to contain, identify, and eradicate the infiltration, and restrict its propagation and spread. It may require specialists from outside or law enforcement resources to get control of the attack. Preparation done in advance including identifying and mapping of systems and data and knowing what is most consequential, and what has been impacted will be critical to any specialist providing response assistance.

By its very definition, regardless of the type of incident, an incident response is after the fact, and too late. Something has happened, and now you must respond. Though not implied in the term 'Incident Response' there is a preparedness component, and it is the effectiveness of that preparedness that determines the effectiveness, cost, and effort of the subsequent response.

There is also an awareness component. An awareness of risk permits actions to be taken, decisions to be made, situations to be avoided - minimizing the occurrence and severity of events. Discussions with an in-country consulate or advisory council about the political climate in a specific country might determine whether a meeting should be held there or moved elsewhere. Knowing the potential impact of Denial of Service on a business that depends on its online presence might suggest the use of a Content Delivery Network to distribute the impact of a DDOS event. A concern for ransomware should encourage limiting data access available to individuals, implementing multi factor access controls, whitelisting permitted software installation, and diversifying backup strategies. Evaluation permits awareness. Awareness permits action. It also permits education.

And now, an apology. I have treated the rest of this section largely as a thought dump, a share of experience and approach, focusing more on checklists than on format. I do not get poetic. It does not lie prettily. It does lend to more rapid access to information you may need for quick reference.

**Executive Crisis Management Teams**

As with the crisis response apparatus in most companies, executive emergency or crisis response teams have no typical in whether formalized, how they are structured, and the types of incidents and episodes they respond to. They often strike a balance between insulation and accountability. The more severe, safety, business or brand impacting the event, the more likely senior most leadership will want, or need to be involved, but where unneeded should avoid being pulled into day-to-day management at the expense of strategic focus.

Whether an accountable executive or individual is appointed for oversight of crisis management, or an executive team performs that function, they are critical in providing the authority to act quickly in response to a crisis. Executive powers are sufficient only to the extent they permit action without the need for further upstream approvals, for decision, authorizing unbudgeted spend, and to approve and commit the company to action, procurement, temporary closure, prioritize or stop activities, dismissal of workforce, relocation, and the execution of contracts.

**Incident management is a comprehensive program**

- Development of a plan and testable execution procedure approved by management
- Infrastructure, skills, budget, and activities to establish preparedness
- Training, rehearsal, and education
- Tools, procedures, knowledge and resources for detection, mobilization, communication, and response
- Corrective and restorative actions to reestablish operations
- Dealing with unresolved issues and secondary events
- Reporting, documentation, and regulatory obligations
- Improvement focused incident review and post-mortem

*An executed plan needs an executive signature for approval.*
*An unapproved plan or a plan designated as 'DRAFT' may be viewed as*
*no plan at all by regulators in audit.*

**Message and delivery**

In the event of a crisis a clear message appropriately delivered reduces confusion, protects relationships, and minimizes potential litigation. What is said to whom and by whom is often one of the most sensitive issues for management in crisis communications. Whereas the impact of the crisis is likely and typically short lived and localized, the impact of words can be devastating to brand, reputation, customer loyalty and executive careers, and will be heard quickly, repeatedly, and seemingly without end, around the globe in some cases, so is, and should be, taken very seriously.

It falls to a designated specialist, communication executive or other, or perhaps the executive Crisis Team to define the message in incident. Once the message is developed and approved (and there may be several), the following needs to be determined and often is best if decided, at least at high level, well before crisis impacts. Unless company policy dictates other, there should be no communication about the incident, outside of the approved and designated channels. Many companies will address these issues as part of the Business Continuity preparedness exercises and plan for the means for these to occur:

- Briefings to executives, LOB technical or operational management

- Communication with investors

- Communications with critical clients

- Communication with public officials (police, fire, FBI) and specialist responders

- Communications with press

- Communications with employees

- Posted notification and broadcast alerts

- Notification requiring response or action

- Group planning and communications

- Helpdesk and support services

- Providing estimates of financial impact and cost of business disruption to insurers

- Communication with state attorneys, regulatory bodies, or international entities

- Public posting on corporate web site

- Testing to assure communications to impacted consumers can scale (statewide, nationwide)

- Testing to assure consumer response can be managed (call volume, website volume)

- Briefings to impacted families where there is death, abduction, isolation, or injury

- Posting of anonymous source threat data to professional threat registers

## CERT Support Teams

Apart from the executive response, a technical, operational, and logistic response will also be required in many or most incidents. As a CISO, whether in the private or public sector, or in academia, the responsibilities for the formation of a CERT team may likely fall to you, as will the requirement for the protection of computer resources, and response to cyber events. Likely, so will preparedness, and knowing what Federal, State, and municipal resources are available to call upon.

For many of us, participation in community CERT teams, and counter terror functions like INFRAGUARD, (https://www.infragard.org/,  a private sector partnership coordinated by the FBI to promote intelligence sharing and preparedness), OSAC (U.S. Department of State Overseas Security Advisory Council, https://www.osac.gov) , local PD, and other areas of public safety and law enforcement, will be part of what we do as CISOs. Much of what we want to protect our companies from is better kept outside of our walls, a case we should all be making to management. We need to encourage their support of work with peer groups, industry ISACs, and with the professional security community, and law enforcement overall.

This, however, is a tangent. There is no typical, and the structures and preparation for crisis, and CERT is as varied as there are companies. With that I will be very generic as to the resources that comprise the CERT team. You may have separate teams for physical crisis (CERT) and computer or cyber security events (CSIRT). One may be the focus of the CSO, and the other the CISO, or they may be the same team, or fall under the same management.

Authority to take the lead in a cyber crisis should fall fully to a designated crisis response leader. The crisis response leader requires trust, and the authority to bring down services, applications, external communications, close off network segments, remove access by executives or power performers, or bring down the network in entirety. An effective Crisis Response leader must be decisive and capable of acting without consensus approvals from management. The Crisis Response Leader also understands proportionality and can assess when an attack or event requires a dramatic action and when it does not.

However structured, recognize that preparedness, physical events, brand protection and reputation, computer, cyber events, and privacy all need to be on your radar, and you need to have the best people lined up from across your enterprise to take part. You also need to have external expertise identified and included in exercises when feasible. At a minimum, external partners should be periodically asked to discuss their capabilities, preparations, and resources, how well they might scale to address an event impacting several to many of their clients, and how they would participate. Where possible external CERT partners should be put under completed and signed contract agreements governing participation and for non-disclosure commitments.

*I just taught my dogma to roll over*

Success requires that you have the support of business and management. You will need the right resources internally and specialists to call upon. You will also need to have the space, tools, and processes to mobilize quickly, assemble in group physically, and virtually, and to reestablish infrastructure, operations, organization, and telecom, and communicate in numerous ways.

The speed and effectiveness of detection, recognition, and response are often decisive as to the impact of the event. Whether the response is with internal security teams, external specialists, or law enforcement cyber investigation teams, having a complete and current description of the environment, systems, and points of transit in and out of the network, will be critical to managing both strategic and day to day security functions, and too, rapidly effecting a crisis response.

*What is said to whom, and by whom, is often one of the most sensitive issues for management in crisis communications.*

*Whereas the impact of the crisis is typically short lived and localized, the impact of words can be devastating to brand, reputation, customer loyalty, and executive careers, and will be heard quickly, repeatedly, globally, and seemingly without end.*

# Response Procedure for breach or cyber attack

Technical attacks, cyber, enterprise, point of sale or other, can be difficult to detect or recognize, devastate swiftly, and sometimes wherever they have gained access, irreparably, and if uncontrolled or unimpeded, completely. Some companies establish default authorities for technical responders specifying pre-approved or immediacy actions to avoid delays prior to engagement of crisis management. Others require direction of a crisis executive to provide authorization on technical action, engagement of specialists and spend. This procedure is provided in example and your procedure or that of others may be ordered differently, be more prescriptive or technically specific, or involve more or fewer steps, but should at a minimum address:

- Initial assessment of what happened.

- Containment of the threat, isolating impacted applications, systems, segments, or components to limit escalation or spread, internally, or to external parties (where possible without causing greater harm)

- Executive notification and crisis updates

- Determine what was attacked, or in theft or breach, what was penetrated or taken, how and from where

- Assess the potential impact of the breach or attack based on the sensitivity of the systems, data, parties and geographies affected and whether there were controls protecting that which was taken or attacked

- Review and analyze attack source and vectors

- Assess effectiveness of controls and determine if any residual risk remains unaddressed

- Implement additional counter measures and controls

- Restore functionality, connectivity, test, and monitor

- Return to normal operations

- Document the incident and the response

- Coordinate with general or internal counsel and engage supporting outside counsel if warranted to meet legal obligations for incident or breach reporting across all impacted geographies

- Manage communications – authorities, employees, clients, investors and press as appropriate

- Involve or engage critical parties, specialists or law enforcement, attorneys, and insurers as needed to manage the mitigation, claims, and prepare for follow up actions, litigation, and litigation defense

- If attack or vector is novel communicate findings to professional bodies to reduce risk to the community

- Evaluate incident and response

*Figure 27 Incident response procedure*

*An incident and the needed response may not be short lived. Plan for rotation, rest, and care of your people.*

# CERT or Crisis Response Team resources

## Operational Teams

- IT Response Area Specialists (Developers, Network Administration, Help Desk)

- Cyber and Technical Security

- Business Continuity

- SOC management

- Engineering

- Public Relations and communications

- Digital Brand Protection

- Legal

- Physical Security

- Facilities protection

- Human Resources

- Purchasing and contracts

- Line of Business Managers and operations

## Law Enforcement

- Federal (FBI, Secret Service, U.S. State Department, Department of Consular Affairs, Homeland Security), State Police, County Sheriff, and Local Police

- International authorities

## Civil Authorities

- City Management

- Fire Department

- Sanitation Department

- Public Health

- Public Safety and Municipal Management

*Threat hunters should not only be our technical best, but also our business brightest.*

## Other CERT External Resources

- Utilities (power, water, telecom, content delivery networks, fuel)

- Technical Solutions Specialists

- Threat Monitors, Investigators, Testers, and Breach Response Teams

- Reputation Management Specialists

- Digital Media Investigation Specialists

- Cloud Security Specialists

- Value Added Resellers

- Specialist Counsel

- Insurance providers

- Facilities Support (electricians, plumbing, air conditioning, general construction)

- Facilities Restoration Services

- Data Restoration Services

- Data Storage Facilities

- Cloud Service Providers

- Colocation Resource support

- Security Guard Services

- Hostage Negotiation / Extrication Services

- Movers and Equipment Transport Specialists

- Temporary power and generator trucks, mobile data transmission units, mobile lighting

- Mobile office and command center facilities

- Assembly, work, and accommodation space available (nearby hotels) when needed

---

Know your risk and the resources you are likely to need. Identify, engage, and plan with them before they are needed

---

*There is no approach that eliminates all risk or the possibility of attack, breach, or compromise of systems or data. Success is measured by the minimization of consequence, and the brief, and uninteresting press, if any, which follows*

Guidance from the NIST 800-61 Revision II Computer Security Incident Handling Guide
*"When reaching out to external parties, an organization can work through US-CERT or its ISAC, as a "trusted introducer" to broker the relationship."*

**Post Incident Procedures**

Even after an incident concludes lingering issues may persist, or secondary issues may arise, and mitigation and response efforts may not be finished.

- Continued monitoring of social media and reputation feeds for evidence of anger, dissatisfaction or threat affords the opportunity to intervene when reputation and brand identity is under attack

- Grievance lines should be established (voice and web)

- Watchdog hot lines should be established for loyal supporters to report threats and disparagement

- Set up a procedure for addressing harassing, threatening or abusive mail or email related to the event

- There may be a need for increased or targeted brand promotion campaigns to restore confidence

- Monitor financial markets as there may be issues of investor confidence to be addressed

- There likely will be a need to offer consumers some reconciliation in the form of identity protection or other means to offset anger and regain client loyalty

- If personal data is involved, there may be a reporting obligation to the state attorney for each state in which the business is operational, has clients known to have been impacted, or has clients that may have had identifying credentials taken or lost whether complaints have been made, verified, or not

- There may be legal consequences and obligations as dictated by the court, or litigation to be initiated against participating parties

- The financial impact, response costs, and other corollary damages brought on by the event should be determined working with risk management and finance specialists in preparation for insurance claims

*Figure 28 Post incident procedures*

*That which we describe as a value chain is at best a loosely structured web constructed of trust and dependency. We build indemnification in contracts as insurance, but in fact it is an acknowledgement of the dirt in the system. There are things we cannot know.*

## Post Incident Evaluation

Was anything learned from the event? Post Incident Evaluation Criteria is important for documenting an event, revisiting aspects blurred by the heat of the moment, and to tune responses and preparations. It is also helpful in lowering the volume again and returning staff to a place of normalcy. It is helpful to have a consistent set of questions, and to pull together the major stakeholders and responders in discussing these.

- What was the nature of the incident, when did it occur, and what systems were impacted?

- How did it impact the business?

- Were any specific measures taken to support or protect the business during the incident?

- How did staff perform; management; external resources; communications throughout the event?

- Were specialists, external counsel, or law enforcement required or contacted?

- Were unbudgeted resources required to address the incident?

- Were the documented plans and procedures accurate, sufficient, and followed?

- What information was missing, insufficient, unneeded, needed sooner, or in other ways?

- What resources were missing, insufficient, unneeded, needed sooner, or in other ways?

- What actions failed, were inadequate, improper, or in any way inhibited the recovery?

- How can the process be improved?

- What controls can be implemented, or vulnerabilities reduced to prevent a similar incident?

- How could an incident like this be better predicted?

- What evidence did the event display that would be an indicator of this attack if seen?

- What artifacts did the event leave behind that can better inform others of its impact?

- What post incident follow up is required or further impact anticipated?

*Figure 29 Post Incident Evaluation*

It is rare that we encounter a threat not realized elsewhere before. Threat information sharing groups can be an effective resource as suggested in the NIST 800-61 Revision II Computer Security Incident Handling Guide. These groups promote information sharing among incident response teams.

- *Forum of Incident Response and Security Teams (FIRST)11,*
- *Government Forum of Incident Response and Security Teams (GFIRST)12,*

Alternatively, contacting a professional security provider can help not just in assessment, mitigation, cleanup, and restoration, but also in coordination of information sharing with sharing facilities and other solution providers if requested.

**Cyber Attack Ready Response Package**

The following documents at a minimum should be at the ready, frequently reviewed for accuracy and currency, and made available to the investigation and CERT response.

- Endpoint count, distribution, and configuration

- IP domain map

- Ingress and egress map

- WAN and LAN architecture

- Server deployment map labeled by location, function, principal applications, and OS

- Storage system and data distribution map

- Database map

- Inventory and map of consequential data

- Mitigation resource deployment map (antivirus, DLP, Firewalls, etc...)

- Log inventory and output reports for critical, impacted or detective systems

- Contact information for critical responders, area and component system specialists, and CERT team members

- Cyber Incident Response Plan

*Consequential data can be breached, compromised, disrupted, or lost through inadequacy or insufficiency of controls, or the vulnerability, extent, porosity, or complexity of the attack surface we present, or where the exploit is attractive due to target recognition or profile.*

# PRIVACY INCIDENT RESPONSE: SOME ADDITIONAL THOUGHTS

The purpose of any effective incident preparedness program regardless of focus (cyber, privacy, enterprise, etc.) is to establish oversight, planning and governance, implement needed or risk reductive protective controls (technical, operational, and contractual), put in place processes for testing, monitoring, and detection, and lastly, facilitate a reactive and corrective response and subsequent examination. It is to monitor for, detect, and then respond to any incident with the intention of isolating the cause and mitigating negative outcomes.

### *Privacy incident response is unique.*

Unlike a cyber or enterprise response where engineers close off networks and systems and deploy counter measures to fend off an attack, a privacy incident response is less real time. It is a deliberative and considered response. It is an informed determination as to whether an event is reportable under any of the laws or policies to which the entity is in scope, and if so, or if ethics dictate, executing obligations, and most often, disclosing to public or regulating bodies. Success is almost entirely dependent on preparation and counsel and an understanding of the regulatory environment, and the response is as prescribed by law.

The effectiveness of any privacy incident response process is determined in large part by the preparation performed beforehand. This would include identifying impactful laws, assessing legal obligations, where multiple laws apply the nuances between them, completing a data inventory, documenting the data that resides on each system, determining its sensitivity and risk, and implementing effective protective controls. It requires an understanding of business structures and the entities that parentally impart guidance or mutually derive benefit that may inherit risk. It includes awareness of markets and consumers, and if impacted, knowing the resources needed to support them. This includes establishing the internal teams, communication channels, irate consumer management processes, and aligning the external resources (regionally localized attorneys, technical responders, reputation, and brand restoration specialists) needed.

The privacy incident response process is deliberative, but under the urgency of regulatory deadlines. And though deliberative, it is not discretional. The decision to report must be aligned to criterion against which the decision to report is consistently tested regardless of event. The thresholds may be a test for harm, number of individuals affected, territorial impact or other as dictated by law or sound practice. But if the thresholds are met regardless of ramifications, consistency should dictate, and if report or other is required by law, obligations met. But a privacy incident response is a terminal reaction. It is an after-the-fact action necessitated by the failure or deficiency of protective controls. Personal data was taken, disclosed, damaged, lost, or rendered unusable or unavailable. A demonstrable investment in a program of data protection, adherence to standards, prudent management, inherent data protection including encryption, a clear and tested plan, and a rapid response, are no longer just strategy, but defensive arguments for the amelioration of liability, and along with transparency, prompt disclosure and cooperation with regulators, possibly reduction of penalty.

What is a data breach?

A breach is any critical disruption in availability, confidence, or control of data or any unauthorized access or disclosure, whether accidental or malicious, and whether resulting in data loss, exfiltration, manipulation, corruption, denial of access or other.

The severity of breach is a function of:

- volume of exposed data
- sensitivity of the data
- vulnerability of populations or individuals whose data is exposed (i.e., children)
- effectiveness of implemented controls like encryption
- protective measures
- rapidity of detection and report

At the risk of oversimplification and irreverence to specific law, operationally response to breach has three goals:

- Judgement - having realized or been informed of an event impacting personal data, whether the data was directly controlled, or indirectly controlled by a service provider under contract, or with a provider in cloud, a determination must be made in accordance with statutory definitions and requirements, whether the event raises to the level where one or more regulatory obligations may be triggered.

- Disclosure - a determination whether notice is required to be given to country, state or other jurisdictional supervisory authorities or courts, offices of state attorney generals, credit monitoring agencies, or federal or state regulators providing specifics as required in formats as specified by law in timeframes as required. It is also a determination whether communications directly or through public notice to any impacted individuals or communities is required by law or should be made as a voluntary disclosure for transparency and good faith, or if the provision of other 'make goods' (compensation, credit monitoring) are needed or should be undertaken for the purposes of maintaining consumer trust.

- Action - required obligations must be met on time and as dictated in conformance with the law. In support, appropriate assessment of the incident and the effectiveness of the response be made, residual risk of recurrence be examined, mitigation be performed, and documentation be maintained of the incident. And though not all events will require report, potentially impactful events, successful or not, should be tracked. The basis of any decisions made should be described and supporting evidence and event logs preserved. Doing so may reveal patterns of exposure that help to identify vulnerabilities, may be required by regulators or courts in determining whether the incident is novel or chronic and whether appropriate efforts had been made to address extant exposures or vulnerabilities.

# BREACH RECORDING AND REPORTING

There are both operational similarities and statutory differences between the CCPA and Europe's GDPR and other data protection laws in the domestic US and globally as to obligations and response in breach. Operationally, many of the same defensive, detective, and responsive controls should be in place to:

- minimize the successful occurrence of a breach impacting personal data

- maximize the resistance to data exposure (using encryption and other protective measures), enable detection, and to permit a successful mitigating response

- demonstrate responsibility, accountability, and provision of reasonable operational and technical measures and compliance with legal requirements

Though requirements and formats may differ by law, all events should be documented, and a templated assessment prepared for consistency and held for comparison and pattern recognition in future events and for regulatory reporting. Not all regulations require the same be reported, or in the same format, but the following brief summation should help preserve record of the incident and get us close:

- time / date / duration / description of event (briefly what happened; how did it happen)

- categories and elements of personal data involved

- individuals, communities, geographic areas impacted

- were individuals or groups harmed or is there a potential for harm

- how the data was protected and was it encrypted or deidentified

- effectiveness of the response in curtailing the incident and mitigating further vulnerability

- actions taken and when including mitigation, reporting, public notice, make goods to consumers

- documents, interviews, testimony, logs, and other evidence preserved

- assessment of participants, victims and responders, corrective training or other action taken

- who to contact for further information (name and contact information)

> Regulatory reporting and public notification obligations should align to the requirements of the law. However, breach response and reporting criteria, formats, and obligations and that which constitutes 'personal information' and therefore determines if a 'breach of personal information' has occurred differs. Where GDPR governs what constitutes breach and triggers reporting under its articles, breach reporting in California is not specifically governed under the CCPA, but by the California's Data Breach Notification Law (Cal. Civ. Code §1798.82)

# CISO
# REDEFINED

*Protecting Business*

Martin Gomberg, CISSP, CIPP/E

## SECTION 16.   PERSONNEL, ASSET, AND BUSINESS PROTECTION

In contemporary architecture, buildings are more open and accessible than ever before. Glass is everywhere in the massive atriums and lobbies, executive conference and dining rooms, and vast social spaces. Lobby security desks have become low profile greeting centers. There are few enclosed offices and the sight of young people on scooters traversing the long corridors and hallways between clusters of low walled modular furniture for socialization, collaboration and group innovation is commonplace. Elevators open to spacious floors and gorgeous designs, and guests walk unimpeded to the beautifully appointed reception areas. So, can an armed assailant or active shooter.

It has been a trade-off. Openness creates beauty and increases accessibility. It provides the feel of collaboration. It also removes the closed doors and offices that offered shelter, a place to hide, and impeded the spread of smoke and flames and the movements of an assailant through the building. The glass enclosed street level lobbies expose often unarmed guards and lobby occupants to the threats of cars, bombs and bullets coming through massive windows with little defense. Often guards and turnstiles are the only barrier between an assailant and full access. And of course, how many buildings in our major cities offer underground parking with no means of screening for explosive or incendiary devices? We live in changing times. This too will change. Chemical or explosive detectors or the presence of leashed shepherds and other trained bomb sniffing dogs walking the garage, or at the entrance, may be evident before too long.

Of course, we have defenses, and many companies have recognized the exposure of their facilities. Large cement planters, fixed bollards, and removable or powered retractable barriers block entrances, driveways and windows from vehicular attacks and accidental crash of cars. Blast and bullet resistant glass reduce the threat to lobby and executive conference rooms. Existing glass can be retrofitted with bullet resistant films. Exposed lobby guards can be afforded some protection as well with free standing branded barriers perhaps displaying a corporate logo. Guards may be armed, an individual company decision. Distance, barriers, use of reinforced supports, smart architecture, and composite column wraps provide some protection to the most exposed or sensitive structural supports in underground garages.

As said above, we live in changing times. These technologies are widely deployed in high-risk consulates and government facilities. Increasingly, concern for attack is a focus of private sector business.

*Where mitigation of a risk whether by direct, compensating, interlaced, or layered controls, is not considered prudent, cost fit, or appropriate to the risk, or the needs of the business, then in the judgment of the business, alternate approaches to the management of risk may be warranted, including insurance or managed acceptance*

*Figure 30 Fixed bollards protect a park*

## Dogs

We all love parks, strolling, people watching, and walking our dogs. Let me take a moment and digress as I share a few words about dogs.

By background, prior to corporate IT governance and security management, I was a forensic anthropologist and identification specialist. I worked with law enforcement and medical examiners. While training in the recovery and identification of human remains at the

Henry Lee Forensic Institute, I had the opportunity to work with a pair of Dedicated Cadaver Detector Dogs brought in by K-9 Trainer/Handler Keith Herron, Sr. out of Kentucky. Keith is a good friend and assists Police departments in remains location and recovery. In one training exercise, to demonstrate the effectiveness of the dogs he buried some blood and decomposed tissue under bleachers at a huge practice field. He released one of the dogs, Vessa, a female shepherd and one of several certified detector dogs that work with Keith. He explains that he can only run one dog at a time when doing their detective work. They are highly competitive. As I remember it, she circled the field perimeter once, a second time in a narrower circle, and then sat down next to the spot under the bleachers where the remains were hidden.

In the picture at top, Vessa, located a small bone dating to a missing persons case from the 1940s!

Mid page, Vessa is detecting material planted in a tree branch.

With another group I had the opportunity to see dogs trained to detect concealed guns. An officer held the leashed dog as nearly an entire room of about 40 unarmed people walked around in a procession, holding the shoulders of the person in front of them. If there was music, it would have looked like a wedding. One officer added to the line, unfamiliar to the dog, had a concealed gun. As the armed officer passed the dog, the dog detected the presence of the gun and jumped up, putting both paws on the identified officer. Well, maybe he was just joining the dance. Dogs are amazing.

But not all of them are cut out for law enforcement or security. Perhaps an undercover detective?

## Evacuation, Reaggregation and Shelter in Place

Building evacuations and shelter in place drills should be well rehearsed under advisement of local law enforcement, or fire and public safety authorities, and should conform to the written plan for evacuations and 'shelter in place' posted by facilities and promoted and reinforced in training drills under direction of building management, or public safety officials. Major metropolitan police offer corporate outreach and will help in conducting training, consultation, and drills. In New York, the NYPD offers the SHIELD program (http://www.nypdshield.org/public/), and Operation NEXUS which provide invaluable guidance.

Evacuation is not intended to be an uncontrolled event. When possible and in many plans, evacuees are responsible to adhere to defined reporting or re-aggregation instructions if not in conflict with personal safety or emotional well-being. A re-aggregation location will be designated typically within a short, but safe distance from the facility where safe evacuation can be confirmed, or additional instructions can be provided. In absence of re-aggregation some companies require that evacuees check in by phone, website, or email to affirm they are safe and confirm that they can be reached so additional instructions as to what to do and when to return to work can be provided to them. Instructions will be defined in the evacuation plan and re-enforced in drills so that evacuees can leave safely and be accounted for.

Above all personal safety is paramount. This should always be true over the protection of systems, data, or physical assets. There may be some who disagree and hopefully the process of natural selection will not have the opportunity to work that out, but in my opinion which I encourage all to accept, there is no data, system, or business important enough to measure against a life. Transfer of business risk to employee safety risk is never the right formula. Regardless of the situation employees should take whatever precautions or actions are necessary for safety and to assure personal well-being and/or adhere to guidance or instructions as provided by public safety officials.

## Crisis Briefings

In the event of an incident resulting in extensive injury, abduction, isolation, or loss of life it should be recognized that there will be an investigation in progress by law enforcement and other public safety authorities, a need for scheduled information updates to concerned family members, and a need to minimize confusion. There may also be a declared crime scene under investigation. Scheduled briefings to impacted families and to employees should be announced and held at a facility away from the impacted facilities to avoid interference with the investigation in process. A large room at a hotel or other available space sufficiently distant, but operationally effective would be a suitable briefing center and would allow fixed schedule briefings without disturbing or interfering with law enforcement or public safety officials.

An executive with authority should conduct or manage briefings, often representing Public Relations or Human Resources, and advisedly with legal presence and/or a grief management or crisis specialist and sometimes law enforcement. Briefings should be held on a consistent and regular schedule. There is considerable guidance published online from Homeland Security and other sources. The NTSB (National Transportation Safety Board) (http://www.ntsb.gov/Pages/default.aspx) may be a valuable source of training for public safety organizations, critical public agencies, and private sector companies.

Be cognizant of the need for nearby accommodations, food, water, emergency medical coverage, rest provisions, security, and the on and off cycling of staff resources and briefing teams. There will also be the need for stress relief facilities (rest spots) and potentially mobile medical facilities. These may be required to manage the post traumatic needs of employees and impacted families.

**Complex Crisis**

Cybercrime, cyber theft, and cyber terrorism are not typically associated with physical damage to structures, injury, or loss of life except where system controls for electrical utility power, environmental systems or operating processes are attacked, medical devices, or where someone seeking to steal data or damage systems does so by gaining physical entry or attempts to obfuscate the commission of a theft of data or other crime with a physical act.

The CISO has not traditionally been directly involved in the management of physical crisis events, typically falling to the CSO or others in facilities, legal or human resources. In many organizations that is changing with the integration of the CISO and CSO functions and the recognition that an attack to one realm may be predictive or a prelude to the other. Threats made in social space materialize as acts on the ground. Riots and cyber events often have the same triggers. Whether as an integrated function or a partnership of specialists the proximity of technical, physical, cyber, industrial and IoT security needs and emerging threats, and the complexity of investigation and the support of law enforcement and investigative professionals require these roles stay attuned and work together.

*We should know where our assets are to know what to monitor and protect, and what data is consequential.*
*The lunch menu needs less protection than does our critical intellectual property, but too often they are treated much the same*

# CISO REDEFINED

*Protecting Business*

Martin Gomberg, CISSP, CIPP/E

## SECTION 17. CYBER, POS, INDUSTRIAL CONTROL, MEDTECH AND IOT

Which of these things does not go together? Well, it depends on perspective. They certainly are different. The devices they employ, technologies and operating systems are unique, tools and languages for their development, monitoring and management differ, and each face different threats. An expert in one is typically not well versed in the others.

From the perspective of management however, they are all in the end, just different environments, as different from enterprise systems as is the remote sales office, mobile, BYOD, Voice over IP, and digital communities. In each case, we need to manage them, and assess, inventory, and mitigate our risks, define, size, recruit and build the teams and organizations with the specialist knowledge appropriate to the environment, expose and correct vulnerabilities, manage procurement and deployment projects, monitor for threats, and respond decisively.

We also need to stay current with changes in technical defenses, and our potential pool of partners, specialists in the environment that possess the expertise to address its risks, and test and validate our defenses, again differing in the skill required.

And we need to appropriately budget for the investments we need to make in assuring effective operations and security. Clean operations, effective account management, awareness, education, and other controls important to our corporate technology operating environments, are equally applicable, and are the most primary safeguards for effective defense. As a CISO tasked with oversight for the care of one of these unique spaces the challenge and enormity of the task may seem daunting and intimidating. There are unique characteristics in each of these environments, and unique skills required, but recognition of the commonalities in the management challenge brings this down to size, an elephant still, but in bite size chunks.

And these environments though individual and unique, participate in the whole of the enterprise from a business sense as sources of growth, opportunity, and competitive advantage. They also participate equally in contributed risk, and as vectors of attack. Weaknesses of one, exposes the other. The compromise of one, is the means to the other. We have all seen less secured remote sales offices leveraged to attack the corporate infrastructure of an enterprise, in even the largest, and best defended corporate environments. We have seen webcams hijacked, and routers, and other unsecured or minimally secured Internet of Things (IoT) devices mobilized and used as "botnets" in Distributed Denial of Services (DDOS) attacks against web properties and businesses. Both Cyber and Point of Sale have been used as vectors of compromise for consequential corporate data. And cyber again in attack on power grids and industrial systems. A PH.D. student at the Georgia Institute of Technology, recently demonstrated that the PLCs (programmable logic controllers) at a water treatment plant would be vulnerable, and that the PLCs of many treatment plants are reachable online, potentially to be attacked or held hostage by Ransomware. This should frighten all of us. http://www.cio.com/article/3169569/security/researcher-develops-ransomware-attack-that-targets-water-supply.html#tk.rss_all

Inadequately protected medical technologies expose individuals to physical harm. Compromised personal health information violates us intimately and exposes hospitals and businesses to regulatory harm and litigation, both in targeted attacks, and inadvertent loss. Where very personal medical data is transmitted for consult, or to inform emergency or critical care, unprotected cached web pages can persist as a residual trail exposing personal data from server to browser, and all the gateways, proxies, and security systems in between. Data moves, and without careful attention, the footprints of data are left everywhere. Corporate, Cyber, Point of Sale, Industrial Control, SCADA, Medical Technologies, and the Internet of Things. We are a multiplicity of diverse environments contributing to the pool of risk, but in exposure, one system.

And if one system, exposed by its component parts, effective defense of any requires an understanding of the touch points for all. It also requires an effective mapping of these touch points, and the identification of the controls needed to secure them, in context of each environment, and where they intersect.

In the realm of corporate risks, "Cyber" is certainly the least understood threat before corporate boards and executive management. It gets most of their attention. Often even traditional IT management is ill equipped with the understanding, tools, and skills, to counter cyber threats, or even effectively discuss them, increasing and supporting the concerns of management. In fact, it may simply be that cyber is the best known of the least understood threats, and so makes more frequent headlines than does point of sale, IoT (internet of Things), SCADA (Supervisory Control and Data Acquisition), ICS (Industrial Control Systems), or Medical Technologies, and so gets greater attention by corporate boards and executive management. It is what is in the newspapers in the morning. And it is in the newspaper just about every morning. And perhaps, some of it the press may simply blend misunderstood, the subtleties of attack sources and vectors lost on writer and reader alike, and so in perception, it is all cyber.

*An incident to a company of one size, with given resources, expertise, and operational maturity, without doubt, is a crisis to another that lacks them*

Perhaps it is also that cyber and point of sale attacks have been around longer than the IoT, Scada or Med Tech threats. We were addressing computer viruses in the 1980s. As for Point of Sale, most cash registers were local with no capability to connect elsewhere. Low speed modems did connect retail bank branches to corporate headquarters and processing centers, well before we had ATMs, and those set to auto answer after the bank had closed were ripe for compromise. Industrial systems had been largely manual or a closed system until recently, also localized, as were medical systems. Internet of Things? Toasters did not speak to anyone except by that ding that communicated that your muffin is burnt. It is a changing world.

But cyber is unique. There have been a few publicly visible cyber incidents in the past years that give us an indication of how bad things can get and bad is an inadequate descriptor for just how bad that is. It is unique in what it attacks, how it attacks, motivations, and impacts. We have seen attacks against domain registries, websites, web applications and the web servers they reside on. The same for internet facing perimeter routers and the protocols on which they run. Even the inability to clean up lingering TCP connection requests has been a source of DDOS attack in widely deployed older routers, these called SYN (synchronization request) FLOOD Attacks.

Ports are scanned constantly to find those that are open, granting access to unprotected services and systems. Excess open services on web servers, passwords left set to the manufacturers default on routers, firewalls, and servers, and attacks at onsite DNS, proxies, and browsers are vectors. Insufficient boundaries, limits and controls on the volume, format, origins, and nature of data input compromises web applications. They are attacked through Cross Site Scripting (XSS), violations of 'same origin' policies, and buffer overflows, sometimes allowing exfiltration of data or access to data resources otherwise unreachable by those outside protected perimeters and corporate boundaries. They also deliver malicious payloads and contaminated content. OMG!! I said this would be in non-technical friendly English! Just a little more.

And now we have containerized scaled down OS, database, application and security components in the cloud and we are configuring these remotely on virtual machines and accessing these as services. How many of our auditors and regulators will be able to check that box any time soon? There is a lot to understand, and to get our heads around, probably mostly good, certainly sounds so, but it just keeps getting more interesting. We have not exactly done a wonderful job with keeping our legacy environments safe and tidy. Maybe this will be better. And it is not the technology, it's the number of moving parts between technology, privacy, compliance, continuity and the digital transformation and our ability to keep up. There is a lot to do.

*It is the application of best practices, vigilance, and shared knowledge, new technologies, and the efforts of CISOs, attorneys, and security experts pushing back against the darker forces globally, that ultimately will advance a slow and sliding success*

## The Kill Chain

The Kill Chain is a phrase coined by Lockheed Martin. It describes the phased anatomy of a successful malware infiltration. It begins with reconnaissance. This is the research, investigation, and interrogation phase of an attack where email addresses for individuals are found, or open ports, services, weak protection, visible topography, system names, or other targetable specifics are identified about a site, a business, or the individuals that they employ in specific roles, and their relationships to systems, data, and other individuals.

Reconnaissance is the goal of *Phishing* techniques that cast a wide net to identify susceptible individuals for subsequent targeted *'Spear Phishing'* against those most likely to succumb, or the *'Social Engineering'* of a relationship of confidence in person, by phone, or by email communications. These are the means used to establish trust, enabling breach.

An email that addresses an individual and makes an acquaintance but asks for nothing only suggesting that they will be back later to bring a gift or a link that would be of interest exploits trust. Returning, they are familiar, and those that are familiar have earned our trust. I recall an Anthropology course I took once with the famed Dr. Elizabeth Langley, an acquaintance of Dr. Margaret Meade, who said that if you want to be accepted by the indigenous people in an area, visit, then leave, and then return at some time later. When you return, you are an old friend. We accept that which is familiar. This and other means of negotiating access with the unsuspecting is social engineering.

Once a target has been identified through *Reconnaissance*, phases of *Weaponization*, the packaging of microcode capable of creating and opening an exploitable back door takes place. The microcode often is designed to do nothing more than install on a vulnerable device and reestablish connection with a malicious website. Delivery of that simple package is by email or other means. Once delivered, exploitation of a vulnerability on the target is leveraged, permitting the microcode to activate, download, and install additional malware from a website, this typically carrying a malicious and deleterious payload. This is the bomb, delivered by a very clever mechanism.

The exploitation is a request, but now initiated by the compromised device from within the less well scrutinized protected perimeter, a request to a website for the delivery of a new package, this one containing the *Payload* intended to do the damage or effect the compromise. Once this payload is delivered and released, finality often involves the establishment of *Command and Control*, allowing the compromised device to be remotely managed, and further activity to take place which might include the compromise of other devices within the protected perimeter, the lateral spread of the infiltrated malware.

And traditionally, infiltration has been the goal. The corporate gold has always been buried deep within the protected perimeter. Giora Engel, a security expert points out in the Dark Reading post "Deconstructing the Kill Chain", that the Kill chain concept reinforces thinking that may no longer be current. It encourages focus on concepts of perimeter and malware defense that are less the reality of the security concerns today.

*Privilege is trust and trust is the cost of doing business*

With data mobile and device agnostic, in the cloud, in virtual instances, traversing a wider array of globally deployed interconnected devices in transit, and created on demand by interrogation of massive data lakes, exploits have a much broader range of opportunities to compromise, capture, or corrupt our most valuable resources, no longer just behind corporate walls.

The targets of cyber have in the past been both known and random. That itself suggests a wide range of motivations, since if you do not know who you are after, you do not know specifically what you are after, or what you will get. But that has changed and in more recent years, attacks in 'the wild' are less a concern than are those that are targeted.

Targeting also better defines motivations. And for cyber the motivation remains broad. Damage, theft, extortion, compromise of systems, and espionage. Motivation is in large part dictated by the actor, and that too for cyber varies, from skilled hackers, script kiddies that borrow code from menu driven sites and launch attacks probably for no reason at all, those that want to just break stuff, thieves, organized criminals (steal, sell or blackmail), unintentional, misguided, or malicious insiders, extortionists that use ransomware for commercial hijack and gain, hacktivists with an agenda, and militarized cyber units supporting nation states.

And who they are in large part dictates what they do. That makes sense. If you want to steal information or search for bank codes that will take time, you need to linger undiscovered, whether within a corporate perimeter, or following the tentacles of partners, resources and remote infrastructure and cloud along which it reaches. It is not in your interest to shut down service or break stuff, or for that matter to give away your presence and risk being exposed and caught. On the other hand, if your motivation is to send a clear message about your ability to shut things down or do damage, that will be very visible and dramatic.

Attackers often opt for anonymity. Most would prefer to avoid getting caught. And most prefer the time to linger. In fact, it is more the norm than atypical that once inside an attacker can quietly explore, co resident with normal activities, undetected for months or years. They employ steganography, hiding deleterious code in normal seeming files, hidden in plain sight. They employ stealth and deception, concealing themselves and their behaviors in the normal stream of activity for a company, not touching too much at one time, not stealing too much, and not creating excessive or unusual traffic, or anomalous activity. They pass outbound traffic through open ports on your routers. They use outbound messaging to establish communication and transfer stolen properties, your properties, elsewhere. They employ tools like encryption to assure their files and outbound communications remain hidden. They bring their own tools to keep their activities hidden and secure, or they borrow yours.

*Controls, sound practices, accountable leadership, standards, and a risk-based strategy get you closer to where you need to be*

It is also often the case that the activities of the uninvited are only detected and brought to the attention of those monitoring the cyber activities for a company by people on the outside, typically security specialists or law enforcement. FBI, Secret Service, NSA, NCIS or others are unexpectedly made aware, your compromise swept up in their surveillance, detecting communication attempts from within some compromised network, in this case yours, to sites actively under investigation.

Attackers also opt for subterfuge, spoofing the attack origin so it appears, or in fact through redirection, comes from someone else. A compromised company might in fact not be a target, simply an unwitting or even witless victim, their equipment employed or confiscated for an attack on someone other. There are many sites, individual homes, small businesses, and large enterprises on the internet, each with insufficient, weak, poorly configured, or no security at all. They are carelessly left open for compromise, their systems, and routers available for misuse, their processing capabilities abducted and conscripted to form armies, so called 'zombie' armies, along with hundreds or thousands of others, mobilized together for 'amplification', converging in an attack. These three mainstays, Subterfuge, Redirection, and Amplification are core to many DDOS Attacks.

Legacy firewalls, anti-virus and intrusion detection are less effective than in the past. New next-gen and heuristic technologies used to detect and mitigate threats are complex and expensive, we make the investments, but are still not confident in our safety. Security expertise is in short supply. In-house investment in developing these skills has a short shelf life given the speed at which new threats emerge.

Keeping our most private, confidential, and critical IP data secure is a top-of-mind issue for every digital age business that collects, produces, or leverages data and most have the same concerns. Cyberattacks and data breaches have become more frequent and more targeted. Successful attacks are occurring against our biggest and presumably best prepared companies, despite that presumably they use the best technologies and are adequately staffed and hire the best expertise.

- New devices, apps and cloud services are emerging faster than people or IT departments can absorb

- Mobility and cloud move operations further from the infrastructure under our control

- Attacks are sophisticated and increasingly more difficult to detect. We have technical solutions for malware, but we do not for human behavior

- Technology and culture are changing too fast for law and policy to regulate.

- The expense and complexity of needed defenses outpace our ability and organization to absorb

- The expectation of consumers that data, apps, infrastructure, and social communities go anywhere, for access at any time, from any device. The culture of immediacy.

- Not just law and regulation, but consumers and investors hold us accountable for breach of data. Whether in dollars or reputation, costs and penalties can be severe.

# CISO
# REDEFINED

*Protecting Business*

Martin Gomberg, CISSP, CIPP/E

## SECTION 18.  THREAT:  THE NEXT GENERATION

Threat has a culture. It is generational. Risk and our security live in context of a universe of change. In one sense, it is our experience with cyber these past forty years or so, the use of common attack vectors, the 'kill chain' model, 'script kiddies' using kits available on the internet to modify and launch attacks, and our 'return-on-investment' approach to risk, that focuses our attention on the risks we know and the defenses which have worked before. That has forced us to fight as if it was the last war. Compliance keeps our focus on the regulatory requirements, and our laws limit our ability to take the offensive.

We defend against that which is familiar because we believe history repeats itself, and in fact it does. With minimal variation, we prepare for that which we have seen before. And because most of our adversaries have traditionally been of the same generation, experience base, mind-set, tools, and skill set, theirs and ours, attackers, and defenders, both much the same, our approach has largely not been wrong. We look at relics of past damage, to predict, plan and justify spending for defense against an unpredictable future. We believe our adversaries attack us because they want to take things, break things, or are simply curious as to how far they can get, or what they can get away with. Again, mostly, we have been right. There have been some glimmers of true evil, and some of exceptionalism, a lot of criminality, and up until recently a minimal rumbling of nation state militarization of cyber, but mostly it has been the same old, sometimes costly, and dramatic, but much the same. Artificial Intelligence (AI) offers a path to the transformational, but as much for them as us.

Sometimes the damage done is significant, we have certainly seen that, but generally not because adversaries have been particularly innovative, in fact usually not. It is often our own inadequate attention to operational cleanliness or defenses. In many of the most glaring of breaches that I can recall, this has been the case. Our improvements have largely been incremental, upgraded routers, firewalls, or intrusion prevention systems, a larger SIEM with better integration and more threat feeds, GRC systems (governance, risk, and compliance) with better risk algorithms and nicer reports, some new products, new tools, faster, better, leverage of cloud models, but mostly finite enhancements on that which has come before. There are some paradigm shifts, but these are rare. We have not seen science fiction yet. And we

 Copyright Martin Gomberg All rights reserved - Do not copy reproduce or distribute without written consent v. 12/1/23

have not walked on the moon in over 40 years. We and our adversaries have grown comfortable, they advance, we advance, we say we have made progress, they hit us again, we make new investments, and management struggles with what to believe. And it has been that way for a generation and more passed.

But now the Baby Boomers are retiring. Gen Xer's are getting on to other things in their lives, and the Millennials are just coming into their own. And of course, those that will follow, whoever they are, and whatever they will be branded, now Gen Z, Centennials, Post-Millennials, next gen whatever, are just around the corner. And with each generation passing, new experience, different motivations. And with geopolitics being what they are, and shifting world and cultural climates, we can only imagine. Technology shifts a moment in time, new ideas, and we are different. The math is the same wherever we are in the world, and we and our adversaries both have that in common. Some of us, constrained by the generational limits of our knowledge, comfort zones, and the anchors of experience, see the exit sign in the not too distant, and will be left behind, true for us, true for adversaries alike. With that, the next reality will be created.

Well, I am being just a bit disingenuous. These past few years have opened our eyes. Focused political manipulation, distortion of message, falsehoods, creation of news, and the targeting and timing of misrepresentation each distort and shape our perceptions and opinions through social media. The impact of these has been grave. There was science and purpose to the ramp up of digital espionage and focused misdirection. And now nation state militarization. Not just a minimal rumbling as I had said in earlier writings. And not just in weaponizing influence but as a weapon of war. Denial of service, attacks on infrastructure, and crippling attacks on hope and confidence and the spread of fear. In truth, we have had ample introduction to the disruptive and destructive capabilities of nation states these recent few with little expectation this will change.

For most of this book I have been talking about a changing culture, transformation in business and business models. Change is not the purview of business alone. Government, politics, cultures, and global relationships are shifting worldwide. The threats we face have transformed and globalized. There are those that hate us, and those we hate, and the math for that leaves that condition true for at least the next two generations, and likely beyond. Terror has gone digital.

So, there is the question. The forty or so year-old cyber war now has a new set of players. Unshackled from the past by generational change, free from the constraints of old experiences, will it still be more of the same, or will our adversaries in cyber and terror move from the predictable, to the terrible, and on to a different set of rules, unidentifiable, unimaginable, and three wars ahead? Will cyber and social be militarized and unleashed as a weapon on populations even more than we have now seen? Will terror adopt cyber as the new paradigm setting the new standard, no longer motivated by 'what we can take or break, or how far we can get', but measured by the ability to corrupt, destroy, devastate, and terrorize?

Even now, a twenty-block ride through a major city is emerging as a privacy threat. Services capture information about who we are, where we travel, and how we behave. Patterns of the places we go can be developed. We can be profiled as to our habits. From our activities, neighborhoods and patterns new information may be extrapolated and derived, assumptions of wealth, the products we might use, purpose of our activities, others that may share similar interest with whom we might be associated, frequency of these interactions, and more. It feels as if we are just on the horizon of a different world.

We know what has passed, but what potentially can we predict that may lay ahead for which we may be unprepared, but need to be thinking about? Speculation from a current perspective says the Internet of things, massive Big Data lakes, 3D printing of critical manufacturing components and replacement organs, digital surveillance, automotive, home, and industrial automation, and wearable or ingestible medical technologies, amongst so much else are all game changers for a potentiated future. But the unpredictable future is fertile ground for all possibilities with the next generation of threat. It can only be imagined.

In this section, I will describe some potential future attack scenarios. The following of course is all fiction. So why is it in a book targeting the emergence of the Redefined CISO? My apologies. For one reason, we have covered a lot of material and I need a break. I am sure you do too. I'll never be a fiction writer. This may be my only opportunity. And for another, I recall the early days of malware, attempting unsophisticated attacks on command executables. Defense was by comparison, easy. We seem to have come light years from those early days, and we will move light years ahead of where we are now. What remains ahead, and how soon until the new reality of what is to come is here?

I have taken significant artistic license to create drama. Science fiction perhaps. Some will consider the picture I am painting unrealistic. Others may not see this as quite so extreme. Some will chastise me for putting these ideas out. We all know that if I can think of them, a thousand capable hackers, bad guys, and military cyber units, in every country, already have. For many my speculation may just be 'yesterday's news'.

Many areas are exposed to digital harm. I just picked a few. These would not need to be sophisticated attacks. Threats that attack through familiar vectors, but in ways not used before, or at least not commonly. Threats that use the technical to disrupt the social fabric and terrorize. Threats that use the technical to attack that which we trust, attacking society in all aspects of the way we live.

I hope that this brief diversion lends more than a brief raise of eyebrows, or a quick thumb through to the next section, but leads us to think about the threats we now face, and potentially will need to think about and confront in the not too distant.

*There is a strategy built into all of the operational and architectural decisions that we make in business. But most often the decisions we make are a tradeoff. A strength in one area is often an exposure in another*

## Attacks at home

Like most, I watch a lot of television. Coaxial cable, digital and optical networks enter every home carrying television signals in to set top boxes, or they wirelessly stream to smart devices and smart televisions, providing entertainment, data, voice, and internet connectivity.

What has always been a closed, proprietary, and well protected network increasingly seems to grow more porous. And what is more inviting a target for terrorism and the delivery of a terrorist message than a few million unsuspecting and unprotected households? Is TV networking a potential vector for digital threats, malicious ad substitution, program disruption, and denial of service, and perhaps for terrorism?

## Attacks that blur Cyber and Societal

Almost every major company in every major city has abandoned their analog telephone system in favor of digital Voice Over Internet Protocol (VOIP) systems. They are better, more flexible to deploy, less expensive, and better integrated with other business systems. Companies can deploy thousands to hundreds of thousands of phones cheaply and quickly. These systems are everywhere.

I wasn't very surprised to learn that a tool we called a War Dialer that rapidly dialed and tested for auto answer on modem lines back in the 80s had reemerged, now available for VOIP systems. It can be used for marketing purposes to dial a number, or all numbers in an area, or multiple areas, to deliver a pre-recorded message. Now we call them Robocalls. "Hi, this is Julia". We all get them.

As I am sure that many of you would agree, amongst so many, one of the great features about digital telephony is caller ID. Caller ID allows screening and blocking of unwanted calls, but on the downside, it can also be spoofed. A call can look like it comes from anyone, and from anywhere. It should come as no shock to anyone that there is free software available on the internet that allows the spoofing of a caller ID such that it replaces the ID of the initiating caller with inserted text. This would be simple to automate and be made iterative, spoofing the ID presented, making the call to one person or thousands look like it is from whomever we want.

Combining the War Dialer that dials a number, or all numbers in an area, or many areas, to deliver a pre-recorded message, with a spoofed ID would allow 'fake news' from a 'fake source' to be delivered to a large population. Malware containing the elements of both a War Dialer and the ability to spoof an ID, targeted to infect inadequately protected VOIP systems (and many are open or inadequately protected), might allow thousands to hundreds of thousands of VOIP phones to call a specific number, a range of numbers, or all numbers in an area, delivering 'fake news', from the 'fake source'.

And now some Si Fi drama. If that call was directed at all of New York, and the surrounding region, New Jersey, Connecticut, and Long Island, and came allegedly from the 'Department of Homeland Security', with the message being 'Indian Point Nuclear Reactor has been compromised, leave the area any way that you can', imagine the effect. There would be panic and confusion. There would be terror.

People would race to pull children out of school and find unprotected elders. They would clog gas lines, law enforcement and 911 would be overwhelmed, and likely cell services as well, as frightened people attempt to call friends and family. Evacuees would jam highways and trains, effectively shut down streets, highways, bridges, tunnels, and transportation systems. There would be lines to pull money out of ATMs everywhere, an automated run on the banks. OK, I am getting crazy so I will stop now. This is exhausting.

What I had hoped to point out is the ultimate terror attack. There is no actual threat. It is the response that is the attack. Malware is the trigger, technology is the vector, and human behavior is the target. The impact is social and societal, devastating, and effective. Science fiction yes, but 'the science' is simple. Maximize the disruptive capabilities of fear. This may be fiction, but however done, not far from possible.

## Attacks against financial integrity and social order

Ransomware is a business, and if you make your Bitcoin payment, most often data held hostage is released. But ransomware is not just a business, it is big business. As per SonicWall, a Dell company, and a leader in advanced network security, there was a 50% increase and millions of attempts in 2016. Now the numbers are off the charts. Ransomware is changing, both in motivation and impact. Per James Lyne, Global Head of Security Research at Sophos, where there was a reasonable assurance that if payments were made, data held hostage would be released, this is no longer always true. In "Shock & Awe' Ransomware Attacks Multiply", by Kelly Jackson Higgins, it was noted that increasingly criminals are demanding ransoms, and even if paid, are demanding more before data is released. They are repeatedly attacking prior victims, threatening the exposure of the data if additional ransoms are not paid, selling the captured data, or simply destroying, or rendering it unusable. There is also another frightening scenario. Ransomware loosed to infect and encrypt the data it targeted but where the thieves were frightened away. There is no longer a criminal enterprise to pay for the key to release the data that has been exposed, and no way to get the data back.

Ransomware can do damage file by file, seemingly at random. It can also be paced slowly over time to be less detectable and obvious. If unnoticed, the damage can percolate from live systems into nightly backups, and remote copies, trickling over an extended period, as we perform our normal operational procedures of backing up data, rendering them useless for recovery. But ransomware does not hold the patent on this means of infiltration. Another malware can be released to behave much the same, but without a profit motive, simply social destruction. And this need not be sophisticated malware. It needs only open spreadsheets, documents, and database files transposing nines and zeroes, avoiding changes to dates and times of course, and preserving original file creation dates so that what has happened is less obvious. We will call it the Nines Virus.

On the surface, this is terrible enough. But think for a moment about the societal impact of no longer relying on the validity of numbers. There would be loss of faith in banking. Credit card balances would be untrusted. Credit would cease. Retirement accounts would be decimated, loans rejected for insufficient resources, banks could not disburse funds lacking confidence in balances and reserves. There would be disruption of our social safety nets as social service and pension payments stop. We would lose the ability to trust transactions or contractual agreements of any type. This is a breakdown of trust and integrity in social order. This is apocalyptic science fiction only missing the zombies. I could take this further but will stop here at the risk someone will offer to buy the movie rights.

**Our responsibility to Next Generation Threat preparedness**

OK. This to many will sound over the top, science fiction, or simply nonsense. Maybe it is, but it does not feel too implausible. The attacks I have described do not require too many moving parts. The question remains as we look at this, Cloud, the Internet of Things, Generative AI, and all the new world defining technology, knowing that we are not the only ones looking, what can we anticipate, and what do we do to prepare? And as much as we may prepare for the technical mode of attack, are we prepared for the human response? The world of the future threats we might face is a world far too big, and perhaps the next attack too dangerous to be left until we see how the movie comes out.

I recall attending a conference where then U.S. Secretary of State John Kerry was asked about the fears that kept him up at night. He responded, and I will paraphrase, that more than the threat of conventional attack, he feared cyber as the next arena in which our battles would take place. I have heard Admiral Mike Rogers, former Director of U.S. National Security Agency, and Michael Chertoff, former Secretary of U.S. Department of Homeland Security express similar sentiments. This said 25 years ago is being said today.

And this is understandable. Even amongst those of us in the profession, knowledgeable about cyber and security, few of us know what the experts know or are concerned about or have a view across all critical infrastructure and sensitive targets and where they may be exposed. We can only imagine what cyber warfare might look like fully unleashed. Attacks against our electrical grid, communications, nuclear power plants, air traffic control systems, medical devices, our ability to pump water or manage pressure behind hydro-electric dams are just a few that I have heard named as concerns, informed or in conjecture. I had never contemplated attacks against the democratic process. Clearly, the melding of physical threat and cyber threat and threats against the way we live is a reality we do not want to face.

A few years back I served as vice-chair of an Overseas Security Advisory Council private sector working group for the U.S. State Department. We brought together resources from numerous law enforcement and Federal agencies, attorneys, security specialists, CSOs and CISOs from the private sector to exercise preparedness for physical, social, and cyber incidents, and to consider future threats. As founder of the Heroes Partnership, I sponsored public safety events and supported public efforts toward counter terrorism including the mock takeover of a high school by active assailants. I am a strong advocate of public – private partnership and cooperation. It is a topic I raise frequently when speaking and on security panels. Many of the threats we face are outside our perimeters and beyond our ability as individual companies to address, yet the consequences to us are potentially enormous. We depend on the effectiveness of the public sector for much of our defense.

That said, the capacity and knowledge of the private sector is critical if those we entrust with our defense are to succeed. It falls to us to work together, with others in our industries, our peers, our competitors, and to align ourselves with law enforcement and federal agencies. This is both an opportunity and a responsibility to public and community, and we should press for acceptance of this responsibility to be recognized and supported in our job descriptions.

*In a practicable sense, there is a lot to do, but much is just good governance and clean operations.*

*Appointing a capable and engaged executive for oversight, designating and certifying qualified, ethical people for required or mandated positions, segregating responsibilities, removing conflicts of interest or authority, knowing our data, understanding business risks, and promoting and implementing an environment of effective policies, procedures, and use of standards will address much of what is required for safer operations and to satisfy 'most' regulations*

# Remember the Joke

*"I can tell you the score of the game before it even starts."*

*The answer, of course is "Nothing to nothing."*

*Well in the world of business continuity I can tell you the lessons of a disaster event even before the stuff hits the proverbial fan. And the reason we know the results before any emergency event, crisis or planning exercise is because we never "learn" from our mistakes – we just repeat them.*

## Communications

The inability to effectively communicate in a timely manner when normal communications become severely challenged or fail completely.

## Roles and responsibilities

The confusion that results from people not knowing what their crisis role is and the crisis roles of others.

## Access

The failure to access key files, documents, equipment, and systems along with the inability to go into impacted work locations.

## Plan activation

The hesitation to implement documented and tested recovery plans or strategies.

## BCP is a people business

Focus on people and their needs. The one question all C-level folks ask immediately following a disaster event is "Are my people, ok?" So, build a plan around people and the resources they need to do their jobs. Give senior managers checklists to remind them of all the immediate concerns they will face from the onset of a crisis event. Let business managers know that since they are responsible for the success of their business. They are also responsible for its failure – including crisis events.

*Mark Haimowitz, CBCP, FBCI*
*Director, Business Continuity Planning*
*Disney ABC Television Network*

# CISO REDEFINED

*Protecting Business*

Martin Gomberg, CISSP, CIPP/E

## SECTION 19. BUSINESS CONTINUITY, DATA PROTECTION AND AVAILABILITY

It is the responsibility of any solvent business to operate, survive and optimally thrive, delivering on its mission in meeting the needs of clients, partners, employees, owners, and investors at the best of times, in adversity, and through change. Business Continuity assessment is a critical lens for examining the structural architecture of a business and how it operates, its underpinnings for effective continuity and adaptability, how it relates to value chain, and clients, and what it requires at different points in the business cycle.

Assessment if properly leveraged presents an opportunity to detect deficiency and limitation, and re-architect the business for efficiency, effectiveness, and improvement, so that it is at the same time a better business, resistant to crisis, and tolerant of change. This is the basis of BC/NT which I will describe in more detail in the next chapter, and a missed opportunity for many.

An effective continuity program positions the prudent company for crisis through preparedness and structure, assures a proper spend tuned to need and risk, and maximizes speed of return to function, while minimizing disruption. It plans, performs assessments, and documents not as a goal, but for a defined purpose, documents only that needed, and assures that relationships, technologies, business structures, and organization are by design sufficiently adaptable to endure crisis, change, and to facilitate swift execution when strategic opportunity presents.

### Lessons from the meltdown

I asked a group of CIOs at a conference if any felt the steps that we had taken in Business Continuity planning had prepared us adequately to respond to the financial and credit crisis of 2007 - 2008, now more than a decade and a half passed, and the Ponzi frauds that had impacted so many companies. Interestingly, several responded that "this was not a Business Continuity issue".

My visceral response was "with companies of all sizes, name players and not all folding left and right including partners, clients, competitors, suppliers and distribution in every industry, staff laid off, budgets being slashed, credit inaccessible, and our business structures and priorities disrupted or changed -- if this is not an issue of continuity …what is?", but in fact I was not surprised by that response.

Perhaps, in the way many have approached Business Continuity they were correct in that statement. Many of us have constrained our thinking to functional continuity of line of business activities. Organizationally, we task planners, analysts, coordinators, or managers with business continuity planning. It is seldom that we see a Senior or Executive Vice President or other title with authority tasked directly with that responsibility.

Often, it is treated as insurance, a required check box for audit, or a regulatory or contractual requirement. It is due diligence and prudent practice. But we create plans that address business interruption. We generally plan for events short term to a few months in duration, and correctable, maybe at great effort and significant cost, of course a business disruption, a fire, hurricane, blackout, building collapse, or other similarly damaging event, but correctable. Most plans for continuity of business are silent on positioning for entity preservation or planning for corporate continuance and viability. If these discussions are held, and I suspect they seldom are even after the experience of the credit crisis, it is by leadership, at the board and executive level, and generally if anything is committed to writing it is limited to a confidential plan for retention incentives and executive succession.

But we were discussing the meltdown. Apart from the structural failures, the economic crisis was a crisis of confidence in our institutions prompting fear that the actions of individuals and the inability of our government to protect us had crippled the financial system irreparably in a manner that we had never seen before. We watched homes foreclose, savings melt away, credit access freeze, markets fall, rising unemployment, and the dramatic failure of some of the most prominent businesses in our country's history. Companies that were well positioned gobbled up competitors. Some with deep reserves hunkered down and decreased spending to slow the 'burn rate' of their resources. Some leveraged reserves to capitalize on the crisis, pursue new markets, and to diversify. Others dried and died on the vine, unable to secure credit, desperate for a 'white knight' merger or acquisition to rescue them as their operating resources depleted, but in a crisis of credit affecting everyone there were simply not enough buyers in the market, even for assets at fire sale prices. Opportunity has a short shelf life.

The inherent strengths and weaknesses in structure and preparedness exposed in companies of all sizes, urban and rural, and in all industries, was revealing, not just about the individual companies, but about our approach to business continuity as a practice.

At the risk of generalizing, it is often not the severity of the crisis, but the duration and complexity that has the greatest impact on business. What we saw during the financial crisis was a laboratory of BC response, some effective, some not, as small companies and multi-billion-dollar enterprises equally struggled to survive using all the tools at their disposal. We saw names like Lehman, Thornburg Mortgage, and Bear Sterns fatigue and fail with the same rapidity as we saw corner stores and favorite restaurants go vacant in our neighborhoods and watched as other big names waited in the wings.

This was absolutely an issue of continuity being played out in real time everywhere we looked, big and small, public, and private, domestic, and global. Faced with entity preservation the full arsenal of continuity measures available to business - cost elimination, reprioritization, workforce reduction, restructuring, liquidation, divestiture, merger, and efforts toward recapitalization – all were invoked in a grand scale as companies struggled to survive. We also saw leadership in companies positioned to acquire, expand, and diversify into competitor spaces and new markets, leveraging preparedness to find and capitalize on opportunity in crisis. This was continuity – but without doubt not the continuity response reflected in most corporate plans.

The success of a business is a function of the ability to create or influence positive outcomes in accordance with the business mission. These are brand recognition, reputation, reach, profitability, growth, and sustainability of operations amongst others. Without this a business cannot survive and thrive. The continuity or sustainability of a company is minimally a factor of the balance and pace of consumption and replacement of both the hard and soft resources on which the business depends in achieving this mission.

The hard asset resources of a company are tangible and measurable. Income (current and pipeline), capital reserves, liquid assets, insurance, and accessible credit. They are also depletable if consumption outpaces creation or replacement. Hard asset resources are consumed in one form or another to service fixed operating expenses, variable operating expenses, procurement and capital investment, and the management of liabilities and incidental costs. The pace of consumption of resources over time is the 'burn rate'. In crisis, some seek to salvage value and decrease burn through disposition of assets. Even for a company rich with hard disposable assets, all very liquid, attractive, and fire sale priced to beat the market, disposition of these can be interrupted by circumstance. This would be the case (and was) for instance with the absence of buyers for otherwise liquid assets, absence of buyers with sufficient cash reserves or access to credit, or a market inundated with sellers attempting to dispose of assets to raise capital.

There are also soft resources on which a company depends to survive. These are employee morale, brand loyalty, consumer confidence, reputation, partner viability, investor tolerance, knowledge, skills, and experience. Just as hard resources, these are equally consumable, and just as depletable with poor management, inadequate attention, and insufficient care and investment. The Burn Rate Model which follows reflects this.

*Opportunity has a very short shelf life.*

*In a crisis of credit affecting everyone there may be fewer buyers in the market for assets, even if liquid and at deep discount to value*

Burn Rate Modeling Tool (hard and soft resource consumption in disaster)

$$Continuity\ (x) = Resources\ /\ Consumption$$

### Where Hard Resources =
- Residual Income
- Reserves
- Accessible Credit
- Consumable Insurance
- Asset Liquidity

### Where Consumption =
- Capital Replacement
- Fixed Operating Expense
- Variable Operating Expense
- Liabilities

### Soft Assets Are Also Consumable / Depletable

- Employee Morale
- Brand Loyalty
- Consumer Confidence
- Investor Tolerance

*Figure 311 Burn rate modeling*

It should be clear that priorities for continuity change with events, business cycles, differ for each company, size of company, and vary by industry. Some may view or prioritize these differently than I do.

- Municipalities will primarily be concerned for human care, social safety nets and restoration of community health, sanitation, and public safety services

- Educational institutions about student safety and educational continuance

- Hospitals about patient safety and facility protection

- Research centers concern for preserving research integrity and subject safety

- Media networks about staying on air, preserving viewer loyalty and advertising revenues

- Banks about capital, transactional safety, records, and execution

- Retail about inventory, distribution, stable markets, and point of sale facilities

- Manufacturing about facilities, operations, and value chain

Irrespective of cause, initiating conditions or circumstance, any crisis can quickly escalate, and the pace of escalation for any number of reasons, resources, training, business cycle, will impact companies differently.

Planning for potential scenarios like flood, fire, blackout, or a cyber-attack, a threat or causative focus, is sometimes less fruitful than examining potential outcomes, a business risk focus. The latter prioritizes impacts and catastrophic exposure of business priorities. It is for each business to give this deep thought and to assess and list what the greatest impacts to their business might be, where their concerns are, and to develop protective strategies for these. I have given a few examples to prime the pump.

- Deprivation of market

- Deprivation of inventory

- Denial of distribution

- Depletion of capital

- Damage of trust or image

Most BC certifications address the commonalities in businesses overall, everywhere, and of every size. They assure us the needed tools are in place, appropriate studies completed, and that risks, needs, and resources are documented. They assure us that there is oversight, a checklist of best practices, each defined by the experience and expertise of others. It is a validation that issues have been examined, thinking has been done, scenarios have been tested, and preparations have been considered or made. Yet, increasingly, for some, there is a perception of difference between the continuity provisions made to protect a company, and that for certifying for compliance with continuity standards, or for regulatory requirements.

Continuity planning as commonly practiced, and as certification typically requires, is often analysis and documentation intensive. It calls for an inventory, inspection, and analysis of risk (RA), a qualitative or quantitative assessment of the impact of risk on the operating business (BIA), defined objectives and priorities for recovery of systems and processes (RPO), acceptable recovery time (RTO), and the people, process, communication, and technology required to ameliorate, mitigate, or moderate identified continuity exposures. As one can imagine the need, scope and magnitude of documentation required should differ with the nature, size and characteristics of a company, degree to which it is regulated, certifications to standards it requires, resources available to implement the assessment, and the approach of the implementer. Plans can be simple checklists, and effective, or copious and detailed to achieve the same result. Need and corporate culture dictate which would be best for a given company, but certification typically has specific requirements irrespective of company size, culture, and perceived needs.

This is understandable. Industry and government regulation, creditors, and investors, often require a proven methodology, framework or structure demonstrating a well-planned posture of continuity, whether requiring certification or not. They expect a minimum standard against which to measure readiness and performance. Regulatory expectations typically align very closely to the documentation and preparation exercises most certifications dictate be performed. Where audits are performed, reviewers assume that the studies they expect will have been done, and that the results of those studies reflect adequate provisioning for continuity.

Commonly Used Terms for the Tools in Business Continuity Planning and Analysis
- BCP = Business Continuity Plan
- RA  = Risk Analysis
- BIA  = Business Impact Assessment
- RTO = Recovery Time Objective
- RPO = Recovery Point Objective

Experienced executives respond to difficult situations and make hard calls every day. When faced with opportunity where it presents, it is often in an unscripted response, and a trust in peer consensus, an inner circle opinion where they are most comfortable. Voluminous plans for continuity often frustrate the executives that receive them. Many will reasonably question the practicality, cost and time investment, and maintainability of the plans. Some question the usability, continued applicability, and effectiveness of the plans through business changes, variance in business cycles, and emerging conditions. They express concern for the rapidity of response that would be possible given plan complexity.

Some see the BC planning and particularly the certification process, and their needs for catastrophic response and BC protection provisions as different. They see business continuity as a situational response, a more adaptive or agile response specific to business impacts or circumstances faced. They prefer a plan that is in accord with budget priorities and the specifics of the operating environment. They prefer a plan that adapts to a cyclic business, reflects change and the continuous development of an evolving company in accordance with its capabilities and resources, with its interests defined by the business, directed by leadership, and those operationally entrusted to protect it. For many companies, this would be a good fit. But not for all.  And of course, for some, without a compliance requirement and specific objectives, nothing would be done at all, and they would be ineffective. Regardless of approach, rapid return to a state of operation from calamity is or should be the expressed purpose of the continuity effort.

That there is a tug of war as to how to view continuity is evident in some of our largest and best run companies. It is not uncommon for leadership to view business continuity as an administrative and operational requirement. It is often not given its due for the business value of the effort, or as a BC colleague once said, is 'treated as the lesser child of security'. It is sometimes unclear to management whether the goal and impetus of the Business Continuity effort is the development, care and feeding of the plan, the accommodation of regulators, and auditors, or the protection of the business. Continuity efforts are often under-funded, delegated to a coordinator or planner role with insufficient authority, or deferred, in companies that consider it of importance only as an insurance in crisis.

*We build indemnification in contracts as insurance, but in fact it is an acknowledgement of the dirt in the system.*

Some of what is considered standard or best practice or required by certification or regulatory compliance may not be pertinent to all situations, and the required studies and assessments may not be the most direct means of getting protection in place quickly. Planning and documentation and situational response are not mutually exclusive. Standards and regulations increasingly do recognize the need for security and protective controls to be sized to fit the needs and capabilities of a company and that the level of detail in planning will differ based on needs, capacity, and complexity.

**Value of Continuity Efforts**

Let me add another perspective. There is probably no other function performed by a business that provides an opportunity to review all the priorities, inter-relationships, and needs of a business by direct scrutiny of all its working components, see its pain points, and understand how it will respond under stress, and through change. Continuity assessment is a critical lens for examining the structural architecture of a business and how it operates, how it relates to its value chain, and what it requires at different points in the business cycle. These are the underpinnings of effective continuity. These are the requirements for understanding risk. However, examination also presents an opportunity to re-architect the business for efficiency, so that it is at the same time resistant to crisis, and tolerant of change. Continuity assessment is a lens that examines and documents how a company works, what it requires, its employees, who they work with, and what they do. It examines key resources, partnerships, suppliers and markets, technologies, contracts, and licenses, and if done well, the structure, priority, interdependencies, and even the liquidity and competitive value of its assets. Too few companies use it in this way.

BC assessments are also of strategic value. They can identify where our markets are too narrow, our support base diffuse, our sources too limited, or where manufacturing, production or fulfillment are at risk. It can expose where our credit lines are inadequate, our contracts too constraining, our licensing insufficient, our staff ineffectively trained, motivated, or deployed, and our facilities and operations at risk.

Continuity assessment is a lens on business. It looks at the effectiveness of succession provisions for management, adequacy of efforts to promote loyalty and morale, sustain partner confidence, and the availability, engagement, and retention protection for key performers, whether in crisis or transformation. It is also a lens on brand. It defines what is needed for communication to investors, business partners, employees, clients, public sector authorities, and press, when, where, what is said, and by whom, assuring the right messages are delivered at the right times and in the right ways.

Of course, continuity provisions are a requirement to meet legal, regulatory, and industrial certifications and standards for compliance, and may be required under contract, but they also serve to maintain employee engagement and sustain company morale in difficult situations. A well-thought-out plan for assuring salary continuance and contract payments sends a clear message to staff and partners. Effective continuity provisions provide confidence to markets, and to business partners, that we have invested in stability in consideration of their interests.

Business continuity is also a light on exposure. An inventory of assets, processes and line of business activities and their dependencies allows these to be prioritized and the sensitivity of each gauged. There are things that we do that are critical and others that are supportive and important but can be deferred. There are lines of business that are cyclical and generate significant revenue at different points in the year when their activities are vital but are far less sensitive outside of these windows. There are activities that are interdependent with others inside the company, or with business partners during the workday, or that touch clients. These must be performed in prime time – during the day – every day and without interruption, and so continuity plans need to account for that. Other activities may be just as important but are self-contained without the dependencies on other business activities and can be resurrected to run after hours or on weekends in a crisis. Still other activities can simply be put on hold. Continuity assessments find that which is most important to the operating business, the revenue streams, the activities that sustain image and maintain relationships, those things that are core to its mission, and by identifying these, and the time sensitivity of these, we can highlight where disruption would be most consequential, and where we need the greatest investment in defenses and supportive controls.

In an interview by TechTarget, John Masserini, CSO at MIAX Options said that "by understanding the revenue generation processes, which are identified and protected under the BC plan, one is able to see how various applied security controls can mitigate the greatest amount of risk with the least amount of effort". He added that he would "encourage every security executive out there to take ownership of – and understand – the business continuity plan as a foundation for their security program. http://searchsecurity.techtarget.com/feature/MIAX-Options-CSO-on-securitys-role-in-business-continuity?utm_content=control&utm_medium=EM&asrc=EM_ERU_75073362&utm_campaign=2017040 3_ERU

Moving people, finding places for them to work or sit, securing space and transportation to temporary locations, allocating equipment, and targeting support resources at recovery are all difficult and expensive processes. Understanding who and what needs to be moved, focused upon, stopped, or started helps in identifying the best formula for accomplishing all this with some semblance of efficiency.

I used the CEAS Corporate Emergency Access System which is available in many to most major cities now to pre-credential those resources that are most critical to a technical recovery and to business resumption. If a crisis has occurred and movement of people has been restricted so that public authorities can restore order and normalcy, but there is not a threat to safety, these systems allow pre-credentialed card-carrying individuals, a percentage of a workforce, access to facilities for work resumption even when closed to normal area traffic.

Opportunity has a short shelf life. Just as crisis is unpredictable, opportunity may equally be, and advantage goes to those that can respond and exploit quickly. These requirements will be called for in assessing, preparing, or executing most major transformative or transitional state events, whether to reduce cost through outsourcing of functions, partner on process, or transform business structure or ownership in spinoff, divestiture, acquisition, or merger, or for the resumption, or resurrection, of a crisis devastated business.

## Assessment and Transformation

Anyone who has managed an IT department through transformation or transition, for any purpose, and in any manner, will recognize that the same efforts, requirements, and documentation that assure continuity, are critical to business transformation, and the pursuit of new opportunities. It should also be obvious that business continuity assessments provide much of the information a company needs to align proper controls to priorities in developing the security plan, and the inventories of entities, processes and teams needed to develop their privacy programs.

- enterprise structure

- entities, what they do, where located

- assess staffing and identify key performers

- inventory skills and resources, documenting roles, and activities

- inventory, aggregate, and prioritize processes and up and downstream dependencies

- identify data, data types and workflows

- identify risks and mapped controls

- determine business needs, timing, cycles, and priorities

- assess 3rd party relationships and performance commitments

- identify and review the transferability and value of assets, licenses, and contracts

- define and map architecture, technology, and operations

- assess operating cost, liquidity, reserves, investments, credit, insurance, and burn rate

- remove impediments to change, adapt, restructure, and transform

- prioritize most consequential business in support of mission

*Along with anonymity, modesty, and sanctity of body and mind, privacy is a derived right. It is derived from the willingness of others, compelled or not, to grant it.*

**Strategic Design**

There is a strategy built into all the operational and architectural decisions we make in business - but most often decisions we make strategically in favor of a specific design, plan, or process, are a tradeoff. A strength, convenience, or competitive advantage in one area, may mean exposure elsewhere.

- Just-In-Time Materials Acquisition might reduce storage requirements, and better utilize credit and cash on hand, but also raises the risk of compromised manufacturing if crisis impacts materials supply.

- Just-in-Time Manufacturing assures efficiency and reduces the carrying cost of unsold inventory, but risks servicing clients if demand exceeds capacity, or if a manufacturing facility fails, or is damaged.

- Geographically distributed fulfillment brings product closer to the client and is more resistant to localized crisis but may be more expensive to support and serve than would a centralized facility.

Risk moves. Each decision we make is a potential tradeoff and part of our operating strategy. The strategy that makes a specific decision also creates, and accepts, the associated risk implied in that decision. Other decisions need to be made to deal with reducing, controlling, or eliminating that risk, or its acceptance. These are no less strategic and equally contribute to the evolving strategy of the company, define its operations, and what is needed to protect it. It is for this reason that although two businesses may be similar and share common industry and operating models, no business continuity plans, or comprehensive protection plans for an operating business are entirely the same. E2E or End to End process modeling whether for a business or its specific processes can expose the deficiencies and highlight the strengths of an operating business.

Each of our businesses, business processes, and critical systems, has an inherent shape or architecture, distributed at some points, consolidated at others, redundant and diverse at some points, and with single points of failure elsewhere. By example, a production process might source raw materials from a single supplier, region, or country, manufacture at several geographically diverse facilities, and leverage a broad channel for distribution and order fulfilment. In this example, where there is adequate capacity and protection in manufacturing and distribution, supply might be a point of compromise, subject to supplier, geographic, currency, sovereign, or other localized risk.

The unique shape of our business expresses the evolving strategy of the company, but may vary for different processes, or at touch points between entities in our business process, or at different times in our business cycle. It likely will have morphed unintentionally over time, or changed with growth, succession of management, and decisions made. Careful inspection will expose points of potential failure, architectural and process weakness, and inefficiencies. It may also reveal competitive and transformational opportunities.

In many companies, it is continuity analysis that provides the holistic and careful inspection of lines of business, external relationships, and market risks and opportunities, that allows rethinking of process and architecture, hardening of infrastructure to crisis, and the positioning and enabling of strategic change.

**Business Continuity Plans**

Enterprise Business Continuity should not be a plan, but a dynamic program that adapts to the swells, contractions, needs and challenges of a viable and vital business over time. In fact, for some it is a program of programs, including Technical Disaster Recovery, Operational Continuity, Crisis Management and more. The sum of programs for in house 'spare and repair' of systems, high availability architecture, and service and support agreements. Equally for some it includes adequacy of product licensing with clearance for use in testing, crisis rehearsals and in responding to crisis, backup and protection of data, training and rehearsals, effective communication, and operational plans for resourcing, relocation, prioritization, and continuation of line of business activities. Effective continuity preparation and business inspection potentiates executive action in pursuit of strategic opportunity, business transformation, and investor protection.

Some businesses or functions will require certification. This may be a requirement of policy, a condition of contracts, investors, compliance, or a minimum qualification to participate in a government or municipal market. For the achievement of continuity preparedness certifications including ISO 22301, there are specific prescriptive requirements. These include for instance the production of specific documents, and the development of specific plans and reports. These include a BCP (Business Continuity Plan), performance of a BIA (Business Impact Analysis) and report, and a formalized Risk Analysis (RA).

In an email from Dejan Kosutic, an expert and exceptional resource on many of the ISO security and continuity standards, he detailed some of the major requirements of an ISO 22301 certification partially listed below.

- Address legal, regulatory, and other requirements

- Scope of the Business Continuity Management System and explanation of exclusions

- Business continuity policy

- Business continuity objectives

- Process for business impact analysis and risk assessment

- Business continuity procedures

- Incident response procedures

- Procedures for restoring and returning business from temporary measures

(Extrapolated from: Dejan Kosutic, https://advisera.com/27001academy/ )

As described in the illustration below BCP (Business Continuity Plans) can vary in scope and documentation detail.

They vary with the size and nature of the organization, certification requirements if any, and expectations of management. There is no one way and the right way depends on objectives. A business continuity plan can be anything from the steps, procedures, processes, and resources needed to mobilize the business, restore communications, and sustain operations, or they may document job descriptions, and how key staff perform critical functions. It may capture detailed manufacturing and product specifications, secure copies of contracts and licenses, and gather all the documentation that might be needed to resurrect a failed company in a new location, under new leadership, or alternate mode of operation. It may be sufficiently detailed to hand over individual processes to external parties to run. Or it may be a simple checklist. Typically, it is some point of balance between.

# The BC Plan

Who goes where, with what, to do what, when, with who.

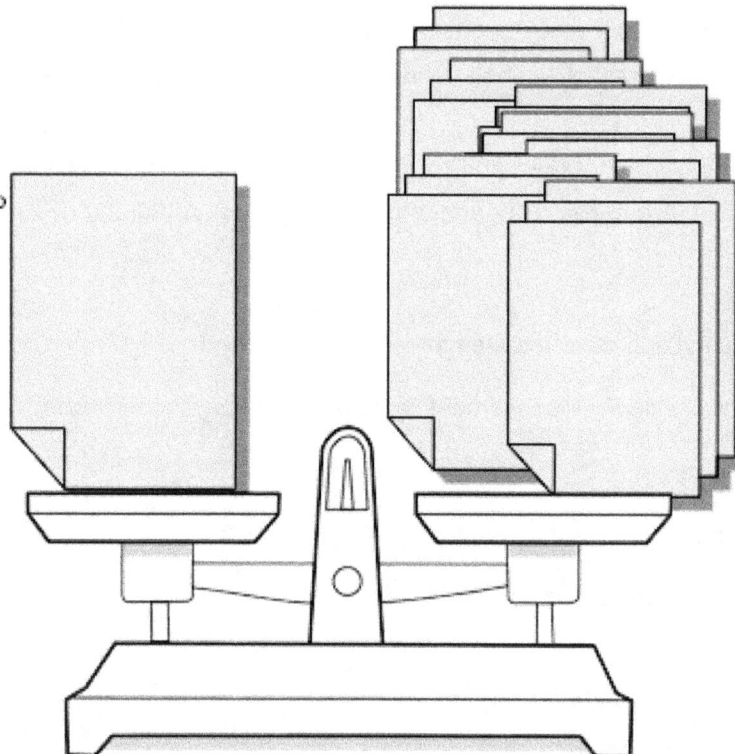

Org charts
Employee lists
Job descriptions
Job function details
Call chains
Process flows
Relocation procedures
Manufacturing plans
Distribution schedules
Suppliers and vendors
Client lists
Contracts
Critical files
Alternate resources
Emergency services
Prioritized plans
Payroll
Payables
Business impact analysis
Crisis communications
Asset inventories
Asset protection plans
Tech Recovery Plan ...

A tangible product of the Enterprise Business Continuity program is the Business Continuity Plan (BCP).

You may be asked as CISO to develop a BC plan or oversee the process. Business continuity planning (development of the plan) is a process. A BCP first defines the analysis it will undertake and the questions that need to be asked of the business. It identifies the information that will be needed to construct the BCP document and the sources of that information. The BCP at this point is simply a list of questions that need answers from management, business, IT, and other stake holders before significant work is done. These according to continuity expert Dejan Kosutic include identifying "what is our goal, are we doing this to meet a regulation, does the regulation impose any requirements as to what needs to be produced and in what format, will there be a formalized Business Impact Assessment, will there be a formalized Risk Assessment, and will we follow a framework for certification" amongst others.
(Dejan Kosutic, https://advisera.com/27001academy/)

Once it has been determined how business needs, risks and tolerances are to be assessed and resources compiled, it is a process of interview, analysis, and the preparation of a write up. The write up typically includes a title page, a summary statement, and a characterization of the study which basically feeds back the answers given to the questions asked at the start of the study. It adds methodologies, team members and roles, and then the substance of findings including the risk analysis, and inventory of risk, business impact statements for each department, mitigation plans, and the resources required.

An effective protocol for analysis is to list the primary processes that drive the business, and prioritize these, and within each process identify and prioritize the associated sub processes, tasks within these, and for each find the dependencies, the inputs, and the outputs of the process. This helps to construct a process map of the business and better focuses the continuity plan. The plan is finalized by detailing proposed options for continuance of operations in crisis. In better programs, the developed plans are challenged for validation, in the best ones, all through the course of development. A summary table listing exposures and mitigating controls in place is often a useful finish.

On completion of the analysis and write up, the draft operational BC plan is developed. The documentation is submitted for review and approval by management. If approved the BCP becomes the mandated means (for some) of coordinating a Business Continuity response assuring the continued operation of the business through crisis, change or transition. It is a living document, revisited and maintained over time, and in some fashion, and for varied purpose, rehearsed.

Risk is inherent in business. Mature businesses develop an understanding of their capacity and tolerance to coexist with known risk. Traditionally, responsible businesses have invested people, time, and dollars in continuity analytics to understand and inventory identified risk. They measure tolerance, anticipate the potency of these events, and plan for the unanticipated, gauging their ability to respond, tested through simulation, and exercise.

With that said, how we plan and where we focus is in debate. With the release of 'The Adaptive BC Manifesto', David Lindstedt, and Mark Armour effectively disrupted the conventional and widely accepted approach to Business Continuity Planning, to which has tacitly been ascribed the label of 'Traditional Business Continuity (BC) or Continuity 1.0. They developed the new Adaptive BC approach, rethinking the Traditional BC practices' that have gone largely unchanged since the early minicomputers and mainframes.

This was effective re-branding, whether intended or not. It clearly contrasted the typically documentation and analysis heavy traditional approach, often frustrating and resource intensive in its demands on a business, to the much leaner, more agile, and more responsive Adaptive BC approach. There is truth in this characterization. I view this as a recognition of difference, and for many a needed rethinking, a retooling of approach, but not necessarily a judgement of value. Both approaches will have their place. Traditional BC is not at risk of the chopping block and is not going anywhere anytime soon.

In fact, the 'legacy methods' and analytic processes (Continuity 1.0) are in common practice, are adhered to by a preponderance of practitioners, are the basis of plans maintained by many companies, and are typically anticipated by auditors. The means and methods of traditional BC remain very useful if relevant to the business, performed for the right reasons, when required, and specifically to suit a purpose, not in itself a goal. An example might be where the pursuit of a certification like ISO 22301 is required which amongst other stipulations calls for a formalized Business Continuity Plan (BCP), Risk Analysis (RA) and Business Impact Assessment (BIA). Another might be where the documents are required in support of contracts that require them or in discussions for change of ownership in one form or another. The company that has done the thinking, kept up on the changes and compiled the documentation is often at advantage when competing for unexpected and rapid moving strategic opportunities.

Whereas Traditional BC is sometimes described as anticipatory, prescriptive, and often analytics and documentation heavy, Adaptive BC is less so, lighter, more agile, and responsive to conditions on the ground. It is targeted at delivering continual value, dismissing much of the analysis of risk and business impact studies. It instead leverages knowledge of the needs of the business and the circumstances before them to guide an appropriately prioritized response. Exercises are performed not for testing, but for continual tuning and quality management.

Adaptive BC Manifesto co-author Dr. David Lindstedt likens the advent and use of Adaptive BC to the Agile movement in project management which began with its own Manifesto in 2001. He writes:

"Agile now offers a proven alternative to traditional project management, focusing on the continued delivery of value in rapid iterations. Likewise, Adaptive BC now offers a robust alternative to Traditional BC, focusing on the continuous improvement of recovery capabilities in lean iterations. Both Agile project management and Adaptive BC recognize the need to provide actual business value to leadership, stakeholders, and the organization. The creation of such value in an era of Lean, Six Sigma, Motivation 3.0, Bitcoin and Blockchain requires a flexible approach to planning, one wedded neither to a linear path of lengthy analysis nor to an emphasis on documentation over capabilities." (Dr. David Lindstedt, personal communication)

Although differing markedly, neither approach is wrong, and except in the eyes of the overly dogmatic, are probably not mutually exclusive. Depending on goals, each brings different value, and in some cases, or at least for some time, may meet somewhere in the middle.

Adaptive BC will prove for many an improvement, and as stated above, some companies will find embracing both traditional BC methodologies modified somewhat to move towards a leaner Adaptive BC approach to be a means to get comfortable, educate their stake holders, and absorb the new methodology into the protective strategies of the business.

Another approach is what I have called BC/NT or New Thinking.

BC/NT differs in an emphasis on architecting inherent resistance and business resilience by design. The BC/NT approach shares some of the conceptual constructs described in Adaptive BC, particularly provision of continuous value, and focus on outcomes rather than causes. It differs, I assume, in the focus on the proactive mitigation of risk through continual identification and correction. I have not spoken directly to the authors of Adaptive BC except in limited email correspondence, and we may in fact be more alike than I presume, but to avoid mischaracterization I refer the reader directly to The Adaptive BC Manifesto at www.AdaptiveBCP.org.

BC/NT has evolved over my decades of experience as a CIO and the recognition that there is often a disconnect between the BC management process and those tasked with BC, and the way business leadership thinks about crisis, makes decisions, and makes business investments. BC/NT has been discussed at several conferences and in a series of papers entitled 'The shell of the Egg. I describe BC/NT and have embedded excerpts of an early blog introducing the approach in the next chapter.

Unfortunately, disasters seldom read your plans, or do as they are supposed to do in accordance with your exercises and tested scenarios. The ability to respond to the conditions on the ground, and play the hand dealt you is critical to business continuation, in the agile approach of Adaptive BC, and the resilience of BC/NT.

*Effective BC plans, performs assessments, and documents not as a goal, but for a defined purpose, documents only that needed, and assures that relationships, technologies, business structures, and organization can endure crisis, change, and facilitate swift execution when strategic opportunity presents*

# Optimizing the Use of Normal Operating Resources to be Effective in Crisis

A Conference Room Seats 8 People

In Crisis an 8 Seat Conference Room Can Seat 192 People or functions

Finding space for people to perform critical business functions is a challenge for every company in crisis.

An 8-seat conference room can be used allocating each seat in 1-hour blocks over 24 hours, in two windows, prime time, and after-hours, as in the television channel model that it emulates.

This provides 192 x 1-hour blocks for seats assignable by business functions. Client facing functions can be allotted a daytime (primetime) slot. Back-office functions an after-hour slot.

Each business function can be assigned as many 1-hour slots as it needs to fulfill a function. For instance, payroll advises that they need two seats, each for four hours, and work can be performed after-hours. Sales may need 12 client facing hours in 3 seats, 4 hours provided for each of 3 salespeople in primetime.

Note: For those that use port based or other 'concurrency based' access, these can be similarly multiplexed, assigning set times to a function.

# PRINCIPLES OF ADAPTIVE BC
## D. Lindstedt & M. Armour

*Deliver continuous value*

*Document only for mnemonics*

*Engage at many levels in the organization*

*Exercise for improvement, not for testing*

*Learn the business*

*Measure and benchmark*

*Obtain incremental direction from leadership*

*Omit the risk assessment and business continuity analysis*

*Prepare for effects, not causes*

*Figure 32 Principles of Adaptive BC*

For a detailed understanding of the Adaptive BC doctrine, I refer you to www.AdaptiveBCP.org, where you can read the original Manifesto and view other resources.

# The Architecture of a Business

*Each of our businesses, business processes, and critical systems, has an inherent shape or architecture, distributed at some points, convergent or consolidated at others, redundant and diverse at some points, and with single points of failure elsewhere.*

*The unique shape of our business viewed end to end expresses the evolving strategy of the company, but may vary for different processes, or at touch points between entities in our business process, or at different times in our business cycle, introducing or shifting risk.*

*In this architectural mapping example, process and continuity risk is concentrated at a centralized fulfillment function. But Sales while diversifying opportunity, will also shift or introduce new business risk as it encroaches new markets, economies, competition, and compliance requirements.*

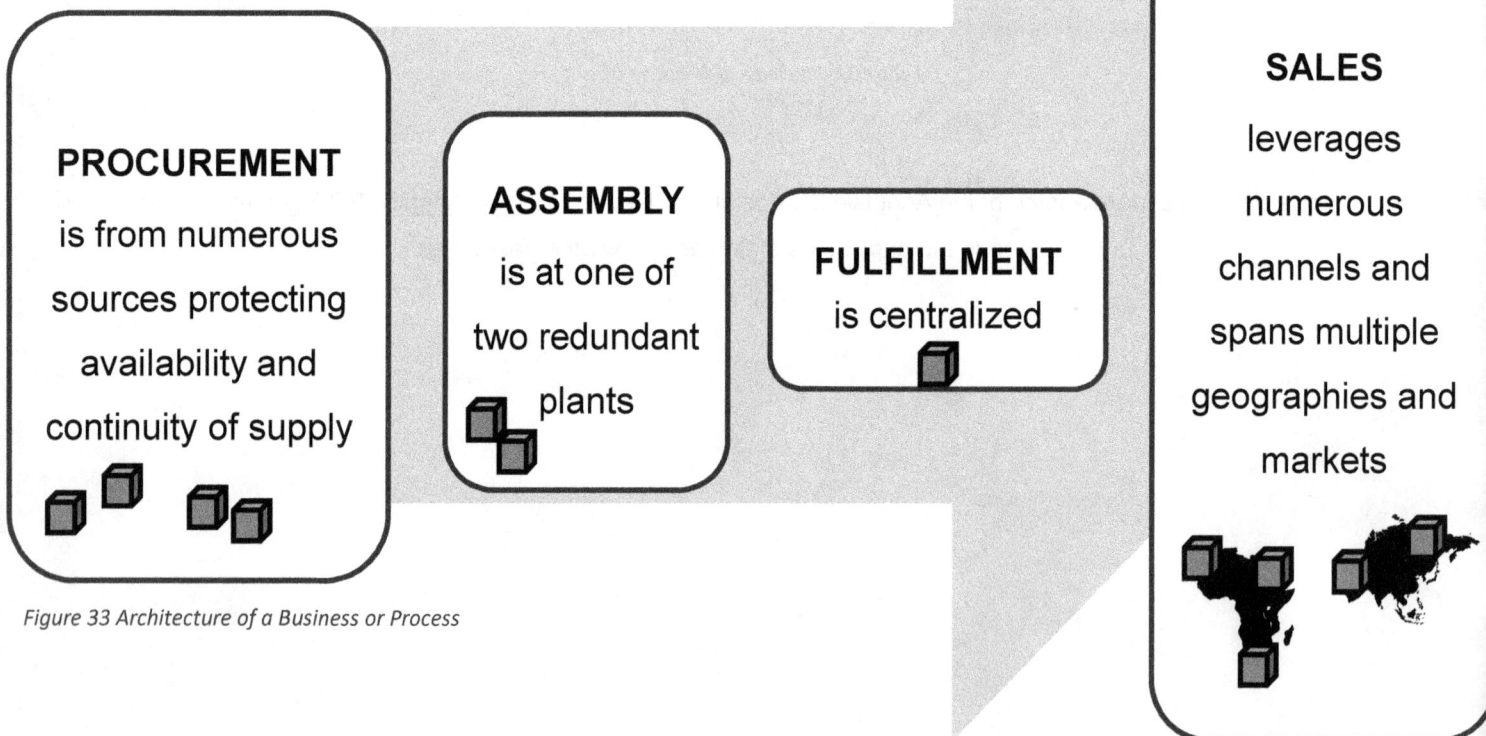

**PROCUREMENT**

is from numerous sources protecting availability and continuity of supply

**ASSEMBLY**

is at one of two redundant plants

**FULFILLMENT**
is centralized

**SALES**

leverages numerous channels and spans multiple geographies and markets

*Figure 33 Architecture of a Business or Process*

# SECTION 20.  THE LESSON OF THE GRAND MASTER

*So, the student turns to the Master of Business Continuity Kung-Fu and says, "master, my enemy's kick is too strong - he repeatedly kicks my leg ... what should I do?*

*The master opens the first book of wisdom which says*
*'Measure the distance, frequency and impact of the kick to better understand the threat it poses, examine the damage resulting from each kick and the duration of the disability caused, determine how much damage you can endure, design a heavy leather protective boot, construct it, repeatedly test it to assure its sufficiency, and then wear it to protect your leg'.*

*The master then opens the second book of wisdom which says*
*'Too much analysis is not useful and takes too long - with the guidance of someone with the knowledge, build a boot and then wear it to protect your leg'.*

*He then opens the final book of wisdom which says*
*'Move your leg'.*

…. Perhaps it is time we think about Business Continuity differently.

# CISO
# REDEFINED

*Protecting Business*

Martin Gomberg, CISSP, CIPP/E

## SECTION 21.  BC/NT - BUSINESS CONTINUITY / NEW THINKING

For any business to survive it must operate, grow, and optimally thrive. Companies are obligated to customers, partners, and investors to protect the availability of the business and assure continuance. Regulations hold public companies and those in specific industries accountable for this. Markets and investors hold the rest of us accountable. Most companies leverage technology and secure the availability of the business with maintenance contracts, high availability systems, protective backups, disaster recovery and incident response procedures.

Many of you will recognize the use of the terms 'Availability, Security and Integrity' from my discussion of controls earlier, recalling (see Section 3) that I derived them from the C-I-A triad (Confidentiality, Integrity, Availability). It applies as much to Business Continuity governance as it does to Security.

A Business Continuity assessment assures the *Integrity* of the procedures that *Secure* the continuance of an *Available* or functioning business. They do this by review and affirmation of the *Presence and Adequacy* of the systems and processes securing the business. Continuity identifies needed assets or functions (availability of an asset or function) and aligns these to alternate means to conduct the business and perform the functions of the business (security of the asset or function). By assuring that the controls needed to secure the availability of the business are present and adequate, continuity planning is itself an integrity control.

As you will recall, we defined integrity as a statement of condition affirming security of an available asset or function at a given time. As such, BC is only valid for the specific conditions it was designed to assure, in the state it was at that time, and for which it has been tested. Despite the best of efforts and most meticulous attention, if business changes, BC lags, if updates are not continuous. This has been a frequent criticism.

And it is for all the above that some in frustration feel they undertake continuity efforts more to satisfy audits and regulations, and less to protect the business. This unfortunately reflects in the shortfalls often seen in BC governance, insufficiently funded, inadequately staffed, given inadequate authority, and typically given little access to company leadership. It reflects why risk, privacy and security assessments repeatedly cover the same ground and ask the same questions of the business when it has already been researched in depth in continuity planning. It is often viewed less for the value of its findings and more as an insurance process.

But I find that continuity is at its best and can better support all other risk initiatives like security and privacy if not treated as an integrity control or point in time check as it traditionally has been, but instead as a continuous process of testing, detecting change, highlighting deficiency, and seeking opportunity, and where weakness and insufficiency is found, identifying and advocating correction, refinement, and improvement.

This is the basis of BC/NT. It is a continual process of validation of the integrity of the controls that secure the availability of an asset or function of the business. It is not a check on a point in time, but an ongoing and continuous program. It is not an annually updated report. It is about continually approaching, challenging, and working with business leadership and key stakeholders on revenue, operations, and safety initiatives and making the business better. It is about organizational and structural advancements, and for opportunities as they present, always with the intended outcome of an improved business and a business that is more resistant to failure, resilient when it needs to be, prepared for that which is anticipatable, and responsive to that which is not, and positioned to support leadership in strategic undertakings. It is examination, inherent and continuous, testing, improving, and continually reassessing the business, risks, and opportunities.

## A Partial Recap of the 2012 Blog 'The Shell of the Egg Revisited: A Case for Re-Thinking Business Continuity' (This blog was the genesis of BC/NT)

*'The shell of the egg is at best under appreciated. Yet the shell provides more than containment and protection. Left encased, shell unbroken, the egg is in context – it can be picked up, manipulated, examined, packaged, moved, and even sold. In context - we get the full picture of a fragile and valuable entity, in a hostile and unpredictable environment, unprotected, except by this delicate natural container, and the cooperation of the external forces with which it interacts.*

*And so, my attention turns to the vital components and activities that comprise our business – an aggregate of complex, interactive, but fragile entities in a hostile and unpredictable environment, unprotected from the vagaries and risk, upstream and down, of partners, industries, and geographies under pressure. Yes, with apologies, I am talking again about Business Continuity.'*

### Why again?

*When in the past we discussed Business Continuity, for many it was synonymous with technical or operational Disaster Recovery. We matured these past years to understand BC to be more specifically business focused, but in the end, for most, still tend to assume an effective holding pattern until operational normalcy returns. These traditional paradigms for DR and BC are responsive, introspective, after the fact, and in my opinion, too little, too late, and insufficient to recognize the magnitude and transformative nature of our current threat environment.*

### The new business continuity paradigm

*Protecting continued operations remains the primary role of BC for certain, but I think there needs to be a new paradigm that broadens the way we think about Business Continuity and that raises focus in our organizations The new paradigm calls for a proactively "hardened" enterprise, designed to resist, and endure crisis, not just respond to it, making continuity inherent in the business model, infrastructure, and in all operating decisions. It calls for a business that is adaptable to change and responsive to opportunity. In addition, in the new paradigm, assurance of continued operations becomes a promotable, leverage-able, and sellable commodity, valuable in exploitation of emerging opportunities, and that increases strategic executive options as they present in crisis, whether affecting us or others.*

### There are new rules in Continuity Assurance:

- *Only a business hardened by design effectively resists crisis*

- *Only a business structured to adapt is malleable enough to weather change.*

- *Only a business structured for change can transform modes of operation when needed.*

- *Only a business structured to endure can entice partnership and strategic opportunities.*

- *Only a business poised to act quickly is at advantage and positioned for whatever arises.*

### The world we live in.

*In the natural order of business, it is typical for individuals, caught in the day-to-day activities of their job, to see only their job, or the needs of their department, and not understand the full value chain, that feeds, or is fed by, the outcomes of their activities. It is often only in business continuity planning that we can step back and examine the business in context, see it in its entirety, and assess the interactions of departments, workflows, and relationships.*

*Our business is not an entity alone but lives in a balanced ecology of internal and external workflows and partnerships, operating within a range of environmental tolerances. Those which affect us, from source, to supply, to production, to distribution, to promotion, and markets - and even to the clients of our markets, and theirs, are now of concern. We need to be vigilant of the businesses, industries, and geographies we feed, or are fed by, and the pressures that affect them. The weak link hurts us all. Even threats to our competitors may prove our threats and the first indication of the tear that rips across our industry.*

*And whatever we thought of our world, and the pressures we assumed we would confront, that environment has changed, and we are increasingly testing the tolerances with which our businesses had been familiar. The world is now a much more dangerous place for the unprepared. It is also a world of immediacy and opportunity for those positioned.*

**I think we can with reflection agree:**

- *We have all witnessed horrendous disasters and malicious attacks*

- *We now live in a world where individuals manufacture disasters.*

- *Most of us live or work near major transportation centers, showcase locations (shopping malls, amusement parks, theatres), in big cities, or in the feeder communities leading to them – each where every targeted physical disaster wants to be.*

- *Cyber makes proximity irrelevant*

- *We now face threats that must be prevented – some from which recovery is not possible.*

- *Our economies, industries, markets, and institutions have proven fragile and exposed*

- *Risks to our businesses and communities are ever present and increasingly severe*

***From my perspective as a CIO, there are a few things that I have come to believe about Business Continuity that have driven me to rethink my approach.***

- *I believe that we are often shortsighted in business. We rarely step back far enough or look deep enough for an unbiased and complete perspective. We grow comfortable with what works well for us, our day-to-day, and we don't often look for new, better, or different.*

- *Business Continuity analysis is often the best lens for examination of structure, process, workflow, interdependency, and organization available to a complex business. Continuity assessments provide the most complete and comprehensive view of the data, technology, and human assets on which a company depends, and their criticality to the mission of the business.*

- *I believe that its understanding of business relationships, priorities and requirements make business continuity programs the best resource to inform other vital programs, strategy, security, staffing, data privacy, 3rd party risk, and to identify where barriers to adherence, uptake and effectiveness exist, and where reengineering would better the business.*

- *I believe that continuity needs to be embedded in the fabric of the business, and by design, should 'harden' business 'structurally' to resist crisis. By example, widely distributed, regional fulfillment centers could reduce the impact of a devastating local event that might cripple or isolate a single centralized facility, or several facilities that had been clustered in an area for operational convenience.*

- *Not all businesses emerge from crisis operating as they had before. Continuity planning needs to maximize options and adaptability - flexibility in how we do business, work from home, relationships and business models, accommodative licensing and contracts - but also be an enabler for operational transformation in crisis, perhaps to allow the outsourcing of technology, manufacturing, or distribution when expedient, or perhaps to allow a change of model from internal sales to online or channel to restore revenue, and by assuring persistence of knowledge through change.*

- *Emerging business models, new trends, consumerization, and transformative technology from internet, to mobility, to cloud, to social media, to AI, are removing barriers to entry in new markets for some, while enabling new and sometimes unexpected competitors to arise. The same forces are exposing barriers to exit from traditional modes of operations for others, and for those the threat of fading to legacy. We are in an environment of rapid change. The response to change is adaptation.*

- *Business Continuity planning needs to by design empower and enable executive options, allowing the business to be forward leaning, transform, merge, grow, diversify, or increase competitive advantage through acquisition, and to seize opportunities in crisis. An effective role for BC is to proactively identify and remove the barriers to executive action, restrictive agreements and licenses, key man knowledge, and to structure partnerships, processes, and technologies that enable change.*

- *I also believe that continuity preparations will be called upon to maximize preservation of value when ownership, structure, or entity, cannot be preserved.*

- *I further believe that no investment in continuity made within any company is sufficient without vocally advocating, encouraging, and supporting the investment in continuity for our industries, partners, and markets. We are only as secure as those on whom we depend, or as I have stated before, "an aggregate of complex, interactive, but fragile entities in a hostile and unpredictable environment, unprotected from the vagaries and risk, upstream and down, of partners, industries, and geographies under pressure".*

- *I believe that it is for BC to promote that message, both within and outside the company, and to advocate for a secure and hardened business environment with our partners, and our communities, allowing all of us to flourish in safety.*

*Understanding what risks move your company beyond a crisis manageable by Technical Disaster Recovery or Operational Business Continuity to one of Enterprise Survivability may help reshape your thinking, approaches, and investments, in DR and BC*

# PRINCIPLES OF BC / NT

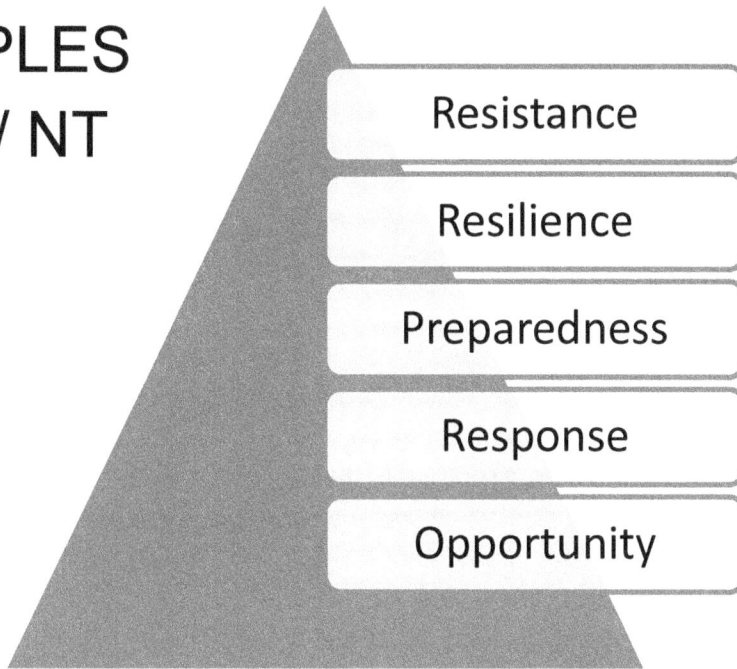

Resistance

Resilience

Preparedness

Response

Opportunity

A business hardened by Resistance to crisis and Resilient to the effects of crisis reduces the effort of Preparing for the events we can see coming and reduces the impact and Response to those that we do not.

Figure 34 Principles of BC/NT

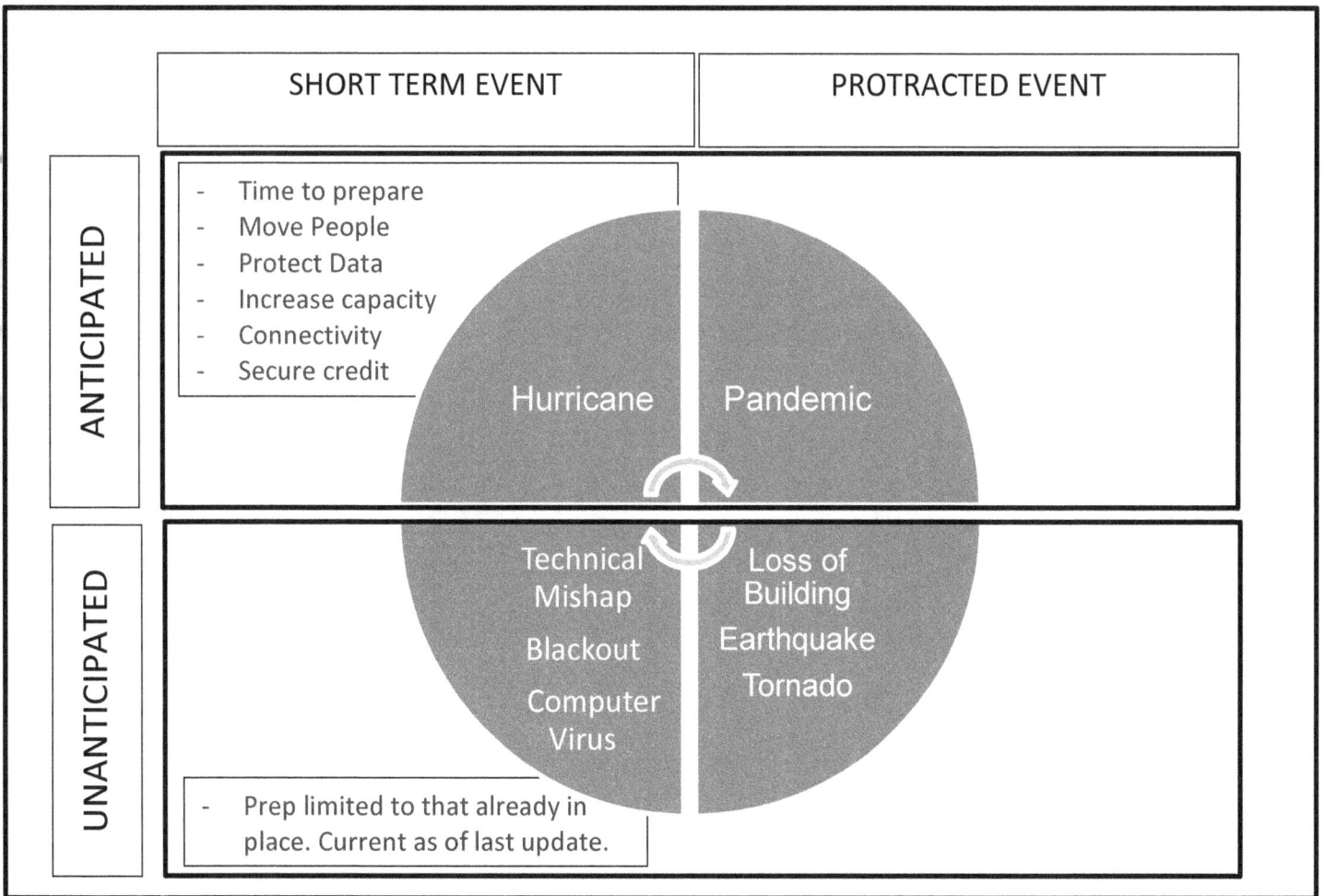

|  | SHORT TERM EVENT | PROTRACTED EVENT |
|---|---|---|
| **ANTICIPATED** | - Time to prepare<br>- Move People<br>- Protect Data<br>- Increase capacity<br>- Connectivity<br>- Secure credit<br><br>Hurricane | Pandemic |
| **UNANTICIPATED** | Technical Mishap<br>Blackout<br>Computer Virus<br><br>- Prep limited to that already in place. Current as of last update. | Loss of Building<br>Earthquake<br>Tornado |

*Continuity Risk*

*The new continuity paradigm emerging may be more about proactive positioning, and enabling adaptability, transition, and transformation, and the potential to co-opt opportunity from crisis, whether our own or others, than we have ever considered before.*

*In assessing risk, it asks the questions:*

- *What about your company, size, message, visibility, location, name, industry, political sensitivity, valuation, technology, or other factors creates your exposure or makes you a target?*

- *How much of your critical infrastructure is exposed because of proximity to a major city or high-profile target, or because it is concentrated along the feeder routes, including highways, freight, and consumer trains, leading to major urban centers?*

- *Has your business, processes, or critical technologies become too diffuse, peripheral, or marginalized to be effectively monitored, secured, or managed?*

- *Most of us understand our financials and can estimate and influence our burn rate in crisis to some degree through cost restructuring, access to credit, and prioritization. Do we understand our soft resources? Just like cash, soft resources, including staff morale, consumer trust, image, brand, and loyalty are consumable. Like any resource these can be depleted.*

- *Are you positioned for change and are critical systems, assets, contracts, licenses, and partnerships constructed to facilitate change?*

- *Have you examined your upstream and downstream "value chain" exposure? What is the risk to the supplies, products, or services that you need, the processes you perform, and the markets on which you thrive?*

- *Is continuity inherent in the design, operation, and philosophy of the business?*

*'Barriers to entry' to new opportunities, and 'barriers to exit' from constraining situations are often the limitations and restrictions imposed by the contracts we sign, and the relationships we choose*

## The Self-Protective Business

I have always believed that if businesses were more 'self-protective' and resistant to crisis, we would need to respond to fewer crisis, and our responses when needed would be easier and less costly. BC/NT advocates that quality management and business protective elements be embedded directly into the business.

Quality and protection should be embedded in strategic decisions, business architecture, selection of physical locations, technologies, protective structures, operational processes, governing policies, data, and in the human elements of a business. This hardens the business to threats by design, while positioning for new opportunities.

BC/NT is the CISO's perfect weapon. It is a means of directly engaging the business as partners in ways that are meaningful to them, bringing quality management to the business through security and good governance, these together, now a better business.

- BC/NT advocates pursuit of opportunities to build a better business, and a safer business.

- The way we 'harden' businesses and make them more secure, resilient, and resistant to crisis is by making them better businesses.

- BC/NT continually reexamines the business and its position of advantage.

- We continuously examine the effectiveness of our decisions and move decisively where opportunities present.

- BC/NT is not a cost, or an insurance. It is not a product that you can buy. It is an approach that you adopt. It is an active program of thought and investment in the tuning and improvement of the business and the safeguards that protect it. The ROI is business.

## An example

In an area that floods regularly each year impacting the operation of a building, incident response teams annually repeat the mitigation and correction steps in the continuity plan, setting up barriers, contracting mobile pumps, relocating key staff to hotel space, repairing the damage or other similar actions. This deals with the symptoms of the impact event, not the root cause. The cost is high, disruption is frequent, access is difficult, and the business is impacted. Moving to a different building in a different location to eliminate this annual impact may be a more appropriate response. Where relocating, or construction of a replacement facility may be the right decision, and an obvious decision for an executive in authority with budgetary powers, operational discretion, and the ear of others in leadership, it may not be the recommendation provided if the authority and executive access of those coordinating the BC process is insufficient.

In stating a concept from Abraham Maslow's 1966 Law of the Instrument on over reliance on familiar tools and the things you know "If the only tool you have is a hammer, treat everything as if it were a nail."

If trained to respond to threat, and not offered the opportunity or empowered to present more strategic options, that is often our default. As such, removing the threat is not always part of the thinking.

A business architecture leveraging several distributed fulfillment centers would be inherently resistant. It is unlikely that the effects of a major storm would impact all centers. More importantly, it also brings product closer to the consumer and reduces time and cost to delivery, an incremental enhancement to business performance. The major threat (the inability to distribute product) is mitigated by the inherent 'resistance' of the multiple facility design which addresses most of the significant risk. Any residual risk (delayed delivery) is now manageable by the 'response' plan and would be focused on adjusting delivery routes and coordinating supply, rather than the complex and expensive recovery of a facility, replacement of merchandise, cancellation of orders, and loss of clients. And with the investment, a significant business improvement has been achieved.

In this way, BC/NT provides an 'inherent ability to sustain sufficiency of service'. In a business impacting event, it assures continuity of operation, sometimes with deficiencies or increased cost for a period, but that is often seen as an acceptable risk by most. Business continues sufficiently until normalcy is restored. In this prior example, deliveries routed from a more distant fulfillment center might be delayed and cost more, an acceptable degradation of performance until the storm damage has been cleared, but they help assure operational continuity, and maintain stability in meeting business commitments.

**Protection is Inherent**

BC/NT is a layered approach, *resistance, resilience, preparation, response, and opportunity*, each layer operating synergistically, each layer reducing the risk succeeding layers need address.

Resistance is the first principle of BC/NT. Resistance to known and potential risk is intrinsically embedded in the business. It is about identifying structures and approaches to the business that are inadequate, exposed or limiting, and correcting them. It is about identifying contexts that are ineffective and changing them, by example, building resistance into technical infrastructure and business operations. It does this through the choices we make, locations we select, business that we do, and the business structures we adopt, and the strategic use of technology. Resistance establishes contracts that support objectives, assuring their effectiveness and transferability, proactive non-disclosures, priority service agreements and other legal structures and relationships. It shapes the strategic choices and changes we make over time, our organizations, relationships, how we deploy and schedule staff and technical infrastructure. Licensing terms that accommodate use for testing, use on alternate systems, or by alternate parties in crisis, and transferability of license in sale or change of ownership. It removes barriers. It requires lines of credit and needed insurance protections are adequate, assured and reviewed. It establishes alternate means of communications and operations.

These provisions all make a business resistant in crisis.

- Removing concentrated risk in supply chain and in geographic or business operations
- Relocation of exposed facilities
- Adaptive sourcing, manufacturing, sales, or distribution models
- Meshed telecom infrastructure assures that if one path is disabled, another exists
- High availability systems and network components assure that one takes over on failure of another
- Continuous replication of data in an active – active or standby design protects databases and data
- Leverages SaaS and cloud.
- Use of application as a service to reduce the impact of a singular event
- Effective network and data segmentation, component hardening, and data protection strategies

Resilience provides options and flexibility. It is the soft stuff. Where resistance is about hardening the business to risk by improving it, resilience is about providing options to make the business fluid and adaptable to change. It begins with implementing flexible HR policies, work from home, a distributed work force, knowledge sharing and cross team competencies, and redundancy of key positions.

*Preparation* supplements innate preparedness over and above the resistant and resilient design. Where an event can be anticipated there are incremental activities that can be done, given that there is time to prepare. By example people can be moved, data additionally protected, equipment, storage capacity, facilities and connectivity procured, hotels arranged to house staff and to provide alternative operating space. Credit can be reassessed, and if needed, additional lines secured. Preparation is an incremental effort targeted to a specific and known event. It is a mechanical and operational layered control that additionally protects, fills in the gaps, and is called upon if needed in anticipation of specific conditions on the ground.

- Encouraging work from home in anticipation of a hurricane to avoid putting staff at risk
- Booking hotel rooms or conference facilities if needed in advance of a storm
- Performing additional backups and moving them off site

*Response* is like the mitigation component one would expect in any continuity plan, but minimized as some of the risk is addressed by the innate resistance and resilience of BC/NT. There are events that cannot be anticipated (data center fire, blackout) or prepared for. They just happen. Preparation is not possible, and a response may be required. Response is dictated by business priorities, prior thinking, planning as to needs and resources by lines of business, and conditions on the ground. It is however a minimized response in many cases as resistance and resilience absorb and mitigate much of the significant risk, leaving only a response to any residual issues that remains. If there is a data center fire, but many of the applications and services are SAAS (software as a service) in the cloud, most workers are mobile, distributed, home based workers, or road warriors that work while traveling, much of the impact of the fire would be diminished by the inherent resistance in the technology and operating model. The business, though impacted, would remain operational. People can still do much of the work they require and remain productive, and response is only required for the residual impact of the event, restoration of the facility, and replacement of the equipment damaged by fire.

Opportunity is unique to BC/NT and atypical of most BC planning processes. BC/NT recognizes that it has a role in enabling and supporting strategic *opportunity* by optimizing the value portfolio of the business.

BC/NT does this by advocating a careful and continual inventory and awareness of value and capability. The assets, people, processes, data, and intellectual property of a company give it its value. This is the portfolio that promotes a company, defines its image, and makes it competitive and recognizable. It is this portfolio of physical structures, investments, trademarks, patents, people, skills, key players, relationships, licenses, and brand that makes a company attractive to investors, merger partners, creditors, and potential acquisition suiter recognizing:

- A widespread or regional crisis may yield opportunity to establish strategic partnerships, acquire a failing competitor at fire sale pricing, move into another line of business through acquisition, or to liquidate underperforming, or at-risk assets for maximum value.

- There may be an opportunity to merge to form a stronger entity acting from a position of power, but often only if prepared to act quickly. Opportunity has a short shelf life and those prepared to execute by design hold the advantage.

- In a regional or industry-wide crisis, or a crisis of credit where pursuit of strategic opportunities is in the interest of the company, a clear and attractive representation of value at the ready enables executives to act from a posture of advantage.

Recognizing under-performing assets or resources also requires an understanding of the value portfolio. Attention to this affords the opportunity to address insufficiencies and tune the business. This is a quality management approach, continually refining the business through inventory and assessment, identifying which delivers and that which does not, tuning and improving and culling the ineffective or obsolete.

- BC/NT is designed inherently to maximize speed to opportunity. It is also designed to assure continuity through transition in support of strategic executive options.

- BC/NT assures that contracts and relationships are built for transfer and price protection, maintaining advantageous terms, and are persistent regardless of the transformational event: launch of a new business, acquisition of a competitor, merger producing a larger entity, a divestiture, or any other strategic change in size, structure, or ownership.

- Continuous review and monitoring ensure adequacy of credit and cash on hand. It ensures systems and organizations built to be flexible with adequate capacity for growth.

- Key man protection and other requirements for sustaining a business through crisis are just as advantageous in transition of a business offshore, or to acquire a business in difficulty.

**BC/NT contracts and relationships:**

Contracts, licenses, and agreements can enable or stifle a recovery, and do the same for an opportunity. Flexibility, persistence, transferability, and protection of contracts and relationships are a theme in many attorney discussions I have had over the years and have been a successful strategy for me through my tenure as a CIO. They are also key enablers giving executives leverage and license for strategic activities in BC/NT. Consider the following for all new contracts and at contract renewals:

- Contracts and relationships that are limiting, acting as a 'barrier to entry' to new opportunities, or as a 'barrier to exit' from constraining situations, are not in our interest. Contracts negotiated should provide exit, transferability, and price protection. These make it easier to seize opportunities and adjust as situations demand.

- The most attractive contracts provide price caps over the term of an agreement which persist at renewal, assure transferability, and sustain over the life of the relationship.

- Provide continuity of service and performance guarantees

- Wording should assure that licenses and agreements anticipate change and assignment

- The option to add new entities to existing agreements, whether internal, a spin off, an acquired external entity, or strategic partner requiring use of common tools or resources, should not be restricted by existing contracts, or limited, or punitive in cost or terms

- Indemnifications and other protections and assurances should persist through transfer

- Agreements should be organized and easily located, periodically reviewed, and replicated securely to an offsite location for protection

**The Role of BC in protecting data and operations**

The protection of data availability is a significant requirement in most regulatory compliance programs and in sound business practice overall. Data protection, recovery, and continuity of business provisions are frequently mandated in federal, state, and non-U.S. law and regulation, and for conformance to required industry standards and codes of practice, implicit or specific. For instance, many Federal and State regulations are specific in requiring good records and record retention and specify how long and in what format classes of data are required to be maintained and protected. From a compliance perspective, testable data and data controls must be available when demanded for validation in audit. Data integrity, preservation, and availability are fundamental in demonstrating effective governance in regulatory inquiries or audits, and sometimes to the courts for matters in litigation.

Protecting data and data availability is a fiduciary responsibility and requires an effective program of data backups, media rotation and tested restoration. It also requires preservation of specific data for legal purposes, a sensible corporate policy on data retention and archiving, and the appropriate application of 'end-of-need / end-of-life' data destruction plans particularly for sensitive data and the media on which it was stored. It requires post life preservation planning for servers, applications, operating system versions, documentation, IDs and other credentials, and restoration devices for any data archived which by law or contract may need to be restored. Additionally, attention should be given to off premise storage, disaster recovery, and business continuity practices and programs.

- From a security perspective, in an environment of pervasive malware, breach and ransomware, the importance of data backup and alternate strategies for data replication and protection are even more evident.

- Backups, snapshots, and data replication strategies including offline storage need to be frequent and varied and even then, without other supporting controls may prove insufficient protection to a ransomware attack trickled in slowly and undetected over time. That said, backups (along with software whitelisting, network segmentation, hardened systems, and data permissions) remain our best defense.

- With cyber, geo-political and natural threats, legal requirements, certifications and standards, strategies for data protection and an effective process for assuring the continuity of an operating business through incidents, challenges and transformation are increasingly critical to business safety and effective operations.

## Contingencies for SAAS

There is a game changer in reducing continuity risk. It is the effective use of Software, Infrastructure, and Platform as a Service, and Software Defined Networking, and security services in the cloud. The game changed is the distribution of risk and the outsourcing of care (not accountability) to those often better resourced to manage it. I have just a few comments, both as an advocate (and I am), and as a caution.

SAAS (software as a service) along with the other manifestations of 'as a service' commodities are strategic, speeds time to market, reduces setup, operating, facilities cost, and capital investment, and allows those most knowledgeable of the application (or infrastructure) to manage its care, as client staff focus on business engagement, performance, and innovation. With the low cost of WAN (wide area networking) bandwidth, SDN (software defined networking), and VPN (virtual private network) infrastructures, access to SAAS has become easier, more quickly established, and access is cheaper to protect.

If careful consideration is given to the selection of secure SAAS providers, and varied providers are selected to provide the services each best provides, a SAAS strategy can be both an effective security, and continuity strategy. It distributes security risk across the selected SAAS providers and hosting facilities and reduces the concentration of data and risk overall. Even the identity management, authentication and authorization that manages secure access to these cloud-based services is available as a cloud-based service making protected access mobile.

The best SAAS providers assure that they have standby DR facilities and continuity of service plans, whether managed in house by them, or contracted through external hosting facilities. They will back up your data, and often protect your data with encryption, sometimes both in transit and at rest, and often will commit in contract, and often in practice, to provide copies of your data deliverable or accessible by you, or to a contingency provider. Some will commit to assuring that the data held and backed up respect's global privacy requirements and will not cross national or legally sanctioned borders.

Despite contractual agreements, if a provider fails, it may not be feasible or possible to resurrect and support a working systems environment, or the business application it supports, even provided escrowed source code and the associated data. And an agreement that assures return of data may be of little value removed from a working and often proprietary systems environment supported by those with the knowledge to run and maintain it. http://www.vorys.com/publications-1139.html

The contingency provider is offered as a promise of continued operation. In concept, having a designated contingency provider offered by a provider of SAAS services will assure that despite the failure of the service provider supporting the applications you need to access, there is another provider ready and willing to keep you running. Be cautious. There may not be great comfort in a contingency provider with whom there is no direct relationship. There is no performance agreement or SLA (service level agreement), and the only contractual agreement providing any protection may be between the contingency provider and the failed service entity, and that entity may or may not have reneged on contract payments, broken commitments, or in other ways soured the relationship.
http://www.bodlelaw.com/saas/saas-agreements-slas-business-continuity-and-escrow-agents

We would have little visibility or means to assure the safety, competency and ethics of a contingency service provider, and the security of their hosting environment, and they may have little incentive in providing significant support. There is also no means to assess the capacity of the contingency provider to satisfy the numerous contract commitments and clients impaired by the failure of the service, all looking to be made whole, and all looking for restoration of normal business operations.

That stated, with scrutiny, and attention to security, there is far more upside than risk in the equation. The likelihood of a failed partner is small, and if leveraging varied providers to deliver service, the risk is limited to the failed service, where an in-house data center disaster likely is comprehensive.

*Even our best companies are not at their best all of the time*

**Continuity in summary**

An effective continuity program positions the prudent company for crisis, assures a proper spend tuned to need and risk, facilitates swift execution when strategic opportunity presents, as well as being an important component of the certifications required for compliance with standards and regulations.

When assessing investments and delegating oversight and authority, it is important to stay cognizant that continuity if effectively managed and given the appropriate executive visibility, is a mechanism to endure crisis, harden structure to be inherently resistant to crisis, but also, is a vital and effective enabler for effective operations and strategic change.

**Support of community and public sector efforts**

Let me take us off track for just a moment. I have been focused on transformative BC through this note, but I have done so at the risk of diverting attentions from a critical focus in the mitigation of risk to our business as stated in the message box below.

> ### *There are threats from which recovery is not an option*
>
> ### *These must be prevented*
>
> ..... Do not miss this message.
>
> We as businesses can no longer just focus inward.
>
> We cannot keep ourselves safe without encouraging strength in our business partners, creating a safer community, and enabling and supporting public sector efforts. This is now more than a civic responsibility or philanthropy. It is a business imperative.
>
> As businesses we have resources, reach and expertise that can be of enormous value to Police, Fire, Health, and Public Safety. Supporting the preparedness efforts of the public sector whether through supplied expertise, resources, services, or dollars, makes good business sense.
>
> Engage public sector partners. It is for all our benefit.

Often, lines seem blurred in what flows from seemingly minor technical
events to the failure incidents and missteps that follow,
to the inevitable operational crisis that impacts business

The speed from one to another is often much faster than one could imagine
in what seems to be just a miserable day with a lot of moving parts,
one flowing inexorably into the other,
limiting clarity to a jaw dropping blur

# E-DISCOVERY: TREVOR M. GOMBERG, ESQ., LEVITT LLP

## E-Discovery and the CISO: Why You Should Care

*This article is for informational purposes only. It is not to be construed as legal advice, nor does it create an attorney-client relationship. Any opinions reflected herein are solely those of Mr. Gomberg and do not necessarily reflect those of Levitt LLP.*

Picture this scenario, maybe you have already encountered it: You receive an email in your inbox from the office of the General Counsel. The email requests you review and comply with the attached Litigation Hold Notice (the "Notice") from outside counsel, about a civil litigation matter the company anticipates will be filed imminently.

The Notice includes all department heads on distribution, including the CISO.

You are the CISO. Upon reviewing the Notice, your first thought probably is: "Why should I care? Isn't e-discovery an operational concern for the CIO, or email administration, or the legal departments problem?"

In some respects, you may be right. However, compliance with e-discovery obligations is not just the CIO's "problem". Rather, it is the "problem" of the whole C-suite. The ramifications for failure to comply may be severe. E-discovery is also the "problem" of the CISO specifically, who is the steward of information security for the company. This article will summarize e-discovery briefly, some of the roles that the CISO may have regarding e-discovery, and some answers the CISO may need to obtain.

## E-Discovery: A Primer

You might be familiar with television legal dramas, where a team of haggard looking attorneys with ties loosened are at work late into the night, pouring through boxes of documents in a conference room. Those boxes are discovery, or documents that must be turned over by the other side in litigation that may support, and may hurt, that party's case.

In my business litigation practice, I have not received this stereotypical "box of documents" in probably over ten years, and for good reason. Today, discovery data volumes that are being sent by adversaries are in gigabytes, if not terabytes of data. This is because documents are no longer just kept in file cabinets, but also in email accounts, networked hard drives, cell phones, the cloud, and practically any "thing" that is hooked up to the internet.

Just one gigabyte of data alone is the equivalent of over 100,000 pages of documents (or about 25 boxes). Thus, today's "box of documents" is instead a USB flash drive, or FTP file transfer.

Federal law, state law, and court-specific rules govern a party's obligations to retain, collect, and then hand over documents.

The need to retain documents for a lawsuit frequently arises before a lawsuit is even filed, when the company reasonably anticipates that there will be litigation. The scope of what must be retained, as captured in the Notice, is generally broad, and may encompass all documents relating to the subject matter at issue, spanning many different categories of business documents, over several years. The Notice should require the IT department to suspend computer backup tape recycling and all document retention schedules under the company's written destruction policy.

All employees are responsible for complying with the Notice, and then cooperating with the IT department, the office of the General Counsel, outside counsel, and any document vendors, in the collection of those documents.

Whether a document is ultimately handed over by counsel (or in other words, whether it is produced) is a function of whether the document is "relevant" and "proportional" to the lawsuit. Each party will request documents and be required to respond to requests from the other side. Those requests will be broad – perhaps even broader than the documents retained – even going so far as to seek every document the company has ever kept. If the parties cannot agree (as is common in litigation), then a court will decide.

In terms of relevance, the CEO's employee file, for example, would probably not have any relevance to whether the company breached a contract, and would likely not have to be produced. In terms of proportionality, if the cost of gathering documents in response to a litigation document request – for example, to produce customer complaints across multiple divisions of the company – outweighs the dollar value of the lawsuit, the request would not be proportional, and the documents would likely not have to be produced.

In a hypothetical civil litigation commenced by shareholders of the company after a data breach, the CISO might have relevant documents in his or her possession. For example, emails might reflect when the CISO first learned of the breach, whether steps were promptly taken in accordance with a company procedure, and whether the breach was from a known vulnerability.

The failure of employees to follow the Notice and search for and retain documents can be severe. Litigants can lose lawsuits by default simply because they have not complied with discovery obligations. In some cases, juries may draw a conclusion that destroyed documents would have been harmful to the company and its litigation position. Thus, e-discovery non-compliance can potentially expose the company to loss in the millions, if not billions, of dollars.

## The CISO's Role

The CISO is responsible for setting procedures for where and how the company's data is secured. However, in e-discovery, the roles seem to change and place lawyers in the driver's seat, directing where and how that data is sent. That means that secure company data will be sent *outside* the company, and ultimately, produced to another party such as a customer, a supplier, or even to a competitor.

But the lawyers are primarily focused on winning the litigation. They may not be focused on what the CISO is focused on. What are the questions that you, as CISO, are (or maybe should be) asking, to be prepared if questioned by other C-level employees, or the board? How are you helping to protect the company from the dissemination of data due to e-discovery?

First, <u>do you know what kinds of data is being captured</u>? The collected documents may contain personally identifiable information, medical information, banking information, or other sensitive information, the unauthorized disclosure of which may trigger notification requirements. The CISO should communicate concerns to counsel regarding types of documents that are likely to contain sensitive information.

Second, <u>where is the data going</u>? Documents are frequently transferred from the company to outside counsel or document vendors electronically. If the documents are going to a vendor, how is the company ensuring that there is no further dissemination? Is there an engagement letter and non-disclosure agreement in place with the vendor? Companies with multiple e-discovery matters may consider a "favored" e-discovery vendor or vendors that have been carefully vetted. This way, the company is more comfortable knowing how its data is being handled across multiple e-discovery matters. The CISO would know, for example, how the vendor is securing the data, whether the data is being kept on its own servers or those of third parties, and to what extent it is conducting penetration testing for vulnerabilities.

Third, <u>how is the data getting there</u>? How are the documents getting to where they need to? For example, are the documents encrypted before they are transferred, such as on encrypted USB devices, and encrypted container files posted to secure FTP sites, with passwords sent separately? As a simple test: if the data got lost in transit, how big of a security threat would it pose to the company?

Fourth, <u>what does the company and counsel plan to do with the data next</u>? This is perhaps the scariest question of all because production of documents is outside the company, its counsel, and its vendors. Lawyers try to manage this huge unknown by entering confidentiality agreements with the other side's counsel, or else seeking an order from the court. Such agreements limit, for starters, who can see the documents to a finite group of people who then need to sign certifications to be bound by and comply with the confidentiality agreement. Confidentiality agreements also limit the ability of documents to be placed in a publicly accessible court file. Finally, confidentiality agreements often include provisions regarding notification to the producing party in the event of an inadvertent disclosure of documents by the receiving party. In addition to confidentiality agreements, parties will often agree to allow "redaction" (obscuring by blacking out) of personally identifiable information or other sensitive information, provided that such information is not an issue within the litigation. The solution for some of these issues may lie, at least partially, in the CISO communicating any concerns, as well as unique knowledge, to counsel, the IT department, and other players in the e-discovery process.

*There are never enough tools, boxes, resources, or appliances, that you can lay on to a business to protect it if basic cleanliness and sensible operations fall short*

# CISO
# REDEFINED

*Protecting Business*

---

Martin Gomberg, CISSP, CIPP/E

## CLOSING REMARKS

Though the position will be defined differently, with different focus for each of us, CISO has emerged as one of the most important growth professions in the protection of business. Confronting challenges to enterprise and cyber security, breaches of privacy, disruption of continuity, and assaults on reputation, while also focused on the surveillance of electronic data, digital media, and virtual communities for evidence of threat to staff, programs, and property, it is a broad scope of responsibilities, and a clearly challenging mission.

The CISO is planner, strategist, architect, and definer of policy, or is the executive that engages these, building, advising, or overseeing the achievement of excellence in staff, and in our relationships with enterprise technical specialists, vendors, and solution providers. The CISO is a factor of maturity for the quality business, working increasingly with executive management and business leaders, in establishing programs and policies enabling the business to accept, measure and incorporate risk into their planning, process, and architecture, to grow and transform, and to comply with regulations and law.

A study by The Hackett Group and SecureState, "Cybersecurity in the Digital Era: How Business Services and Security Leaders Can Work Better Together to Reduce Cyber Risk' highlights the "disconnect' between internal cyber security professionals, and the business stakeholders, who as they clearly state, "must ultimately own cybersecurity risk". Yet, according to this study, corporate leaders not only recognize that cyber security is a foundational digital business capability, but they rank cyber risk as the number one threat to their businesses. These business leaders ranked cyber risk higher than competitive threats, talent shortages, and global political turmoil. Less than half expressed confidence that they were reasonably well protected from the impacts of cyber risk. I suspect that even at less than half, that number is high.

Those that have expressed or achieved a reasonable position of effectiveness and capability, irrespective of technical capacity, share a few operational commonalities according to the study. Each have pursued 'mutual education of security and business executives, clear assignment of responsibilities, and consistent and early engagement of security' in business process and initiatives. These are clearly critical to understanding and addressing cyber risk in business and are certainly success factors for business differentiation and digital transformation.

Whether through operational or technical insufficiencies, accidents, malware, targeted attacks, or in breach of our defenses, putting our most sensitive data and assets at risk, we are all susceptible to compromise. This is a primary area of focus for all of us, but it is not just averting compromise where our focus is required. We, our organization, our business, our industries, and our markets are all undergoing change. In one way or another transformation will require us to think differently, reevaluate our assumed strengths, watch new horizons for threat, and meet a new environment of risk to succeed. And we need to do all of this while speaking the language of business and recognizing a new realm of emerging business concerns.

I have attempted to reexamine our competencies, exercise some, and introduce some where we are certain to be deficient. This for all of us is an exercise of reinvention. The CISO as it has been redefined is a new and growing executive role, steeped in business as much as it is technical. A valued member of the C-Suite, an enabler of strategic business pursuits, empowering transformation in the contemporary business enterprise through management of risk as a barrier to success.

I wish you all well in the journey.

# SOME USEFUL RESOURCES

- FBI – Public / Private Partnership https://www.infragard.org/

- Federal Sentencing Guidelines http://www.ussc.gov/guidelines

- FIPS PUB 199: Standards for Security Categorization of Federal Information and Information Systems

- COSO http://www.coso.org/audit_shop.htm

- COSO https://www.protiviti.com/en-US/Documents/Resource-Guides/Updated-COSO-Internal-Control-Framework-FAQs-Second-Edition-Protiviti.pdf

- https://ico.org.uk/

- FDIC Cybersecurity Assessment Tool https://www.fdic.gov/news/news/financial/2015/fil15028.html

- Schneir On Security  https://www.schneier.com/blog/archives/2008/09/security_roi_1.html

- US Department of Homeland Security www.dhs.gov

- Information Security Governance Simplified – From the Board Room to the Keyboard – Todd Fitzgerald https://www.crcpress.com/Information-Security-Governance-Simplified-From-the-Boardroom-to-the-Keyboard/Fitzgerald/p/book/9781439811634

- Information Security Risk Assessment Guidelines:  Risk assessment methodology based on the Centers for Medicare and Medicaid Services (CMS) Information Security RA Methodology

- Institute of Internal Auditors, Three Lines of Defense Model https://na.theiia.org/standards-guidance/Public%20Documents/PP%20The%20Three%20Lines%20of%20Defense%20in%20Effective%20Risk%20Management%20and%20Control.pdf

  http://www.inconsult.com.au/understanding-the-three-lines-of-defence/

- IRS Pub 1075 (PDF):  Tax Information Security Guidelines for Federal, State and Local Agencies and Entities http://www.irs.gov/pub/irs-pdf/p1075.pdf

- ISACA Website: COBIT V http://www.isaca.org/COBIT/Pages/default.aspx(ISACA COBIT 5)

- ISO: International Standards Organization http://www.iso.org/

- http://advisera.com/27001academy/knowledgebase/list-of-mandatory-documents-required-by-iso-27001-2013-revision/?utm_source=infusionsoft&utm_medium=email&utm_content=follow-up-sequence-text-list-of-mandatory-documents-required-by-iso-27001-2013-revision&utm_campaign=greatest-barriers-27001&inf_contact_key=9b63a4ef1a4dce18f6c3b40bf01538a652a9d614ba94d439408196a10445d87a

- Mintz Levin Data Breach Matrix https://www.mintz.com/newsletter/2007/PrivSec-DataBreachLaws-02-07/state_data_breach_matrix.pdf

- National Transportation Safety Board Website http://www.ntsb.gov/Pages/default.aspx

- Network Abuse Clearinghouse    http://www.abuse.net/lookup.phtml

- New Jersey Homeland Security www.njhomelandsecurity.gov

- NIST 800-60 (PDF), Guide for Mapping Types of Information & Information Systems to Security Categories http://csrc.nist.gov/publications/nistpubs/800-60-rev1/SP800-60_Vol1-Rev1.pdf; http://www.nist.gov/manuscript-publication-search.cfm?pub_id=150439

- NIST https://www.nist.gov/sites/default/files/documents/cyberframework/cybersecurity-framework-021214.pdf

- NIST 800-61 Revision II Computer Security Handling Guide  http://nvlpubs.nist.gov/nistpubs/SpecialPublications/NIST.SP.800-61r2.pdf

- NYS DFS Cybersecurity Rule – New York State Department of Financial Services 23 NYCRR 500 - https://www.dfs.ny.gov/docs/legal/regulations/adoptions/dfsrf500txt.pdf

- Overview of cybersecurity laws, regulations, and policies: from "best practices" to actual requirement, David Thaw, University of Maryland http://www.umiacs.umd.edu/mc2symposium/slides/UMD_MC2_SymposiumSlides-DavidThaw.pdf

- Perkins Coie Security Breach Notification Chart https://www.perkinscoie.com/en/news-insights/security-breach-notification-chart.html

- Proskauer Privacy Blog: A Primer on the GDPR: What You Need to Know, Courtney Bowman http://privacylaw.proskauer.com/2015/12/articles/european-union/a-primer-on-the-gdpr-what-you-need-to-know/

- Resolver: On Risk and ROI

  http://www.resolver.com/blog/the-roi-that-comes-from-understanding-risks-or-managing-compliance-requirements/

- Risk Based Security Investments http://www.tripwire.com/state-of-security/featured/justifying-security-investments/

- UK Information Commissioners Office: GDPR Consent Guidance

  https://ico.org.uk/media/about-the-ico/consultations/2013551/draft-gdpr-consent-guidance-for-consultation-201703.pdf

- European Commission: https://commission.europa.eu/system/files/2023-07/Adequacy%20decision%20EU-US%20Data%20Privacy%20Framework.pdf

- US International Trade Association: https://lnkd.in/eqCJwDx2

# INDEX

---

## Let me close with a repeat of my message to All CISOs

*The most effective CISO is visibly active outside company walls*

*It is the responsibility of every CISO and the teams they manage to collaborate with law enforcement, security providers, and each other, to build a presence capable of acting in the defense not only of our individual companies, but the business community, our markets, and the communities we live in and serve.*

*We do this as engaged CISOs, speaking, writing, sharing information, and collaborating on strategy and providing resources. We are operating in dangerous times. This threat cannot be beaten from behind our walls, or alone. It must be taken on together.*

Visit the website at: www.cisoredefined.com

www.ingramcontent.com/pod-product-compliance
Lightning Source LLC
Chambersburg PA
CBHW081804200326
41597CB00023B/4146